THE RIPPER & THE ROYALS

INSPECTOR
ABBERLINE

CRIMINAL
INVESTIGATION
DEPT.
SCOT.º Yª

A 49.30.1.

Unimportant scraps
(miscellaneous suggestions)

HO 144/220/A 49301

$\frac{1}{1-3}$ attend to $\frac{B}{1-3}$

$\frac{1}{4.5}$ destroyed

$\frac{1}{6-7}$ missing

$\frac{1}{8}$ destroyed.

$\frac{1}{}$ ~~missing~~ now $\frac{C}{1}$

$\frac{1}{10}$ J. W. Anderson

$\frac{1}{11.12}$ now $\frac{C}{2} + \frac{C}{3}$

$\frac{1}{15-20}$ destroyed

$\frac{1}{21}$ now $\frac{..}{4}$

$\frac{1}{22}$ " $\frac{E}{1}$

$\frac{1}{23.24}$ destroyed

$\frac{1}{25}$ now $\frac{C}{5}$

$\frac{1}{26-35}$ destroyed

$\frac{1}{36}$ now $\frac{B}{5}$

$\frac{1}{37}$ " $\frac{C}{5-a}$

$\frac{1}{38-43}$ destroyed

$\frac{1}{}$ now $\frac{C}{}$

E 300

$\frac{1}{51.56}$ destroyed

$\frac{1}{57}$ missing

$\frac{1}{58.59}$ destroyed

$\frac{1}{60}$ now $\frac{C}{8}$

$\frac{1}{61}$ destroyed

$\frac{1}{62}$ now $\frac{C}{11a}$

$\frac{1}{63-68}$ destroyed

$\frac{1}{69}$ now $\frac{D}{1}$

$\frac{1}{70-75}$ destroyed

$\frac{1}{77}$ destroyed

$\frac{1}{78}$ now $\frac{E}{3}$

$\frac{1}{79-90}$ destroyed

$\frac{1}{91}$ J. W Anderson

$\frac{1}{92-100}$ destroyed

$\frac{1}{161.162}$ missing

$\frac{1}{163.164}$ destroyed

$\frac{1}{165}$ missing

$\frac{1}{166-168}$ destroyed

$\frac{1}{169.170}$

$\frac{1}{171}$ missing

Index of Scotland Yard Ripper files.

The Ripper
& The Royals

Melvyn Fairclough

Foreword by Joseph Sickert

Second edition

Duckworth

Second paperback impression 1995
Second edition (corrected and augmented) 1992
First published 1991
Gerald Duckworth & Co. Ltd.
The Old Piano Factory
48 Hoxton Square
London N1 6BP

ISBN 0 7156 2444 X

A catalogue record for this
book is available from the
British Library

Photo credits: 1, Barbara Bagenal Collection, Tate
Gallery Archive; 2, 6, 7, 11, 24-9, Joseph Sickert
Private Collection; 3, Islington Public Libraries; 4, 5,
8-10, 22, Hulton Picture Company Ltd; 12, Greater
London Record Office; 13, 14, 16-18, 21, Public
Record Office, Crown copyright; 15 a & b, London
Hospital Medical College; 19, 31, British Newspaper
Library; 20, Mary Soames Collection; 30, Popper-
foto; 32, 33, private collection of Reginald
Hutchinson.

For Selina, Daniel, Guy,
Rebecca and Andrew

Photoset in North Wales by
Derek Doyle & Associates, Mold, Clwyd.
Printed in Great Britain by
Redwood Books, Trowbridge, Wiltshire

Contents

Plates between pages 146 and 147

METROPOLITAN POLICE

Memorandum

Whitehall

5th day of Dec 1889-92

Sir 52913

With respect reference to your last instruction my interview with J.K. Stephen. Lord Randolf Spencer Churchill Sir W. Gull were confirmed I am sending this report for you personal Attention no further investigation will be made I leave this in your hand I have done our duty. Rest of my report will be sent on I shall now heed to my burns

your respectfully
D.I. F.G. Abberline

Reference to Papers

from 52933
TE 3941

To G.J. Goschen
MI.F.36

Letter from Inspector Abberline (see Appendix 8).

Foreword by Joseph Sickert

Some years ago I agreed to cooperate with the journalist Stephen Knight by recounting to him my family history, which involved the story of the Ripper murders of 1888. I told him a good deal of what I had heard from my father, Walter Sickert. But during the course of our cooperation I began to realise that he was misinterpreting the material, and we quarrelled. I decided not to give him the whole story, and though his book *Jack the Ripper: The Final Solution* (1976) was broadly on the right lines it was not only wrong on many points but missed out many vital details.

It has always been a regret to me that the story has not been presented properly, and I am grateful to Melvyn Fairclough for agreeing to set the record straight. His book has my blessing. My sole purpose in cooperating with him here is to vindicate the reputation of my family – not only of my father, but of my mother and grandmother, and of my grandfather, the Duke of Clarence.

Drawing of Joseph Sickert,
aged 1, by his father

Preface

Joseph Sickert first came to public notice on 17 August 1973 when he took part in a BBC television series on the identity of 'Jack the Ripper'. He revealed that the Ripper murders were the work not, as had always been thought, of a lone maniac, but of a group of high-ranking Freemasons determined to cover up a scandal surrounding Edward VII's eldest son, the Duke of Clarence, who had secretly married a Roman Catholic commoner, Annie Crook, and fathered a child by her. Joseph's information came from his father, the celebrated painter Walter Sickert (1860–1942). Joseph's mother, Alice Crook, had been the child of the Duke of Clarence. Joseph is the natural son of Alice and Walter Sickert.

These startling revelations were later elaborated by Stephen Knight in a book, *Jack the Ripper: The Final Solution* (1976). Knight, who took his basic information from Joseph, described in detail the role in the Ripper murders played by members of the Royal Family, the Royal Physician (Sir William Gull), the Chief Commissioner of the Metropolitan Police (Sir Charles Warren) and others. All this and a good deal more had been told to Joseph by his father.

After a quarrel Joseph decided not to tell Knight the whole story. Above all, he did not reveal to him the the identity of the man who orchestrated the murders. Knight was therefore compelled to construct a theory of his own – which included the suggestion that Joseph's father himself was one of the Ripper gang who operated at the scene of the crimes!

Apart from the quarrel, Sickert had a natural reluctance to divulge everything he knew about the Ripper murders. It took three years of weekly visits before he finally revealed to me the names of all those involved – names which are put forward here for the first time. This is not just another 'Ripper book', however, since it goes far beyond the murders. (Some of the details presented, particularly those of the murders, will be familiar to readers of Knight's book. They are sketched in here to make the picture complete. No knowledge of Knight's book is presumed in the reader.)

Joseph was later accused of fabricating the whole of his Ripper story. This was his own fault. After the appearance of John Wilding's play *The Secret of Jack the Ripper*, which was loosely based on Knight's book, he announced to the *Sunday Times* that it was 'a hoax ... a whopping fib'. The play had been shown at the Queen's Theatre, Hornchurch in May 1978. Joseph was offended by its portrayal of his grandmother as a cockney whore alongside the Ripper victims. It soon closed, which of course was exactly what he had intended.

Some years ago it was alleged that the Duke himself was the Ripper. The charge was first made by T.E. Stowell, CBE, in an article in the *Criminologist* in 1970. Stowell later withdrew the charge just before he died. Frank Spiering also tried to prove it in *Prince Jack* (1978), a lamentably poor book, relying on feeble evidence.

In *Clarence* (1972) Michael Harrison pointed to J.K. Stephen, the Duke's Cambridge tutor. Stephen, as it happens, was also a relation of Joseph's, albeit a distant one. The relationship, disclosed for the first time in this book, may come as a surprise to 'Ripperologists'. It is one of the least of the surprises in the book, however.

Recently, in *Sickert and the Ripper Crimes* (Mandrake, Oxford, 1990), Jean Overton Fuller claimed that the murderer was Walter Sickert, working alone. Joseph acknowledges that his father was associated with those involved, but he rejects entirely the suggestion that he was the actual murderer. For my part, while I too reject Fuller's conclusion, I am pleased that she has provided exciting new evidence which corroborates independently much of Joseph's story.

Most authors writing about the Ripper have bolstered their theories by reference to police and Home Office files, often claiming that these support their case. Yet they almost all agree that there was a cover-up at the highest level. This is inconsistent and absurd. Anyone organising a cover-up would hardly expose his efforts in a file. If, as many believe, there was a cover-up, nothing in the files can be expected to lead the enquirer anywhere near the truth.

There were three men, however, who did write about the murders, in their diaries. One was an actual member of the Ripper gang – John Netley, the coach-driver who drove them into the East End. Another was Walter Sickert, who was closely associated with everyone else involved. The third was Walter's friend Inspector Frederick George Abberline, one of the senior police officers in charge of the enquiry, who gave Walter three diaries. He also left him material evidence found at the site of the last Ripper murder. Until recently nobody knew this evidence existed.

Apart from these written sources, I have been able to draw upon the wealth of oral tradition given to Joseph by his father, his mother and others. Though this material is 'hearsay', it nevertheless supports, along with circumstantial evidence, what is contained in the diaries.

According to John Rothenstein, Director of the Tate Gallery, Walter Sickert, whom he knew, declared that his father, Oswald Sickert, 'never forgot anything he told him'. Rothenstein added that Walter Sickert himself 'possessed an extraordinarily retentive memory'. Joseph has inherited this faculty and remembers everything his mother and father told him. He has also gleaned background information from distinguished people who, as we shall see, have been closely involved with the Royal Family and with members of the British aristocracy.

Joseph had a friend in Sir Bernard Marmaduke Fitzalan Howard, the 16th Duke of Norfolk. He also knew Lady Bridget Paget, who before her marriage had been a mistress of the Duke of Windsor when he was Prince of Wales. As a boy of 13, Joseph spent time at the home of the Bowes-Lyons, the family of Queen Elizabeth the Queen Mother, where he talked to Queen Mary. As a young man during the Second World War he was helped by the Prime Minister, Winston Churchill.

In addition to these distinguished acquaintances, Joseph's connection with the Ripper saga has brought him to the attention of cranks and people interested only in the lurid and morbid aspects the case. Though in the past he has been mindful of other people's feelings and demonstrated remarkable diplomacy, he now wishes to counteract the hostility that has dogged and injured his family for more than a century. One of those whom he was unfortunate to meet was Peter Sutcliffe, dubbed the 'Yorkshire Ripper'. In Chapter 11 I relate how Sutcliffe pestered Joseph's family.

In recent years various people have tried to obtain the Abberline diaries through British government agencies. My belief is that they intended to suppress them, aware that they might contain the embarrassing story of how and why the Ripper murders occurred and reveal the names of the eminent people responsible.

The three diarists told different sides of the story and together their documents provide overwhelming evidence for the truth.

*

I am grateful for the expert help and advice given by the staff of the following: Borough of Camden Libraries, at Holborn and Swiss Cottage; Borough of Lambeth History Library and Archives at the Minet Library; Borough of Southwark Libraries, specifically Kingswood Library and Dulwich Library; Tower Hamlets Libraries, specifically Whitechapel Library and the Local History Library; the Greater London Archives and Records Office; the Public Records Office, at Kew and Chancery Lane; St Catherine's House Register of Births, Marriages and Deaths; the British Newspaper Library, Colindale; the Corporation of London Records Office, Guildhall; Guildhall Library; the Medical School Library, Guy's Hospital; the Archivists of the Charing Cross Hospital, the National Temperance Hospital and University College Hospital; the Limerick City Library; the Limerick County Library, particularly Christopher O'Mahony of the Limerick Regional Archives.

Michael Bott, Keeper of Archives & Manuscripts, University of Reading, provided information from the Medical Directories from 1924 to 1964. Jean Overton Fuller allowed me to quote from her book, and answered all my questions. Information concerning Eton College was provided by Penelope Hatfield, the College Archivist.

My thanks go to L.J. Baker of South Australia for his information about the rifling of the police files on the Ripper. Paul Begg gave me photocopies of portions of Inspector Abberline's memoirs so that I could compare the handwriting with that in the diaries.

For information regarding John Netley's masonic career I am grateful to a Freemason who wishes to remain anonymous. Details of the masonic careers of other persons were provided by Katrina McQuillan, the Assistant Librarian, Library and Museum of the United Grand Lodge of England, and Alexandra Ward, the Curator, Grand Lodge of A.F. & A. Masons of Ireland. Rev. Daniel Harrison, Administrator of St John's Catholic School for the Deaf, Boston Spa, provided a copy of the nineteenth-century records concerning Joseph Sickert's 'father', William Gorman. Special thanks go to Ellen Lackner for telling me about her family, particularly Annie Elizabeth Crook and Alice Margaret Crook. She also provided family photographs and documents.

Anne Morabito, Ben Whur, Francis Jevons, Philip West, Frannie Rackow, Sarah Rackow, Archie Brown, Michael Pearce, Peter Lewis, John Windsor, Kit Miller, Simon Adamczewski, Martin Fido, Paul Begg all helped. My apologies to anyone whose name I have inadvertently omitted.

*

When I first met Joseph Sickert, I found him to be both genial and receptive. I talked, he listened. He talked, and I listened – and listened and listened. He was fascinating and infuriating at the same time: infuriating because there was always something that at first he kept in reserve. I had to keep going back, and just when I thought I had heard all of it there was more. Eventually he entrusted me with the most fascinating story I have ever heard, a story both complex and simple: complex, because there were so many names to remember, so many families involved, so many twists and turns: simple, because it was based on things we all understand and readily recognise: love, tragedy, greed, power and despotism, all the age-old ingredients of intrigue and corruption.

For the privilege of relating this story, this cornucopia of crime, this Ripper revelation, this tragic tale – my thanks go to Joseph Sickert.

London, October 1991   M.F.

Preface to the Second Edition

For this reprint I have corrected various typographical and other errors that I noticed in the original edition, or that have been brought to my attention by readers. I am grateful to everyone who has gone to the trouble of writing, both in this country and from abroad.

I have also taken the opportunity of including some new material which has come to light. Some extra paragraphs of text and four new appendixes have been added to take account of it. The pagination alters from p. 222 of the previous edition.

The most important item is a curious letter from Inspector Abberline to the Chancellor of the Exchequer, G.J. Goschen, reproduced above (p. vi). Whatever the full explanation of it may be, it seems to prove beyond doubt the Churchill connection put forward in this book. It is discussed in Appendix 8.

Five recently discovered letters from Queen Victoria's physician, Sir William Gull, to Princess Alexandra in 1877 were kindly made available to me by Tim Haydock, who bought them at auction. They are discussed in Appendix 11. Gull's prescription for an apparent abortifacient is reproduced on p. 210.

Earlier this year Joseph Sickert and I had the good fortune to interview Reginald Hutchinson, the son of George Hutchinson, who was the only witness to see Mary Kelly's murderer (p. 179), whom he was able to identify but whose name he was paid to conceal. Reginald Hutchinson gave us the photograph of his father which is reproduced as Plate 32 – the only known photograph of George Hutchinson, published here for the first time. The interview is recorded in Appendix 9.

The post-mortem report on Mary Kelly was acquired by Scotland Yard in 1987 and has only recently been released. It is printed in Appendix 10.

I am grateful to Anne Thompson, who reviewed the book in the Dundee *Sunday Post*. Her subsequent letter, reproduced at the end of Chapter 9, lends support to the story of the Duke of Clarence's enforced stay in Glamis Castle after 1892.

*

I am impressed by the keen response the book has evoked both from the reading public and from reviewers. I realised that not all the reviews would be favourable. Many reviewers had written their own books, each pursuing a different 'lone maniac' theory of the Ripper's identity, and there was bound to be opposition to a book which advanced a complex thesis. The reaction was seen to startling effect in *Jack the Ripper A to Z*, edited by the veteran 'Ripperologists' Paul Begg, Martin Fido and Keith Skinner, with a statutory Foreword by Donald Rumbelow. Though my book appeared after the *A – Z*, I had sent a summary of its main points to the editors. All the entries relevant to it in the *A – Z* were dismissive. I was gratified, therefore, on receiving a long letter from Paul Begg commenting on my book after publication, to find that in fact so few details in it needed reappraisal. (I am most grateful to him nevertheless for the points he raised.)

Both books were reviewed together by Richard Whittington-Egan –

according to the *A – Z* 'the doyen of British true-crime writers' – who hailed the *A – Z* as 'the magisterial offering of the most respectable and respected "Ripperological" trinity ...'. As for my book, he advised potential readers 'not [to] take it seriously', endorsing the *A – Z*'s view that 'extreme caution is recommended in examining any story emanating from or otherwise associated with Mr Sickert'.

Whittington-Egan thus appears to have changed his mind radically since he wrote his Foreword to Stephen Knight's book sixteen years ago, judging that Knight presented 'a most cleverly worked out, plausible – brilliant, even – solution'. Why the U-turn? Did he, like his medieval namesake, hear the bells of Bow pealing out: 'Turn again Whittington.' Or was it, perhaps, that my book, by offering more evidence than Knight's and solving the Ripper mystery for good and all, did precisely the opposite of his wishes as stated in the Foreword: 'I don't want the answer found, the guessing game to end.'

*

A refreshing alternative to the Ripper cabal proved to be the independent investigator Tim Haydock, a scholar with a formidable grasp of detail. Though flattering me with the claim that I hold the 'high ground of Ripperology' he nevertheless disagrees with me on certain points. I maintain that three of the five women were killed in a coach. He concedes that Nichols may have been, but holds that the rest were killed where their bodies were discovered. For my part, I concede that Chapman may have been killed in the back yard where she was found, but I still strongly maintain that the murder of Eddowes was performed in a coach, and that Joseph Lawende was mistaken when he asserted that the woman he saw talking to a man in the recess of Church Passage was not Eddowes (see below, p. 39). When Walter Sickert told Joseph that the murders were done in a coach, he may have meant that the gang were operating from a vehicle rather than on foot, though that is not how Joseph remembers it.

*

I am pleased that the book has established itself as a bestseller. Even a member of the Royal Family read the first edition and judged it 'fascinating', and bought a dozen copies. Let us hope that this new edition achieves an even wider circulation, both inside and outside Royal circles.

London, June 1992   M.F.

Chronology

1843	January 8	birth of Inspector Abberline
1849	February 13	birth of Lord Randolph Churchill
1860	May 31	birth of Walter Sickert (Munich)
1864	January 8	birth of D. of Clarence (Eddy)
1864	Jan. or Feb.	birth of Annie Elizabeth Crook
1883	September	Order of the Garter conferred on D.of Clarence
1883	October	D. of Clarence enters at Trinity College, Cambridge
1883-4		D. of Clarence meets Annie Crook
1885	April 15	birth of Alice Margaret Crook
1885		D. of Clarence initiated into Royal Alpha Lodge
1887	November 13	'Bloody Sunday', Trafalgar Square
1888	April 3	Emma Smith murdered
	June 8	D. of Clarence dines with Lord Randolph Churchill and Lord Salisbury at Cambridge
	August 31	Mary Nichols murdered
	Sept 8	Annie Chapman murdered
	Sept 30	Elizabeth Stride and Catherine Eddowes murdered
	November 8	Sir Charles Warren resigns
	November 9	Mary Jane Kelly murdered
1889	July	police raid Cleveland Street brothel
1891	November 1	fire at Sandringham
1892	January 14	official death of D. of Clarence. J.K. Stephen begins to refuse food
	February 3	death of J.K. Stephen
	February 6	John Netley runs down Alice Crook and fakes his own death
	February 7	Insp. Abberline retires from police force
	November 9	sudden death of D.of Marlborough (Lord Blandford)
1895	January 24	death of Lord Randolph Churchill
1899		Walter Sickert moves to Dieppe
1903	September 20	death of John Netley close to Clarence Gate
1905		Walter Sickert returns to London, births of Prince John and Alice Crook's son Charles
1910	May 6	death of Edward VII
	?	Queen Alexandra takes photograph of D. of Clarence at Glamis
1915	March 20	Insp. Abberline at Buckingham Palace – asks to see D. of Clarence
1916	November 17	death of Sarah Crook
1918	July 14	Alice Crook marries William Gorman
1920	February 3	death of Annie Elizabeth Crook
1925	October 22	birth of Joseph Sickert
	November 20	death of Queen Alexandra
1933	?	death of D. of Clarence, according to Walter Sickert
1942	January 22	death of Walter Sickert at Bathampton
1950		death of Alice Margaret Crook

CHAPTER ONE

Clarence's Contretemps

Towards the end of 1883 Princess Alexandra, wife of the Prince of Wales, later to be Edward VII, asked a young painter, Walter Richard Sickert, to introduce their eldest son, Prince Albert Victor, to the artistic and literary society of London.

Walter Sickert had not yet attained the fame and prestige he was later to acquire. He was only 23. Nor had he long been a painter. He had made several drawings in Dieppe in 1879, but his painting career can be said to have begun in 1881 when he enlisted, for a fee of 15 guineas, in a course of Fine Art at the Slade, where he studied under Alphonse Legros. During this period he also attended Heatherley's School, where he was taught by Otto Schölderer, an old friend of his father's.[1]

Princess Alexandra chose Sickert because of his many artistic friends. Through his parents he had become acquainted with Holman Hunt, Burne-Jones, William Morris and Lord Leighton. He had known Whistler since 1879, or perhaps before, and by the end of 1883 had become his apprentice and etching assistant. In the master's company his circle of artistic friends widened. It was extended even further when he travelled to Paris, whither he escorted Whistler's famous 'Portrait of the Artist's Mother'. His friends included not only painters but writers, such as his parents' friends Shaw and Wilde. Before his disgrace Wilde had stayed with the Sickert family at Dieppe. Walter's brother Oswald attended Trinity College, Cambridge, where he made friends with Roger Fry and Bertrand Russell. The actor Ian Forbes-Robertson visited the Sickerts at Dieppe; and Walter also knew other actors, having himself performed with the great Henry Irving, in whose troupe he toured the provinces before his entry to the Slade.

Walter's father, Oswald, and his grandfather had been employed by the Danish Royal Family, which may have been how he became known to Princess Alexandra. His grandfather, Johan Jurgens Sickert, who was Danish, had, according to Walter, 'been a painter of easel pictures and head of a firm of decorators, who were employed in the Royal Palaces by Christian VIII of Denmark ... who conferred on him a travelling purse to Copenhagen ...'[2] Walter did not make clear whether or not his father availed himself of the purse, but said he studied in Paris under Courture. If he did take up the offer before going to Paris he must have visited the Yellow Palace at Copenhagen and the Royal Hunting Lodge at Bernstorff. Princess Alexandra's father was Prince Christian of Schleswig-Holstein-Sonderburg-Glucksberg. In 1868, five years after she moved to England to marry Edward Prince of Wales, Oswald Sickert settled in England with his family.

She may also have come to know of Walter through J.K. Stephen who in 1883 became Prince Albert Victor's Cambridge tutor. Walter was fond of St Ives, a favourite Cornish haunt for artists. In 1881 James Stephen's uncle, Sir Leslie Stephen, father of Vanessa Bell and Virginia Woolf, purchased Talland House at St Ives. The family, which sometimes included cousin James, spent their summers there and received many visitors from London. Walter Sickert was one of them. Indeed his earliest known painting (1883) and the only one known to be signed with his Christian name, rather than its initial, is 'On the Sands, St Ives'.

Like his mother, Prince Albert Victor was congenitally deaf, a condition whose effects were aggravated by his poor education. Many regarded the Prince as backward. Being deaf herself, Alexandra could understand his problems, and she came to realise that he was of an artistic, rather than an academic, bent. Like other disabled people he found it easier to express himself in art than in the classroom.

Walter Sickert, who was four years older than Albert Victor, was old enough to be his teacher and young enough to make a suitable companion. At this time (1883) Sickert was lodging at Claremont Square off Pentonville Road, Islington; but he had a studio at 15 Cleveland Street, in the centre of what was then a bohemian area near Fitzroy Square. Fitzrovia, as the district came to be known, had long been the home of artists for whom the Georgian houses, with their large rooms and floor-to-ceiling windows, were perfect premises. Holman Hunt had shared for a while a studio at 7 Cleveland Street with Gabriel Rossetti. Millais lived round the corner at 83 Gower Street. In the closing years of the century Cleveland Street and its environs, with its village atmosphere, was the Montmartre of London. The Post Office Directory shows that Sickert was surrounded by artists, writers, colourmen, bookbinders, engravers, woodcarvers, cabinet-makers and French-polishers: an ideal creative melting-pot for a young artist.

Sickert's studio was at the southern end of Cleveland Street.* It was here, at No. 15,† while he was visiting Walter Sickert in his studio, that

---

* Earlier in the nineteenth century Cleveland Street was called Norfolk Street, and the building where Annie Crook worked at No. 22 had been No. 10 Norfolk Street, where Charles Dickens had twice lodged with his parents, once when he was two and again as a young man from 1829 to 1831. The building still exists with a shop, but today it sells medical supplies.

† See Appendix 1.

Prince Albert Victor was introduced to Annie Elizabeth Crook. Across the road was a tobacconist and confectionery shop at No 22. It was here that Annie Elizabeth Crook was employed when she first met Albert Victor. Annie lived a few doors away down the street, in the basement of No. 6. She sometimes modelled for Walter Sickert, who introduced the Prince to her as his brother, Albert Sickert. This subterfuge, which had been Walter's idea, enabled the Prince to enter the area and pass among the locals without being noticed. Among his family and friends he was affectionately known as 'Eddy', and when the secret of his identity was revealed to Annie she too called him that. (I shall refer to him thus from now on.)

Eddy fell in love with Annie Crook, not least because she resembled his mother, Princess Alexandra, to whom he was deeply attached. Annie was of Scottish descent* and the partially deaf 18-year-old prince found it easier to understand the clear vowels and distinct consonants of her brogue than the soft southern accents of Court.

*

It is not difficult to understand why Annie fell in love with a fairy-tale figure like Eddy. This young Prince of the Blood Royal was tall and dark, and women were drawn to his sensual, almost feminine, features. The love affair did not begin immediately they met, but was encouraged and nurtured by Eddy's Cambridge tutor, J.K. Stephen. Stephen was related to Annie, a fact I shall discuss presently, when I shall link it to other, even more surprising family connections within this story.

From what Walter told him, Joseph believes that Eddy met Annie when they were both 18 or 19, but that nearly three years elapsed before they became lovers. Annie became pregnant almost as soon as they did. On 18 April 1885 she gave birth to their daughter Alice at the Marylebone Workhouse, a massive building in Euston Road which was demolished in the 1960s to make way for the Polytechnic of Central London.

We must remember that in the 1880s a woman's virtue was of paramount importance and, if she became pregnant outside marriage, she was considered to be without virtue: a 'fallen woman'. It would follow that a man who, in society's eyes, was 'respectable' could not and would not marry her, even though he might be the father of her 'fatherless' child. Many other men of the period who found themselves in the same predicament, but with much less than a throne to lose, found it easy enough to send the girl off to the country or to another town, with an allowance to sustain her and the child. We may conclude that the only reason Eddy could have had for marrying Annie was a deep attachment.

Walter told Joseph that Eddy and Annie twice went through a form of

* See Appendix 2.

marriage, once at an Anglican and subsequently at a Roman Catholic ceremony. The Anglican marriage, which was for Eddy's benefit, took place near Cleveland Street, at St Saviour's Parish Hall, which stood on the corner of the northern side of Maple Street where it crosses Whitfield Street. The Catholic marriage, which was for Annie's benefit, was in St Saviour's Chapel attached to St Saviour's Cancer Hospital, 10–12 Osnaburgh Street, near the top end of Cleveland Street.* (Bernard Shaw was living thirty yards along on the same side at No. 36. Further along still was the studio of Signor Raggi who was commissioned by the loyal colonists of Hong Kong to sculpt a colossal statue of Prince Eddy's grandmother, Queen Victoria.) The choice was rather odd since the hospital was not a Roman Catholic establishment. In fact I was assured by a representative of St Saviour's in Hythe, Kent, where the hospital moved to, that the Sisters of Mercy who ran the Hospital were the first order established after the Reformation. According to an article in *The Graphic* of 6 November 1886 (p. 489), St Saviour's 'was founded about 14 years ago [1872] by a lady ...' The article went on to show that the 'lady' established ecumenical principles which may have led to the granting of permission for non-Anglican weddings to take place in the Chapel:

> The Chapel of the Hospital is very beautiful and the services there are greatly appreciated by the household. The sick of all denominations are received and no attempt to interfere with their religion is allowed.

The Act of Settlement, passed by a majority of one in the House of Commons in June 1701 had eight clauses in addition to those settling the succession, one of which had a direct bearing on Eddy's marriage to Annie. (It is to this Act that our present sovereign, Elizabeth II, as a direct descendant of Sophia of Hanover, owes her crown.) It declared that all future sovereigns must belong to the Church of England, and in addition excluded any person who married a Roman Catholic from 'inheriting the crown'. Under this statute, therefore, Eddy forfeited his rights to the throne when he married Annie. The Bill of Rights of 1689 also declared that no Roman Catholic, and no one married to a Roman Catholic, could inherit the throne because 'it hath been found by experience that it is inconsistent with the safety and welfare of this Protestant kingdom to be governed by a popish prince'.

Further to confound Eddy's future was a curious piece of legislation in the Royal Marriage Act of 1772. This forbade him from marrying without the monarch's consent. The measure was demanded by George III after both his brothers had contracted secret marriages with women of humble birth. The Act passed into law despite considerable opposition, and is still in force. Though Eddy's marriage to a Catholic was proscribed by the Bill of Rights and the Act of Settlement, it was, in the eyes of the Church,

* See Appendix 3.

canonically valid, and Annie could have been accepted as a morganatic wife. There had been several precedents. Before 1923, when the Duke of York married a commoner, Elizabeth Bowes-Lyon, seven women started life as commoners and subsequently received royal status after marrying a king or future king. The queens of Edward IV and Richard III, four queens of Henry VIII and the wife of Catholic James II all began life as commoners, though only five were commoners at the time of their marriage.

On 17 April 1759, eighteen months before becoming George III, the Prince of Wales, was married by the Rev. James Wilmot to Hannah Lightfoot. Documents exist in the Royal Archives at Windsor signed by George P. and George Guelph* and witnessed by J. Dunning, afterwards Lord Ashburton, and Lord Chatham. The documents, which handwriting experts of the day considered to be genuine, recorded a marriage which, if it took place, meant that George III's subsequent official marriage to Charlotte of Mecklenburg-Strelitz was bigamous and that his descendants from this second marriage, beginning with George IV and continuing to our present monarch, Queen Elizabeth II, were all usurpers with no right whatever to occupy the throne. The documents were impounded by the Lord Chief Justice, who considered them to be treasonable.[3] According to Compton Mackenzie, the author Mary Pendered in 1910 wished to examine the documents 'in the interests of research' but permission was refused.[4]

Rumour had it that George III fathered three children by Hannah Lightfoot. If any of their descendants are alive today, they would have a better claim to the throne than the present Queen, even though George and Hannah's marriage, if it took place, would have been morganatic.

Twenty-six years after George III's marriage to Hannah Lightfoot his son, the Prince of Wales, later George IV, secretly married a twice-widowed Roman Catholic, Maria Fitzherbert.[5] The marriage, which took place in Mrs Fitzherbert's drawing-room in Park Street, Mayfair, became an open secret.

I mention these two morganatic marriages to show that what was possible for George III and George IV was also possible for Eddy. (Incidentally, the person conducting the ceremony would not necessarrily know who Eddy was, since photographs had not yet appeared in newspapers, and false names could have been used.)

Joseph has no direct proof that his grandmother married Eddy, no marriage certificate. He is merely repeating what both his mother, Alice Crook, and his father, Walter Sickert, told him. Walter Sickert even

---

* Guelph was the name of the family to which the Electors of Hanover, and therefore the sovereigns of Great Britain from 1714 to 1837, belonged. A morganatic marriage is one between a member of a royal or princely family and a person of lower rank. The children of such a marriage are legitimate, but are debarred from succeeding to their father's titles.

claimed to have been a witness at the ceremony and mentioned that when it took place at St Saviour's Chapel two people who should not have known about it accidentally discovered what had taken place. One was a nun, who was subsequently transferred to another establishment; the other was a cleaning lady, Mrs Elgar. The ceremony took place in the early evening just as Mrs Elgar, who lived in nearby Stanhope Street, began work. The following day she was sacked.

There is now much less concern in England about religious differences than there was in the 1870s and 1880s. Many of us may therefore find it difficult to understand the strong anti-Catholic feeling that existed. Though such attitudes have changed, however – everywhere perhaps except in Northern Ireland – the lawmakers have not taken it into account.

*

The French Revolution had precipitated many changes in the political map of Europe, and many believed that they would culminate after Victoria's death in the abolition of the British monarchy and the establishment of a republic.

On 22 September the *East End News* referred to a sermon by the Rev. W.E. Kendall which highlighted the common apprehension:

> Next year Paris celebrates the centenary of her great revolution. He [Kendall] feared the French people are more than one hundred years ahead of us in revolutionary experience. Unless something was done and done soon, for the destitute masses of London and other great cities of this Empire, we should have not a centenary of revolution, but a revolution itself. It was all very easy to drive 10,000 men and boys before you; but when a half-million people spring up, there would be another kind of reckoning. We must see that those in high authority deal with this matter, and that the people be not driven to excesses in their despair.

The socialist Margaret Harkness, a feminist forced by convention to write under the male pseudonym 'John Law', observed:

> The whole of the East End is starving. The West End is bad, or mad, not to see that if things go on like this we must have a revolution.[6]

After Victoria's death historians tended to portray her as a monarch who had been universally loved by her people. Later generations have accepted this interpretation, but the truth is that she was unpopular. Often she was hissed in public. The true climate of feeling towards her can be seen from six separate assassination attempts, the last in March 1882. On one occasion a retired lieutenant of the 10th Hussars – Eddy's regiment, whose Colonel-in-Chief was his father, the Prince of Wales – hit her over the head and knocked her out.[7]

The obsessional mourning affected by Victoria after Albert's death did nothing to endear her to the common man. On 6 November 1871 a radical MP, Charles Dilke, called her seclusion a 'dereliction of duty', and pressed for the elimination of the monarchy and the establishment of a republic. Victoria herself feared the spectre of revolution – what she called 'a new French revolution in England'.[8] Criticising Lord Salisbury, a writer in the *East London Observer* noted that 'men and their families are hovering on the brink of starvation, and there is grave reason to fear that a social revolution is impending'.[9]

In the 1880s socialism was gaining more and more disciples. Karl Marx died in 1883. The following year the Fabian Society was formed to promote the principles of socialism. Jews were flocking to England from eastern Europe to escape the pogroms, and some, reacting to the harsh experiences in the countries they had left, adopted socialist and radical ideas. The East End, where many of them settled, was home to more than two dozen Jewish Socialist Institutes, and their radicalism and growing numbers were seen as a threat to the social order. The truth was very different, however, because the Jews organised themselves to protect the deprived, and crime engendered by poverty and hopelessness was averted. Unity and order were created where resentment and revolution might otherwise have flourished.[10]

On 8 February 1886 unemployed dockers and labourers rallied at a mass meeting in Trafalgar Square to hear the socialists Henry Champion and John Burns and the Marxist H.M. Hyndman. Later they marched to Hyde Park, intending to disperse; but they were provoked by clubmen in Pall Mall, and the march turned into a riot. About 3,000 looted their way to Oxford Street, where they were scattered by the police. A special committee of enquiry chaired by the Home Secretary sat for nine days. The Chief Commissioner of the Metropolitan Police, Col. Sir Edmund Henderson, was made a scapegoat and resigned. He was succeeded by another military man, General Sir Charles Warren, who set about militarising and disciplining the force.

During the summer of Queen Victoria's Jubilee, 1887, the weather was fine and many of the homeless unemployed slept rough in St James's Park and Trafalgar Square. By the autumn, when the weather deteriorated, they were in almost permanent residence in Trafalgar Square. Individuals and charitable organisations took them food and clothing, but the general feeling, particularly among local shopkeepers and business men, was that something drastic needed doing. It was Warren, the new Police Commissioner, who took action. He cleared the square, but he came into conflict with the Home Secretary, who rescinded the order. West End shopkeepers now felt that their only option was to take the law into their own hands, and they threatened to hire gangs to keep the square empty. Warren demanded additional powers and, with the approval of the Home Secretary, banned the use of the square on certain days. On 12 November 1887 large notices were posted at every entrance, proclaiming, in heavy type, printed with large wooden blocks:

NO ORGANISED PROCESSION
SHALL BE ALLOWED TO APPROACH
TRAFALGAR SQUARE ON SUNDAY
THE 13th. INST.

Defiance culminated the following day in a pitched battle – the original 'Bloody Sunday'. Three hundred Life Guards and three hundred Grenadiers, supporting 4,000 constables in reserve, confronted a mob nearly 100,000-strong converging on Trafalgar square. The crowd surged forward urged on by radicals, and armed with knives and sticks. The Guards had loaded muskets and fixed bayonets. Surprisingly, at the end of the day only one person was killed, though more than 150 were injured.

It was against this background of radicalism and social unrest lit by republican fervour that Eddy married his sweetheart, Annie Crook. If the scandal had become known it would have been exploited by the radical elements. Class resentment and rampant anti-Catholic feeling would have been mobilised. Crowds might have united to form a dangerous revolutionary force. Those in power would do almost anything to conceal the fact that Eddy, the heir to the throne, had married a Catholic commoner and fathered her child. Concealment, said Walter Sickert, was the whole purpose of the Ripper murders.

*

Walter made it clear to Joseph that the real power behind the throne in the 1880s was Freemasonry. The Prince of Wales was the Grand Master of England. In 1901, when he became king, he was succeeded by his brother, the Duke of Connaught. Eddy, around whom the whole Ripper story revolved, was initiated by his father into the Royal Alpha Lodge No.16 in 1885, the year his daughter Alice was born. Many peers of the realm, especially those close to the throne, were Freemasons.

Eddy's secret marriage was sure to enrage powerful courtiers. His father had been involved in several serious scandals, but this one was potentially far more dangerous. When Lord Salisbury heard of it, he did the only thing he could in the circumstances: he ordered a cover-up.

Walter, according to Joseph, witnessed the first phase one day while walking down Cleveland Street towards his studio at No.15. Stephen Knight placed the event in 1888. This cannot be true since No.15 was demolished in 1887 to make way for a Nurses' Institute (see Appendix 1). It must have been earlier, perhaps in 1885, when Annie, according to her daughter's birth certificate, was definitely living at 6 Cleveland Street.

Walter noticed a gang of 'ruffians' standing on the corner of Howland

Street. They were strangers, an unusual sight in that community. Suddenly a shout went up and they began to brawl among themselves. One can imagine how this would make passers-by turn their heads. People would open their windows to see what was happening. Some of those in the street would turn to watch, while those at one end might turn and walk back towards the spectacle. Meanwhile two coaches which had been waiting in Goodge Place moved into Tottenham Street and then into Cleveland Street. Walter saw one of them stop outside his studio at No.15, while the other continued until it stood outside No.6, where Annie lived in the basement. Two men in brown suits entered the studio, to reappear moments later with Eddy between them. They entered the cab, and as it pulled away Annie could be seen struggling with a man and a woman who were bundling her into the second coach. It was all over in a few minutes, and when the coaches turned in opposite directions at the end of the road the men brawling, who had successfully distracted the locals and passers-by, stopped fighting and dispersed. Eddy was confined to Court and supervised, but Annie was not so fortunate.

*

At some point before the clandestine marriage the proprietor of the confectionery and tobacconist's shop where Annie worked asked several customers if they knew of a suitable girl assistant. (The rate books for 1884 and 1885 show Charlotte Horton at 22 Cleveland Street. The Post Office Directories from 1883 until 1886 list James Currier, Confectioner.) Walter had an acquaintance, one Edmund Bellord, a partner in the Cleveland Street firm of solicitors Perkins & Bellord. Knowing that Bellord was a founder and leading committee member of the Providence Row Night Refuge for Women in Crispin Street in the East End, he asked him to find a young woman from among those there. This was done, and Mary Kelly was soon to be seen alongside Annie serving snuff, cigars, cigarettes and sweets. The proprietor, aware that Annie was pregnant, made her train Mary so that she could take over her job when she left to have her child. But when the baby was born Walter asked Mary to move in with Annie so that she could serve in the dual role of companion to Annie and nurse to the child. She became the last Ripper victim.

That Annie Crook and Mary Kelly worked at 22 Cleveland Street has been circumstantially confirmed by Walter Sickert's friend and fellow-artist Florence Pash. Florence knew Kelly, and said so to Violet Overton Fuller, who repeated it to her daughter Jean in 1948. Jean herself met Florence at an exhibition that year, where pictures by both Florence and Violet were hanging. Jean Overton Fuller writes:

> Florence knew [Sickert] from 1885, when he was twenty-five. She knew him right through the Ripper period. Florence has an authority with which the

friends of his mellowing years, and later Ripperologists, cannot compete. Florence knew Mary Kelly.[11]

Indeed Fuller reports (p.17) that Florence not merely knew Kelly but was her friend.

Mary Jane Kelly, who was about the same age as Annie, told her lover, Joseph Barnett, that she was born in Limerick on the west coast of Ireland. She said that when she was young her father had moved the family to Wales, where he became a foreman at an iron foundry in Carmarthenshire. She had six brothers and sisters, and when she was 16 she married a collier named John Davis. A mining explosion made her a widow when she was 18, and two years later she moved to London.[12]

Florence Pash, according to Fuller (p.17), confirmed the Welsh connection, stating that Kelly 'had come to London from Wales. She had a job in an infirmary in Cardiff, washing floors'. She also confirmed (p.12) that Kelly was nanny to Annie Crook's daughter Alice:

> There was a little girl born illegitimate, to some male member of Queen Victoria's family.

This child's nanny, said Florence, was Mary Kelly, who was 'not a trained Governess ... her previous employment had been as a shop assistant. Later she became a prostitute.'

Florence Pash, according to Fuller (p.15), said that Kelly was

> ... strong willed, with ideas of her own. She was dissatisfied. She did not think Sickert treated her with sufficient respect and consideration. She was ambitious for better things, and not really cut out to be a nanny. Indeed she could have made a career as an artist's model, if only anyone had thought of it. She was quite good looking. Good hair, dark, bushy.

When Annie was snatched from her home at 6 Cleveland Street, neither the baby Alice nor Mary was at home. Mary may have been out pushing the child in her pram. By walking up Cleveland Street and crossing Euston Road she would soon have arrived in Regents Park, where nannies met daily to chat while giving the children an airing.

With some embarrassment – and also, I noted, a degree of shame – Joseph admitted to me that his grandmother, Annie Crook, was rather neglectful of Alice. Walter told him that Annie had sometimes allowed Mary Kelly to take Alice away with her when she visited her friends. Once, according to Walter, while visiting Annie in Cleveland Street, Prince Eddy was horrified to discover fleas on Alice's shawl after she had returned with Kelly from the East End. Sometimes Kelly would be away with the child for days at a time, often in the East End. It was on one such occasion that Annie was snatched from her home.

From Cleveland Street, according to Walter Sickert, Annie was taken to Guy's Hospital in south London, where she was confined for 156 days and certified insane. This was ordered by Sir William Gull, Queen Victoria's Physician-in-Ordinary and physician also to the Prince of Wales and Prince Eddy. Gull was a Lecturer and Professor at Guy's Hospital Medical School and, as Royal Physician, with considerable influence, could persuade the Treasurer of Guy's to turn a blind eye.

According to Walter, rather than that her real name should be used in the hospital she was referred to as 'Mrs Mordaunt'. She was looked after by a Dr Broadbent. Registers of patients at Guy's are available at the Greater London Record Office, but they are incomplete, and I found no record of any patient under the name Mordaunt. Perhaps I should not have expected to! There was, however, a Dr Broadbent.

The name Mordaunt was deliberately chosen as a joke. Eddy's father, the Prince of Wales, had been drawn into a divorce scandal in 1869. He was subpoenaed as a witness when Sir Charles Mordaunt sued his wife Harriet on grounds of adultery with Viscount Cole, Sir Frederick Johnstone and 'other persons'. It was well-known that Sir Charles included the Prince of Wales among those unnamed, and the Prince was subjected to a courtroom cross-examination during which he denied any improper familiarity with Lady Mordaunt. The evidence against him had been circumstantial, and there was nothing to prove that he had seduced her. In fact it appeared that it was she who had chased him. Unfortunately for Sir Charles, his wife was found unfit to plead, because of her insanity, and the cuckolded husband lost his case. The oblique parallel between the cases of Bertie and Lady Mordaunt and of his son Eddy and Annie Crook gave Annie's imprisoners an opportunity to display their wry masonic humour. Because Sir William Gull was to certify Annie insane, she was lent the name of someone they knew who was similarly afflicted.

Annie's mother was an epileptic, but though epilepsy is often inherited it had so far not affected Annie. Nevertheless Walter learned that, while Annie was confined in Guy's, Gull had some kind of operation performed upon her which led to her partial paralysis and later epilepsy. Gull was an expert on paraplegia and diseases of the nervous system, the spinal cord and the brain. Annie's memory was impaired. She could now be set free without endangering Gull and his accomplices.

From then on, though she could still walk and occasionally found menial work, she was never again her old cheerful self. She drifted in and out of hospitals and workhouses, at least twice with Alice in tow; this was after the child was returned to her from France some time before she was three (see below). On 12 March 1913 she entered Hendon Infirmary, suffering from 'spells of amentia'. After that date her whereabouts are unknown because Hendon Infirmary, like many other institutions, has lost its records for the war years. On 18 February 1920 her name reappears in the records for St George's Union Infirmary in Fulham Road (now St Stephen's Hospital, which is being re-built). She was now completely insane and was sent next door to the Lunacy Observation Ward of St George's Union Workhouse. Her case notes for 20 February 1920 read:

> Confused – sometimes noisy and hilarious, at other times almost stuporous – has delusions that she is being tortured – takes no interest in her surroundings.

The end came three days later when she suffered cardiac arrest. Her death certificate, dated 23 February 1920 and certified by D.S. Sandiland MRCS, states: '(1) Myocardial degeneration. (2) Dementia.'

Although Annie was insane at the end, was the 'delusion that she was being tortured' really a delusion? Or did her memories take her back to the time when she was carried off to Guy's Hospital to suffer at Gull's hands, never again to see Eddy?

*

When Mary Kelly returned with Alice to Cleveland Street and Walter told her of Annie's fate, she fled back in terror to the anonymity of the East End, leaving Alice with him. This is what Walter told Joseph and his mother, and it was confirmed by Walter's friend Florence Pash. Fuller (p.15) reported her as saying that Kelly 'eventually flounced off, leaving Sickert holding the baby, almost literally'. Florence also claimed (p.14) that she often looked after Alice herself, when Sickert needed to go out.

Walter eventually sent Alice to Dieppe, where she stayed for a year or so with his relations and often returned during her childhood. She travelled with a nanny, who was appointed by none other than her grandmother, Princess Alexandra. When she was about 2½, towards the end of 1887, she was given back to her mother. The nanny was a Mrs Bratton. Alice told Joseph that she was taught by Mrs Bratton to dance the can-can.

One of Joseph's acquaintances was Air Marshall Sir Hugh Dowding GCB, GCVO, CMG, hero of the Battle of Britain, later Lord Dowding. His widow, his second wife, Muriel, sent Joseph a copy of a letter she had received from Mrs Bratton's grandson, Frederick Bratton. Here is part of it:

> I was especially interested in particulars of the Duke of Clarence. My grandmother was commanded to court to foster-feed a child of the Duke's. She was selected from a number of 'possibles' after countless tests and interviews.
>
> At the last moment her uncle, Dr J Bratton (Mayor of Shrewsbury, etc.) put his heavy foot down and sent regrets on her behalf.
>
> He told the family that Court life was 'frivolous' and that she might 'get

into trouble'. (Whatever that might mean.)

It could well be, for she was very young and pretty, had been a dancer, and was nursing her first-born.

In the top left-hand corner of this type-written letter, Baroness Dowding has written in her own hand:

Thought the bit about the nurse might interest you, Joseph.
    Blessings
    Muriel.

Despite Dr Bratton's putting his foot down, his niece did for a time become Alice's nanny. Perhaps the reason he claimed to have refused permission was that he was told to by the Royal Family. That Mrs Bratton became Alice's nanny is made likely by the fact that Alice herself said that Mrs Bratton taught her to dance.

*

Mary Kelly disappeared and was not heard of again until the spring of 1888. By then she had exchanged confidences with three middle-aged women who, in order to survive, occasionally resorted to prostitution. She was still only in her early twenties, but she had already become a regular drinker and had settled in among the East End whores and broken-down gin-tipplers. Life for London's poor in the 1880s was a constant battle against unemployment, starvation, homelessness and cold, which drove thousands of otherwise respectable women to prostitution. For most of them the only relief from shame was cheap drink. Mary Kelly was an attractive young woman easily distinguished by her long hair, which she allowed to fall unfashionably over her shoulders. She could often be seen parading it, her crowning glory, when she solicited for customers in Leman Street or outside The Ten Bells in Commercial Street.

Kelly and her three friends devised a scheme to lift themselves out of the gutter. Knowing Walter Sickert's connection with the Royal Family, they approached him with a blackmail demand, threatening to make public everything they knew about Eddy's wife and daughter: unless of course they were paid for their silence.

Sickert told Florence Pash, who told Violet Fuller, who told her daughter Jean: 'After [Kelly] had gone she started blackmailing.' Jean Fuller writes (p.139): 'Sickert told Florence he had received a black-mailing letter or letters from Mary Kelly.'

Walter immediately communicated the news to Eddy. Eddy turned to his younger brother George and his father, who informed the Prime Minister, Lord Salisbury, and some of his father's friends.

Walter made it clear to Joseph that neither Lord Salisbury nor the Royal

Family meant the four blackmailers to be murdered, merely to be silenced in some way. They believed that if this latest scandal was exposed at this time of political unrest the throne might be swept away forever and with it the real strength behind it: the brothers of the Freemasonic Royal Alpha Lodge No. 16, who were then, as they probably are today, the leading Freemasons in the country.

Stephen Knight set out to show that Gull was the merciless force behind the Whitechapel atrocities. Joseph, however, has made it perfectly clear to me that though it was he who actually killed and mutilated four of the victims, he was acting under orders, and that it was men more prominent than he, more eminent by virtue of their birthright, who were really responsible.

Engraving of Alice Crook by Walter Sickert

SKETCHES AT THE INQUEST

P.C. NIEL J.97. DR. LLEWELLYN INSPR. HELSON THE CORONER

EAST London has a terror that must be stamped out. We illustrate on this page, and describe in another, Police-Constable Niel's discovery of murdered Mary Ann Nicholls in Buck's-row, Whitechapel, on the early morning of August the Thirty-first. This crime has so many points of similarity with the murders of the two other women in the same neighbourhood—one, Martha Turner, as recently as Aug. 7, and the other less than twelve months previously—that the police admit their belief that the three crimes are the work of one individual. All three women were of the same class, and each of them was so poor that robbery could have formed no motive for the crime. **The three murders were committed within a distance of 200 yards of each other**

THE WHITECHAPEL MYSTERY.

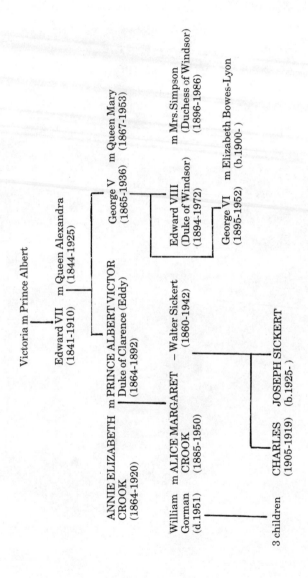

Victoria m Prince Albert

Edward VII   m Queen Alexandra
(1841-1910)   (1844-1925)

ANNIE ELIZABETH   m PRINCE ALBERT VICTOR   George V   m Queen Mary
CROOK   Duke of Clarence (Eddy)   (1865-1936)   (1867-1953)
(1864-1920)   (1864-1892)

                                                                                        Edward VIII   m Mrs.Simpson
                                                                                        (Duke of Windsor)   (Duchess of Windsor)
                                                                                        (1894-1972)   (1896-1986)

William   m ALICE MARGARET   – Walter Sickert   George VI   m Elizabeth Bowes-Lyon
Gorman   CROOK   (1860-1942)   (1895-1952)   (b.1900-)
Crook   (1885-1950)
(d.1951)

                                              CHARLES   JOSEPH SICKERT
                                              (1905-1919)   (b.1925-)

3 children

CHAPTER TWO
The Murders

Most authors who have written about the Ripper murders, certainly most of those who published before 1974, had no access to the official files on the case. Subsequent writers who have seen the files have discovered that they hold little of real value and no concrete evidence pointing to any particular suspect. This has led many to invent theories and then search for suspects to fit them. There has even been widespread disagreement on such fundamental issues as the number of murders actually committed by the Ripper. Some writers, for instance, believe that Elizabeth Stride was not one of them and claim only four victims. Michael Harrison postulated as many as ten (he actually said eleven but counted two in one night as one).[1] Most writers, however, have agreed with Sir Melville Macnaghten. Macnaghten joined Scotland Yard in 1889, the year after the murders and, as Assistant Chief Constable with the Criminal Investigation Department, wrote the following in his confidential notes:

The Whitechapel Murderer had 5 victims and 5 victims only.
    (i) 31st Aug. '88. **Mary Ann Nichols** – at Buck's Row – who was found with her throat cut – & with (slight) stomach mutilations.
    (ii) 8th Sept. '88. **Annie Chapman** – Hanbury St: – throat cut – stomach & private parts badly mutilated & some of the entrails placed round the neck.
    (iii) 30th Sept. '88. **Elizabeth Stride** – Berner's Street: throat cut, but nothing in shape of mutilation attempted, & on same date **Catherine Eddowes** – Mitre Square, throat cut, & very bad on mutilations, both of face and stomach.
    (iv) 9th November. **Mary Jane Kelly** – Miller's Court, throat cut, and whole of the body mutilated in the most ghastly manner.[2]

Though the bodies were not found within the boundary of one parish or within the domain of a single police force, they were geographically in the same area: the East End, a large section of metropolitan London lying east of the City. It consisted of twelve main areas: Whitechapel, Spitalfields, Shoreditch, Bethnal Green, Mile End, Stepney, Limehouse, Poplar, St George's in the East, Old Ford, Bow and Bromley-by-Bow.

It was through the 'rookeries' of the East End that Bill Sykes ran for his life in *Oliver Twist*. It was here, in Limehouse, that Sherlock Holmes went snooping and sleuthing among the opium dens of the Chinese quarter. It was to the East End that the City of London banished its more undesirable industries – undesirable by virtue of their smell or their noise: fish-curers, animal slaughterers, skinners, furriers and bell-makers. Slaughterhouses could be found at every corner, but they were not the hygienic places of modern times, regularly visited by diligent Health Inspectors. Many were in ordinary houses, and the blood and urine running out of the front doors on to the pavement and into the guttter were a smelly attraction for starving dogs and a slippery hazard for passers-by.

The nearby docks provided work for many, but the pay was poor and employment irregular. A man might work for two days unloading a ship and not get chosen for the next job, since the pool of available men was bottomless. The meagre pay he received would barely support him, his wife and their children for two days. After several days without money and with little food, he might eventually be taken on to load or unload another ship, only to be too weak from hunger to be of much use to his employer.

Children in rags playing barefoot outside, even in the harshest weather, were a shameful feature of every Victorian city, but nowhere more so than in London's East End. Without contraception many couples had six or more children, and thousands of families could be found huddled together in rooms twelve feet by ten. It was not rare for a child to be found in the morning accidentally suffocated in the overcrowded bundle of rags used as a bed. Sleeping bodies huddled together for warmth and companionship, their only comfort during the struggle against deprivation. Incest between father and daughter, or brother and sister, was commonplace. So was wife-beating. As Jack London, who lived among the derelicts for a time, perceptively observed:

> The men are economically dependent on their masters, and the women are economically dependent on the men. The result is, that the woman gets the beating the man should give to his master, and she can do nothing. There are the kiddies, and he is the breadwinner, and she dare not send him to jail and leave herself and the children to starve. Evidence to convict can rarely be obtained when such cases come into the courts; as a rule the trampled wife and mother is weeping and hysterically beseeching the magistrate to let her husband off for the kiddies' sake.[3]

The Lancet estimated that between 60,000 and 80,000 women resorted to prostitution, and in October 1888 the Metropolitan Police estimated that there were 1,200 in Whitechapel alone.[4] Most of the middle and upper classes believed that prostitutes were women of low morals and refused even to contemplate the real reasons for their number. When a woman was widowed, or her husband unemployed, leaving the children to starve, a few minutes spent 'servicing' a stranger offered a quick and easy means of support for many a desperate mother. Once the first step had been taken, it was but a short way from a single 'fall from grace' to a regular way of life.

Sometimes the prettiest daughter of the family would be lured by the illusion of financial freedom apparently offered by life 'on the game' and many an East End girl could be found in the West End. One night flirting with the wealthy toffs under the bright lights 'up West' in the Haymarket offered a more attractive prospect than, and as much money as, a week of drudgery in a Spitalfields sweatshop. It was of the East End that Arthur Morrison wrote, in words which today may be thought reactionary:

> There is no need to say in the East End of what. The East End is a vast city, as famous in its way as any the hand of man made. But who knows the East End? It is down through Cornhill and out beyond Leadenhall Street and Aldgate Pump, one will say: a shocking place, where he once went with a curate; an evil plexus of slums that hide human creeping things; where filthy men and women live on penn'orths of gin, where collars and clean shirts are decencies unknown, where every citizen wears a black eye, and none ever combs his hair. The East End, says another, which is given over to the Unemployed. And the Unemployed is a race whose token is a clay pipe, and whose enemy is soap: now and again it migrates bodily to Hyde Park with banners, and furnishes adjacent police courts with disorderly drunks. Still another knows the East End as the place whence begging letters come ...[5]

To Gareth Stedman Jones the East End was *Outcast London* (1971), while to Jack London its inhabitants were *The People of the Abyss* (1903), The Ripper murders were at first known as the 'Whitechapel murders', and Whitechapel was described by J.H. Mackay as 'The East-End in the East-End'.

Commercial Street cuts a dog-leg diagonal through Spitalfields, from Shoreditch High Street to Whitechapel High Street. Issuing from this relatively wide thoroughfare in the 1880s were three mean, inhospitable, narrow streets known as the most evil in London: Thrawl Street, Flower & Dean Street and Dorset Street. James Greenwood, a journalist, wrote of the Flower & Dean Street rookery:

> Within a short distance ... of the heart of the centre of the City of London, there existed for the past fifty years, and still exists and flourishes, what is perhaps the foulest and most dangerous street in the whole of the metropolis.[6]

The 'Flowery Dean' consisted almost entirely of lodging houses. As long as the bed was paid for there were no questions asked, and prostitutes would use them as brothels, flopping down with their clients into an

infested 'double' for eightpence a night. A criminal could enter the street
at one end with the police on his tail and, by means of connecting
passages and doors, flee through courtyards leading to other streets. It
was here that three of the Ripper victims occasionally stayed: Annie
Chapman and Elizabeth Stride at No. 35, and Catherine Eddowes at No.
55. Next door, at Nos 56-57, known as the White House, stayed the
sometime lodger Mary Anne Nichols, the first 'unfortunate' singled out by
the Ripper.*

Murder No. 1: Mary Anne Nichols   31 August

The local police were baffled by the crime, and Inspector Abberline,
former head of the Whitechapel Criminal Investigation Department, was
drafted from Scotland Yard to co-ordinate the ground-level enquiries. His
private diaries feature in subsequent chapters, but here is the official
account of his first enquiry:

> About 3.40 a.m. ult. as Charles Cross, carman of 22 Doveton Street,
> Cambridge Road, Bethnall Green, was passing through Bucks Row,
> Whitechapel (on his way to work) he noticed a woman on her back on the
> footway (against some gates leading into a stable yard). He stopped to look
> at the woman when another carman, also on his way to work, named Robert
> Paul of 30 Fosters Street, Bethnal Green, came up and Cross called his
> attention to the woman, but being dark he did not notice any blood, and
> passed on with the intention of informing the first constable they met. On
> arriving at the corner of Hanbury Street and old Montague Street they met
> P.C.55H Mizen and acquainted him of what they had seen and on the
> constable proceeding towards the spot he found that P.C.97J Neil had found
> the woman, and was calling for assistance.
> P.C. Neil turned on his light and discovered that the woman's throat was
> severely cut. P.C.96J Thain was also called and sent at once for Dr
> Llewellyn of 152, Whitechapel Road, who quickly arrived on the scene and
> pronounced life extinct and ordered the removal of the body to the
> mortuary. In the meantime P.C. Mizen had been sent for the ambulance
> and assistance from Bethnal Green station, and on Inspector Spratling and
> other officers arriving, the body was removed to the Mortuary. On arriving
> there the inspector made a further examination and found that the
> abdomen had also been severely cut in several places, exposing the
> intestines. The Inspector acquainted Dr Llewellyn who afterwards made a
> more minute examination and found that the wounds to the abdomen were
> in themselves sufficient to cause death, and he expressed an opinion that
> they were inflicted before the throat was cut.
> The body was not then identified. On the clothing being carefully
> examined by Inspector Heston he found some of the underclothing bore the
> mark of Lambeth Workhouse which led to the body being identified as that
> of a former inmate named Mary Anne Nichols, and by that means we were

* 'Unfortunate' was the Victorian euphemism for prostitute, but in reality best describes the
sad plight of these women. See W.J. Fishman, *East End 1888* (1989) pp. 122-5, 221.

able to trace the relatives and complete the identity. It was found she was the wife of William Nichols of 37, Coberg Street, Old Kent Road, a printer in the employ of Messrs. Perkins Baker and Co., Whitefriars Street, City, from whom she was separated about nine years through her drunken and immoral habits, and that for several years past she had from time to time been an inmate of various Workhouses and entered the service of Mr Cowdry, Ingleside, Rose Hill Road, Wandsworth. She remained there until the 12th July when she absconded stealing various articles of apparel. A day or two after she became a lodger at 18, Thrawl Street, Spitalfields, a common lodging house, and at another common lodging house at 56, Flower and Dean Street up to the night of the murder.

About 1.40 p.m. that morning she was seen in the kitchen at 18, Thrawl Street when she informed the deputy of the lodging house that she had no money to pay for her lodging. She requested that her bed should be kept for her and left stating that she would soon get the money. At that time she was drunk. She was next seen at 2.30 a.m. at the corner of Osborne Street, Whitechapel Road by Ellen Holland, a lodger in the same house, who seeing she was very drunk requested her to return with her to the lodging house. She however refused, remarking that she would soon be back and walked away down the Whitechapel Road in the direction of where her body was found. There can be no doubt with regard to the time because the Whitechapel clock chimed 2.30 and Holland called attention of the deceased to the time.

We have been unable to find any person who saw her alive after Holland left her. The distance from Osborne Street to Bucks Row would be about half a mile. Inquiries were made in every conceivable quarter with a view to trace the murderer but not the slightest clue can at present be obtained.

A description of Mary Nichols was given in a special report by Inspector J. Spratling of J Division, which can be seen in the Metropolitan Police files on the case in the Public Records Office at Kew. Spratling wrote :

P.C. J Neil reports at 3.45 a.m., 31 inst. August, he found the dead body of a woman lying on her back with her clothes a little above her knees, lying with her throat cut from ear to ear on a yard crossing at Buck's Row, Whitechapel. P.C. [Neil] obtained assistance of P.C.s 55H Mizen and 96J Thain. The latter called Dr Llewellyn. No. 152, Whitechapel Road. He arrived quickly and pronounced life to be extinct, apparently but a few minutes. He directed her removal to the mortuary, stating that he would make a further examination there, which was done on the ambulance [a sort of handcart].

Upon my arrival there and taking a description I found that she had been disembowelled, and at once sent to inform the doctor of it. He arrived quickly and on further examination stated that her throat had been cut from left to right, two distinct cuts being on the left side. The windpipe, gullet and spinal cord being cut through, a bruise apparently of a thumb being on the lower left jaw, also one on left cheek. The abdomen had been cut open from centre of bottom of ribs on right side, under pelvis to the left of the stomach, there the wound was jagged. The omentum or coating of the stomach was also cut in several places, with a strong bladed knife, supposed to have been done by some left handed person, death being almost instantaneous.

Description: age about 45, length 5ft 2 or 3; complexion dark; hair dark brown turning grey, eyes brown, bruise on lower right jaw and left cheek, slight laceration of tongue, one tooth deficient front of upper jaw, two on left of lower.

Dress: brown ulster, 7 large brass buttons (figure of a female riding horse and a man at side thereon), brown linsey frock, grey woollen pettycoat, flannel drawers, white chest flannel, brown stays, black ribbed woollen stockings, men's spring sided boots, cut on uppers, tips on heels, black straw bonnet, trimmed black velvet.

I made enquiries and was informed by Mrs Emma Green, a widow, New Cottage adjoining, and Mr Walter Purkis, Eagle Wharf opposite, also of William Louis, nightwatchman to Messrs. Brown Eagle at wharf near, none of whom heard any screams during the night, or anything to lead them to believe that murder had been committed there.

P.C. states he passed through the Row at 3.15 a.m. and P.C.10 Kirley about the same time, but the woman was not there then and is not known to them.

Buck's Row was a narrow and forbidding street, and in the 1880s the high warehouses which dominated the northern side cast a malevolent shadow over most of its length. The entrance to the stables where 'Polly' Nichols was found was about sixty yards from the nearest gaslamp which stood on the opposite side, level with the back wall of the Board School building: a monstrous monolith, now derelict and deserted, which still looms at the junction of Buck's Row and Winthrop Street. Once, the playful screams and laughter of children spilled down from the playground, which unusually stood on the building's flat roof ringed by iron railings which can still be seen on its perimeter. Opposite where Nichols was found was Essex Wharf which Inspector Spratling, in his report, incorrectly called Eagle Wharf. The name could still be seen in bold red-brick lettering upon the wall facing west up Buck's Row until the building was demolished in 1991. It was later renamed Durward Street after local residents appealed to be released from the notoriety created by the murder.

The manager of Essex Wharf, Mr Walter Purkis, slept in his bedroom at the front of the house directly overlooking the stable entrance where Nichols was found, only twenty-five to thirty feet away. He was awake between 1 a.m. and 2 a.m. and at other times during the night. Neither he nor his wife, who was awake most of the night, heard any unusual noise. The stable stood between the end of a long wall stretching from the school and an even longer terrace of houses, the last of which, New Cottage, was the home of Mrs Emma Green and her daughter and two sons. Like Mrs Purkis opposite, Mrs Green had endured a night of insomnia, but she had heard nothing suspicious beneath her first-floor bedroom window, which was only about fifteen feet from where the body was found. Two nightwatchmen, one from a wool depot in Buck's Row, the other from a nearby tar factory, also maintained that they neither heard nor saw anything out of the ordinary, adding that it had been an unusually uneventful night. This tallied with the testimony of Mizen and Neil, the two policemen who patrolled Buck's Row every half-hour and had seen no one acting suspiciously.

No one in fact had seen or heard anything odd. How then had the murderer managed to locate Nichols, force her to the ground, open her abdomen from the ribs down and under the stomach, slash the stomach lining and stab the genitals, all within the sight and hearing of two households and between the beats of two patrolling policemen? Finally, the murderer had cut her throat back to the spine before leaving the scene of the crime unnoticed by either of the two policemen patrolling the ends of Buck's Row. It was this swift, silent technique which evoked, in the nightmares of a panic-stricken public, the image of an invisible fiend.

Murder No. 2: Annie Chapman   8 September

The history of Spitalfields is the history of London's East End, and the Great Mosque at the corner of Fournier Street and Brick Lane exemplifies its historical pattern. It was built in 1743 as a chapel for the Huguenot silk-weavers, Protestant master-craftsmen who had fled religious persecution in France. From 1809 to 1819 it was occupied by the London Society for Promoting Christianity among the Jews and later became a Wesleyan Chapel. From then until 1976 it was the Great Synagogue of the Machzike Hadeth Community serving the eastern European Jews who, after fleeing the pogroms arrived in east London and succeeded the Huguenots in the manufacture of clothing. The Jewish community has now mostly left Spitalfields for the suburbs of north and west London, and its place has been filled by a large, close-knit community of Bangladeshi immigrants, who have not only converted the former synagogue into a mosque but taken over the rag trade and the houses used by the eighteenth-century silk-weavers. Some of these four-story houses topped with weaver's lofts, with their long rows of windows, have survived to the present day. Many have recently been restored for occupation by architects, journalists, historians and yuppies. In the 1880s they had degenerated into squalid slums; hellish havens for derelicts and other wanderers of the night. It was to one of these that Inspector Chandler was quickly summoned from Commercial Street Police station on a cold September Saturday in 1888.

No. 29 Hanbury Street, a lodging house run by 58-year-old Amelia Richardson, a maker of rough packing-cases, lay less than half a mile northwest of Buck's Row, the site of the first murder. It was here, in the back yard, that the ripped remains of Annie Chapman were discovered.

Hanbury Street was named after the local firm of brewers, Truman,

Hanbury & Buxton, whose beers are still brewed at their Black Eagle Brewery. No. 29 stood in the middle of an early eighteenth-century terrace which was pulled down in the 1970s to give way to the Truman Brewery's concrete monstrosity that now dominates the whole northern block between Wilkes Street and Brick Lane. To visualise what Hanbury Street looked like in 1888 the reader need only walk up Brick Lane and turn right into Cheshire Street, where the grimy East End of yesteryear reappears: sad streets of shuttered shopfronts and dingy dwellings: a place of peeling paint, where hollow-eyed hunger stared from broken windows and children's faces.

Some of the houses in Hanbury Street had two front doors. This was so at No. 29. One door led into the ground-floor shop. The adjacent door opened into a narrow passage dimly lit by a small gas-lamp on the wall. The passage, with its warped wooden painted panels, widened half way along where, on the left side facing the front door, a worn staircase led to the rooms upstairs. A few yards beyond the stairs was the back door, which opened onto two stone steps leading down to the back yard. Seventeen people lived at 29 Hanbury Street. So that they could come and go as they pleased the front door was customarily kept unlocked. Strangers could therefore go from the street to the back yard without disturbing any of the lodgers, or being seen by them. A few local prostitutes had discovered this and would sometimes take their clients through to the yard to be serviced with a fourpenny 'knee-trembler' against the back wall of the house.

At five minutes to six on the morning of 8 September, just eight days after the murder of Mary Anne Nichols, John Davis, a market porter who lived on the third floor of 29 Hanbury Street with his wife and three sons, went into the back yard before he left for work. As soon as he opened the back door he saw, to his everlasting horror, lying between the two steps and the rickety fence separating the yard from the one next door, the disembowelled remains of Annie Chapman. Though the handkerchief round her neck hid the jagged cut which had all but decapitated her, Davis could not miss the bloody butcher's mess that began at her abdomen and stretched up, past her neck, to where her intestines were thrown over her shoulder, like a casually tossed, blood-spangled scarf. Davis was still dressing himself, and when he ran into the street to escape the horror and to raise the alarm he still had his trouser belt in his hand. There he met PC Pinnock, who returned with a crowd at his heels, including two workmen from three doors away and some of the lodgers. Though they entered the passage of the house, they could not bring themselves to enter the yard, and after a few seconds' deliberation PC Pinnock sent some of the men for assistance. They ran off up Hanbury Street towards the red-bricked building which housed the Commercial Street police station. Inspector Joseph Chandler was on duty, and later wrote this report:

I at once proceeded to No. 29 Hanbury Street and in the back yard found a woman lying on her back, left arm resting on left breast, legs drawn up, abducted, small intestines and flap of the abdomen lying on right side above right shoulder, attached by a cord with the rest of the intestines inside the body; two flaps of skin from the lower part of the abdomen lying in a large quantity of blood above the left shoulder; throat cut deeply from left and back in a jagged manner right around the throat.

I at once sent for Dr Phillips, divisional surgeon, and to the station for the ambulance and assistance. The doctor pronounced life extinct and stated the woman had been dead at least two hours. The body was then removed on the police ambulance to the Whitechapel Mortuary.

On examining the yard I found on the back wall of the house (at the head of the body) and about 18 inches from the ground about six patches of blood varying in size from a sixpenny piece to a point, and on the wooden paling on left of the body near the head patches and smears of blood about 14 inches from the ground.

The woman has been identified by Timothy Donovan, deputy of Crossingham's lodging house at 35, Dorset Street, Spitalfields, who states he has known her about 16 months as a prostitute, and for the past four months she has lodged at above house. At 1.45 a.m. 8th instant she was in the kitchen, the worse for liquor and eating potatoes. He (Donovan) sent to her for the money for her bed, which she said she had not got and asked him to trust her, which he declined to do. She then left stating that she would not be long gone. He saw no man in her company.

Description: Annie Siffey, age 45; length 5ft; complexion fair, hair wavy, dark brown; eyes blue; two teeth deficient in lower jaw, large thick nose.

Dress: black figured jacket, brown bodice, black skirt, lace boots, all old and dirty.

A description has been circulated by wire to all stations and a special enquiry called for at lodging houses etc., to ascertain if any men of a suspicious character or having blood on their clothing entered after 2 a.m. 8th instant.

The inquest was opened by Coroner Wynne E. Baxter in the Alexandra Room of the Working Lads' Institute in Whitechapel Road. One of the first witnesses was Amelia Farmer, a friend of the dead woman. She told the hearing that, about two years before her death, Chapman had been living at 30 Dorset Street with a man who made sieves. For this reason Chapman had named herself after his trade and called herself Annie Sivvey, or Sievey. Farmer stated that Chapman sometimes sold matches or flowers, and that she was skilled in crocheting antimacassars for sale. Apparently she had only resorted to prostitution when the ten-shillings-a-week allowance from her husband ceased at his death on Christmas day 1886. Inspector Abberline stated that the victim had been positively identified as the widow of John Chapman, a Windsor coachman. He added that whoever killed Polly Nichols had also killed Chapman, stating that there was 'no doubt that the same person committed both murders'.

The police divisional surgeon, Dr George Baxter Phillips, who had twenty years' practical experience to draw upon and had examined the bodies of countless murder victims, stated that when he examined the body of Annie Chapman 'the deceased had been dead at least two hours and probably more'.

Mrs Elizabeth Long, the wife of a park-keeper, testified that at 5.30 a.m. she had seen a woman whom she believed to be Chapman talking to a man of 'shabby genteel' appearance who looked like a 'foreigner' outside 29 Hanbury Street. Ten minutes before this Albert Cadosh had gone into the yard next door to where Chapman was found dead and heard what he thought was a woman's voice from the far side of the fence, followed by what sounded like someone falling down. If the body which Cadosh thought he heard falling by the fence was Chapman's, clearly Mrs Long could not have seen her ten minutes later outside in the street. Conversely, if Mrs Long had seen Chapman, it could not have been Chapman's murder that Cadosh had heard ten minutes earlier. Alternatively, Mrs Long could have mistaken someone else for Chapman, and Cadosh could have heard a woman other than Chapman 'servicing' a client against the fence. Of course, either could have been mistaken about the time. Further evidence emerged to perplex the investigators when a certain John Richardson testified that he had entered the yard at 4.45 a.m. and seen nothing. This statement, which was noted by Chief Inspector Swanson, could not be reconciled with the time of death established by the doctor called to the grisly scene.

Dr Phillips examined Chapman's body at 6.20 a.m and expressed the opinion that she had been dead at least two hours. We have no reason to doubt this; after all, he had examined countless bodies in similar circumstances. Chapman must therefore have died about 4.20 a.m. and, he suggested, probably earlier. If so, she could not have been alive an hour or more later, at 5.20 and 5.30, the times specified in the statements of Cadosh and Long. Even the effects of massive blood loss and the exposure of the remains to the cold morning air would not have led Dr Phillips to overestimate the time of death by at least an hour and 'probably more'.

John Richardson was the son of Amelia Richardson, the landlady of No. 29, though he was not living there at the time of the murder. On that day he visited his mother's home at about 5 a.m. He went into the back yard to check that she had padlocked the cellar where he kept his tools. Afterwards he sat on the steps and, with a table knife, trimmed a loose piece of leather from his boot. The knife, which he usually employed to chop carrots for his rabbit, proved too blunt for the job in hand, and he went away to borrow another from a workmate in the nearby market. When he sat on those steps it would have been impossible for him to miss Chapman's lifeless body, if it had been there. The gory sight which later horrified Davis would have stretched out below him to his left. Indeed it would have been difficult for him to avoid touching Chapman's billowing skirts with his foot. Since it was light enough to trim away a small piece of leather it was obviously light enough to see the body. This was made abundantly clear from Richardson's statement at the inquest:

> ... I was there about a minute and a half or two minutes at the outside. It was beginning to get light but not thoroughly. I could see all over the place. I couldn't have failed to notice the dead woman if she'd been lying there.

This all tallies with what Walter Sickert maintained: that four of the five Ripper victims were not killed where they were found. Probably Albert Cadosh, the man who lived next door to where Chapman was found, heard her body being thrown to the ground by her murderers after they had carried her into the yard. Supporting Sickert's assertion was the reporter of the *East London Advertiser*. He was no doubt one of the first journalists on the scene, and he reported that blood could be seen leading down the passage and into Hanbury Street itself.

Inspector Chandler had searched the yard and discovered near the body a piece of muslin and a comb in a paper case. By her head were two pills and a torn-off piece of envelope which had been used to wrap them and must have fallen from her hand when she was placed on the ground. Dr Phillips thought that the muslin and comb had been placed there; and this led to speculation that, with some coins and rings, they had been arranged ritualistically by her feet. In fact no rings or coins were found. Chapman had been wearing three brass rings which, according to Eliza Cooper – a woman she had recently fought with – had been bought from 'a black man'. The rings were missing from the body and there was an abrasion on the ring finger apparently caused by rings being recently wrenched off. If the murderer removed the rings, he must have known, from her obvious penury, that they were brass, not gold. Was there perhaps another reason for their removal?

As well as cutting her throat and opening her abdomen, the murderer laid the intestines over her shoulder and removed her uterus and two-thirds of her bladder. These parts were not found. Dr Phillips said at the inquest, 'There were indications of anatomical knowledge. The whole of the body was not present, the absent portions are from the abdomen. The way in which those portions were extracted showed anatomical knowledge.'

The Lancet commented that the murders were 'obviously the work of an expert – of one, at least, who had such knowledge of anatomical or pathological examinations as to be enabled to secure the pelvic organs with one sweep of the knife'.

On 27 September a letter arrived at the Central News Office. It was written in red ink to simulate blood and was signed:

Yours truly Jack the Ripper.

This was the first time the sensational name had been used, and when news of it was made public it captured the imagination of hundreds of hoaxers whose letters now fill three large loose-leaf catalogues in the Metropolitan Police file. The name proved a godsend to the press, and not surprisingly many observers thought that the original letter was the work of an enterprising journalist trying to add yet more colour to an already lurid story.

There was an extraordinary number of murders in the East End of London in 1888. Yet none of them, no matter how brutal or bloody, had created as much panic as the death of Annie Chapman. Events three weeks later gave new impetus to the feeling of terror.

Murder No. 3: Elizabeth Stride   30 September

Next to the East End is the City of London, which in 1888 was, without rival, the wealthiest square mile in the world. Major Henry Smith, the Acting Deputy Commissioner for the City of London Police, drafted extra constables into his territory, which, then as now, separated the fashionable West End from the slums of the East End. This precautionary measure, however, was insufficient to prevent the first Ripper murder within the City boundaries. It occured on 30 September.

At about eight o'clock the audience were beginning to take their seats at the Lyceum Theatre to watch the American actor Richard Mansfield brilliantly portray the two title roles in Henry Irving's production of R.L. Stevenson's *Strange Case of Dr Jekyll & Mr Hyde*. The men arrived carrying silver-topped canes, resplendent in their blue-black top-hats and fur-trimmed overcoats, while their bejewelled ladies, silk bustles rustling, sparkled beneath the recently installed electric lights. In a world which could have been a thousand miles away, but was in reality less than three, Catherine Eddowes, wearing an old black jacket with an imitation fur collar and a drab linsey skirt covered with a dirty cotton apron, was seen shuffling her scuffed men's laced boots up Aldgate High Street in the heart of the East End, stupidly drunk and imitating a fire-engine. She had sunk to the pavement by the time City PC931 Lewis Robinson arrived on the scene. With the help of PC George Simmonds he half carried her to Bishopsgate Police Station, where the policy on peaceable drunks was to keep them till they were sober enough to be released.

Five hours later Louis Diemschutz reined his pony into Berner Street, which runs south from the Commercial Road. He had arrived from Upper Norwood where he sold cheap jewellery from a stall in Westow Hill, which was then overlooked by the southern water-tower of the Crystal Palace. Diemschutz was the steward of the International Working Men's Club at 40 Berner Street. This Saturday the club was as lively as usual, and after a debate on 'The Necessity for Socialism among Jews' the audience could be heard enjoying a communal sing-song. The music was still going strong when Diemschutz turned his pony into the yard by the side of the club building. The animal shied at the entrance to the yard and refused to proceed.

After prodding around with his whip, Diemschutz discovered the body of a woman he thought to be drunk. He could not see properly in the darkness and it crossed his mind that she might be his wife. He ran into the club to check if she was there, and also to get a candle, and returned to the body with another member. The candle was blown out in the wind almost as soon as it was lit, but in the light from the briefly flickering flame the two men saw that the woman was dead. Her throat had been cut and the blood was still oozing onto the cobbles. Screaming murder at the top of their voices, they ran towards Commercial Road, where they were met by PC Lamb.

The body was later identified as that of Elizabeth Stride, known among her friends as 'Long Liz'. In his official Home Office report, dated 19 October, Chief Inspector Donald Swanson took up the story:

I beg to report that the following are the particulars respecting the murder of Elizabeth Stride on the morning of 30th September.

1 a.m. 30th.Sept. A body of a woman was found with the throat cut, but not otherwise mutilated, by Louis Diemschutz (secretary to the socialist club) inside the gates of Dutfields Yard in Berner Street, Commercial road east, who gave information to the police. P.C. Lamb proceeded with him to the spot and sent for Drs. Blackwell and Phillips.

1.10 a.m. Body examined by the doctors mentioned who pronounced life extinct, the position of the body was as follows: – lying on left side, left arm extended from elbow, cachous lying in the hand, right arm over stomach, back of hand and inner surface of wrist dotted with blood, legs drawn up, knees fixed, feet close to wall, body still warm, silk handkerchief round throat, slightly torn corresponding to the angle of right jaw, throat deeply gashed and below the right angle apparent abrasion of skin about an inch and a quarter in diameter.

Search was made of yard but no instrument found.

Swanson went on to summarise his report as follows:

The body was identified as that of Elizabeth Stride, a prostitute, and it may be shortly stated that the enquiry into her history did not disclose the slightest pretext for the motive on behalf of friends or associates or anybody who had known her. The action of police being continued in the direction mentioned in the report respecting the murder of Annie Chapman was as follows.

A. Immediately after the police were on the spot the whole of the members who were in the Socialist Club were searched, their clothes examined and their statements taken.

B. Extended enquiries were made in Berner Street to ascertain if any person was seen with the woman.

C. Leaflets were printed and distributed in H Division asking the occupiers of homes to give information to police of any suspicious persons lodging in their houses.

D. The numerous statements made to police were enquired into and the persons (of whom there were many) were required to account for their presence at the time of the murders and every care was taken as far as possible to verify their statements.

Swanson next described the thoroughness with which the search was conducted, saying that 80,000 pamphlets were distributed, 80 persons detained at various police stations and 76 butchers and slaughterers investigated. It was even thought necessary to question visiting Greek gypsies; also three cowboys who had been touring Europe with Buffalo Bill's American Exibition. The consensus was that the murders were so 'un-English' in character that they must have been committed by a foreigner.

On the Monday following the murder of Stride *The Times* described the Berner Street locale thus:

The scene of the ... crime is a narrow court in Berners [sic] Street, a quiet thoroughfare running from Commercial Street down to the London, Tilbury and Southend Railway. At the entrance to the court are a pair of large wooden gates, in one of which is a small wicket for use when the gates are closed. At the hour when the murderer accomplished his purpose these gates were open, indeed, according to the testimony of those living near, the entrance to the court is seldom closed. For a distance of 18ft or 20ft from the street there is a dead wall on each side of the court, the effect of which is to enshroud the intervening space in absolute darkness after sunset. Further back some light is thrown into the court from the window of a workmen's club, which occupies the whole length of the court on the right, and from a number of cottages occupied mainly by tailors and cigarette makers on the left. At the time when the murder was committed, however, the lights in all the dwelling-houses in question had been extinguished, while such illumination as came from the club, being from the upper story, would fall on the cottages opposite and would serve to intensify the gloom of the rest of the court.

The same newspaper also reported that Stride had been found clutching grapes in her right hand, while the *Evening News* even found a witness who claimed to have sold the grapes to a man who was with Stride. Matthew Packer's fruit shop was at 44 Berner Street, two doors along from the entrance to Dutfields Yard. I have included here a previously unpublished photograph taken at the turn of the century. It shows Packer's house and the entrance to Dutfields Yard. Packer's house-cum-shop was next to the corner shop shown in the photograph, which at the time of the murder was a public house. The cartwheel which can be seen hanging on the wall of the building housing the Working

Men's Club hangs above the very spot where Elizabeth Stride's body was discovered in the 9-foot-wide gate entrance to Dutfields Yard.

In 1870 at 18 Stepney Causeway Dr Barnardo, the Irish philanthropist, opened the first of his Homes for Destitute Boys. In a letter to *The Times*, after the Ripper murders had begun, Barnardo highlighted the physical and moral danger facing children when they entered the common lodging houses, and he advocated the provision of special shelters for homeless children under the age of 16. This was not his own idea, he said, but one put to him when he had visited the common lodging house at 32 Flower & Dean Street. He was reported in the *Penny Illustrated Paper* of 13 October as saying:

> In the kitchen there were many persons ... the female inmates of the kitchen seemed thoroughly frightened at the dangers to which they were presumably exposed. The pathetic part of my story is that my remarks were followed with deep interest by all the women. Not a single scoffing voice was raised in ridicule or opposition. One poor creature, who had evidently been drinking, exclaimed somewhat bitterly to the following effect: 'We're all up to no good, and no one cares what becomes of us. Perhaps some of us will be killed next!' And then she added: 'If anybody had helped the likes of us long ago, we would never have come to this!' I have since visited the mortuary in which were lying the remains of the poor woman Stride, and I at once recognised her as one of those who stood around me in the kitchen of the common lodging house on the occasion of my visit.

Murder No. 4: Catherine Eddowes   30 September

At 1 a.m., the very moment that Stride's body was being prodded by Louis Diemschutz's horsewhip, Catherine Eddowes, who had sobered up in her cell at Bishopsgate Police Station, was being released by the gaoler, PC George Henry Hutt.

'What time is it?' she asked.

'Too late for you to get any more drink.'

'I shall get a damn fine hiding when I get home,' she observed, after being told that it was 1 o'clock in the morning.

'And serve you right, you have no right to get drunk. This way, missus.' He directed her along the passage to the outer door. 'Please pull it to.'

'All right, good night, old cock.' She closed the door behind her, and turned south towards Houndsditch, Aldgate and her death.

Less than three-quarters of an hour after Eddowes regained her freedom she was found in the darkest corner of Mitre Square by City PC 881 Watkins. She was lying in a pool of blood, 'like a pig in the market', as Watkins said later. At night Mitre Square was in almost total darkness. In the actual square there was only one lamp, which stood sixty-five feet away from the body. Victorian gas lamps shed a feeble light which penetrated the darkness only a few feet. There was also a lamp by Church

Passage, one of three passageways to the square, about seventy-five feet from the body. Church Passage led from the east of the square to Duke Street, while a covered passage near the north-east corner led into St. James' Place, known as 'Orange Market' because of the numerous establishments which once sold foreign fruits – pineapples, grapes, coconuts, melons and oranges. The main entrance to the square, the only one wide enough to allow a carriage, was a cobbled roadway 25 ft wide leading from Mitre Street.

The corpse was discovered in the south-west corner on the pavement overlooked by an empty house. Diagonally opposite was a large ware-house owned by Kearley and Tonge, Tea Merchants. Directly across the cobbled square was No. 3, a house occupied by a policeman, Richard Pearce. Next to it was another, older and empty.

Immediately after discovering the body Watkins ran across the square to Kearley & Tonge's, where he knew he would find the nightwatchman, George Morris, an ex-policeman.

The inquest was held at the City Mortuary, Golden Lane, before the Coroner, Mr M.S. Langham, who asked Morris, 'What happened at a quarter to two o'clock?' Morris told the court that his door to the warehouse was slightly 'on the jar' and, as he was sweeping the steps to the door, it was pushed by someone on the other side. He opened it wide to find PC Watkins pleading, 'For god's sake mate, come to my assistance.'

He thought at first that Watkins had been taken ill, but when asked what the matter was Watkins replied, 'There's another woman cut to pieces.'

Having ascertained that the body was in the opposite corner, he ran and shone his lamp where the corpse lay. Leaving PC Watkins to guard the body, with a shrill blast on his police-whistle, which he had retained after his retirement from the force, he ran out of the square and up to Aldgate, where he found two more policemen, PC James Harvey and PC Holland.

Dr Frederick Gordon Brown gave his medical report at the inquest on Eddowes. (It can be found among the coroner's papers which have recently been made available in the archives of the Corporation of London.) Some of the horror which Dr Brown found during his examination is seen in what follows.

> The body was on its back, the head turned to left shoulder, the arms by the side of the body as if they had fallen there. Both palms upwards, the fingers slightly bent. A thimble was lying off the finger on the right side.
>
> The clothes drawn up above the abdomen, the thighs were naked. Left leg extended in a line with the body. The abdomen was exposed, right leg bent at the thigh and knee.
>
> The bonnet was at the back of the head – great disfigurement of the face. The throat cut. Across, below the throat, was a neckerchief. The upper part of the dress was pulled open a little way. The abdomen was all exposed. The

intestines were drawn out to a large extent and placed over the right shoulder; they were smeared over with some feculent matter. A piece of about two feet was quite detached from the body and placed between the body and the left arm, apparently by design. The lobe and auricle of the right ear was cut obliquely through.

There was a quantity of clotted blood on the pavement on the left of the neck round the shoulder and upper part of the arm, and the blood coloured serum which had flowed under the neck to the right shoulder; the pavement sloping in that direction.

Body was quite warm, no death stiffening had taken place. She must have been dead most likely within half an hour. We looked for superficial bruises and saw none. No blood on the skin of the abdomen or secretion of any kind on the thighs. No spurting of blood on the bricks or pavement around. No marks of blood below the middle of the body. Several buttons were found in the clotted blood after the body was removed. There was no blood on the front of the clothes. There were no traces of recent connection.

Brown conducted the post-mortem at the City Mortuary in Golden Lane. (The building is now used as a library, and I caused some consternation among the staff when I mentioned in passing that the white-tiled room they were using as a canteen was originally the post-mortem theatre in which a Ripper victim had been examined.)

After the opening of his post-mortem report, in which he mentioned that a piece of Eddowes's ear dropped off her clothing when it was removed from the body, Brown continued:

The face was very much mutilated. There was a cut about a quarter of an inch through the lower left eyelid, dividing the structures completely through. The upper lid on that side, there was a scratch through the skin on the upper eyelid, near to the angle of the nose. The right eyelid was cut through to about half an inch. There was a deep cut over the bridge of the nose, extending from the left border of the nasal bone down near to the angle of the jaw on the right side of the cheek. This cut went into the bone and divided all the structures of the cheek except the mucous membrane of the mouth. The tip of the nose was quite detached from the nose by an oblique cut from the bottom of the nasal bone to where the wings of the nose join on to the face. A cut from this divided the upper lip and extended through the substance of the gum over the right upper lateral incisor tooth. About half an inch from the top of the nose was another oblique cut. There was a cut on the right angle of the mouth as if the cut of a point of a knife. The cut extended an inch and a half, parallel with lower lip. There was on each side of the cheek, a cut which peeled up the skin forming a triangular flap about an inch and a half. On the left cheek there were two abrasions of the epithelium under the left ear.

The throat was cut across to the extent of about six or seven inches. A superficial cut commenced about an inch below (and about two and a half inches below and behind the left ear) and extended across the throat to about three inches below the lobe of the right ear. The big muscle across the throat was divided through on the left side. The large vessels on the left side were severed. The larynx was severed and below the vocal cord all the deep structures were severed to the bone, the knife marking intervertebral cartilages. The carotid artery had a fine hole opening. The internal jugular vein was opening an inch and a half; not divided. The blood vessels contained clot. All these injuries were performed by a sharp instrument like a knife, and pointed.

The cause of death was haemorrhage from the left common carotid artery. The death was immediate and the mutilations were inflicted after death.

We examined the abdomen. The front walls were open from the breast bone to the pubes. The cut commenced opposite the enciform cartilage. The incision went upwards, not penetrating the skin that was over the sternum. It then divided the enciform cartilage. The knife must have cut obliquely at the expense of the front surface of that cartilage.

Behind this the liver was stabbed as if by the point of a sharp instrument. Below this was another incision into the liver about two and a half inches, and below this the left lobe of the liver was slit through by a vertical cut. Two cuts were shewn by a jagging of the skin on the left side.

The abdominal walls were divided in the middle line to within a quarter of an inch of the navel. The cut then took a horizontal course for two inches and a half and made a parallel incision to the former incision, leaving the navel on a tongue of skin. Attached to the navel was two and a half inches of the lower part of the rectus muscle on the left side of the abdomen. The incision then took an oblique direction to the right and was shelving. The incision went down the right side of the vagina and rectum for half an inch behind the rectum. There was a stab of about an inch on the left groin; this was done by a pointed instrument. Below this was a cut of three inches going through the peritoneum about the same extent.

An inch below the crease of the thigh was a cut extending from the anterior spine of the illium obliquely down the inner side of the left thigh and separating the left labium, forming a flap of skin up to the groin. The left rectus muscle was not detached. There was a flap of skin formed from the right thigh, attaching the right labium and extending up to the spine of the illium. The muscles on the right side inserted into the frontal ligaments were cut through. The skin was retracted through the whole of the cut of the abdomen, but the vessels were not clotted. Nor had there been any appreciable bleeding from the vessels. I draw the conclusion that the cut was made after death and there would not be much blood on the murderer. The cut was made by someone on the right side of the body, kneeling below the middle of the body.

I removed the contents of the stomach and placed it in a jar for further examination. There seemed very little in it in the way of food or fluid, but from the cut end partly digested farinaceous food escaped.

The intestines had been detached to a large extent from the mesentery; about two feet of the colon was cut away. The sigmoid flexure was invaginated into the rectum very tightly.

Right kidney pale, bloodless, with slight congestion of the base of the pyramids.

There was a cut from the upper part of the slit on the under surface of the liver to the left side, and another cut at right angles to this which were about an inch and a half deep and two and a half inches long. Liver itself was healthy.

The gall bladder contained bile. The pancreas was cut, but not through, on the left side of the spinal column. Three and a half inches of the lower border of the spleen by half an inch was attached only to the peritoneum. The peritoneal lining was cut through on the left side and the kidney carefully taken out and removed. The left renal artery was cut through. I should say that someone who knew the position of the kidney must have done it.

The lining membrane over the uterus was cut through. The womb was cut through horizontally leaving a stump of three quarters of an inch. The rest of the womb had been taken away with some of the ligaments. The vagina and cervix of the womb was uninjured.

The bladder was healthy and uninjured and contained three or four ounces of water. There was a tongue like cut through the anterior wall of the abdominal aorta. The other organs were healthy.

There was no evidence of recent connexion.

I believe the wound in the throat was first inflicted. I believe she must have been lying on the ground.

The wounds on the face and abdomen prove that they were inflicted by a sharp pointed knife, and that in the abdomen by one six inches long.

I believe the perpetrator of the act must have had considerable knowledge of the position of the organs in the abdominal cavity and the way of removing them. The parts removed would be of no use for any professional purpose. It required a great deal of knowledge to have removed the kidney and to know where it was placed. Such a knowledge might be possessed by one in the habit of cutting up animals. I think the perpetrator of this act had sufficient time, or he would not have nicked the lower eyelids. It would take at least five minutes.

I cannot assign any reason for the parts being taken away. I feel sure there was no struggle. I believe it was the act of one person.

The throat had been instantly severed so that no noise could have been emitted. I should not expect much blood to have been found on the person who inflicted these wounds. The wounds could not have been self-inflicted.

My attention was called to the apron. It was the corner of the apron, with a string attached. The blood spots were of recent origin. I have seen the portion of an apron produced by Dr Phillips and stated to have been found in Goulston Street. It is impossible to say it is human blood. I fitted the piece of apron which had a new piece of material on it which had evidently been sewn onto the piece I have, the seams of the borders of the two actually corresponding. Some blood and, apparently, faecal matter was found on the portion found in Goulston Street.

I believe the wounds on the face to have been done to disfigure the corpse.

A quarter of an hour after the discovery of the body Inspector Edward Collard arrived from Bishopsgate Police Station and ordered his men to search the neighbourhood. Nothing was found. Later the head of the City of London Police Detective Department, Superintendent James McWilliam, arrived. He ordered a second search of the area, including the lodging houses, and one of his men, Detective Constable Halse, worked his way east until he arrived in Goulston Street at around 2.20, returning to Mitre Square, whence he accompanied the body to the Golden Lane Mortuary.

While her clothing was being removed, it was observed that a portion of her apron had been cut away and was missing. Detective Constable Halse returned with Major Henry Smith to Mitre Square where it was learned that a piece of apron had been found in Goulston Street thirty-five minutes after DC Halse had patrolled there. At the junction of Goulston Street and Wentworth Street stood the recently erected Wentworth Model Dwellings. Like many of the tenements built in London during the 1880s, it had been financed by black-suited city speculators posturing as philanthropists. Like many others it was built on a system of staircases leading to apartments from open landings. Entry to the stairwell was obtained through doorways open to the street. Wentworth Model Dwellings, though still standing, is now a model only of inner city dereliction and, like most of the doorways in the building, the one to apartments 108-119 is now bricked up to prevent entry because of the dangerous condition of the building.

It was inside this doorway that PC254 Alfred Long of A Division shone his bull's-eye lantern at 2.55 a.m. and found the blood and faeces-stained piece of cloth which later proved to be a portion of Eddowes's apron. On the black brick door-jamb, between the mortar separating the bricks, written with a piece of chalk in what was described by one witness as 'a good schoolboy hand', the beam of PC Long's lamp fell upon this message with its enigmatic double-negative:

> The Juwes are
> The men that
> Will not
> be Blamed
> for nothing

Believing that there might be another body somewhere in the building, PC Long searched the staircase after blowing his whistle. There was no body, but the call for help soon brought another constable who was left to stand guard while PC Long took the piece of apron to his superiors. Though it was Metropolitan territory, the City Commissioner, Major Henry Smith, rushed to Goulston Street and ordered photographs to be taken. This, however, was not possible as it was still dark, and the photographers stood around kicking their heels waiting for dawn to break.

When Metropolitan Police Superintendent Arnold arrived he suggested that the words should be washed away for fear that Jews living in the building should become incensed and cause a riot. The Metropolitan Police Commissioner, Sir Charles Warren, agreed. Various options were suggested: the word 'Juwes' for example, with its curious spelling, could be erased, leaving the remainder to be photographed: or the whole thing could be covered with a blanket until daylight, when it could be erased after being photographed. The piece of apron was the one and only piece of forensic evidence that Jack the Ripper had left behind, making the chalked message almost of equal importance. The police had every reason to believe that the message was writen by the Ripper. DC Halse, for instance, thought that it had been chalked recently. This makes it all the odder that Warren ordered the whole of the message to be sponged away before it could be photographed in daylight. Some observers have even stated that it was Warren himself who sponged it.

Martin Fido was the first author to make known the existence of PC James Harvey.[7] Harvey's beat took him down the length of Church Passage, the way into Mitre Square from Duke Street. After walking its length he stopped at the entrance to the Square and peered into the inky darkness. He did not enter Mitre Square – that was PC Watkins's territory – but turned round and walked the thirty or so feet back to Duke Street. Fido showed that Harvey's beat took him to the entrance of Mitre Square less than five minutes before PC Watkins discovered the body. He therefore believed that the murderer took less than five minutes to kill and mutilate his victim. If so, the murderer displayed not only a metronomic sense of timing, but a skill more than humanly possible. In fact the following account shows that Fido was right.

PC Watkins testified at the inquest that he passed through Mitre Square as a church clock struck 1.30, adding that he returned to find Eddowes's body 'about twelve or fourteen minutes later': that is between 1.42 and 1.44. PC Harvey stated that he went down Church Passage, looking into the square at 'about 18 or 19 minutes to 2': that is 1.41 – 1.42.

Between 1.41, the earliest time given by Harvey for going down the passage, and 1.44, the latest time given by Watkins for the discovery of the body, there are only three clear minutes. Between the latest time given by Harvey (1.42) and the earliest time at which Watkins claimed to have found the body (also 1.42) there is no time at all.

It is altogether more likely that the body was lying in the court when Harvey looked into it, between 1.41 and 1.42, and failed to see it because of the gloom, thus allowing the murderer 12 to 14 minutes during Watkins's beat. During that time both policemen were patrolling all three entrances and every street around the square. Using the scale-drawing by Frederick W. Foster, which was produced at the inquest, it is possible to work out that PC Watkins was never more than a hearing distance of forty feet away from where Eddowes was found, and never more than thirty-five yards' walking distance.

A simple stabbing or battering would have been easy to accomplish in three minutes, but the internal exploration and intricate mutilations which characterised this murder would not have been possible in that time. And darkness made it impossible no matter how much time there was. Dr Brown pointed out at the inquest that 'it would take a great deal of skill and knowledge as to the position of the kidney to remove it. The kidney could easily be overlooked, for it is covered by a membrane.'

Since the only feeble gas-lamp in Mitre Square was sixty-five feet away, the kidney would not merely be overlooked, it would be unseen. Divisional Police Surgeon George William Sequeira made the following statement at Eddowes's inquest, which can be seen in the Corporation of London records at Guildhall.

> I know this locality. This is the darkest portion of the square. There would have been insufficient light to enable the perpetrator of the deed to have committed the deed without the addition of any light.

One thing is obvious. No one, no matter how expert or swift or deft with a knife, could have murdered Eddowes, disembowelled her, removed an organ difficult to locate and cut intricate markings on her face all within, at the very most, fourteen minutes and at the very least three minutes – and, what's more, have done so in almost total darkness.

The only explanation that fits the circumstances is that there must have been some light falling on Eddowes when the mutilations took place. But if the murderer had taken a lamp into Mitre Square he would have risked being seen, either by PC Harvey when he peered into the square from Church Passage, or by PC Watkins when he hurried from the scene of the crime, still carrying the lamp. There is only one reasonable conclusion: Catherine Eddowes was not killed in Mitre Square.

Joseph Sickert has always maintained, as he told Knight, that three of the five Ripper victims were not killed where they were found, but behind curtains within the confines of a coach which transported the bodies to the place where they were later discovered. In this way too the mutilations could be performed carefully in the light of a lamp.

A second drawing made at the murder scene, and produced at the inquest, shows what appears to be two large dark pools of blood billowing from Eddowes's throat, making it seem unlikely that she was murdered anywhere other than where she was found. The drawing, however, when examined closely, explains that one pool is of 'clot blood' while the other is of 'fluid blood'. In other words, by the time the artist arrived the blood had separated, and the serum had run down the slope of the footpath and under Eddowes neck, to form a distinct pool, making it look, at first glance, as if there was twice as much as was actually spilled. In an experiment performed by a butcher of my acquaintance, a mere quarter of a pint of blood poured onto the ground created a pool as big as the one in the drawing.

The diligent enquirer may reasonably ask why no one heard or saw a coach in the vicinity of the murders. As we have already seen, the people living near the murder site of the first victim, Mary Anne Nichols, heard no scream or sound of any struggle. In the case of Catherine Eddowes no sound was heard to arouse the suspicion of the two policemen close by. How in either case did no one remember seeing a coach, or hearing the sound of coach wheels on cobble-stones? Coaches and carts were as commonplace then as cars and taxis today. They were part of the scenery, as 'invisible' as the lamposts every few yards or the post-box on the corner. During the first murder, in Buck's Row, the police on their beats, two night-watchmen and occupiers of houses within yards of the murder site all claimed to have heard nothing, even remembering what a quiet night it was. Yet there had been a constant coming and going of knackers' wagons to and from the nearby yard of Barbers the horse-slaughterers in Winthrop Street. This backed right onto the house where Nichols's body was discovered. Just as city people sleep all night undisturbed, failing to notice the trains and large lorries which pass close by their homes, because they are used to the sound, so in 1888 the sound of horses' hooves failed to register in the minds of those living near where the Ripper victims were found.

Coaches carrying late-night revellers from club to home were so common in 1888 that even policemen would not recall any one in particular. One such club, The Imperial in Duke's Place, was emptying out at the very time Eddowes was discovered in nearby Mitre Square. At 1.35 three of its members, Joseph Lawende, Joseph Levy and Harry Harris, were waiting for hansom-cabs while standing at the end of Church Passage which led into the square. They were later interveiwed by the police. Lawende said he saw a man and woman talking amicably in the dark passage from Mitre Square to Duke's Place. He said later that the clothing of the woman was the same as Eddowes's. PC Harvey, however, saw no one there a few minutes later.

The coach conveying the murderer was just one among the many that went about their business that night unnoticed.

It was shortly before the night of the second and third murders that the first letter bearing the *nom de guerre* 'Jack the Ripper' was received and its details published in the press. Two weeks after the murder of Stride and Eddowes a parcel was sent to George Lusk who presided over a Vigilance Committee which, along with others, had been formed to help the police suppress crime in the East End. The parcel contained a letter and part of a kidney. This letter, the only one regarded by the police as 'important', was as follows:

From Hell

Mr. Lusk
 Sir
  I send you half the
Kidne I took from one women
prasarved it for you tother piece I
fried and ate it was very nise. I
may send you the bloody knif that
took it out if you only wate a whil
longer

                    signed   Catch me when
                              you can
                          Mishter Lusk.

The kidney proved to be human, but medical opinion was divided over whether or not it belonged to Catherine Eddowes. It had clearly been preserved in spirit, which led some to believe that it had been sent by a medical student as a prank.

Prank or not, when news of it hit the streets, London went into a paroxysm of fear. Not even the extra police drafted into the area could dispel the feeling of terror. People asked themselves how the police could hope to catch a killer who, under their very noses, had, in one night and in the space of 45 minutes, murdered two women, extensively mutilating one of them.

On Monday 8 October 1888 the remains of Catherine Eddowes were removed from the City Mortuary at 1.15 p.m. for interment in grave No. 49336 at the City of London Cemetery opposite Wanstead Flats, Manor Park. Her body was carried there in a glass-sided coffin, conveyed in an open hearse with a wreath on either side. Among the mourners were her sisters, Eliza Gold and Elizabeth Fisher. *The Times* of 13 October pompously observed:

> Following the remains were two mourning coaches, and in the rear of these, were a large waggon crowded with women, the majority of whom were attired in a style not at all becoming to the occasion.

Murder No. 5: Mary Kelly   9 November

After a respite of five weeks the terror was revived when Mary Kelly was murdered in her room. This was only yards from the Women's Refuge out of which Walter Sickert had brought her a few years before to be the nanny to Annie Crook's daughter Alice.

Half way up the east side of Commercial Street stands Christ Church. Built of Portland stone under an act of Parliament by Wren's pupil Nicholas Hawksmoor, it is one of the finest churches to survive from the eighteenth century. Attached to it is a parcel of land known locally since the nineteenth century as 'Itchy Park', owing to the many homeless, lice-infested people who could be seen scratching themselves as they fell asleep on the benches. Facing this park, on the opposite side of Commercial Street, was Dorset Street.

In 1883 part of the rookery of Flower & Dean Street was demolished to make space for the Charlotte de Rothschild Buildings, which were occupied the year before the Ripper murders. The slum clearance was intended to secure the 'scattering of individuals'. The individuals in question were the troublesome itinerants and 'criminal and semi-criminal classes'. The plan was not entirely successful, however. All that happened was that the undesirable elements transferred themselves into other local lodging-houses, often called doss-houses. Nowhere was there such a dense concentration as in Dorset Street which, even after it was renamed Duval Street, after Mary Kelly's murder, was still known locally as 'Dosset Street'. Though it was a narrow street of squalid slums, with a well-deserved reputation as the centre of the most sordid part of the East End, Dorset Street, unlike many of the unlit nearby streets, was ablaze with lodging-house lamps burning brightly over doorways. These were usually large enough to carry sign-written advertisements announcing the nature of the establishment and its tarriff. Out of thirty-three houses in Dorset Street listed in the 1881 census, there was a public-house at No. 32, The Blue Coat Boy, a milk-house at No. 8, three boarding-houses and sixteen private houses. The remaining twelve were listed as lodging-houses. By 1888, because of the many people made homeless by the destruction of the Flower & Dean Street rookeries, most of the sixteen private houses in Dorset Street also conducted business as lodging-houses, omitting to register as such in order to evade constrictions imposed by the lodging-house regulations.

Both Annie Chapman and Elizabeth Stride lived at No. 35, known as Crossingham's Lodging House. William and Mary Crossingham owned another lodging-house in Dorset Street, also known by their name. This was massive, comprising Nos 16, 17, 18 and 19 at the Commercial Street end. Opposite was the narrow entrance to Millers Court where Mary Kelly rented the room where her body was discovered on the morning of 9 November 1888.

A number of statements taken by the police that morning are copied verbatim below.

Statement of Thomas Bowyer, 37, Dorset Street, Spitalfields, in the employ of John McCarthy, Lodging house keeper, Dorset Street.

Says that at 10.45 a.m. 9th instant, he was sent by his employer to number 13 room, Millers Court, Dorset Street for the rent. He knocked at the door, but not getting any answer he threw the blinds back and looked through the window, which was broken, and saw the body of the deceased woman whom he knew as Mary Jane. Seeing that there was a quantity of blood on her person and that she had been apparently murdered, he immediatly went and informed his employer Mr McCarthy, who also looked into the room and at once dispatched Bowyer to the police station, Commercial Road, and informed the inspector on duty (Insp. Beck) who returned with him and his employer who had also followed to the station. He knew the deceased and also a man named Joe, who had occupied the room for some months past.

Statement of John McCarthy, Lodging House Keeper, 27 Dorset Street, Spitalfields.

I sent my man Thomas Bowyer to No. 13 room, Millers Court, Dorset Street owned by me for the rent. Bowyer came back and called me, telling me what he had seen. I went with him back and looked through the broken window, where I saw the mutilated remains of deceased whom I knew as Mary Jane Kelly. I then despatched Bowyer to the Police Station, Commercial Street (following myself) to acquaint the police. The Inspector on duty returned with us to the scene at Millers Court. I let the room about ten months ago to the deceased and a man named Joe, who I believed to be her husband. It was a furnished room at 4/6 per week. I sent for the rent because for some time past they had not kept their payments regularly. I have since heard the man named Joe was not her husband and that he had recently left her.

Statement of Joe Barnett, now residing at 24 and 25 New Street, Bishopsgate (a common lodging house).

I am a porter in Billingsgate Market, but have been out of employment for the past 3 or 4 months. I have been living with Marie Jeanette Kelly who occupied No. 13 room, Millers Court. I have lived with her altogether about 18 months, for the last eight months in Millers Court, until last Tuesday week (Ulto) when in consequence of not earning sufficient money to give her and her resortimg to prostitution, I resolved on leaving her, but I was friendly with her and called to see her between seven and eight p.m. Thursday (8th) and told her I was very sorry I had no work and that I could not give her any money. I left her about 8 o'clock same evening and that was the last time I saw her alive.

Elizabeth Prater, wife of William Prater of No. 20 room, 27 Dorset Street, states as follows:

I went out about 9 p.m. on the 8th and returned about 1.30. I was speaking for a short time to a Mr McCarthy who keeps a chandler's shop at the corner of the court. I then went up to bed. About 3.30 or 4 a.m. I was awakened by a kitten walking across my neck, and just then I heard screams of murder about two or three times in a female voice. I did not take much notice of the cries as I frequently hear such cries from the back of the lodging-house where the windows look into Millers Court. From 1 a.m. to 1.30 a.m. no one passed up the court, if they did I should have seen them. I was up again and downstairs in the court at 5.30 a.m. but saw no one except two or three carmen harnessing their horses in Dorset Street. I went to the 'Ten Bells' P.H. at the corner of Church Street and had some rum. I then returned and went to bed again without undressing and slept until about 11 a.m.

The following statement seemed to confirm the screams of murder heard about 4 a.m:

Statement of Sarah Lewis, No. 24 Great Pearl Street, Spitalfields, a laundress.

Between 2 and 3 o'clock this morning I came to stop with the Keylers at No. 2 Millers Court as I had had a few words with my husband. When I came up the court there was a man standing over against the lodging house on the opposite side in Dorset Street but I cannot describe him. Shortly before 4 o'clock I heard a scream like that of a young woman, and seemed to be not far away. She screamed out murder. I only heard it once. I did not look out of the window. I did not know the deceased.

Sarah Lewis further said that when in company with another female on Wednesday evening last at Bethnal Green, a suspicious man accosted her. He carried a black bag.

Statement of Mary Ann Cox, No. 5 Room, Millers Court, Dorset Street, Spitalfields.

I am a widow and an unfortunate. I have known the female occupying No. 13 room, Millers Court about 8 months. I knew her by the name Mary Jane. About a quarter to twelve last night I came into Dorset Street from Commercial Street, and saw walking in front of me Mary Jane with a man. They turned into the court and as I entered the court they went indoors. As they were going into her room, I said good night Mary Jane. She was very drunk and could scarcely answer me, but said good night. The man was carrying a quart can of beer. I shortly afterwards heard her singing. I went out shortly after twelve and returned about one o'clock and she was still singing in her room. I went out again shortly after one o'clock and returned at 3 o'clock. There was no light in her room then and all was quiet, and I heard no noise all night.

The man whom I saw was about 36 years old, about 5ft 5in. high, complexion fresh and I believe he had blotches on his face, small side whiskers and a thick carroty moustache, dressed in shabby dark clothes, dark overcoat and black felt hat.

Mary Jane was dressed I think, last night when I saw her, in a linsey frock, red knitted cross-over around shoulders, had no hat or bonnet on.

Statement of Julia Venturney.

I occupy No.1 room, Millers Court. I am a widow but now living with a man named Harry Owen. I was awake all night and could not sleep. I have known the person occupying No. 13 room opposite mine for about 4 months. I knew the man who I saw down stairs (Joe Barnett) he is called Joe, he lived with her until quite recently. I have heard him say that he did not like her going out on the streets. He frequently gave her money. He was very kind to her. He said he would not live with her while she led that course of life. She used to get tipsy occasionally. She broke the windows a few weeks ago whilst she was drunk. She told me she was very fond of another man named Joe, and he had often ill used her because she cohabited with Joe (Barnett). I saw her last yesterday, Thursday about 10 a.m.

Statement of Maria Harvey of 3, New Court, Dorset Street.

I slept two nights with Mary Jane Kelly, Monday and Tuesday last. I then took a room at the above house. I saw her last about five minutes to seven last night in her own room, when Barnett called. I then left. They seemed to be on the best of terms, I left an overcoat, two dirty cotton shirts, a boy's shirt and a girl's white petticoat and black crape bonnet in the room. The overcoat shown me by police is the one I left there.

At Kelly's inquest, Maria Harvey also reported that Kelly was much better educated than other women of her class.

The following statement has been the subject of some debate, since the person making it claimed to have seen Mary Kelly on the morning she was found dead, when medical evidence showed that she had been murdered five or six hours before.

Statement of Caroline Maxwell, 14 Dorset Street, Spitalfields, the wife of Henry Maxwell, a lodging house deputy.

I have known deceased woman during the past 4 months, she was known as Mary Jane, and that since Joe Barnett left her she has obtained her living as an unfortunate. I was on speaking terms with her although I had not seen her for 3 weeks until Friday morning 9th instant about half past 8 o'clock. She was then standing at the corner of Millers Court in Dorset Street. I said to her, what brings you up so early. She said, I have the horrors of drink upon me as I have been drinking for some days past. I said why don't you go to Mrs Ringer's* and have ½ pint of beer. She said, I have been there and had it, but I brought it all up again. At the same time she pointed to some vomit in the roadway. I then passed on, and went to Bishopsgate on an errand, and returned to Dorset Street about 9 a.m. I then noticed deceased standing outside Ringers public house. She was talking to a man, age I think about 30, height about 5ft 5in, stout, dressed as a Market Porter. I was some distance away and am doubtful whether I could identify him. The deceased wore a dark dress, black velvet body, and coloured wrapper round her neck.

Four people assisted Dr Bagster Phillips in the post-mortem. In addition to his junior partner there were Dr Duke of Spitalfields, Dr Gordon Brown and Dr Thomas Bond, the consulting surgeon to the Metropolitan Police 'A' Division. Dr Bond was also a lecturer in forensic pathology, and his presence was specifically requested by Robert Anderson, the Assistant Commissioner and head of the Metropolitan CID.

A letter from Bond confirms Bagster Phillips's belief that Kelly died about twelve hours before they examined her remains: that is, at about 2 a.m. Thus when Mrs Maxwell claimed that she saw Kelly alive at 8.30 a.m, six and a half hours after the estimated time of death, it was thought that she mistook either the day or, less probably, the person.

The key to Kelly's room had been missing for some time, and Barnett confirmed that he and Kelly used to open the door by reaching through a broken window pane at the side to draw the bolt, locking it by the same means. The window had only been broken since their quarrel on 30 October, ten days before the murder. Yet the key had been missing for some time before that. Someone, it was reported, must have had a key, for the room was found to be locked from the inside and the police could not

* The Britannia, a public house at the corner of Dorset Street and Commercial Street. It was run by Walter Ringer and his wife Matilda.

open the door merely by reaching through the broken window and slipping the bolt; they had to break in.

After his arrival in Millers Court, Inspector Abberline gave orders for it to be sealed off; no one was to leave or enter. Soon afterwards he sent a telegram to Sir Charles Warren suggesting that bloodhounds be brought. The police then stood around waiting for the Commissioner's arrival. Unfortunately they did not know that he had resigned the day before.

By 1.30 Superintendant Arnold decided that they had waited long enough and ordered the window to be removed. What they had been able to see through the broken pane had been sickening enough, but the sight which greeted their unimpeded view, once the whole frame with its dirty panes had been taken out, was one of unmitigated horror and desecration, a charnel house of profanity. The *Illustrated Police News* reported:

> The throat had been cut right across with a knife, nearly severing the head from the body. The abdomen had been partially ripped open, and both of the breasts had been cut from the body, the left arm, like the head, hung to the body by the skin only. The nose had been cut off, the forehead skinned, and the thighs down to the feet, stripped of the flesh. The abdomen had been slashed with a knife right across downwards, and the liver and entrails wrenched away. The entrails and other portions of the frame were missing, but the liver etc., it is said were found placed between the feet of this poor victim. The flesh from the thighs and legs, together with the breasts and nose, had been placed by the murderer on the table, and one of the hands of the dead women had been pushed into her stomach.

A press agency report which was immediately syndicated to several newspapers, such as *The Times*, gave further details. They included the following:

> ... while the face was slashed about, so that the features of the poor creature were beyond all recognition...The clothes of the woman were lying by the side of the bed, as though they had been taken off and laid down in the usual manner.

Though there were reports that the uterus was missing, the examining doctors confirmed that this was not the case. In 1987 Scotland Yard recovered the original post-mortem report on Kelly, written by Dr Thomas Bond (see below, Appendix 10).

It was disclosed at the inquest, and reported in some newspapers, that Kelly had two children, but no one knew their names or their whereabouts.

After the police had entered through the window and taken photographs, the landlord, John McCarthy, broke open the door with a pick-axe. No one has yet tried to explain why the window was removed. The simple procedure would have been to break open the door straight away. Fresh information, which has never before been discussed, let alone published, will enable us to explain (in Chapter 12) exactly why the police could not enter 13 Millers Court by the simple expedient of going through the door.

Millers Court was a narrow yard of six houses, white-washed up to the first story, the window-frames showing the remnants of green paint. Entrance to the court was obtained through an arched, tunnel-like passage which ran between Nos 26 and 27 Dorset Street, both of which were owned by Kelly's landlord, John McCarthy, a 37-year-old naturalised British subject born in France. No. 27, to the left of the passage, was McCarthy's chandler's shop, but the building doubled above and behind as a lodging house. No. 26 was also a lodging house and the rear ground-floor had been partitioned, so that a second room was created. This was Kelly's room, No. 13. It was small, about twelve feet square, and was entered through a door at the right-hand side of the passage at the furthest end from the street. Apart from the bed, there were two tables (one holding portions of Kelly's body), another small table and two dining-type chairs, one of which had a broken back. A fierce fire had been burning in the grate and the ashes, after being sifted, disclosed the remains of clothing left by Kelly's friend Maria Harvey, which she alluded to in her statement. Above the fireplace opposite the door hung a print entitled 'The Fisherman's Widow'. In a small wall-cupboard next to it there was some crockery, some empty ginger-beer bottles and a piece of stale bread. A man's pilot coat doubled as a curtain over the window, one of two looking out into the courtyard at right-angles to the door of the room.

*

On the day of Kelly's funeral her body was conveyed from the mortuary attached to St Leonard's Church, Shoreditch, to St Patrick's Roman Catholic Cemetery at Leytonstone. St Leonard's is immortalised in the traditional 'Oranges and Lemons' nursery rhyme with the words: 'When I grow rich, say the bells of Shoreditch.' When one one of the bells began tolling at noon on the day of Kelly's funeral, they acted as a signal to draw together a large crowd of local residents. As the coffin appeared at the main gate of the church, borne upon the shoulders of four men, the crowd seemed to be suddenly agitated, and as the coffin was placed in the open car people rushed forward desperately trying to touch it. All the men had respectfully removed their hats, and several women, with tears rolling down their rouged cheeks, cried out, 'God forgive her.'

The coffin was carried in the open horse-drawn car, followed by two mourning carriages with three people in one and five in the other. Joe Barnett was there of course, as well as the women who had given evidence at the inquest. In deference to the French style in which Mary

Kelly preferred to be known, someone, probably Barnett, had seen fit to
have the following words engraved on the coffin plate:

Marie Jeanette Kelly, died 9th November, 1888, aged 25 years.

When Father Colomban read the service by the side of Kelly's final
resting place, an unmarked pauper's grave, the mourners had no way of
knowing that the spectre of Jack the Ripper had retreated into the
shadows, his ghastly work complete, his reign of terror ended.

"I COULD SWEAR TO THE MAN ANYWHERE"
HUTCHINSON.

CHAPTER THREE

Masonic Mutilation

Not since James II fled the country in 1688, taking refuge with Louis of France, has a Roman Catholic monarch ruled England. The year 1988 marked not only the centenary of the Ripper murders, but the tercentenary of the landing in England of William of Orange, invited by the Protestant leaders to seize his father-in-law's throne.

If the Vatican wished to extend God's Kingdom on earth by having a British monarch bend the knee before St Peter, a first step, a sort of Popish foot in the front door of Buckingham Palace, would be for the heir presumptive to the throne to marry a Catholic. This was the fear of those in power at the end of Queen Victoria's reign when they learned that her grandson, Prince Albert Victor, had married Annie Elizabeth Crook.

We need hardly wonder that leading Freemasons of the day wished Eddy's marriage to a Catholic to remain a secret. Enmity between Catholics and Freemasons had existed for a century and a half. The Vatican first showed its hostility in 1738 with *In Eminenti*, Clement XII's famous Bull which condemned 'the society, Lodges and Conventicles of Liberi Muratori, or Freemasons, under pain of excommunication to be incurred ipso facto ...' This anathema continued until 1975, when it was ordained that a Catholic could become a Freemason if he obtained the consent of his bishop.

Throughout the last two decades of the nineteenth century a torrent of condemnation of Freemasonry poured from the Vatican. Leo XIII issued three denunciations, the first, his famous Encyclical of 1884, has been described by an eminent authority as 'perhaps the severest attack the Papal See has ever made upon Freemasonry, and is of such immense significance in respect of what happened to Freemasonry round about the turn of the century ...'[1]

A strong anti-Catholic sentiment existed at that time, particularly among Freemasons, but also in the rest of the population. Walter Sickert told Joseph that all the troubles suffered by Eddy, Annie and their daughter Alice, and later by Joseph himself, only happened 'because you are all bloody Catholics'. This judgment, however simple, shows the importance he attached to the anti-Catholicism of leading Freemasons before the Second World War, and to its prevalence especially at the time of the Ripper murders.

Faced with the blackmail attempt of Mary Kelly and her three friends (Kelly too was a Catholic), certain leading Freemasons felt compelled to cover up Eddy's indiscretion. They belonged to a particular lodge, the Royal Alpha Lodge No. 16, a brief history of which may be of interest.

When the Duke of Sussex became Grand Master of the United Grand Lodge in 1813, he decided to form a private lodge under his personal control, the members of which were to be hand-picked. The 'Well Disposed Lodge', which met in Waltham Abbey, was chosen for the role. It was renamed the 'Alpha' and moved into Kensington Palace. In 1824 it left the palace and met in various places. These, according to Lane's *Masonic Records* of 1895, included Willis's Rooms, King Street, St James's Square, and the Hotel Metropole in Northumberland Avenue.

Masters of this lodge have always been eminent masons: Grand Masters, Provisional Grand Masters and Princes of the Blood Royal. Initiations have been relatively rare, but some have been particularly notable. In 1885, the year Alice Crook was born, Eddy, her royal father, was initiated by his own father, the Prince of Wales, who was Master of the lodge in that year. The present-day Grand Master of England, the Duke of Kent, and his brother Prince Michael are two recent admissions.

Notable members in the 1880s included the Duke of St Albans, the Earl of Carnarvon, the Earl of Derby, the Earl of Limerick, the Marquess of Lincolnshire and the Earl of Euston, who was to figure in the Ripper murders. According to Walter Sickert two other Freemasons were also deeply involved: the Physician-in-Ordinary to Queen Victoria, Sir William Withey Gull, and the Chief Commissioner of the Metropolitan Police, Sir Charles Warren. Neither is listed as a member in either of the two histories of the Royal Alpha published by the United Grand Lodge after the Ripper murders, the first in 1891, the other in 1963. The former lists its officers. The Most Worshipful Brother HRH Prince of Wales was the Immediate Past Master; the Senior Warden was Lord Balfour of Burleigh, the Fellow Warden the Earl of Limerick. In 1888 Prince Eddy was the Right Worshipful Master of the Lodge.[2] Since neither is listed, Gull and Warren may simply have been regular visitors to the lodge as guests of their friends. Sickert may have assumed that they were members because of their association with the two Princes.

*

Walter told Joseph that when Mary Kelly returned to the East End after Annie's incarceration she was utterly distraught. Some women sitting around the fire with her in the kitchen of a lodging house asked what was wrong, and she blurted out the whole story of Prince Eddy, Annie and their child Alice. When they heard this they decided to blackmail Sickert, assuming that as he lived in the West End, took holidays in France and hobnobbed with royalty he must be a wealthy man.

Their demand, however, was very modest. Women who earned a mere fourpence, the price of a night's lodging, by 'entertaining' a stranger who paid for the bed in which he was entertained, could doubtless be fobbed off with a paltry sum. Though these women worked when they could – sewing sacks, selling flowers, making matchboxes at twopence farthing per gross, or, like Annie Chapman, crocheting antimacassars, they would often, out of sheer desperation, earn a crust and a night's lodging by selling their bodies. The story of a prince marrying a commoner would hardly be shocking to them. Indeed they probably found it both amusing and romantic. Walter told Florence Pash, as we noted in Chapter 2, that Kelly sent the blackmail letter. According to Florence Pash (above, p. 10) she was resentful of Sickert, who had not 'treated her with sufficient respect and consideration.'[3]

The blackmail demand, as we have seen, finally reached the Prime Minister, Lord Salisbury. According to Joseph, Walter believed that Salisbury was a Freemason in the Royal Alpha Lodge and so knew all about the masons' involvement in the Ripper murders. In none of the masonic literature I have read, however, is he ever mentioned among the eminent statesmen claimed by the Grand Lodge. Indeed in 1986 the United Grand Lodge stated categorically that he was not a Freemason. His father, the 2nd Marquess, had been the Vice Grand Master of All England, and one of his own sons was also a mason. The son of a mason is known as a 'Lewis', and it is the usual practice for Freemasons, particularly among peers, to invite their sons into the fraternity. The Grand Lodge may have denied Salisbury's affiliation either to distance him from recent theories suggesting masonic influence in the Ripper murders, or more probably to distance themselves. Walter's assertion that Salisbury was a member of the Royal Alpha Lodge, though not proved, is probable, since Sickert had an intimate working knowledge of Freemasonry and was aware of the masonic connection with the Ripper gang, most of whom he knew well. But even if Salisbury was not a mason it would still have been in his interest to support any plan to maintain his position and, more especially, that of the Royal Family. The scandal was, after all, a serious threat to the monarchy and the Establishment.

Here it is worth digressing to note the family's anti-Catholic history, particularly as exemplified by Robert Cecil, the 1st Earl. Many who annually celebrate the Gunpowder Plot of 5 November 1605 do so in the mistaken belief that it was conceived by Guy Fawkes. Historians know otherwise, since there is abundant evidence pointing to Robert Cecil as the one who – through Thomas Percy, beneath whose lodgings by the House of Lords the gunpowder was placed – surreptitiously nurtured and encouraged the plot. He intended the plotters to be 'discovered', tried and found guilty so that the Catholics would fall into disrepute. In this he was successful. Catholics suffered merciless persecution during the seventeenth century.

Cecil did not oppose Catholics in general, only political Catholics likely to upset the established order.[4] His descendant inherited not only his family title but also its inbred need and unquestioned ability to foil any faction which threatened the national church. This was how he chose to view the threat of Irish Catholic Mary Kelly and her friends to expose Eddy's marriage to a Catholic, and why he aligned himself with the Ripper coterie. Walter Sickert's contention, as we have seen, voiced several times to his son Joseph, was that the Ripper murders only occurred 'because you're all bloody Catholics'.

According to Sickert, as we have noted, Salisbury never intended the four women blackmailers to die, merely to be silenced. Sickert knew that the Ripper plan was not conceived by the Prime Minister but by the country's leading Freemason. The Prince of Wales, though he was Grand Master of the United Grand Lodge of England, was not the supreme mason. (A similar situation exists today. The present Grand Master, the Duke of Kent, holds a largely titular position, and is not the country's leading mason. This is Major-General Sir Ralph Hone, KCMG, KBE.)

*

Two masons who were part of the Ripper conspiracy were Sir Charles Warren and Sir William Gull. Warren, head of the Metropolitan Police, was in an ideal position to ensure a successful cover-up. Gull killed and subsequently mutilated four of the Ripper victims. He can therefore be said to be 'Jack the Ripper'. When Joseph ended his collaboration with Stephen Knight, Knight had learned from Joseph that it was Gull who had carried out the actual killings, and he therefore told his readers that Gull was the leader. But Knight was mistaken. Gull was working under orders from another member of the Royal Alpha Lodge – a man on close terms both with the Prince of Wales and with his son Eddy, whose family sometimes employed Sir William as their family doctor. It was this man who had once been in Lord Salisbury's Cabinet and was a member of the English nobility, who orchestrated the affair, directing the murders and the disposal of their bodies. He was the last person seen with Kelly at the approximate time of death as estimated by the doctors.

Before revealing his name and the names of the rest of the Ripper gang, we must explain briefly why the murders were executed with such gruesome finesse. This requires some basic background information about Freemasonry.

*

Fremasonry began life as a mediaeval sow's ear. By the middle of the last century it had become a Victorian silk purse. Conceived originally as a craft guild, in the first quarter of the eighteenth century it had been taken over by the landed gentry, the aristocracy and the Royal Family.

In the Middle Ages members of the craft guilds were known to one another because they worked together in the same place. Silversmiths, for instance, received customers in their workshop. So did shoemakers, milliners and joiners. Even carpenters building houses or the local tavern at the village crossroads needed only to walk down the lane a short way, seeking other local work when the tavern was completed. Stonemasons were different. The stone buildings erected in the Middle Ages were mostly cathedrals, castles, churches or abbeys, and they were spread around the country. Only cities had cathedrals. Castles were comparatively few and far between, while abbeys, self-governing monasteries, were even fewer. Consequently the stonemason had to travel round the country from job to job, wherever work was available, or under compulsion when royal buildings were being erected. When he arrived at his next job he was often a complete stranger to those already there, particularly to those overseeing the work. Stonemasons soon devised a system of secret signs and passwords which enabled strangers applying for work to prove that they were properly qualified. In this way they were able to maintain a closed shop, with the highest standards of workmanship. The place where they kept their tools was called the lodge.

Unlike almost every other craft, in which the craftsmen required the 'freedom' of the city to pursue his occupation, the travelling masons needed to be 'free' to build anywhere, unimpeded by local by-laws and regulations. This is one reason why they became known as Freemasons. Eventually they became more than a guild, growing beyond their special role as a trade union and, by the end of the sixteenth century, becoming a covert organisation of mutual assistance with its own philosophy. At this stage they allowed other tradesmen and gentlemen into their lodges. Those who had trained as stonemasons were known as 'operative freemasons', the rest as 'speculative freemasons'.

Modern freemasonry is thought to have begun in Scotland. The first non-mason to be initiated was John Boswell, Laird of Auchinlech and ancestor of Dr Johnson's biographer, who became a member of the Lodge in Edinburgh in 1600. The first non-mason in England is thought to have been Sir Robert Moray, who was initiated at Newcastle-upon-Tyne in 1641.

*

By the end of the seventeenth century 'accepted masons', as speculative masons were also called, outnumbered operative masons, and soon the 'gentlemen of fashion and taste', who saw no reason why they should associate with 'common' artisans, began to form their own lodges. In 1716 four London lodges were united in the Grand Lodge and 'resolv'd to hold the Annual ASSEMBLY and feast, and then chuse a GRAND MASTER from among themselves, till they should have the Honour of a Noble Brother at their Head'.[5]

The election of one Anthony Sayer on St John the Baptist's Day 1717 fulfilled the first part of this resolution. It was a token appointment, as the upper-class brothers wished to consolidate their influence steadily without antagonising the established membership. Just as the speculative membership had overwhelmed the original operative brothers, so the nobility now sought to dominate the accepted masons. The second part of the resolution was realised when the 2nd Duke of Montague was appointed Grand Master – the first, long-awaited 'Noble Brother'. Since then dozens of noblemen have been initiated into Freemasonry: Earls, Marquesses, Dukes and Princes of the Blood Royal. The last have included five future Kings of England: George IV, William IV, Edward VII, Edward VIII and George VI. Edward VII's two brothers were both Freemasons, as was his father-in-law, Christian IX of Denmark.

Other eminent English masons have been the Duke of Wellington, Earl Kitchener, Earl Jellicoe and Field-Marshalls Earl Haig and Earl Alexander of Tunis. Prince Philip was initiated in December 1952. The present Grand Master of England, as we have noted, is the Duke of Kent. The Grand Patroness is Her Majesty Queen Elizabeth II.

One's imagination may well be stretched by the thought of a Royal Prince or Field-Marshal or famous statesman baring his breast and rolling up one trouser leg during what seems to many to be a rather childish initiation rite. Yet this ritual is only a small part of the first of the installation ceremonies.

In the Middle Ages a young man wishing to become a stonemason did so by entering his craft as an apprentice. Traditionally, Accepted Freemasons are ceremonially initiated as 'Entered Apprentice'. This is known as the first degree. In the second degree the Entered Apprentice 'passes' into the position of 'Fellow Craft', and from this intermediate position he can become a 'Master Mason', being so 'raised' in the third-degree ceremony. These three degrees – Entered Apprentice, Fellowcraft and Master Mason – comprise Craft Freemasonry, which is under the jurisdiction of the United Grand Lodge. There are, however, other, higher degrees, of which many masons are unaware and which are not supervised by the Grand Lodge.

Many men 'raised' to the status of Master Mason believe that they have reached the top of the masonic ladder, since the higher degrees are never mentioned, except to a person invited to enter them. Despite the connotations of the term 'Master Mason', it is only the highest of the lower degrees. If the Master Mason has any ambition it is usually within his own lodge where, with the passage of time, he can rise to become the

Worshipful Master. The ambitious can aim for rank in their Provincial Grand Lodge, or even within the United Grand Lodge itself. But beyond these 'Craft' degrees, there are some thirty higher degrees which are under the jurisidiction of the Supreme Council, which meets at No. 10 Duke Street, St James, an Edwardian building known among masons as the 'The Grand East'. A brass plaque by the door announces innocently: 'Supreme Council 33°.'

As a first-degree Entered Apprentice the initiate swears on pain of death and horrible mutilation to obey the precepts not only of the brotherhood, but of the Bible and the laws of the land in which his lodge is located. (This feature has been omitted since 1988 because of adverse publicity caused, in the main, by Stephen Knight's attack in *The Brotherhood*.) As a third-degree Master Mason the initiate swears to keep the secrets of another Master Mason, saying: '... my breast shall be the sacred repository of his secrets when entrusted to my care – murder, treason, felony, and all other offences contrary to the laws of God and the ordinances of the realm being at all times most especially excepted.'[6] In other words a Master Mason is required to keep the secrets of his masonic brothers, unless they engage in murder, treason or felony.

A Freemason of the third degree wishing to be elevated to the higher degrees has to be selected by the Supreme Council, and if he is chosen he has the opportunity to rise to the 33°. In practice, however, only a few are selected. Beyond the third degree it takes another fourteen degrees to become 'perfected', to pass through the Holy Royal Arch. Once he has passed the Royal Arch, the mason's vows undergo a grave change and during his initiation he swears '... that a companion Royal Arch Mason's secrets, given me in charge as such, shall remain as secure and inviolable in my breast as in his own, murder and treason not excepted ... that I will aid and assist a companion Royal Arch Mason when engaged in any difficulty, and espouse his cause, so far as to extricate him from same if in my power, *whether he be right or wrong*' (my italics).[7]

William Morgan, an American Freemason, author of *Freemasonry Exposed* (1836), who was, as rumour had it, murdered for his pains, stated:

> The oath taken by Royal Arch Masons does not except murder and treason, therefore under it, all crimes can be perpetrated.[8]

Not only is the Royal Arch Mason prohibited from exposing his brother on pain of death, he is compelled to assist in covering up his crimes.

All but two of the group of masons responsible for the Ripper murders were Royal Arch Masons. One, as already stated, was the Metropolitan Police Commissioner, Sir Charles Warren. He passed the Royal Arch in 1861 at the remarkably early age of 21, the age at which it is usual for a young man to be invited to join the brotherhood. As the Met's top man he was in a unique position to fulfil his Royal Arch oath: to assist a brother in difficulty. The ruling masons behind the Government believed themselves to be in danger, and since Eddy was a fellow Freemason he could expect their help. He received it when they silenced Mary Kelly and the other blackmailers, and they were killed according to masonic ritual.

*

To enhance their credibility and give an air of authority to their beliefs, the masons claim certain ancient events to be at the root of their order. Not least is the story of the building of Solomon's Temple at Jerusalem.

The master builder of the temple was Hiram Abiff. This at least has Biblical foundation, but masonic legend adds to the scriptures with its unattributable claim that Hiram Abiff had three apprentice masons who murdered him because he would not divulge to them his masonic secrets. These three were called Jubela, Jubelo and Jubelum. After murdering their master they fled, but they were hunted down and found at the coast near Joppa, whereupon they themselves were put to death 'by the breast being torn open and the heart and vitals taken out and thrown over the left shoulder'.

In the first degree of Freemasonry, that of Entered Apprentice, part of the penalty for revealing masonic secrets is to have one's throat cut. The 'penal sign' of the Entered Apprentice is a left-to-right movement, the extended thumb of the right hand being passed across the throat. Ripperologists have generally accepted that four of the five Ripper victims had their throats cut exactly that way. There has been some debate about whether or not Elizabeth Stride did, but the medical evidence gives an accurate account of how she died. Both Dr Baxter Phillips, who examined her corpse, and Dr Thomas Bond, the consulting surgeon for the Metropolitan Police's 'A' Division, agreed that her throat had been cut in the same way, that is, from left to right. In addition to having their throats cut, Annie Chapman and Catherine Eddowes had their intestines torn out and 'placed' over their shoulders, like the three legendary apprentices. It is perhaps unnecessary to add that Freemasons are not generally thought to reward treachery with ritualised murder. The Whitechapel atrocities were planned by the warped minds of men belonging to one particular lodge.

*

When Prince Eddy ventured into Cleveland Street to see Sickert or to meet his sweetheart Annie, he left Marlborough House by coach from the Royal Mews. Out of discretion he later transferred from this coach, with the Royal Arms emblazoned on its door, to a privately hired coach. The driver was John Netley.

Walter Sickert described Netley as only about 5 ft 5 ins tall, but with broad shoulders. He added that Netley was insecure about his height and, to compensate, ingratiated himself with eminent people. As he was already aware of the secret trysts between the Prince and the shopgirl, and of their marriage and child, he was later recruited by the Ripper gang to convey Sir William Gull to the East End to murder Mary Kelly and her blackmailing associates.

The prospective victim was first located and then invited into the coach to be murdered by Gull. This took place behind drawn curtains, where the victim was mutilated by the light of a lamp. The Royal Physician's gory work complete, Netley drove to a pre-arranged place and deposited the body on the ground, arranging it in the manner prescribed by his masonic masters. In the 1880s it was not uncommon for customers to invite prostitutes into coaches for illicit sex, rather as kerb-crawlers invite them into cars today. Once they were inside, Gull gave the women grapes which had been liberally treated with laudanum, an alcoholic extract of opium. It was Gull's habit to carry grapes and raisins as a refreshing snack to relieve weariness. This fact is supported in a letter to Dr Duckworth (later Sir Dyce Duckworth, Consulting Physician to the Prince of Wales) found by Stephen Knight in the library of the Royal College of Physicians. Sir William Gull wrote:

> I believe in the use of wine as I have said ... but I repeat that in my work when fatigued I prefer grapes and raisins and water ... 16 Dec 1877.

When, in 1973, Joseph Sickert first made his claim that Gull was the actual murderer and that he used poisoned grapes, he had no way of knowing that Gull habitually ate grapes to refresh himself. Nor could he have known of Gull's letter to Dr Duckworth.

According to the testimony given at her inquest by Dr William Sedgewick Saunders, the City of London analyst, it appears that Eddowes was not drugged in this manner. His report can be examined in the Corporation of London Records Office. A Fellow of the Institute of Chemistry and a Fellow of the Chemical Society, Saunders stated unequivocally:

> I carefully examined the stomach and the contents more particularly for poisons of the narcotic class with negative results there being not the slightest trace of these or any other poison.[9]

Dr Saunders was a Freemason.

Eddowes was released from her cell only four and a half hours after she had been unable to stand without support. Most people in such a condition would need at least eight hours to rid their bodies of the alcohol. Though she was capable of leaving the police station, we can assume that her brain was still so befuddled by alcohol that she was easily enticed into the coach. Since one murder had been committed already that night, the murderers probably wished to deal quickly with Eddowes so that they could leave the area. They dispatched her immediately.

*

Once the women were in the coach, Gull could begin his grisly work. The inside of the coach was lined with 'American cloth', a waterproof material made to look like leather and normally used to cover chairs and carriage seats, which prevented the victim's blood from soaking into the floor of the coach. The material was later removed by Netley and washed down.

Much of the medical evidence indicates that Nichols, Chapman and Eddowes were not killed where they were found. It will be recalled that Nichols, the first victim, who was found in Buck's Row, had her throat cut and her abdomen slashed so that her intestines were exposed. Dr Llewellyn believed that the mutilations had been inflicted before the throat was cut. They could not therefore have been done primarily to kill her. Clearly it was for some other reason, as part of a ritual. Dr Llewellyn had first examined Nichols where she was found and noticed that there was only a small amount of blood on the ground. At the inquest he stated that there was '... not more than would fill two wine glasses, or half a pint at the outside.'[10] Some writers, trying to show that Nichols was killed where she was found in Buck's Row, point to the fact that a large quantity of blood had run from her throat and was soaked up by her clothing, accounting for the lack of blood on the ground. But if her blood was going to be soaked up by her clothes, this would happen wherever she was killed. The blood had run from her throat and down her back to her waist. This would have been unlikely if she had been killed on the ground where she was found. If, on the other hand, as Sickert said, she was killed in Netley's coach and carried to the gateway in Buck's Row, the blood would have run down to her waist if she was carried in the way one would expect: that is, with one man holding her legs and another clutching her under her shoulders, the body bending in the middle.

When the second victim, Annie Chapman, was examined in the yard of 29 Hanbury Street her uterus not only had been removed but was not to be found. According to *The Lancet* (29 September 1888): 'The intestines, severed from their mesentric attachment had been lifted out to a large extent and placed on the shoulders of the corpse.' At the inquest on Eddowes, Dr Brown said: 'The abdomen was all exposed. The intestines drawn out to a large extent and placed on her shoulder. A piece of the intestine was quite detached from the body and placed between the left arm and the body.'[11] Note: the intestines were *placed* – not thrown, not fallen, not discarded, but placed. In other words they were put there deliberately.

Here it is pertinent to recall the story – a crucial part of masonic lore – of the execution of Jubela, Jubelo and Jubelum. When this trio of murderers was found, they were heard lamenting their fate in the following manner:

> *Jubela:* O that my throat had been cut across, my tongue torn out and my body buried in the rough sands of the sea, at low water-mark, where the tide ebbs and flows twice in twenty-four hours, ere I had been accessory to the death of so good a man as our Grand Master, Hiram Abif.
>
> *Jubelo:* O that my left breast had been torn open and my heart and vitals taken from thence and thrown over my left shoulder ... ere I had conspired the death of so good a man as our Grand Master, Hiram Abif.
>
> *Jubelum:* O that my body be severed in two in the midst, and divided to the north and south, my bowels burnt to ashes in the centre and the ashes scattered by the four winds of heaven ... It was I who gave him the final blow. It was I who killed him outright.[12]

The similarity between the treatment of the Ripper victims – the mutilations and deliberate arrangement of the bodies – and the treatment of the three murderers of Hiram Abiff is unmistakable, and confirms Walter Sickert's assertion that the Ripper murders were masonic. All five victims had their throats cut in the manner of Jubela, while four were torn open in the manner of Jubelo. (Elizabeth Stride was spared these mutilations because the killer was disturbed by Louis Diemschutz and his pony and cart.) When Eddowes was examined, she was found slit from her groin to her breastbone, reminding us of Jubelum's 'O that my body be severed in two'. Three of the victims – Chapman, Eddowes and Kelly – had their 'vitals' torn out and removed. Two, Chapman and Eddowes, had them thrown over their shoulders according to Jubelo's description. In the last chapter we explained how little time the murderer had to place Eddowes's body in Mitre Square and demonstrated the impossibility of performing the delicate mutilations on her face in the murky corner away from the square's single gas-lamp. The mutilations were undoubtedly conducted in a well-lit coach, behind closed curtains.

The final stage, the delivery and arrangement of the body, was hampered by lack of both time and illumination. It will be remembered that, according to Dr Sequeira, Eddowes was found in 'the darkest portion of the square'. This may have been why her intestines were thrown in error over her right rather than over her left shoulder as specified in the masonic ritual. Walter told Joseph that it was the coach driver, John Netley, who was responsible for taking the body from the coach and arranging it where it was found later. Netley was not a Royal Arch mason and would not be as particular over masonic ritual as those issuing the orders. And we may imagine the revulsion he felt in having to handle the bloody intestines. If he had realised that there had been a mistake he would have been loath to handle them a second time. He was no doubt as much concerned with avoiding the blood and feculent matter as with the arrangement of the victim's body. Time too was at a premium. Escape would have been jeopardised if he had bothered about a ritual he barely understood.

*

The third victim, Elizabeth Stride, was killed where she was found in Dutfields Yard. According to Walter, Stride was drunk and refused to enter the coach. I find it difficult to accept that she was drunk, because contemporary records show that she spent two hours before touting for business. It is hard to believe that she refused the chance to earn money in the relative comfort of a coach. Gull was a bird in the hand (forgive the pun) worth more than a possible two in the alley.

What seems certain is that her murder was committed literally seconds before Diemschutz turned his pony and cart into the yard. Probably Netley heard the sound of the pony's hooves, killed Stride immediately and hid himself behind the gate until the danger had passed. He probably expected the cart to pass by the yard entrance and Stride's body to remain unseen in the gloom of the unlit passage. When Diemschutz examined her body, her throat was still bleeding profusely, oozing onto the cobbles away from the body. Diemschutz told the *Evening Standard* that when Dr Blackwell examined her he found cachous in one hand and grapes in the other. Dr Baxter Phillips found fruit stains on her handkerchief but stated at the inquest: 'I am convinced that the deceased had not swallowed either skin or seed of grape within many hours of her death.'[13] But Walter Dew, a Detective Constable in Whitechapel, recollected that 'detectives searching every inch of the ground came upon a number of grape skins and stones'. It seems likely that Stride ate the grapes but, like many people, disliked the skins and pips and spat them out, leaving the soft pulp which had been chewed virtually undetectable among the contents of her stomach. It has to be remembered also that forensic medicine in 1888 was not the exact science it is today.

A greengrocer from 44 Berner Street, next door but one to Dutfields Yard, was reported in the *Evening Standard* as having sold grapes to a man with Stride shortly before her body was discovered. This was regarded as important by Scotland Yard, as can be seen from the following report by Sergeant Stephen White, countersigned by Superintendent Arnold and Inspector Abberline:

> I beg to report that acting under the instruction of Inspector Abberline, I, in company with P.C. Dolden, C.I. Dept., made enquiries at every house in Berner Street, Commercial Road, on the 30th. ult, with a view to obtain

information respecting the murder. Any information that I could obtain I noted in a book supplied to me for that purpose. About 9 a.m. I called at 44, Berner Street, and saw Mathew Packer, Fruiterer in a small way of business. I asked him what time he closed his shop on the previous night. He replied, 'Half past twelve in consequence of the rain. It was no good for me to keep open.' I asked him if he saw anything of a man or woman going into Dutfields Yard, or saw anyone standing about in the street about the time he was closing his shop. He replied, 'No, I saw no one standing about, neither did I see anyone go up the yard. I never saw anything suspicious or heard the slightest noise, and knew nothing about the murders until I heard of it this morning.'

I saw Mrs Packer, Sarah Harrison and Harry Douglas residing in the same house but none of them could give the slightest information respecting the matter.

On the 4th inst. I was directed by Inspr. Moore to make further inquiry and if necessary see Packer and take him to the mortuary. I then went to 44, Berner Street, and saw Mrs. Packer, who informed me that two detectives had called and taken her husband to the Mortuary. I then went towards the Mortuary where I met Packer with a man. I asked him where he had been. He said, 'This detective asked me to go to see if I could identify the woman.' I said, 'Have you done so?' He said, 'Yes, I believe she bought some grapes at my shop about 12 o'clock on Saturday.' Shortly afterwards they were joined by another man. I asked the men what they were doing with Packer and they both said that they were detectives. I asked for their authority. One of them produced a card from a pocket book but they would not allow me to touch it. They then said that they were private detectives. They then induced Packer to go away with them. About 4 p.m. I saw Packer at his shop. While talking to him the two men drove up in a hansom cab, and after going into the shop they induced Packer to enter the cab, stating that they would take him to Scotland Yard to see Sir Charles Warren.

From enquiry I have made there is little doubt that these are the two men referred to in the attached newspaper cutting who examined the drain in Dutfields Yard on the 2nd inst. One of the men had a letter in his hand addressed to Le Grand & Co., Strand.

These two so-called 'private detectives' were also referred to in another report in the Home Office file written by Inspector Swanson who was heading the enquiry:

Two private enquiry men acting conjointly with the Vigilance Committee and the press, upon searching a drain in the yard found a grape stem which was amongst the matter swept from the yard after its examination by the police ...[14]

Whoever these two men were, the surprising thing is that they did take Mathew Packer to see Sir Charles Warren. The police files contain a statement by Packer, hand-written by Sir Charles himself, in a script so difficult to decipher that it took me an hour to read. The following is the first complete text of Packer's statement ever published:

Matthew Packer

Keeps a small shop in Berner Street with a few grapes in window. Black and white.

On Sat night about 11p.m. a young man 25 – 30, about 5. 7 with a long black coat buttoned up, soft felt hat, kind of hawker hat, rather broad shoulders rather quick in speaking. Rough voice. I sold him ½ pound Black grapes 3d. A woman came up from back church street end (the lower end of the street) she was dressed in black frock and jacket, fur round bottom of jacket a black crepe bonnet, she was playing with a flower like a geranium white outside & red inside. I identify the woman at the St. George's Mortuary as the one I saw that night.

They passed by as though they were going up Com. Road but instead of going up they crossed to the other side of the road to the Board School & were there for about ½ an hour till I shd say 11.30 talking to one another. I then put up my shutters. Before they passed over opposite to my shop they went near to the club for a few minutes apparently listening to the music.

I saw no more of them after I shut up my shutters.

I put the man down as a young clerk.

He had a frock coat, no gloves.

He was about 1½ inch or 2 or 3 inches a little bit higher than she was.

It was initialled 'C.W.' and dated 4.10.88.

Sergeant Stephen White did not trust the two 'private detectives', as is evident from the fact that he twice used the word 'induced' when describing how the two men persuaded Packer to go with them. It seems fairly obvious that these two were working on Sir Charles Warren's behalf, quite independently of the official CID and the uniformed section of those assigned to the case. Packer's statement was the only one in the police files that was taken by Warren. All the other documents dictated or written by him are of an administrative kind, unconnected with the actual ground-level police investigations. This makes Packer's statement all the more curious, for it is apparent that Warren did not want the officers officially assigned to the case to know of Packer's evidence about the grapes, which might have led them to Warren's brother mason from the Royal Alpha Lodge, Sir William Gull. I am surprised that Packer's statement was left in the file at all and can only surmise that, because it was so difficult to read, no one bothered to unravel its contents.

*

There was a rather more dramatic but equally important statement given by Israel Schwartz, a Hungarian Jew, which is contained in Chief Inspector Swanson's report, first revealed by Stephen Knight:

12.45 a.m. 30th Israel Schwartz of Helen Street, Back-church Lane stated that at that hour on turning into Berner Street from Commercial Road and had got as far as the gateway where the murder was committed he saw a man stop and speak to a woman, who was standing in the gateway. The man tried to pull the woman into the street, but turned her round and threw her down on the footway and the woman screamed three times, but not very loudly. On crossing to the opposite side of the street he saw a second man standing lighting his pipe. The man who threw the woman down called out apparently to the man on the opposite side of the road: 'Lipski' and then Schwartz walked away, but finding that he was followed by the second man he ran as far as the railway arch, but the man did not follow so far. Schwartz cannot say whether the two men were together or known to each other. Upon being taken to the mortuary, Schwartz identified the body as that of the woman he had seen and thus describes the first man who threw the woman down: – age about 30, ht 5ft. 5in. comp. fair, hair dark, small brown moustache, full face, broad shouldered; dress dark jacket and trousers, black cap with peak, had nothing in his hands.[15]

Second man age about 35, ht. 5ft. 11in. comp. fresh, hair light brown, moustache brown; dress, dark overcoat, old black hard felt hat, wide brim, had a clay pipe in his hand.

Schwartz's testimony was reported in one newspaper only, *The Star*. Schwartz could speak little English, and his statements both to Abberline and to the *The Star* were made through an interpreter, which would account for the variance. Even so the police considered his statement important, and Schwartz is generally regarded as the one man who saw Jack the Ripper.

According to Robert Anderson:

The only person who had ever had a good view of the murderer unhesitatingly identified the suspect the instant he was confronted with him; but he refused to give evidence against him. In saying that he was a Polish Jew I am merely stating a definitely ascertained fact. And my words are meant to specify race not religion. For it would outrage all religious sentiment to talk of the religion of a loathsome creature whose utterly unmentionable vices reduced him to a lower level than those of the brute.[16]

This is complete nonsense. Anderson, a born-again Christian, was here rehashing the anti-semitism which was prevalent in the 1880s and caused several Jews to be accused without evidence. Anderson sent a copy of his book to Chief Inspector Swanson. It was found among the possessions left to Swanson's grandson by his last surviving daughter who died in 1981. In it were some marginalia written by Swanson in which he said that Anderson's Polish Jew was a man called Kosminski. He also stated that the reason Anderson's witness refused to testify against the Polish Jew was that he too was Jewish. Kosminski was also one of three suspects named by the Metropolitan Chief Constable CID, Sir Melville Macnaghten, in his notes written in February 1894, six years after the murders. The notes were written to refute an accusation made in *The Sun*, against one Thomas Cutbush who had been arrested in 1891. The other two named were Montague John Druitt and Michael Ostrog.

No hard evidence exists against Druitt. Ostrog, a thief and confidence trickster, was wanted by the police, but not for the Whitechapel murders. Referring to Druitt, Ostrog and Kosminski, Macnaghten wrote:

> *any one of whom* would have been more likely than Cutbush to have committed this series of murders. (My italics)[17]

In other words, for all Macnaghten knew, any one of them could have been Jack the Ripper. Or, for that matter, none of them.

A recent Thames TV programme in the Crimewatch series (August 1990) tried to show that Kosminski was the Ripper. It was pointed out that the witness noted by Anderson who refused to testify against the Polish Jew was Israel Schwartz, who saw a man throw Elizabeth Stride to the ground. In his marginalia in the copy of Anderson's autobiography Swanson noted that the witness refused to testify against Kosminski because he was 'also a Jew'. In other words the witness, Schwartz, was a Jew. As can be seen in Schwartz's statement, the assailant he saw shouted out the name 'Lipski'. This was a term of anti-semitic abuse derived from the name Israel Lipski, a Jew convicted of murder the year before. Home Office reports show that Stride's assailant was referring to Schwartz. If, as Swanson claimed, the Ripper suspect was Jewish, it is unlikely that he would have used a derogatory anti-semitic term in reference to another of his race.

Incidentally, Israel Lipski was a Polish Jew, and his trial for murder in 1887 served to fuel existing anti-semitism. Clearly Anderson was feeding this racism, and his claim that Jack the Ripper, like Lipski, was a Polish Jew was no coincidence.

The man whom Schwartz saw throwing Stride to the ground, 'aged about 30, height 5ft. 5in.' and described as 'broad shouldered', is probably the man seen earlier by Packer, who sold him grapes and described him as 'a young man 25 – 30, about 5 . 7 ... rather broad shouldered'.

According to Walter Sickert the man seen by Schwartz was John Netley.

*

Catherine Eddowes, the fourth victim, the second that night, was found dead in Mitre Square about 45 minutes after Stride. Her murder exhibited more obvious masonic significance than the first three. Both the mitre and the square are tools of the stonemason and potent emblems of Freemasonry. In his initiation ceremony, full of shadowy symbolism, the Entered Apprentice is given stonemason's tools and told, 'These tools we apply to our morals.' The square is one of the working tools of second-degree Freemasons and forms a distinctive feature of the Master of the Lodge's jewels. Freemasons 'square' their lodge, and fellow masons are said to be 'on the square'.

A mitre is a tool used by stonemasons to check right-angles. It is also a bishop's hat. The main Ripper conspirators, with the exception of Netley, had 'passed' through the 'Royal Arch'. The three principals of the lodge, known in the brotherhood as Zerubbabel, Haggai and Joshua, wore headresses. The first two wore crowns, while Joshua wore a mitre.

Another pertinent association of Mitre Square with Freemasonry is the Mitre Tavern, which was demolished in the nineteenth century. It was situated at No. 3 Mitre Street and gave its name both to the street and the square. It became a meeting place for Freemasons in the eighteenth and early nineteenth centuries. Standing near the entrance to the Square, it was used for lodge meetings by the Union Lodge in 1751, the Hiram Lodge in 1797 and the Lodge of Joppa in 1817 and 1823. The Hiram Lodge, one of the most distinguished, also met at The Crown in Duke's Place on the east of the square, while the Lodge of Judah met at The Tailor's Arms in Mitre Street on the west side. This Lodge also met at St James's Tavern, St James's Place, a small court at the end of a covered passage at the north-east corner of the square. By 1888 Mitre Square had been associated with, and indeed literally surrounded by, Freemasonry for a hundred and fifty years. Outside the West End since 1737, the Royal Alpha had only two other meeting places, and one was The Mitre Tavern.

J.F. Brewer wrote that in 1530 Mitre Square had been the scene of another brutal murder of a woman, citing a document he had found in the British Library. In the sixteenth century Mitre Square was the site of the Priory of the Holy Trinity. A blue tile set into the wall can be seen today marking the spot where it stood. According to Brewer, a woman was praying in the Priory at the high altar when she was set upon by a mad monk, Brother Martin. Like Eddowes in 1888, the unknown sixteenth-century victim was butchered with a knife, which the insane monk then turned upon himself.

This event – if indeed it ever happened – parallels in a number of ways the mythical slaying of Hiram Abif in the masonic allegory. The sixteenth-century woman was murdered while praying in a holy place, and the mad monk who murdered her died under violent circumstances, as did the three apprentices who killed Hiram Abif: Jubela, Jubelo and Jubelum. It was as if the masonic killers linked the mythical story of Hiram Abif, who plays a central role in Royal Arch Masonry, and the slaying of the unknown woman in 1530 to the murder of their own victim, Catherine Eddowes.

Among the claims made by Brewer, was the following.

Measure this spot as carefully as you will, and you will find that the piece of ground on which Catherine Eddowes lies is the exact point where the steps of the altar of Holy Trinity existed.[18]

*

The land upon which Mitre Square is situated once belonged to England's premier duke, the Duke of Norfolk. Mitre Square was once called Duke's Place, and the street by the side of the square retains the name. As Britain's most eminent lay Catholics, the Dukes of Norfolk might, in the minds of the Ripper gang, have been used to symbolise the threat which Eddy's marriage to a Catholic presented. Eddowes's body lying upon that particular piece of ground might have been a deliberate insult to Catholicism. Fanciful as this may appear, it has to be remembered that, as I have been assured by more than one Freemason, masons are very partial to esoteric humour.

Eddowes had cuts on her cheeks. They formed two lines meeting at right-angles, similar to a capital 'A', but with legs wider apart and without the crossbar, another reminder of a mason's square. The pairs of joining cuts created a triangular flap of skin on each cheek. This too is significant for Freemasons, particularly for Royal Arch masons. The triangle has long been used to represent the Trinity in orthodox Christian dogma. But the union of two triangles has been used since medieval times as a stonemason's mark. In 1949, during the rebuilding of the Houses of Parliament, such a mark was uncovered in the crypt of St Stephen's, built between 1135 and 1154. Just as stonemasons proudly left their individual marks to identify their handiwork and craftsmanship, so the Ripper murderers identified themselves by the two triangles on Eddowes's cheeks, proclaiming to other Royal Arch masons that it was they who had brought terror to London. By the masonic designs which mutilated their victims, they declared the extent of their power.

A design of two triangles interlaced, forming a six-pointed star, an Hexalpha, is regarded by Freemasons as the Seal of Solomon and the Shield of David. It is called Hexalpha because the six-pointed star is an arrangement of six 'A's. A in Greek is alpha. This is a further reminder of the name of the lodge which the masonic killers of 1888 belonged to or were associated with: the Royal Alpa Lodge, whose members also regard the double triangle as the representation of their altar-top.

Another piece of the regalia worn by Freemasons in their lodge meetings is the ceremonial apron. Shoemakers, blacksmiths, butchers, bakers and even candlestick-makers wear aprons. The stonemason wears an apron too, but it is made of leather. Any other material would quickly wear out. The speculative masons, instead of using bull hide, as stonemasons did in the fourteenth century, refined their aprons by making them of white lambskin, and in 1731 the Grand Lodge allowed that 'Masters and Wardens of particular lodges may line their Leather aprons with white Silk, and may hang their jewels at white Ribbons about their Neck'.[19]

It was a curious feature of the Ripper murders that after the second killing, that of Annie Chapman, the rumour spread that the person responsible for the crime was someone called 'Leather Apron'. Eventually a man known by that nickname was arrested. As a bootmaker he wore a leather apron. His name was John Pizer, and after being exonerated he successfully sued several newspapers and was awarded substantial damages.[20] One wonders whether the rumour was spread by the Freemasons themselves, as a veiled means of proclaiming their responsibility?

Bernard E. Jones explains that at one time the Master's apron was flung into the grave at his funeral.[21] Not only did the police spend some time seeking someone known as 'Leather Apron', but part of the apron which had been worn by Catherine Eddowes was cut off and flung, not into her grave, which would hardly have been possible, but into the dark hole of a doorway in Goulston Street, to be found later underneath the chalked message, an enigmatic epitaph. The words 'The Juwes are The men That Will not be Blamed for nothing' were written down in the pocket book of the constable, PC 254A Alfred Long, who found both the message and the apron. Sir Charles Warren had the words washed away (above, p. 36), explaining later in a letter to the Home Secretary, Henry Matthews, his reason for eradicating this piece of forensic evidence.

*

Once the information about the writing and the apron had been reported to the nearest police station, at Leman Street in the City, detectives converged on Goulston Street, as we have seen. City Detective Daniel Halse had messages sent to the heads of both the City and the Metropolitan Police, and stayed by the doorway with a photographer waiting for daylight when the writing could be photographed for evidence. The doorway stood at the foot of Wentworth Dwellings which housed many Jewish families.

The first Metropolitan officer to arrive at the scene was Superintendent Arnold, who was in charge of that division. Despite the odd spelling of the first word, Arnold, as we noted, warned that the writing might inflame local prejudice against the Jews and, in order to avoid a riot, suggested that it should be rubbed out. Not wishing to be the one to shoulder the responsibility for destroying evidence, however, he ordered an inspector to wait by with a dry sponge, until Sir Charles Warren arrived.

When he did arrive, a row between the City Police and the Metropolitan Police was in full swing. The City Police insisted, quite rightly, that the message was important evidence and should be photographed. There was considerable rivalry between the two forces, and Sir Charles loyally sided with his own man, Arnold. Several suggestions were made by the City men, which would have both preserved the evidence and avoided a riot. A blanket could be hung over the whole message until daylight made photography possible, or the offending word 'Juwes' could be rubbed out, leaving the rest to be recorded. Both suggestions, as we have seen, were rejected by Warren and, since Goulston Street was in Metropolitan territory, the City men had no power to veto him and he ordered the whole message to be rubbed out.

Warren became a Freemason in 1859. He was initiated at Gibraltar while there with the Army, when he was only 19. At 21, as we noted, he passed the Royal Arch. In 1863 he became a Knight Templar and two years later an officer of Grand Lodge and a Past Grand Sojourner of the Supreme Grand Chapter. Two years before the Ripper murders he had been instrumental in founding the Quatuor Coronati Lodge No. 2076, the Premier Lodge of Masonic Research. If anyone knew the real meaning of the message found above Eddowes's apron it was Sir Charles Warren. It was precisely because he understood the message that he had it permanently obliterated. 'Juwes' in the message was not a misspelling of the word 'Jews'. Rather it represented *Ju*bela, *Ju*belo and *Ju*belum, known collectively as the three *Ju*wes. Jubela, Jubelo and Jubelum featured in British masonic ritual until 1814 when the rituals were revised. Men like Sir Charles Warren, however, were deeply interested in masonic history and were well-versed in the Hiramic legend. Since 1814 the three assassins have been known as the 'ruffians'. According to Bernard E. Jones, an expert on Freemasonry, the names apparently derive from the word 'ghiblim' or 'giblim',[22] which were regarded in early rituals as the name of a mason. Early eighteenth-century French masons turned the hard English 'g' into their soft 'g', so that 'giblim' became in effect 'jiblim'. Speculative masonry went from England to France, and when some of it returned it did so in distorted forms, and we may suppose that the three names are examples of the process.

Jones states categorically that 'there is good ground for the word giblim meaning mason'.[23] The words on the wall found by PC Long were therefore a message proclaiming that it was really Freemasons who were the men 'who will not be blamed for nothing'. Freemasons I have met have made it clear that masons are fond of puns, puzzles and double negatives.

One Freemason had the message chalked up, another had it removed. The first, the leader of the gang, was displaying characteristic rashness and arrogance, while the second, Warren, was displaying characteristic caution. The unholy Ripper gang were beginning to show differences of opinion among themselves, a schism which ultimately resulted in one of them breaking ranks to tell an outsider, a non-mason, why the murders were committed. A few years later the outsider recorded everything he was told, as well as everything he subsequently discovered through his own detective work. In a remarkable series of diaries he provided Walter, and ultimately Joseph, with documentary evidence for the story which was related to me.

*

The fifth and last murder was the most bestial of all. Mary Kelly had been the intended last victim, but somehow despite the impeccable planning, Catherine Eddowes was mistaken for her. In the few weeks before her death, Eddowes had acquired a healthy suntan, when she spent a working holiday hop-picking in Kent with her common-law husband John Kelly and her friend Emily Birrell. When she was found in Mitre Square, there was a mustard tin beside her body containing two pawn tickets; one was issued to her friend Emily, the other to Anne Kelly. Since 'Kelly' was the name of the man she was living with, she used it for propriety's sake, in order to appear to be his legal wife. When she was taken to Bishopsgate Police Station on the night of her death she was asked her name and said 'Nothing'. Later, at 12.55, when she was sober enough to be released, she said her name was 'Mary Anne Kelly'.

In October 1888 the Metropolitan Police estimated that in Whitechapel alone there were about 1,200 prostitutes. It can hardly be mere coincidence that two of them who became Ripper victims – the last two – shared the same name, Mary Kelly.

The last victim, Mary Jane Kelly, was the most important of the four, and the Freemasons responsible wished her to be found in Mitre Square – a place, as we have seen, of particular significance to them. But they made a mistake and killed the wrong Mary Kelly. When the error was discovered, they decided not to kill the real Mary Kelly in the same manner, or in the same place. Something even more horrible was reserved for her. Anyway Mitre Square could not be used a second time since, after Eddowes's murder, it would be patrolled even more vigilantly by the uniformed police.

Stephen Knight (p. 170) drew attention to an engraving by William Hogarth, which mirrors the dreadful scene that greeted the police when they broke down the door of Mary Kelly's room in Millers Court. Hogarth was a Freemason, a member of the Lodge at The Hand and Apple Tree, Little Great Queen Street, close to the site of the present Great Freemasons Hall. He was a steward in the Grand Lodge and designed a 'jewel' for the Grand Steward's Lodge. Among his patrons was the Duke of Montagu, who was Grand Master in 1721. The engraving, the last in a series entitled 'The Four Stages of Cruelty', appears to the uninitiated to be nothing more than a caricature of the medical profession. As Knight showed, it represents a ritualised masonic killing in progress, a scene minutely mimicked by the mutilations performed on the Ripper victims, particularly Mary Kelly.

The corpse has a cable-tow round its neck. Freemasons use this device to represent the cutting of the throat. One is actually worn round the neck of a novice during his initiation ceremony as an 'Entered Apprentice'. As noted, all the Ripper victims had their throats cut. Hogarth's engraving also shows the post-mortem subject with mutilations on the face; one of the eyes is shown cut into, reminding us that Eddowes had cuts on her face and eyelids.

Chapman, Eddowes and Kelly had their intestines dragged out. Hogarth's subjects' intestines are seen drawn out onto the floor. Eddowes's intestines had been cut and, according to Dr Brown's testimony, a piece was 'quite detached from the body and placed between the left arm and the body'. Hogarth's corpse also has a piece of intestine between the body and the arm – in both cases the left arm.

Kelly's heart was missing, while in Hogarth the corpse's heart is on the floor being eaten by a dog. One of the medical operatives is seen about to skin one of the legs. Dr Bond's post-mortem report on Kelly (Appendix 10) states that her right leg had been skinned and 'denuded in front to the bone'. This feature is a masonic allegory, a reminder of the initiation of a Master Mason when the candidate, in reference to his two previous initiations, says: 'And my right leg bare.' As he utters these words he has to roll up his trouser leg. With Kelly they rolled away the flesh.

Finally, in Hogarth's engraving there are three men dismembering the body, a reminder of the three Juwes in the Hiram Abif legend.

In the previous scene in the series 'Cruelty in Perfection' the viewer sees the remains of a woman lying with her throat cut. She is lying against a fence, like Annie Chapman. In the engraving the victim is surrounded by her belongings, as Chapman was surrounded by hers. Moreover Hogarth's victim is pregnant; Chapman had her uterus removed.

At his initiation the aspiring Freemason is divested of all metal, including jewelry and coins. When the Ripper victims were found dead, none of them had a single item of jewellery or coin, either in their pockets or in their purses. Admittedly they were all living in poverty and had no jewellery, apart from Chapman's valueless brass rings. She was divested of these.

There was some indication that Stride had serviced at least two men immediately before her demise. Where was the money she earned? Mary Kelly was also seen in the company of at least two men, both of whom were seen going with her into her room; yet no money was reported among her belongings. Obviously simple theft was not the motive for this odious series of murders. Everything points to a powerful connection between the murders and Freemasonry.

*

A further fact supports the view that top-ranking Freemasons were the

Ripper killers: the date of the final murder – 9 November.

The City of London has managed to mix the everyday business of commerce and finance with the ceremonial pageantry of yesteryear. Although the residential population is quite small, about 4,000, this swells each morning with the influx of commuters. The City then has the highest density of Freemasons in the world. With its several thousand men 'on the square', the City has good reason to call itself the 'Square Mile'.

Various institutions within the City boundaries have their own masonic lodges. Lloyd's Bank has its Black Horse Lodge of Lombard Street, Lodge No. 4155. The Bank of England – which acts as banker to the Government and performs many other state functions – has a masonic lodge with its own name, one of the earliest, consecrated in 1788. The City is sectioned for administrative purposes into twenty-five 'wards'. Ten have their own lodge.

The Livery Companies deriving from mediaeval craft guilds and certain religious societies, are peopled almost exclusively by Freemasons. Today they comprise about 15,000 men, all of whom qualified for membership when they became 'Freemen of the City'. With notable exceptions most are Freemasons, and it is they who nominate the City's twenty-six Aldermen from whom the Lord Mayor is selected. The Guildhall, the official residence of the Lord Mayor, which is used for his election and for the election of Sheriffs and City MPs and for state banquets, also has its lodge. Since its establishment in 1906, sixty-six Masters of the Lodge have been elected Lord Mayor of the City of London.

Every year, usually on the second Saturday of November, the Lord Mayor's Show parades through the streets of London. In 1888 the pageant was held on 9 November, and as the procession passed before St Paul's Cathedral carrying the Lord Mayor-elect down Ludgate Hill, the newsboys pushed through the crowds waving placards and shouting: 'Murder – horrible murder!' The crowd's thoughts were turned to Jack the Ripper, who became the main topic of conversation. Jack had stolen the day and would be forever linked, in the mind of the crowd, with the Lord Mayor's Show. If, as *The Star* later reported, the Ripper craved notoriety and wished 'to be the sensation of the hour', his timing could hardly have been bettered. *The Star* added: 'He got his sensation.'

November 9th was not only the Lord Mayor's day. More significantly it was the birthday of the Grand Master Mason of England, the Prince of Wales – Eddy's father. As the future King of England he embodied the future of the British monarchy, the very establishment the Freemasons had been protecting when they murdered the four blackmailing women. The original intention was that their most important victim, Mary Kelly, should be found in Mitre Square, a place which, as we have seen, was highly significant to Freemasons. When they realised that they had killed Catherine Eddowes by mistake, something even more significant than

Mitre Square had to be found for Kelly who threatened their figurehead, the Prince of Wales, in two ways: as Grand Master and as future king. They therefore waited nearly six weeks until his birthday – just as the head of John the Baptist was presented to King Herod, when Salome danced before him, at his birthday celebration.

On 8 November, the day before the murder, Sir Charles Warren tendered his resignation. His main purpose as Commissioner was fulfilled. He knew that later that night his masonic brothers would find and kill Kelly, their last victim. He was no longer needed to cover up or suppress evidence, as he had with Mathew Packer's statement and the writing on the wall. That same evening he met some of his other masonic brethren, those of the Quatuor Coronati Lodge No. 2076 which Warren founded. Quatuor Coronati – 'the four crowned ones' – were Christian martyrs who had been put to death at Rome in AD 304 for refusing to offer incense before an image of Aesculapius. They became the patron saints of stonecutters and, by extension, of Freemasons. This lodge, world-famous among Freemasons, was established in 1884, and its first Master was Sir Charles Warren. It met on 8 November in Great Freemasons Hall, as always on the 'saint's day' when the four martyrs are remembered. That evening they installed their new master, William Simpson of the *Illustrated London News*. Warren wished him well, toasting him before the assembled throng. The Treasurer was the novelist Walter Besant who was closely associated with Warren through their mutual interest in Palestinian exploration. Subsequently Warren had time to meet up with his murderous friends in the East End and learn what progress had been made in pursuit of Mary Kelly. In one of his last acts as Commissioner, performed before the acceptance of his resignation, he signed a document authorising a poster promising a pardon to anyone giving information leading to the arrest of the Whitechapel murderer. It read:

MURDER – Pardon – Whereas, on November 8 or 9 in Millers Court, Dorset Street, Spitalfields, Mary Jane Kelly was murdered by some person or persons unknown, the Secretary of State will advise the grant of Her Majesty's pardon to any accomplice not being a person who contrived or actually committed the murder who shall give such information and evidence as shall lead to the discovery and conviction of the person or persons who committed the murder.

Apart from his inside knowledge, Warren knew that the medical evidence showed that Kelly died in the early hours of the 9th. Yet with the poster he strongly linked the deaths of the 'four crowned ones' and the Quatuor Coronati Lodge, which he founded, and which he celebrated on the 8th, to the death of Kelly. Discounting Eddowes, since her murder was a mistake, the Ripper's intended victims numbered four. Doubtless

Warren saw a parallel between the ancient story of the 'four Crowned ones', who died for refusing to show proper respect to the image of Aesculapius, and the then modern story of the four women, killed for daring to defy the monarchy, which was an image of the real power behind it: the Freemasonry of the Royal Alpha Lodge No. 16.

A Freemason who was associated with the Ripper gang, and who will be named in the following chapter, died mysteriously and unexpectedly in 1892 – on 9 November.

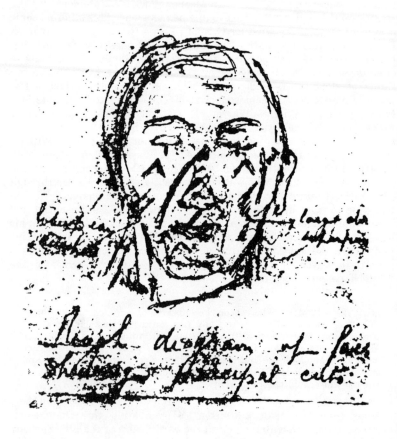

Sketch made of Catherine Eddowes' facial injuries

CHAPTER FOUR

Magister Magistrorum

Stephen Knight believed that there were only three men who actually ventured into the East End to carry out the murders, though they had help from those connected with the cover-up. According to him they were: Sir William Gull, who did the killing and mutilations of four of the victims; John Netley, who ferried Gull into the murder locale and also killed Elizabeth Stride; and Walter Sickert, who acted as look-out man. According to Knight, Joseph told him that the look-out was Robert Anderson, the Assistant Police Commissioner and head of the CID. But Knight was sure that Walter Sickert could only have known as much as he did if he himself was the look-out. What Joseph did not tell Knight was that the reason his father knew as much as he did was that he had been given the whole story by one of the police investigating officers, Inspector Frederick George Abberline, who had learned the truth directly from one of the actual gang members. Abberline chose to remain silent at the time, but he later wrote down all the relevant details – the reasons and the names of those responsible – in his diaries.

In 1927 the diaries were given to Walter. Walter left them with Alice Margaret Crook to be kept safe for Joseph, so that if he ever needed to, he could prove he was who he claimed to be: the grandson of Eddy. When Joseph was a boy his father told him a good deal of the contents of the diaries, clarifying the story with additional information which he had gleaned himself. The first diary, which named those responsible for the murders, was sealed with wax. The other two had locks, but Joseph received the keys when his mother left the diaries to him. In order to check certain details for my benefit, he has frequently referred to the contents of the two locked diaries. He kept the third sealed until a contract should be drawn up between us, when I should be given full and free access to all three. The whole of Joseph Sickert's account, which is really a series of related accounts, stretches from the early 1880s to the present day. To maintain continuity I have confined to a later chapter (Chapter 8) the reasons why the diaries were written. At that point, however, the narrative of Joseph's story will be seen to be substantiated. Until then, I beg the reader to bear with me. I may add that the story is unfolding here in the same way it was given to me by Joseph, and that it was quite a time before I saw any actual evidence concerning his account of Jack the Ripper.

*

John Netley's coach with Sir William Gull inside was not the only vehicle to ferry the gang of masonic murderers in and out of the East End. Other gang members went along to oversee the job in hand, or to act as look-outs, or simply for the ride. Like a shooting party making a foray into the country, they would fortify themselves against the night air with nips of brandy from hip-flasks. This was slumming with a difference, and as many as twelve made up that band of misogynists. One of them was Dr Robert Anderson, head of the Metropolitan CID. His father was the Crown Solicitor for the County and City of Dublin. The son followed the father's profession and read Law at Trinity, and was called to the Irish bar in 1863. His wife, Agnes Alexandrina, was the brother of Ponsonby Arthur Moore, who succeeded his cousin as 9th Earl of Drogheda.

Before the murders Warren's Assistant Commissioner was James Monro. The son of an Edinburgh solicitor, Monro was educated in Scotland and Germany and at the age of 19, in 1858, entered the Indian Civil Service. In less than twenty years he rose to be Inspector General of the Bengal Police, when he was universally recognised for his professional efficiency. Resigning in 1884, he was recalled to London to become head of the CID with the newly created rank of Assistant Commissioner. He felt that his department needed to be expanded and enlarged, and to be independent of the Commissioner.

The most pressing political problem of the day was Home Rule for Ireland. The Chairman of the Home Rule Party, Charles Stuart Parnell, was pressing for an independent Parliament in Dublin and adopting obstructive methods in the House of Commons, where he held the balance between the Liberals and the Conservatives. But there were others who had decided that peaceful methods were futile. These were the Fenians, the Irish Revolutionary Brotherhood, whose plans for their two Irish and American branches had been drawn up in Paris in 1848. Since then they had committed several bomb outrages, notably the Clerkenwell Prison bombing of 1867, which led the following year, on 26 May, to the last public hanging in Britain, and an explosion in the precincts of Scotland Yard.

In 1867 Anderson was called to London to enquire into the Clerkenwell bombing, and the Home Office gave him 'control of the various secret agents whose main occupation was that of infiltrating the Irish Nationalists'. According to his son he held 'uncompromisingly Unionist views'.[1]

Anderson was on fairly close terms with the Royal Family. An evangelical fundamentalist, he wrote more than a dozen exegetical books and pamphlets, several of which were read by Queen Victoria, Queen Alexandra, Queen Mary and the German Emperor. One of his closest friends was Major-General J.C. Russell, Extra Equerry to Edward VII. As a staunch Protestant he spoke out often against Roman Catholicism, as when he chaired the 62nd Anniversary Meeting at the London City Mission:

Protestantism is no anchorage of faith, but it is like the breakwater which makes our anchorage secure – it shields us from influences that make Christianity impossible. While priestcraft would set up a Church to mediate between God and man, Protestantism points us to the only Mediator – our Lord Jesus Christ.[2]

Anderson had been a member of the Secret Service and his main job for the Home Office was to process intelligence. He co-operated with Monro, and together they helped organise the Special Irish Branch, the forerunner of today's Special Branch.

Warren felt that Monro had turned the CID into a political police force, and objected to the way he had spied on the Irish MPs in his attempt to connect them with the Fenians. In the summer of 1888 Monro demanded the appointment of Sir Melville Macnaghten as Assistant Chief Constable in his section. At first Warren agreed. Later, however, *just before the start of the Ripper murders*, he changed his mind, refusing to say why, and suggested Anderson instead. Warren threatened to resign, but eventually it was Monro who resigned after Warren made life intolerable for him. Warren was now free to bring in his toady, Anderson, from the Home Office, and he made him his own Assistant, as well as head of the CID.

The Home Secretary, Henry Matthews, a staunch Roman Catholic – the first Catholic to sit in the Cabinet since the Emancipation Act – was useful to Lord Salisbury for his influence in Irish Catholic circles. Despite his high office, he was prevented by his religion from joining the masonic brotherhood, but he could not fail to notice that the leadership of the Metropolitan Police was largely comprised of Freemasons. Little has changed today.

When Warren forced Monro out of office, replacing him with his friend Anderson, Matthews must have realised that the two Protestant leaders were up to no good. His response was to take Monro into the Home Office where he was appointed head of the Detective Service, a meaningless position at the time; and he encouraged him to continue liaison with the CID behind Warren's back, to find out what they were planning. A significant feature of the episode was the Home Office's insistence that the two new appointments, of Monro and Anderson, should be kept secret. Anderson admitted that he was sworn to secrecy when he wrote that 'for some some occult reason the matter was kept secret, and I was enjoined not to make my appointment known'.[3] He took up his post as Warren's Assistant on 31 August, only hours after the discovery of the body of Polly Nichols. After working there for a week he commenced the sickleave which he had demanded as a prerequisite of the job. The night before he left for Switzerland Annie Chapman was murdered, and it was not long before the newspapers were commenting on his absence from duty. On the morning of 30 September, after the discovery of Stride and Eddowes, the Home Secretary made an urgent appeal to Anderson to return, and he did so the following day.

Walter Sickert made it clear to Joseph that Anderson was a member of the Ripper gang, and Joseph told me that this was confirmed by the diaries. Of course Anderson could not have played an active part in the murders of Stride and Eddowes if he was out of the country at the time, but Walter was sure that Anderson was actively involved collecting intelligence on the whereabouts of the victims. It was Anderson's expertise in correlating information that encouraged Warren to use him instead of Monro.

The next two names Joseph was to produce were those of the Earl of Euston, eldest son of the Duke of Grafton, and Lord Arthur Somerset, younger son of the Duke of Beaufort. Both were Royal Arch Masons, and the Earl of Euston was later to become the Grand Master of the Mark Masons. Somerset – known as 'Podge' to his close friends – was the Extra Equerry and Superintendent of the Prince of Wales's Stables and, like Lord Euston, one of the Prince's close friends. In 1889, the year after the Ripper murders, both their lordships were to feature prominently in the 'Cleveland Street Scandal', which focused on the homosexual brothel at 19 Cleveland Street, two doors away from Walter Sickert's studio at No. 15. The scandal had several links with the Ripper murders, as will be shown in Chapter 7.

Neither Walter nor Joseph, nor even the diaries, make clear what roles were played by Lord Arthur Somerset and Lord Euston. They were probably not in the coach when Gull performed the mutilations, if only because there was no room. Nor is it likely that a lone woman, even a prostitute, would enter a coach containing three men. All Joseph learned from Walter was that Euston and Somerset were definitely in the East End on the nights of the murders: that they gave support to those responsible and acted as look-out men.

The seventh name to add to Joseph's list was that of John Courtenay, an elusive character about whom I could discover little. When Joseph first mentioned him I had seen one of the diaries, but had not read any of them, and I had no way of discovering for myself who he was. Most of the time Joseph did not have the diaries at home, but they were kept elsewhere, for safety. Courtenay became a phantom figure to me, since Joseph seemed to know so little about him, though he had met him as a boy. 'I think he was a Lieutenant Commander in the Royal Navy, but then I seem to remember that he might have been a naval attaché in the Diplomatic Corps. I'm not sure. He was killed when he was run over by a tram, when his foot got caught in a tramline in the Hampstead Road.'

Armed with this item of information I went to the British Newspaper Library in Colindale and looked through the two local newspapers covering the Hampstead Road area. I scanned every page of both papers for 1936, the year Joseph said Courtenay met with his accident with a tram. I found nothing. I checked the same papers for 1935 and 1937. Still nothing. My next stop was St Catherine's House, where I went through the Register of Deaths, but I found no John Courtenay who died in London in 1935, 1936 or 1937 and concluded that Joseph must have been mistaken about the year of his death.

I had learned during my research that Courtenay was the family name of the Earls of Devon who for many centuries have lived in Powderham Castle. I asked Joseph if he knew whether or not John Courtenay was related to them – not an unreasonable question, considering that so many of those involved in the Ripper murders were aristocrats. Joseph said he remembered that in Courtenay's last years his eccentric lifestyle was causing the family some embarrassment and his relations had been to London to find him and bring him back. He remembered an incident outside Warren Street Underground station. Courtenay was talking to a newspaper vendor by his stall when a taxi pulled up. The people who clambered out shouted and ran towards him; but he ran off, disappearing into the maze of the underground. They were Courtenay's family – 'a well-to-do lot', according to Joseph.

Walter told Joseph that Courtenay had worked for the leader of the Ripper gang, acting in the capacity of man-servant, or 'batman', when they went into the East End. When I read the diaries I discovered nothing apart from Courtenay's name, and the fact that he was 'working as a servant'.

I have no wish to link anyone's name unjustly to this sordid case, and I have to say that I have found no evidence whatever that any member of the Earl of Devon's family was linked to the Ripper murders.

*

At this point in Joseph's narrative I did not know who the leader was, and Joseph tantalised me with clues to his identity. 'He was the brother of a duke,' he said at one point. At another time: 'He was the son of a duke.' I thought he was being deliberately vague, or even cryptic. It did not occur to me that a man could be both the son of a duke and a duke's brother, and it was only when I finally knew the man's identity that the penny dropped and I realised that Joseph had spoken the literal truth both times. The obvious had not dawned on me: that if a man was the younger son of a duke, he would also be the brother of a duke when the father died and his elder brother succeeded to the title.

I asked Joseph why he had never disclosed any of this information, incomplete though it was, to Stephen Knight. He said that he came to distrust Knight, adding that certain members of the family to which the leader of the gang belonged had helped his own family: specifically, his mother, Alice Crook, and also himself. He had no wish to visit the sins of the fathers upon the sons, and felt it would be unfair to embarrass the Ripper's present family, since they had nothing to do with the Whitechapel murders.

For at least eighteen months, every time I met Joseph I dared myself to ask the question outright, 'Who was he? Who was the Ripper leader?' I remained silent, however, fearing that I could easily lose the trust he had so far put in me. Eventually something happened which led him to disclose further secrets contained in the pages of one of the diaries: the undisclosed names of the remaining three members of the gang, including their leader.

On New Year's Eve 1985 there appeared on British television a feature film *Murder by Decree*, a UK/Canada Production, which fictionalised the Ripper story by presenting it as a Sherlock Holmes thriller, woven round the story of Annie Crook and Eddy and their child. Christopher Plummer played Holmes and James Mason Dr Watson. It boasted many other luminaries of stage and screen, notably John Gielgud as the Marquess of Salisbury, Anthony Quayle as Sir Charles Warren, Donald Sutherland as Robert Lees – a clairvoyant alleged to have helped the police in the Ripper hunt – and David Hemmings as a 'radical' police officer. It was loosely based on *The Ripper File* by Elwyn Jones and John Lloyd (1975). That book was itself based upon the 1973 BBC series 'Jack the Ripper,' in the last programme of which, as we have noted, Joseph had first come to public notice.

The film told the story of Annie Crook's marriage to Prince Eddy and their unnamed child. The murders were master-minded by Lord Salisbury, Sir Charles Warren and a royal physician. The physician was 'Sir Thomas Spivey' and his coach driver 'William Slade'. Annie Crook was played by Geneviève Bujold, who spoke with a pronounced French accent.

None of this bothered Joseph too much, but he could not dismiss as mere poetic licence the insulting manner in which the persons of Eddy and Annie were portrayed. It is true that both were long dead and could not be hurt by anything said about them. Nevertheless they were his grandparents, and it is hardly surprising that he was indignant about the actions and motives the film attributed to them. Eddy was Annie's 'seducer', who became 'tired of her' after he had 'cynically taken her in marriage'. Joseph accepts that Eddy was dissolute, but he sees no reason why anyone should suggest that the affair between his grandparents was anything but reciprocal, or that Annie did not enter into it with her eyes open. Without contrary evidence, there was no reason to suggest that the marriage was not regarded as seriously by Eddy as it undoubtedly was by Annie. He was also annoyed that in the final scene his grandmother was made out to have committed suicide. To Roman Catholics suicide is a mortal sin.

Joseph was in fact consulted by the film-makers over one item: the secret handshake employed by the 33° Freemasons. He showed them how to do it, and Holmes is seen using it to greet Sir Charles Warren. Walter Sickert had taught it to Joseph and his mother when Joseph was a small boy. During the last years of her life Alice was not only deaf but blind, and when he entered her home Joseph identified himself with the handshake. When he was a boy, he and his mother used to greet one another this way as a joke. (The handshake is used only in secret masonic ritual. Therefore Walter Sickert could only have known it if he too was a 33° mason, unless another mason broke his oath and showed it to him. The former is, I think, more likely.)

The film makers could not portray Walter Sickert as a Ripper gang member, as Knight had done, without possible litigation by Joseph. Instead they used his initials for the name of the coach driver, William Slade. 'Slade' was a reference to the fact that Walter attended the Slade School of Art and 'coveted the post of Slade Professor'.[4] (One amateur Ripperologist told me that he had read that some of Sickert's students called him Walter Slade on account of his keenness for the coveted post. Unfortunately he could not remember where he had read it, and I was unable to verify it.)

When Joseph finally saw the film he felt betrayed and hurt. 'Didn't they suffer enough,' he asked, 'when they were alive, without their having to do that to them now that they're dead?' He decided to name everyone responsible for the Ripper murders, and when I telephoned him the day after he led me by hints and clues to the name of the leader of the gang. He had just arrived home with a friend with whom he had spent New Year's Day. He does not drink very much, but on this occasion he had enjoyed a convivial evening and was in a mood more mischievous than usual. He told me: 'The main one had an American mother and was a member of an old and noble family.' He added nothing more, and I went to bed that night more confused than ever. The only person I could think of who had an American mother and came from a noble family was Winston Churchill, but he had been too young in 1888. I had visions of reading Burke's Peerage page by page looking for a likely candidate. Fortunately that was not necessary, because Joseph had decided to tell me the whole Ripper story. When I telephoned next day I told him that he had told me nothing, and that the only person I could think of was Winston Churchill.

'Yes, that's right,' he said. 'It was his father, Lord Randolph Churchill.'

Taken aback, I asked: 'Joseph, are you saying that Winston Churchill's father was Jack the Ripper?'

'Yes. He and his brother, the Duke of Marlborough. But Randolph was the leader.'

All those wonderful stories about Winston Churchill crowded into my mind: the deeds of heroism, the witty responses to silly remarks, the silver phrases that had adorned the language. Joseph was asking me to believe that the father of this man who had given courage to the British during the Second World War – the leader who had given the roar to the British lion – was Jack the Ripper!

*

Lord Randolph Henry Spencer Churchill was the younger of two surviving sons of the 7th Duke of Marborough. His brother George, the Marquess of Blandford, succeded to the dukedom in 1883. Lord Randolph's wife, Winston Churchill's mother, was Jennie Jerome, an American beauty with Red Indian blood, the daughter of a wealthy New Yorker, Leonard Jerome.

Lord Randolph was a member of the Privy Council, an Oxford MA and a Cambridge LLD, a Justice of the Peace, MP for Woodstock from 1874 to 1885 and for South Paddington in 1885-86, Secretary of State for India in 1885, Chancellor of the Exchequor and Leader of the House of Commons in 1886. Was I to believe that in 1888 he was Jack the Ripper?

The idea seemed preposterous! Why on earth would this 'political star of eccentric orbit'[5] involve himself in the sordid murders of five East End women? I wondered whether Randolph had strong ties of friendship with the Royal Family. Or was his involvement due to some personal idiosyncrasy, a hatred of women in general, or of whores in particular?

I still had not read the diaries, though Joseph had once brought one out to show me, saying that it was one of his father's. I made the mistake of thinking that he meant that the diaries had been written by Walter Sickert personally. He said he would let me see the journals at a later date. I would not be disappointed, he said, since they confirmed everything he had told me.

*

In 1876 Lord Randolph's brother, the Marquess of Blandford, the heir to the dukedom, had courted Lady Edith, Countess of Aylesford while her husband was absent in India with the Prince of Wales. Aylesford was only twenty-six, but from his love of the turf, pugilism and cock-fighting, and his generally violent disposition he had already earned himself the nickname 'Sporting Joe'. While he was in India Blandford took up residence in an inn near Packington Hall, the Aylesford country seat in Warwickshire, to be near Lady Aylesford. She wrote to her husband and confessed her infidelity. The Prince of Wales commiserated with his friend, and Aylesford set off from India on the back of an elephant and returned to England. On his arrival he began divorce proceedings, citing Blandford. After denouncing Blandford as 'the greatest blackguard alive', the Prince of Wales supported Aylesford and suggested that Blandford should also divorce his wife, so that the two could marry. Lord Randolph was furious and defended his brother with typical loyalty and recklessness. Lady Aylesford gave Blandford some admiring letters she had received from the Prince of Wales, and they were handed to Lord Randolph. With these in his pocket he went to Marlborough House to see the Princess of Wales and told her that he had the means to prevent the case ever coming to court, that if it did the Prince would be subpoenaed to give evidence, and that 'His Royal Highness would never sit on the Throne of England'.[6] He threatened to publish the letters unless the Prince stopped leaning on Blandford and put pressure instead on Lord Aylesford to drop his divorce. Randolph, with typical arrogance, boasted to his friends that he 'held the Crown of England in his pocket'.[7]

When the Prince received this news in Cairo, where he was resting, exhausted after five months' travelling, he flew into a rage and dispatched Lord Charles Beresford to London to demand an apology from Randolph: otherwise he would name his seconds and arrange for a duel in France with pistols (duels were illegal in England). It would have been political and social folly for Lord Randolph to fight a duel with the Prince and risk the life of the Heir Apparent. The Prince could not seriously have expected he would. Randolph replied with a curt and insolent letter saying that a duel was absurd and impossible, as the Prince himself knew, better than anyone.

In July a letter of apology from Randolph was rejected by the Prince. The Lord Chancellor, Earl Cairns, drew up another, which was approved by Disraeli and Lord Hartington. By now Randolph was in America touring with his wife, who had begged 'for a breath of fresh air',[8] and the letter was sent to him for signing. Sign it he did, choosing to do so in Saratoga, New York, where a century earlier General Burgoyne had been forced to surrender his British Army to the Americans, claiming that he was signing a convention rather than a capitulation. Like the General, Randolph also felt that signing the apology was a defeat for British honour. He added a postscript saying that he felt compelled 'as a gentleman' to accept the Lord Chancellor's phraseology. He sent the letter to his father, who forwarded it to the Prince. The intentional irony was not lost on Bertie, and though he sent the Duke a formal acknowledgment he refused to communicate with Randolph on account of the ungracious postscript which, he said, proved that Randolph 'was not a gentleman'. On Christmas Day the Queen wrote to the Prince to say that now that Lord Randolph had apologised he could not be entirely excluded from Court festivities. The Prince agreed but said that on such occasions he would bow, but not speak, to Lord Randolph. Thereafter he made it known that he would enter no house in which the Randolph Churchills were entertained. This meant that they were virtually banished from society, and when, at the end of 1876, his father left for Ireland where he had been appointed Viceroy, Randolph went with him as his Private Secretary, taking Jennie and young Winston.

Among the Irish Tory friends made by Randolph in Ireland, the closest was George FitzGibbon, the newly appointed Irish Solicitor-General. They shared the same sense of irony and had an immediate rapport when they first met at Dublin Castle. It was through the influence of FizGibbon and his friends that Randolph became a Unionist deeply committed to the Irish Protestant cause. FitzGibbon was also a friend of another member of the Ripper coterie, Sir Robert Anderson, with whom he had studied law at Trinity College, Dublin. Anderson was a frequent visitor to Dublin Castle in the course of his duties at the bar. FitzGibbon was also an influential Freemason.

Ireland provided the opportunity for Randolph to express his Protestant sentiments and show his opposition to Roman Catholisism. In the next few years he was to make many speeches on the subject of Ireland, allying himself to the Protestant cause. In 1886 plans were made for him to tour Ulster. The tour was stage-managed by the Rev. R.R. Kane and William Johnston. Both were in the Orange Order, an Irish political association founded in Armagh in 1794 for the defence of Protestantism and the maintenance of Protestant ascendancy. The United Grand Lodge of English Freemasons deny that the Orange Order is masonic. But though there is indeed no official association between the Orange Order and Grand Lodge, it cannot be denied that many of the Orangemen's ideas, ceremonies and regalia are masonic in character. It is also true that a great many members of the order are Freemasons. On 13 February in a speech at Paddington Randolph incautiously declared his violent Unionism, stating: 'England will not leave the Protestants in the lurch.'[9] His arrival in Ulster eight days later became the focal point of an hysterical Protestant demonstration, and Randolph was to become a figurehead for Irish Protestants in general and Orangemen in particular. He even attended meetings at their Lodges. It could be said of him, as he once said of his mother in a letter to Jennie dated 12 December 1873, that he 'hat[ed] Romish practices like poison'.[10]

Eight years passed before Bertie spoke to Randolph again, but, at a dinner-party given by the Attorney-General, Sir Henry James, in March 1884, he consented to eat at the same table. He later said that 'R. Churchill's manner was just what it ought to have been'.[11] The Prince had completely forgiven Randolph when, two years later, he dined with the Churchills at their home in Connaught Place. By then Randolph had been appointed Secretary for India, while his brother, Lord Blandford, who was also present, had succeeded as 8th Duke of Marlborough. Lady

Churchill's charm and beauty helped thaw the ice, and the Prince was pleased to be able to renew his friendship with her, thereafter giving her presents of expensive jewellery and making her his mistress.

The renewed friendship flourished, and Bertie began to look upon Randolph as an ally: so much so that Sir Philip Magnus could say:

> Lord Randolph Churchill, who was appointed Chancellor of the Exchequer and Leader of the House of Commons in August, 1886, when he was aged 36, became the Prince's principal political confidant, in place of Sir Charles Dilke.[12]

Their association was not one of mere political confidentiality, however, as can be seen a few pages later:

> The Prince continued, nevertheless, to treat Churchill as an intimate friend.[13]

According to Giles St Aubyn:

> The Prince and Randolph became inseparable companions, and were seen together at most of the principal race meetings. H.R.H was tireless in pressing the claims of his friend on anyone willing to listen.[14]

In fact by this time Lord Randolph was a close friend of the whole Royal Family, and on 8 June 1888, less than three months before the Ripper murders began, he dined at Cambridge with Eddy, who was there to receive his honorary degree.[15] There were other eminent men around the table, some from the most distinguished families, including an ex-Lord Chancellor, the Earl of Selborne, a future Prime Minister, the Earl of Roseberry, and the Prime Minister, the Marquess of Salisbury.

*

The Royal Physician, Sir William Gull, was also a friend of Lord Randolph and enjoyed a close association with his family. In December 1882 Randolph's wife was ill with typhoid and was being treated by the Court physician Dr Francis Henry Laking. Randolph was in Algeria, and in a letter to him dated 19 December Jennie wrote that her mother-in-law, the Duchess of Marlborough, had asked Gull to call on her to make sure that Laking was treating her correctly. She mentioned Gull again in subsequent letters. In a reply to her on New Year's Day 1883 Randolph mentioned that Gull had telegraphed to say that Jennie was 'going on well'. On 17 January he wrote and asked her to see Gull again before she left London to join him in Monte Carlo.[16] This was six years before the Whitechapel murders. Moreover Gull's daughter Caroline had married the son of Sir Henry Wentworth Acland, who was family physician to Lord Randolph's father, the 7th Duke of Marlborough.

*

According to Joseph, Walter also implicated Lord Blandford. (Even after succeeding to the dukedom he was still generally referred to as Lord Blandford.) Expelled from Eton, he has been variously described as wilful and wayward.[17] He was notoriously lecherous, gaining the sobriquct 'the wicked Duke'.[18] He treated his wife appallingly and advised Randolph against marriage, regarding it as 'a delusion and a snare' which was 'irrevocable'.[19] Yet there were those who considered him angelic compared with his brother Randolph. During the Aylesford affair Disraeli remarked to Queen Victoria: 'Blandford I always thought was a scoundrel, but this brother beats him.'[20]

Blandford was something of an amateur scientist, and he installed in Blenheim Palace the first private telephone system, which was independent of, and it was said superior to, the systems of either Alexander Graham Bell or Thomas Edison. In 1883 his first wife divorced him, and early in 1888 he travelled to America to find a rich successor, a practice that had become almost commonplace among English aristocrats who wished to secure new money for old estates. In June 1888 he married the wealthy widow Lillian Hammersley (who, it was rumoured, because her name had the embarrassing misfortune to rhyme with 'million', preferred to be called Lily). While he was in America wooing Lily, Blandford called on Thomas Edison, the 'Wizard of Menlo Park'. In a letter to Jennie's brother-in-law, Moreton Frewen, Edison was later to praise Blandford with the words: 'I thought the English Duke was a fool with a crown on his head. But this one knows a great deal which I do not intend inventing until next fall.'[21] Blandford installed a dynamo in the cellar of Randolph's house at 2 Connaught Place, enabling him to boast that his was the first house in London to be lit by electricity. Randolph and Blandford were to maintain a close friendship, occasionally marred by violent arguments, and it was said of both of them that they had 'hereditary rudeness'.[22]

Whatever Blandford's part in the murders, one fact stands out. He died suddenly in 1892, at the age of 48. He was found in his laboratory at Blenheim Palace with, according to his housekeeper, 'a terrible expression on his face'.[23] It was four years to the day after the last Ripper murder: 9 November.

*

Lord Randolph was as erratic as his brother. Like his son Winston, he appears to have been a manic-depressive, swinging between black depressions and exhilarating brilliance. Effusive charm alternated with withering sarcasm. His talk was punctuated by abusive epithets, and he enjoyed embarrassing people by sudden bursts of bad behaviour. He was once described as 'a throwback to feudal times, when a duke believed himself to be equal to kings' and as speaking 'with the infallibility of a Pope and the readiness of a cheap Jack'.[24]

Randolph had no notions of equality. During his election campaign at Woodstock he complained to Jennie that he had to shake too many unwashed hands and enter too many dirty cottages. The common man was to be kept at arm's length and in his lowly place. Arriving in Woodstock and overhearing one of the 'lower orders' say of him, 'There's a rum specimen', he remarked that he wished he were an Ashanti king so that he could have the man executed.[25]

By 1885 the word 'insanity' was being frequently applied to Randolph. Lord Derby in his diary for 19 May described him as 'thoroughly untrustworthy: scarcely a gentleman, and probably more or less mad.' Both Lord Salisbury and Queen Victoria thought him mad,[26] and in his final years he became completely unhinged.

Randolph's speeches in the House of Commons were frequently acerbic, usually controversial and always brilliant. Members who heard the cry 'Randy's up' echoing through the corridors and hallways would come scurrying to their seats. His magnetism, his oratorical skill, his very manner were inherited (some believe copied) by Winston. Winston even adopted his pose, standing with hand on hip, elbow pointing out behind him. Both men had sonorous voices. Both adopted a studied seriousness and a ham theatricality. Both made great use of epithets and metaphors. Both lisped, but this did not mar their skill with spoken language – if anything, it added gravity. Listening to any of Winston's famous wartime speeches, we hear paternal echoes.

Perhaps the only real difference between Winston and his father lay in his attitude to the man in the street. It would never have occurred to Lord Randolph to wonder about the opinions of his local blacksmith or house-painter. Why should he care what the peasants thought? Winston, on the other hand, took a genuine interest in the views of ordinary people. When, for instance, builders went to Chartwell from Westerham to restore the house, he would ask their opinion about politics, listening intently to gauge the general mood. He had a streak of humility quite absent in his father.

Of average height with a wide, turned-up moustache, Randolph appeared every inch the rakish son of a duke. According to the *Pall Mall Gazette* (28 June 1884), he was:

> ... beautifully dressed, his linen is glossy, and evidently carefully superintended in the best laundries, his gold chain has the solid appearance of real 18 carat, his tiny shoes, rosettes, and silk socks are the daintiest of their kind. His manner is typified by his own phrase: 'COME ON.'

According to Marian Fowler:

> Underneath this son of Blenheim's suave façade – violet waistcoat, tan shoes, diamond-studded amber cigarette-holder – there had always been a smouldering violence; now it erupted more and more frequently. 'So mad and odd,' sighed Queen Victoria.[27]

*

None of the names given to me by Joseph were to be found in any of the Home Office or Police files. This is hardly surprising since Warren and Anderson used their position to organise a cover-up. Most of the items which were originally in the files are missing. For example, the first page of the file which held accusations against policemen and doctors, No. HO 144/220/ A 49301, lists the contents as follows:

> 2 items went to Anderson.
> 1 item went to the police.
> 10 items missing.
> 176 items destroyed.

Out of these 208 separate items listed, only 19 remain. Many are simply newspaper cuttings. The rest, as the last compiler of the file has stated on the front, are an 'unimportant series' of 'miscellaneous suggestions'.

In 1988 a representative of Scotland Yard explained that in the nineteenth century the Yard's files were kept on long shelves. When these were full, space was made for new files by throwing away the oldest ones. If so, the Ripper file should have been thrown out long ago. The fact is, files on sensational murders were kept for ever, which is why the Ripper file is available today. The statement will hardly satisfy serious investigators, since it does not explain why individual papers are missing from a file which still exists. Many police officers have looked into the file over the last hundred years and were easily able to remove items to impress their friends with, or keep as souvenirs.

The following is an interesting story about police tampering with the file, which was given to me by L.J. Baker, a septuagenarian who visited Britain recently from South Australia:

> I was born in England in 1921, and emigrated to Australia in 1958. Whenever things went wrong my mother always used to say: 'If it hadn't been for that Ripper we wouldn't be in the mess we're in today.' Years later she told me she remembered her grandfather coming home once from the Lodge, where he was Master of the Lodge, throwing his masonic apron into the fire and saying: 'No one in this family, from now on, will have anything

to do with the lodge.' In 1929, the year Abberline died and I was about eight or nine years old, my uncle Sidney – my mother's brother – visited us. He had once been a sergeant in the Metropolitan police as a mounted policeman. He was invalided from the force because of the severe beating he took from a gang who dragged him from his horse and left him permanently crippled. This was about 25 years after the murders [about 1913]. He walked with a stick from then on.

When I was a teenager talking to Det. Inspector Thomas Erry, who was in the CID in Accrington, Lancashire, I mentioned the story of my uncle to him, and he said: 'I have it on good authority – mentioning no names of course – that though the general belief is that the Ripper files were stolen to prevent the truth coming out, the real reason they were taken was to make sure they were preserved. The masons run the force, and there's always this division between them and the non-masons. The masons didn't want the contents of the file to be known, so certain non-masonic police officers took it upon themselves to break the law by taking the files and preserving them. Your uncle was one of those involved and got on the wrong side of the masons. There were a large number of Freemasons who left their lodges over the Ripper murders. It caused quite a stir. The official line regarding your uncle was that his horse stumbled and rolled over on him.'

The inference is clear. When it was discovered that certain police officers who were not masons took the files to preserve the truth, the masons retrieved them and had them destroyed.

*

In the 1880s and early 1890s it became fashionable for the upper classes to visit the slums of the East End, sometimes to distribute charity to the 'lapsed masses', but often just to see how the the other half lived. This is how the word 'slumming' entered the language. If in the autumn of 1888 any of the uniformed constables plodding the streets of Whitechapel and Spitalfields had recognised Sir Charles Warren they would have assumed that he was there on police business, while the others with him would have been accepted as his upper-crust society friends who had simply accompanied him on a slumming excursion. If the police patrols noted some of the gang in passing, the files could later be rifled so that no suspicion could attach to the Ripper conspirators.

On Randolph's death, just before his 46th birthday, in 1895, Winston vowed to pursue his father's aims and vindicate his memory. When he became Home Secretary in 1910 he had access to all the Home Office and police files, secret or otherwise, and could remove any incriminating reports of his father's presence in the East End at the time of the murders. Such an act of devotion might be based not only on respect for his father's name but on loyalty to the Freemasons, because Winston was himself a Freemason, having been initiated into the United Studholme Lodge No. 1591 in May 1901. The United Studholme, which has a Royal

Arch Chapter attached, now meets at 10 Duke Street, St. James: the
same address as the present Supreme Council 33°, the premier masonic
council in England. In April 1990 an original letter of invitation to the
'raising' of Brother Winston to the third degree, which took place at 33
Golden Square on 25 March 1902, was on exhibition in the Library of
Freemasons Hall, Great Queen Street. It was signed by the Secretary,
Lord Euston, a member of the Ripper coterie who was later to figure in
the Cleveland Street scandal (see Chapter 7).

Winston resigned from the Freemasons in July 1912. It is not
unreasonable to suggest that he had learned about his father's
involvement in the murders and felt so ashamed of what he and other
masons had done that he refused to have any further connection with the
brotherhood. Clearly Winston invented an idealised image of his father,
not realising later that he was modelling himself on a fantasy figure he
had invented. He drove himself to become the statesman he wished his
father had been and the great Prime Minister his father never was, and
with his own children he became the caring father he never had. In 1906
he published a biography of Randolph which, in the words of Ted Morgan,
'was in fact one of the most systematic whitewashings that any
biographer, whether related to his subject or not, had ever attempted'.[28]

*

In the 1880s, in the swelling tide of republican sympathy, Eddy's
marriage to a Catholic commoner might easily have swept away the
monarchy, the aristocracy, the landed gentry and the government: in
short, the whole established order. Near the pinnacle of this pyramid
stood Lord Randolph, who would be bound fervently to defend the status
quo, particularly the interests of the monarchy. This was well illustrated
in 1873 when he passionately supported the Royalist cause in France
where, he said, he was ready to 'hang the left en mass' (sic) in Paris.[29]

Randolph's motives were often unaccountable, even mystifying, to his
son, who wrote of him:

> A veil of the incalculable shrouded the workings of his complex nature. No
> one could tell what he would do, or by what motive, lofty or trivial, of
> conviction or caprice, of irritation or self-sacrifice, he would be governed.[30]

Whatever his motives, Randolph was a determined man not easily
thwarted by the inconveniences of conscience. According to Marian
Fowler:

> What Randolph wanted, using fair means or foul, Randolph always got.[31]

When Randolph's parents first opposed his marriage to Jennie Jerome,
he admitted to her in a letter, 'All tricks are fair in love as well as war & if
I am crossed, I can plot and intrigue like a second Machiavelli.'[32] We need

not doubt it. He further proved his ability to plot ahead when he became a first-class chess player. He once played against the chess champion of the world in a game described by Winston as 'original, daring, and sometimes brilliant.'[33]

It was not difficult for Randolph to obtain Gull's cooperation in the murders. Not only was he Gull's masonic superior, but Gull, now aged 72, was suffering from the inroads of age and beginning to display signs of cruelty. Mutilating the victims' bodies would hardly have been too obnoxious to him, since he frequently conducted post-mortems in his medical research. When he died, his son-in-law, Thomas Dyke Acland, wrote page after page of eulogy in his *In Memoriam: Sir William Gull*, but another side of Gull's personality also makes itself felt (p. xxxix):

> He had been attending a poor patient with heart disease, and after his death was extremely anxious for a post-mortem examination. With great difficulty this was granted, but with the proviso that nothing was to be taken away, and the sister of the diseased patient, a strong-minded old maid, was present to watch proceedings. Gull saw that it was hopeless to conceal anything from her, or to persuade her to leave the room. He therefore deliberately took out the heart, put it in his pocket and, looking steadily at her, said, 'I trust to your honour not to betray me.' His knowledge of character was justified by the result and the heart is now in Guy's Museum.

In relating this anecdote to demonstrate, as he thought, his father-in-law's knowledge of character, Acland unintentionally provided insight into Gull's own character. Gull displayed a callous disregard for the feelings of another, a woman already suffering the pains of bereavement. The story graphically reminds us too that the only organ missing from Kelly's body was her heart.

Within a month of Winston's birth in 1874 Lord Randolph made repeated visits to the family doctor, Oscar Clayton, for an undisclosed ailment. It was likely to have been syphilis which he was treated for in later years. His physician, Dr Robson Roose, believed that Randolph had contracted syphilis, and in October 1885, though he continued to treat him himself, he placed him in the care of a specialist, Dr Thomas Buzzard.[34]

Winston wrote in his autobiography:

> It was an axiom with my parents that in serious accident or illness the highest medical aid should be invoked.[35]

In accordance with this principle Lord Randolph obtained – according to Walter Sickert – the aid of Sir William Gull who was not only his masonic companion, but one of the most esteemed physicians in the land. Gull was also an expert in the treatment of syphilis. According to his son-in-law 'he would give mercury in syphilitic cases with the utmost confidence'.[36] (This, together with potassium iodide, was the only effective treatment: there was no known cure.)

No one can say with certainty how Lord Randolph contracted the disease, but according to his nephew and godson, Shane Leslie, as reported by Ted Morgan, he caught it from 'a Blenheim housemaid shortly after Winston's birth in 1874'.[37]

A well-known story of Randolph's supposed encounter with a prostitute as an undergraduate at Oxford is related by Frank Harris in his scurrilous autobiography *My Life and Loves*. Whether or not the story – told to him by Randolph's political friend and follower Louis Jennings – is true in all details, or indeed in any, it reflects a contemporary view of Randolph's proclivities, from which one may conclude that he had reason to be 'down on whores':

Randolph was not a success at Oxford at first, [Jennings began]. He never studied or read; he rode to hounds at every opportunity and he was always imperious as the devil. But after all he was the son of a Duke and Blenheim was near and the best set made up to him, as Englishmen do. He was made a member of the Bullingdon Club, the smartest club in Oxford, and one evening he held forth there on his pet idea that the relationship of master and servant in the home of an English gentleman was almost ideal. 'Any talent in the child of a butler or gardener,' he said, 'would be noticed by the master, and of course he'd be glad to give the gifted boy an education and opportunity such as his father could not possibly afford. Something like this should be the relationship between the aristocratic class and the workmen in England: this is Tory-democracy as I conceive it.' Of course the youths all cheered him and complimented him and made much of him, and when the party was breaking up, one insisted on a 'stirrup-cup.' He poured out a glass of old brandy and filled it up with champagne and gave it to Randolph to drink. Nothing loath, Randolph drained the cup, and with many good wishes all the youths went out into the night. Randolph assured me that after he had got into the air he remembered nothing more. I must now let Randolph tell his own story.

'Next morning,' Randolph began, 'I woke up with a dreadful taste in my mouth, and between waking and sleeping was thunder-struck. The paper on the walls was hideous – dirty – and, as I turned in bed, I started up gasping: there was an old woman lying beside me; one thin strand of dirty grey hair was on the pillow. How had I got there? What had happened to bring me to such a den? I slid out of bed and put on shirt and trousers as quietly as I could, but suddenly the old woman in the bed awoke and said, smiling at me, "Oh, Lovie, you're not going to leave me like that?"

'She had one long yellow tooth in her top jaw that waggled as she spoke. Speechless with horror, I put my hand in my pocket and threw all the money I had loose on the bed. I could not say a word. She was still smiling at me; I put on my waistcoat and coat and fled from the room. "Lovie, you're not kind!" I heard her say as I closed the door after me. Downstairs I fled in livid terror. In the street I found a hansom and gave the jarvy the address of a doctor I had heard about. As soon as I got to him, he told me he knew my brother and ...' I broke out in wild excitement, "I want you to examine me at once. I got drunk last night and woke up in bed with an appalling old prostitute. Please examine me and apply some disinfectant." Well, he went to work and said he could find no sign of any abrasion, but he made up a strong disinfectant and I washed the parts with it; and all the time he kept on trying to console me, I suppose, with cheap commonplaces. "There isn't much serious disease in Oxford. Of course there should be licensed houses, as in France, and weekly or bi-weekly examination of the inmates. But then we hate grandmotherly legislation in England and really, my dear Lord Randolph, I don't think you have serious cause for alarm." Cause for alarm, indeed; I hated myself for having been such a fool! At the end I carried away a couple of books on venereal diseases and set to work to devour them. My next week was a nightmare. I made up my mind at once that I deserved gonorrhea for my stupidity. I even prayed to God, as to a maleficent deity, that he might give me that; I deserved that, but no more, no worse: not a chancre, not syphilis!

'There was nothing, not a sign, for a week. I breathed again. Yet I'd have to wait till the twenty-first day before I could be sure that I had escaped syphilis. Syphilis! Think of it, at my age, I, who was so proud of my wisdom. On the fateful day nothing, not a sign. On the next the doctor examined me again: "Nothing, Lord Randolph, nothing! I congratulate you. You've got off, to all appearance, scot-free."

'A day later I was to dine with Jowett, the Master of Balliol. It was a Sunday and he had three or four people of importance to meet me. He put me on his left hand; he was always very kind to me, was Jowett. I talked a lot but drank very sparingly. After that first excess, I resolved never to take more than two glasses of wine at any dinner and one small glass of liqueur or brandy with my coffee. I wouldn't risk being caught a second time. I was so thankful to God for my immunity that vows of reform were easy.

'In the middle of dinner suddenly I felt a little unwell. Strange! At once I was alarmed, and cold with fear, excused myself and left the room. Outside I asked a footman for the lavatory. I also asked the butler to excuse me to the Master. "I am feeling very ill," I said, "and must go home."

"You don't look well," he replied, and in a minute I was in a hansom and on the way to the doctor's. Luckily he was in and willing to see me.

'To cut a long story short the Oxford doctor and later a London man said I was quite clear of all weakness and perfectly cured.'[38]

*

In later years Jennie took many lovers, who included Count Charles Kinski, Henry Breteuil, William Waldorf Astor, Herbert von Bismark, Sir Harry Cust, Viscount D'Abernon, Lord Dunraven and the Prince of Wales. The lack of sexual intimacy with his wife and the decline of his marriage made Randolph isolated and bitter, and explains his remark to Lord Rosebery that 'no man is so entirely alone and solitary as I am'.

Frank Harris's account has been doubted. Harris, it is said, was someone with a lively and flamboyant imagination who was not averse to biographical invention and who took liberties with the truth.

Nevertheless he was a friend of both Lord Randolph and Winston. Indeed when Winston was writing the biography of his father, it was Harris who negotiated an £8,000 advance from the publisher, Macmillan. This was particularly laudable since he had wanted to write the biography himself.

That Randolph had syphilis has been contested by Richard Hough.[39] In this he has the support of Peregrine Churchill, trustee of Winston's archives who, in a letter to the *Sunday Telegraph* on 29 April 1990, named Professor Roy Foster as one historian who denied that Randolph had syphilis. But Foster in fact wrote that 'Lady Randolph's correspondence with her sister, as well as the belief of his (admittedly ineffectual) doctors, leaves little doubt that Churchill's later debility was the result of syphilis'.[40] Randolph's grand-niece, Anita Leslie, agrees.[41]

There seems little doubt that Randolph had syphilis, but whether he did or not, or whether he suffered from an overdose of prescribed drugs as Peregrine Churchill claimed, or had a brain tumour as argued by Hough, the important thing is that he and his doctors believed that he had syphilis, and he was treated by them accordingly. He became extremely bitter. As Ralph G. Martin wrote, 'it was as if he blamed all women for the syphilis which destroyed his brilliant career'.[42]

*

Randolph had an important source of influence on the eminent men he recruited: he was their masonic superior. He was the highest Freemason in England. The supreme position he held, according to Walter Sickert, though Grand Lodge deny that he was ever a mason, was that of Magister Magistrorum – Master of Masters. None of his biographers mentions his Freemasonry, and I have been assured by an apparently reliable masonic source that the records at Freemasons Hall contain no mention of him. Nor are there any paintings of him in Freemasons Hall, as there are of other aristocratic Freemasons. This was officially confirmed to me in a letter from the Assistant Librarian, Katrina McQuillan, dated 15 February 1991. An explanation suggests itself.

According to the records in the library at Freemasons Hall, one Rudolph H. Spencer was initiated in 1878 into the First Lodge of Ireland under the Irish Constitution. In London later that year, at the request of Joseph W. MacMullen, the Worshipful Master of the Lodge, he was passed and raised in the Westminster and Keystone Lodge No. 10, under the English Constitution. The ceremony took place during the Summer Banquet held at the Star and Garter at Richmond.[43] According to Alexandra Ward, the Curator of Freemasons Hall, Dublin, there is no record of Spencer's name in the Irish archives. In 1878 Lord Randolph was still in Ireland as his father's secretary, but made frequent trips to London. *Rudolph H. Spencer and Randolph H. Spencer Churchill were one and the same.* 'Mr Spencer' was the alias used by Lord Randolph and his brother Blandford. When Blandford lived in France with Lady Aylesford they did so as Mr and Mrs Spencer.[44] According to two of Lord Randolph's relatives, Anita Leslie[45] and Peregrine Churchill,[46] 'Mr Spencer' was the name Lord Randolph used as an alias when he travelled on the continent. Clearly he used it when he entered the masonic fraternity in Dublin after his probable introduction by the closest of his Dublin friends, the influential Freemason Lord Justice FitzGibbon.

Were it not that *The Pocket History of Freemasonry* by Fred L. Pick (Past Master of the Quatuor Coronati Lodge, the world premier lodge of masonic research) and G. Norman Knight lists Lord Randolph among statesmen who were Freemasons, no one might ever have known of his connection with the brotherhood.[47] The book, which is freely available from the Quatuor Coronati Lodge and from the officially sanctioned regalia shop opposite Freemasons Hall, Great Queen Street, was first published in 1953. Presumably they found Lord Randolph's name in the records before its subsequent erasure.

An odd coincidence, if coincidence it be, adds a curious feature to the story. St Saviour's Infirmary and Chapel in Osnaburgh Street, where, according to Walter Sickert, Prince Eddy and Annie Crook were married, was pulled down in the 1930s and replaced by a red brick building now used for offices. A large plate by the front door proclaims its name:

Marlborough House.

It is difficult to escape the feeling that another wry masonic joke was being played when the name was chosen. Marlborough House, in the Mall, was the home of the Prince and Princess of Wales and their son Eddy. Moreover Lord Randolph Churchill was the son of the Duke of Marlborough, and a member of the 'Marlborough set', a social circle headed by the Prince of Wales, who founded the Marlborough Club, which flourished until 1914. Of course when Marlborough House in Osnaburgh Street was built both Lord Randolph and the Prince of Wales had been dead for years, and it is now impossible to discover who chose the building's name or why it was chosen. If it is mere coincidence, it is a remarkable one.

Lord Randolph suffered his first paralytic attack, which affected his gait and speech, in 1881. He had all the symptoms of syphilis in its tertiary stage, when the spirochaetes establish colonies in various parts of the body, causing inflamation and obstruction of the small arteries. When this happens the aorta can become permanently stretched by the pressure of blood; later the valve that prevents the blood pumped into the aorta from returning into the heart leaks. When his doctors realised that his heart was affected they prescribed digitalis to slow it down and strengthen the contractions. They also prescribed belladonna to allay the pain, and laudanum as a tranquilliser. Of course none of this could cure him, and he began taking the drugs in increasing doses. The drugs and the alcohol, which had also been prescribed along with tobacco, led to the debilitation noted by his associates.

By 1886 Jennie was aware of the nature of Randolph's disease which had caused him to cease conjugal relations. At first she thought another woman was involved but, after a fearful row, he told her the truth. At least now she could understand, and thereafter treated him with her usual affection.[48] In 1892 she paid a secret visit to his doctor. Randolph found out and they had another row. He refused to believe he was dying.[49]

In January 1894 Randolph and Jennie went on a world cruise, accompanied by a young physician, Dr George Keith. By then he seems to have been in the fourth and final stage of the disease, when the nervous system is severely affected so that deterioration of the personality, delusions and finally insanity set in. Jennie told her sister Leonie that at one point in their journey Randolph drew a loaded revolver in their cabin and threatened her, but she snatched it from him and pushed him back onto his berth.[50] They returned to London on Christmas Eve, after which he fell into a stupor. He died on 24 January 1895. (His son Winston died on the same day seventy years later.)

Three weeks before his death Jennie wrote to Leonie. She was speaking of Randolph's disease, but her words could as easily be applied to the more sinister secret of his Ripper involvement:

> Physically he is much better but mentally he is 1000 times worse ... Up to now the General Public and even Society does not know the real truth, and after all my sacrifice and the misery of these six months it would be hard if it got out. It would do incalculable harm to his political reputation and memory and be a dreadful thing for us all.[51]

Since this letter is quoted by Peregrine Churchill, it is difficult to see why he does not believe that Lord Randolph had syphilis.

*

Joseph, it will be remembered, had told me that he hesitated to reveal Lord Randolph's name because Randolph's family had helped him and his mother. I asked if that help had come from Winston.

'Yes,' said Joseph, 'he was a friend of my dad's. Dad used to give Winston painting lessons.'

This was something that could be checked. I could not discover anything linking Randolph directly to Walter Sickert, but I was reassured to find that Joseph was right in saying that Walter had taught Winston to paint.[52] Moreover Walter had been a friend of the Churchill family for more than half a century. Nevertheless it was to the friendship between Walter and Winston's wife, Clementine, that my researches first led me.

Clementine Hozier's mother, Blanche, had been estranged from her husband since 1891, and in 1899 she took Clementine and her other children to stay in Dieppe, a popular summer resort of the period. In Neuville-les-Dieppe, away from the bustle of the fashionable town centre, and across the harbour where the fishing community was established on the hillside, lived Madame Augustine Eugénie Villain, known for her mop of red hair and fiery temper as La Belle Rousse. Not only was she Walter Sickert's landlady and model; she became his mistress and bore him a son, Maurice. It was said that as a boy Maurice loved fire engines and often went to bed in his boots. He lost an eye in the First World War and was awarded the Croix de Guerre. A Sickert painting of Maurice in uniform displaying his medal was exhibited in 1916, but its whereabouts are now unknown. Maurice himself declined into dissipation.

It was inevitable that the Hoziers should meet Sickert, who was one of the more colourful English residents of Dieppe. The 14-year-old Clementine was much taken by this handsome artist with the green eyes and eccentric manner, and she would sometimes walk up the hill to his lodgings and take tea with him. She would accompany him to an art gallery, or he would take her to meet his friends, many of whom were also artists, such as Degas, an acknowledged influence on Sickert's work.

Clementine and Walter were to remain lifelong friends, and when in 1927 she was knocked down by a car in the Brompton Road Walter paid her a visit at 11 Downing Street. Winston took an instant liking to him, and from that moment he often visited them at Chartwell where he encouraged Churchill's growing passion for painting. With his influential friends in society and in government, Churchill was perfectly placed to give Sickert any help he might need, either for himself or for Alice Crook, or for their son, Joseph. The first occasion was in 1937.

When Joseph was 12 Winston arranged for him to meet some people at a house in Queen Anne's Gate, between St James's Park and Parliament Square. He cannot remember exactly which house. (The Home Office, a hideously modern building, now stands at one end of Queen Anne's Gate overlooking splendid examples of early Georgian houses, while the Crown Prosecution Service is at the other end.) From there he was accompanied to Nova Scotia Farm, Elmset, near Ipswich, where he met several well-known people, one of whom was Ivor Novello. After a short stay Churchill had Joseph transferred to St Paul's, Walden Bury, four miles from Hitchen in Hertfordshire. St Paul's was the birthplace of Queen Elizabeth the Queen Mother, and in 1937 it was the home of her brother, David. Joseph does not know precisely why he was sent there, and can only surmise that it was regarded as a place of safety. As we shall see, there had already been two separate attempts on his life.

About a year after Joseph went to St Paul's, while making a toy revolver from balsa wood for Simon, the son of David Bowes-Lyon, he overheard a conversation between David and a stranger. They were discussing the possibilty of sending Joseph away. Before they could send him anywhere he ran away and returned to his mother in Drummond Street. From there Churchill had him sent to St Thomas's Roman Catholic School in West Grinstead and afterwards to Guernsey, where for a while he was educated at Elizabeth College, a public school in the capital, St Peter Port.

At the outbreak of war Guernsey was invaded, but before the Germans arrived all the English pupils at Elizabeth College returned to England. Once again Joseph found himself in West Grinstead. After visiting his mother in Drummond Street he went to Carlisle, before spending a short time in Ireland, where he had relations on his father's side.

On his return to Drummond Street in 1942, the year his father died, he was the victim of a murder attempt.

I joined the army when I was about 17½, but lied about my age. I trained in Ireland and then joined the Royal Army Ordnance Corps in England. From there I went into the Royal Corps of Military Police but later went back to the RAOC. Somehow they discovered my real age and I was sent home.

One day I was in my room at home in my mother's house in Drummond Street. It was nighttime during the 'blackout' and there had been an air-raid warning. I could hear the hob-nailed boots of soldiers running about outside. I was lying on my bed looking at some sketches. I knew every sound in that house. You know how you can recognise every sound in your own home. If someone you know – a friend or a member of your family – walks upstairs, you hear bump-bump-bump as they bound up, and that's alright. But if you hear just the creak of a stair, your ears prick up because it's suspicious. That's what happened, and I looked up and saw the door-knob move. It wobbled, and then the door opened, and I went like that [demonstrating] and kicked the door. Bang! I'd been shot.

There was a scuffle on the other side of the door and a whistle blew and there were cars arriving outside. Two men in suits came into my room. I was shattered. Anyway, this man – I'll never forget his name, Captain Duke: he was an agent in the Secret Intelligence Service – he said, 'Are you all right?' I said, 'I don't know. I think my leg fell off', and I asked, 'Is my head all right?' because it was hurting. He said, 'Oh yes, you've got a scratch!'

The bullet shot off the third toe on my right foot, skimmed my knee and chest and caught my forehead as it went past my head into the wall behind me. I've still got the bullet.

Anyway, these men kept waiting, looking at their watches, and I was given an injection by this Dr Kerr brought from the National Temperance Hospital. The men waited a bit longer and then Captain Duke pulled out a revolver and – Bang! – he shot it into the floor. 'All right take him out,' he said. And they took me out. I asked, 'What was that for?' He said, 'There's been a gun accident', and he gave me an old-fashioned look. They took me to the National Temperance Hospital.

A few years afterwards I heard that Captain Duke was murdered in France. His body was found down a well. He'd been carrying money for the French Resistance and he was murdered for the money.

Because he had been lying down, Joseph had presented a relatively small target and, with his shoulders bracing him against the bed as he kicked the door, the bullet had passed through his foot and along the upper line of his body. It went through his foot beneath his toe, which is now missing, leaving a large gap between his second and fourth toes. The scar on his upper left forehead also provides visible evidence of his ordeal.

After a couple of days in the National Temperance Hospital in Hampstead Road, around the corner from Drummond Street, he was visited by some army officers. They decided to send Joseph to a military hospital at Shenley, and he soon realised that the establishment was, in his idiom, a 'nut-house'.

Joseph never learned who had tried to murder him, or why.

*

Finally, after Walter's death in early 1942, Winston Churchill, who was Prime Minister, returned Joseph to St Paul's, Walden Bury. David Bowes-Lyon was now working for the Ministry of Economic Warfare, spending most of his time in the USA, where he was too busy to concern himself with the problem of Joseph. During his stay there, Joseph met Winston, who spoke to him briefly when he visited St Paul's.

Joseph has a few memories of St Paul's, such as the following. There were many servicemen there during his second stay, most of whom were recovering from wounds received in combat. Occasionally some of them would visit the nearest cinema, and when Joseph asked if he could go with them he was refused on the grounds that he would stand out from the rest because they were all in uniform and he was not. Whoever the authorities were at St Paul's at that time, they were well aware that an attempt had been made on Joseph's life and that there could be another one at any time. They reasoned that, as the only one in a large group not wearing uniform, he would present an easy target. With schoolboy simplicity, he suggested that a uniform be found for him, and the next time a group of soldiers went to the cinema Joseph was among them, proudly dressed as an army cadet.

On another occasion he was in the grounds sketching the scene before him and failed to hear someone coming up behind. There was a light breeze blowing round him, and being deaf in one ear he failed also to hear what was being said to him. Unaccustomed to being ignored, the person prodded Joseph sharply in the back. Naturally he was startled, and his pencil slipped across the page. Expecting to see one of the more mischievous cadets, he wheeled round and shouted, 'Fuck off.' Immediately he recognised the regal bearing. It was Queen Mary, who because he had seemed to ignore her had prodded him with her umbrella. She chose diplomatically not to hear the expletive and proceeded to spend some time with him discussing art.

MATHEW PACKER TELLS
A STRANGE STORY TO THE
POLICE.

The Juwes are
The men that
    Will not
In Blamed
    for nothing

TEMBER 22, 1888.   Price One Penny.

READY FOR THE WHITECHAPEL FIEND. WOMEN SECRETLY ARMED.

CHAPTER FIVE

The Changeling

Prince Eddy's deafness was caused by otosclerosis, a condition he had inherited from his mother, Princess Alexandra, who had inherited it from her mother, Princess Louise of Hesse-Cassell. Passing from Eddy to his daughter Alice, it continued to blight Joseph's own family, infecting both his children and his grandchildren. Of his three daughters, Carol and Theresa have been spared it but Patricia, the youngest, has not. Nevertheless, with the love and encouragement of her parents, Patricia has grown up to lead a full and productive life, assisting teachers of profoundly deaf children. Her own two offspring, Benjamin Alexander and Abigail, are both deaf, Benjamin profoundly so. The taint of otosclerosis is an enduring proof of his connection with the Duke of Clarence.

There was one problem, however. Joseph was not the only son born of his mother's relationship with Walter Sickert. The first affair led to the birth of a son in 1905, who was called Charles. There is no record of his birth at St Catherine's House. The following account shows why.

When Joseph was a boy his mother told him that his brother was taken from her when he was a baby and that she believed him to be dead. She explained the circumstances of their separation as follows.

One day when she was living with her grandmother in Pancras Street, she was walking from her home towards Tottenham Court Road. On the corner stood a public house where the police had arrived to halt an affray. A crowd had already gathered, which prevented her progress, so she stopped and watched. A woman stood next to her, edging closer, until eventually she stood on her foot. The woman may not have realised she was hurting her, but Alice's reflex was to push her away. A policeman noticed and the woman complained to him. Alice was arrested.

Though she never appeared in court, Alice found herself confined in Holloway Prison for two weeks. Perhaps the police had found it difficult to communicate with her because of her deafness. Moreover she may have wished to remain silent because of her suspicion of those in authority. Her mother and grandmother were eventually told where she was. They told Walter Sickert who, in turn, asked one of his friends, Jim Driscoll, to see if he could obtain her release. A more unlikely person for the job can hardly be imagined. Driscoll was a professional boxer. One of his sparring partners was William Gorman, who was later to marry Alice.

Driscoll was born in Cardiff in 1880. In 1910 he became featherweight champion, winning the Lonsdale Belt. Joseph does not know why his father asked Driscoll to intervene on Alice's behalf, but assumes that Walter did not wish to get involved with the authorities. Moreover since Driscoll was a friend of both Sickert's and Gorman's he must also have been acquainted with Alice. The authorities would have thought it perfectly natural for him to be concerned about her.

During Alice's two weeks in Holloway they told her that her son Charles would not be returned to her. She was unable to care for a child properly, they said, since, in the language of the day, she was stone deaf.

In the early 1970s Joseph tried to discover what had become of his brother Charles.

Eventually someone telephoned Joseph, introducing himself as a person who had been investigating Charles's story on behalf of Stephen Knight. He told him the following:

> We've been working on it for about six weeks, but we don't think we should carry on with it. We can't go any further. We went as far as we could and we're willing to give the money back. The only thing we could glean was that your brother Charles was taken to Mill Hill, to an orphanage and then to Brent, another school associated with the one in Mill Hill. From Brent he was taken to America or Canada. All we can say is that Charles is dead. We've had to sign the Official Secrets Act; so we can't tell you any more, except that Charles is definitely dead.

Joseph got the impression that this information was taken from the records of the Mill Hill establishment but had been subsequently obliterated. The investigators were warned off and forced into virtual silence by the Official Secrets Act.

Joseph's close friend Harry Jonas mentioned this to Lady Dowding, who invited Joseph to her home. She said she knew an American, Henry Bailey Stevens, who had once mentioned knowing another American, Curtis Freshel, who had a connection with the Royal Family. Stevens was traced, and in due course Joseph received the following letter from him. Though it provided no clue to Charles's whereabouts, it did reveal a gobbet of information which students of the Royal Family may find of interest:

Dear Mr Sickert,

I deeply appreciate your letter of August 28. Although I have to report that Curtis Freshel could not have been your brother, he must have been some sort of cousin.

He was born in Detroit on April 22, 1886. Most of his boyhood was spent in England, graduating from the International College in 1908. He died in his apartment in New York July 1 1968.

I do not know his grandmother's name, but she was a Lady-in-Waiting at Queen Victoria's court and was seduced by Prince Edward Albert probably in the early 1860's. The understanding was that if the child proved male he would be in line to the throne. She took her child to America and possibly with help from the Queen brought her up well. Curt's father was a successful industrialist with important holdings in both Detroit and Brazil.

In 1914 Curt married M.R.L. Sharp (nicknamed Emarel by Bernard Shaw, who was a warm friend of them both) in Boston. There they used their beautiful home, 'Providence House', as a cultural center and home for their Millennium Guild. My wife and I came to know and admire them. The inflation caused by World War I nearly bankrupted them, and they moved to New York, where Curt developed Bakon [sic] Yeast, a profitable industry in the Vitamin B class. He kept his lineage a complete secret until he knew Death was taking him.

I am enclosing two photographs of him, young and old.

Yours sincerely,

[signed] Henry Bailey Stevens.

Twelve years later, in 1985, Joseph received another telephone call in connection with his brother Charles, this time from his original caller's son, who said that his father had died but had told him before his death what had befallen Joseph's brother. Furthermore, as he himself had never signed the Official Secrets Act, he could let Joseph know exactly what had happened to him.

On 12 July 1905 Eddy's younger brother, Prince George, the Prince of Wales and future King George V, was pleased to be informed that his wife, May of Teck, later Queen Mary, had been safely delivered of their fifth son, whom they christened John Charles Francis.

According to the son, the investigator had discovered that Prince John had died in his first year but that his death had not been announced. Instead Joseph's brother Charles had been taken from his mother's care and brought up by the Royal Family in John's place.

Members of the Royal Family and some of their advisors had been worried that Charles might one day prove an embarrassment to the monarchy since, as Eddy's grandson, he was in line to the throne. A modern pretender was to be avoided at all costs. Having the child within the confines of the palace walls, they could make sure he was well cared for and also forestall any complications his existence might create. Since John and Charles were born at about the same time, and so were almost the same age, the exchange was never suspected.

The BBC knew all this but refused to feature it in the 1973 programme. They told Joseph and Harry Jonas that Prince John was medically examined at an age when he ought to have been able to talk properly but instead made unintelligible noises. The doctors believed he was mentally retarded. Two years later he was examined again, this time by a Dr Corder, who established that he was deaf and that this was the cause of his inability to speak properly. The doctors also discovered that 'Prince John' was suffering from an incurable epileptic illness. He had inherited both conditions from his mother, Alice Crook. Alice's own mother, Annie Crook, and her grandmother, Sarah Anne Crook, had both suffered from epilepsy. Alice and her father, Eddy, both had otosclerosis. Neither Prince George nor Princess Mary had it. That Alice Crook had it has been ascertained from her medical file.

How, we may wonder, did George and his wife treat Charles? Did they distance themselves from this cuckoo-in-the-nest? Or did he receive from them the love which they would have given him, had he been their natural child?

The sad fact is that George and Mary saw very little of the new Prince John. The one member of the royal family whose affection for him put the rest to shame was Queen Alexandra. Perhaps this was only natural since she knew that John's real mother was Alice Crook, and that John was therefore her only great-grandchild. In her biography of Queen Mary, Anne Edwards wrote:

> Prince John celebrated his fourth birthday in July of 1909. He was a winsome child, painfully slow, and he began the first stages of an incurable epileptic illness. Grave doubts now existed that he would survive to adulthood. Placed entirely in Lala Bill's [the nanny's] care, he remained in the nursery at York Cottage, at Sandringham, where his brother Georgie [Duke of Kent], treated him in almost parental fashion. John did not often see his parents. His grandmother, the Queen [Alexandra], however, favoured him above all the other Wales children, and spent long hours amusing him whenever she was at Sandringham. John's epileptic fits had become more frequent and intense. A decision had, therefore, been made that his presence with his parents and brothers and sisters – now that they were the royal family – was an undesirable image. Thereafter, John remained segregated from his family. Georgie, who was nine, was the most affected by his brother's absence. He went to see John every day, as did Queen Alexandra and Mr Hansell. But the other members of the family and Household found it too heart-wrenching a task. Queen Mary's emotion towards John's disablement is hard to assess. No mention of John was made in any of her correspondence – not even to Helène Bricka or her Aunt Augusta, to whom she might have confided her fears, guilts or unhappiness with considerable intimacy and ease. Nor did she appear to have discussed John with any of her Ladies-in-Waiting or members of the family, such as her brothers and their wives. Her overt acceptance and avoidance of the situation set the tone for those close to the royal family.[1]

Queen Mary's attitude towards John's disablement – her coldness and indifference – which, as we saw in the above paragraph, Anne Edwards found 'hard to assess', can now be properly understood in the light of Joseph's claim that 'Prince John' was really Joseph's elder brother Charles, and could never hope to attract from her the love and concern of his natural mother.

Charles was not taken directly to Buckingham Palace, or to any of the other royal residences, but to a Roman Catholic orphanage in Mill Hill, in what was then countryside, on the outskirts of north London. Alice told Joseph that he was taken there by a nurse and a man called Lascelles. Joseph vaguely recalls the name Gerald Lascelles, but is not certain. Lascelles is the family name of the Earls of Harewood, who have had a close association with the Royal Family for many generations. Indeed the 6th Earl Harewood was particularly close since he married the eldest daughter of King George V. He was also a leading member of the masonic fraternity and was personally installed as Grand Master by King George VI in 1943. There were two Gerald Lascelles in 1905: Gerald William, and his son Gerald Hubert. Both died in 1928. Gerald William was the third son of the 4th Earl of Harewood.

The boy Charles who grew up believing himself to be Prince John died on 18 January 1919, at the age of 13 years and 6 months. In modern times every Prince of the Blood Royal has been buried at Windsor, but not the boy the world thought was Prince John. He was buried in the churchyard of Sandringham Church of St Mary Magdalen, to the right of the path leading to the porch. By denying his burial at Windsor the Royal Family symbolically denied that he was their son.

Worthy of note in connection with 'Prince John's' illness is that there has never been any history of epilepsy in the Royal Family.

*

One day in 1932, when Joseph was about seven, Ethel Brown and her husband paid him and his mother a visit. Ethel Brown was Annie Crook's niece and Alice's cousin. She said she was visiting out of concern for Alice's health, and to give her a break she offered to look after Joseph for a couple of weeks. Since she was a member of the family, Alice had no reason to doubt her motives and got Joseph ready for the short journey to the Brown home in Sandwich Street, not far from St Pancras Railway Station.

From his home in Drummond Street they took him to Warren Street Underground station nearby. Their destination was Mill Hill. Here, in his own words, is Joseph's account of what happened to him when they arrived there:

> I was near the corner of Stanhope Street and Drummond Street. There was no traffic at all, and all of a sudden came the cry 'Joseph'. I looked at one of the boys first. Then I saw my mother. It wasn't just her, there were some people there. I waved to her and said: 'I won't be a minute.' And I ran down – and there was my mum and an aunt – name of Brown, Ethel Brown. She

had a large family, about seven or eight children, and her husband was a sailor – ex-sailor. And they said: 'Oh, you're all wet.' They took me into the house and my mum was crying. It frightened me. 'Oh no,' she said. 'It's all right, don't be alarmed, everything's all right.' They put my new clothes on. I was so excited I thought, 'Another part of the celebrations!' What with Christmas and New Year, I'd made friends with everybody.

This was about 11 o'clock in the morning, on a Sunday. I had nothing else on my mind. The drowning, the attempted drowning, that was gone.* They had a bag for me, and they said this was my mother's cousin Ethel Brown. I thought – well, you know, I was quite happy because I used to play with her sons where they lived in Sandwich Street. They took me to Warren Street and we got on a train.

I said: 'Where's my mother?'

'Oh well, she's coming later on. Be a good boy.'

We sat there and the train went off. I was a small boy, remember, and I think about this – even one second is a long time for a fidgety child.

We went on and on, in the train, and I thought, 'I'm leaving everything. I've been playing. Why have I stopped playing with my friends?' I wanted to get back to playing in the snow. And it came to the point that I started crying.

All of a sudden there was a shock when someone shouted: 'All change.'

We got out of the train, and in front of me on the left was a wooden hut. I worked out later that it was a waiting-room. Next to this waiting-room was an exit – three red-tiled steps – in front of the booking office on the right. This bloke, an enormous bloke, and this woman, my aunt, my mother's cousin, took me through, but I wouldn't go any further. I wanted to go back on the train and go home.

'Now, come along,' they said, and I kicked Ethel Brown, and the chap picked me up and held me and I nearly cried.

They got me into a car. There must have been a car-park, a sort of car-park, outside. They drove along this road – all snow everywhere – and we came to these big gates with a lion on either side of the gates. We went through along this sort of S-bend to this enormous red-brick house.

As they took me in, a smell of wax-polish and carbolic disinfectant hit me. It's a unique smell that seems to get into everything.

My mother's cousin and the man went to the right, with a lady with my bag. Oh no, my bag stayed with me, and they took me to the left, into the kitchen, because I was shivering, and it was a big kitchen with nuns there with a couple of these bigger boys. I was crying and shaking and the boys were talking and laughing. They were quite happy and content, but I wasn't. This was about two hours, and I'd been at home playing, and I said I wanted to go home to my mother. As soon as I said 'my mother' they laughed, the boys laughed. From that minute I had to think about something different, or I would have remembered what happened to me when I was drowning, because the drowning came back to me. I thought, 'Well, I'll make my mind blank and I'll wake up again and my mother will be there.'

So I lay down on the floor. As I lay there someone poured water on my face. It was this horrible nun pouring water on me from a cup, and the boys were laughing.

So they got me up and I said I wanted to go home. They gave me a slice of bread and dripping and some cocoa and a rosy-red apple. I'd never had cocoa

* For the near-drowning incident, see below, p. 112.

before in my life. I tried to drink it and it made me shiver. I couldn't take it, and she gave me a drop of milk. I couldn't eat the bread and I kept the apple, and they took me out through another door, a different way. I never saw Ethel again.

They took me across a yard. This was in the evening. You know, it was becoming evening. I suppose about five or six because, though it was dark in the winter, it seemed quite light with snow on the ground. They took me up about fifty steps – wooden steps – into a sort of dormitory. There were about five rows, five or six rows of beds. And she took me into the centre where there was a red light. I'd never seen it because we had gas at home, you see, and this was unusual – to see a little red bulb, an electric bulb. And it was marvellous, but it didn't really appeal to me. It was alien to me, you see.

I had to take my clothes off and put a nightgown on. No, not a nightgown – a sort of nightgown with trousers. Like pyjamas, but a sort of nightgown. I put these on, and my own clothes were folded at the bottom of the bed. I lay there crying and shivering because I couldn't get warm.

I heard this voice say, 'Oh, you poor boy, have you lost your mummy and daddy, are they both dead?'

That sort of thing the boys were saying, but I refused to answer and I covered myself up to comfort myself.

I must have sobbed myself to sleep, but I woke up terrified because of the awful clanging of a bell. I still had this apple in my hand. The scent reminded me of my mother. It's a silly thing, but it was a comfort. I've never eaten an apple since.

I looked up and everybody was rushing about – all bigger than me, all their actions going. I was sitting there like a fool – you know, completely lost. Then this nun came in and threw me this bundle of clothes, all grey and rough, and a pair of heavy boots.

'Put your clothes to the side and put these on.'

I waited until she went out. I think it was just a bored routine on this nun's part. Everyone had gone out, but instead of putting on the clothes they'd left I put my own on. 'Ah, I'm half home now, because I've still got my clothes,' I thought.

I'd got the apple in my hand and I went to the door. It was at the bottom of some steps. It was so dark down there, and when I opened the door the snow was so bright, it hit me. You know, such a shock – and cold.

But my heart was pounding. I wasn't going to be confined here. I would do what I always did, I'd run away. I just stepped into the light and bent over to tie my shoelace. I'd no idea how to, really. Well, I had a rough idea, I just tied them in a knot.

I looked to my right and saw these lights twinkling, on the outside twinkling. I realised that it was car lights flickering through the railings. I got this bag and – well, you know, put it over the top and got over on top of the railings. I started to follow this car back. I ran, and as I was running the echo of my feet pounding on the snow made me think someone was behind me, and I ran a bit faster, and I wet myself, you know. 'I'm going home, I'm going home' – that's what I was saying to myself. That's the only thing that kept me going.

Then I saw the station, and there were people – early rush hour, I suppose – going to work. And I followed them in onto the station and there was a train waiting and I got on and sat next to a woman – and then off it went. I didn't know what was going to happen but I thought I'd get off at the next stop. They kept calling names at each station. Then came the name I wanted – 'Warren Street!' I went up the stairs and played on the side because I was home again.

A porter said, 'Come on get out, don't play about on the stairs.'

So he took me out. This was at the top end of Tottenham Court Road. I was going to run home. Then I realised, 'My mother's betrayed me. She hasn't bothered to come and fetch me'.

I thought, 'The only person who's shown any concern for me was Lloyd.' So I went down to Euston Station to the taxis lined up waiting for passengers. I went up to one of the drivers and said. 'Will you take me to my father, Lord Lloyd?' I called him Lord, you see, I don't know why. I was asking him to take me to T.O. Lloyd, my sort of godfather.

The cab driver took me to a policeman on Euston Station. He took me into this warm office. It was lovely but I shivered even more for some reason. The policeman wrapped me up in his cape which was heavy and warm, and then made some phone calls.

They took me out to the cab. I think they had instructions not to take me in a police car. The car journey wasn't far and I was taken to Lloyd's home in Francis Street near Westminster Cathedral. While Lloyd made a phone call, his wife made me some sweet tea, and I fell asleep. I woke up to hear some voices. I was told later that one of them had belonged to Marmaduke, the Duke of Norfolk.

I used to meet Lloyd a lot in Francis Street after that, at a club or something there. He always came out and pressed a five pound note into my hand. Not a half-crown, a five pound note, which was a fortune in those days, especially for a young boy.

We were left alone after that, really – for a long time.

Thomas O. Lloyd, says Joseph, was the link man between Queen Alexandra and Joseph's mother. He and his first wife, Emily, lived at 'Little Croft', The Street, Mortimer, Berks. Emily died in 1950 and Lloyd subsequently remarried. Before this he lived in Durham Place, Chelsea.

A relative of Thomas Lloyd, who wishes to remain unidentified, told me that Thomas O. Lloyd was the brother of Lord Lloyd of Dolobran (Sir George Ambrose Lloyd). During the First World War Lord Lloyd served in Egypt, Gallipoli, Russia and Mesopotamia, and campaigned with Lawrence of Arabia. He held many high positions and in 1918 was Governor of India. From 1925 to 1929 he was High Commissioner for Egypt and the Sudan. He was mentioned in dispatches six times. In 1940 he was appointed Colonial Secretary by Winston Churchill, who had become Prime Minister in May that year.

It is my belief that Joseph overheard someone refer to Thomas O. Lloyd's brother Lord Lloyd and assumed that the title belonged to Thomas. I believe that when Joseph asked the taxi driver to take him to Lord Lloyd, that is where he was taken, and not to T.O. Lloyd's home. Lord Lloyd lived at 11 Morpeth Mansions, Morpeth Terrace, near Westminster Cathedral. The whole terrace of Edwardian luxury apartments runs into Francis Street – where Joseph said he was taken.

Lord Lloyd's neighbour was Winston Churchill who lived in a six-bedroom four-reception-room flat in Morpeth Terrace until 1940.

Lord Lloyd's wife, Blanche Isabella, was the daughter of Commander Frederick Canning Lascelles, RN, brother of the 5th Earl of Harewood. She was Maid-of-Honour to Queen Alexandra. T.O. Lloyd probably became the link man between Alice and Queen Alexandra, through his brother and sister-in-law.

Thomas O. Lloyd was a convert to Roman Catholicism. As often happens with converts, he became more devoted to his new-found creed than many who were born into it. I learned that he travelled by train from London to the Midlands to receive instruction from a priest at the Birmingham Oratory. His unnamed relative said he was 'an exceedingly clever and intellectual man, widely read in the Latin and Greek classics. He was also well-read in the religious field and said the Divine Office daily in Latin by himself – some 1½ hours of prayer in those days, normally only done by priests.' The Lloyd family are Welsh landed gentry but were bankers and engineers in Birmingham in the eighteenth and nineteenth centuries. Though he was a man of independent means he chose to live simply and devoted himself to charitable works, using much of his time and energy helping the deaf on behalf of the Sisters of Charity of St Vincent de Paul, Carlisle Place. Carlisle Place abuts on Francis Street – where Joseph said he often met Lloyd.

Lloyd's relation told me that giving a young boy £5 was entirely characteristic of him. 'He was an extremely private person,' he added, 'and never revealed even his membership of the St Vincent de Paul to his family during his lifetime.'

It was because of his work with the deaf, and because he was a Roman Catholic, that Alexandra chose Lloyd to act as a link between herself and Alice and Joseph. Through him they were introduced to many eminent Catholics, including Monsignor Rivers of St Patrick's Church, Soho Square, and Sister Clare, the Mother General of St Vincent de Paul. As noted, they were also befriended by the Duke of Norfolk, who no doubt became friends with T.O. Lloyd because Lloyd was one of the very few upper-class Roman Catholics.

In a letter to Joseph dated 23 January 1959, five months before his 86th birthday, Thomas Lloyd wrote:

> I hope your wife and little Theresa have kept well in the cold weather ... you have always been such a good steady man. You are sure of a reward & your good parents, I am sure, watch and pray for you & your family.
>
> Sister Clare always admired your Father & Mother so much. If you write again please give me any news of your sister. I hope someone is looking after her and taking care of her.
>
> May God bless you, dear Joseph – please pray for me.
> Yours sincerely
> (signed) Thomas Lloyd.

Joseph's father mentioned here is William Gorman. Joseph's sister is Anne, who is also deaf. Both were helped by the charity of St Vincent de Paul.

*

By the time Joseph was taken to Mill Hill an extensive catalogue of terror had accumulated in his mother's memory, all of it caused by people in power and authority. Not surprisingly she developed a suspicious nature and constantly impressed upon Joseph the need for vigilance when approached by strangers.

Walter never advertised his affair with Alice, though it was known to some of his close friends. We have to remember the twenty-five-year age gap. In Edwardian England, with its rigid, hypocritical attitudes, Sickert understandably wished to avoid broadcasting their affair.

Sir William Orpen once lived and painted at Thackeray House, 35 Maple Street, the studio home of Harry Jonas. He painted a full-length portrait of Alice, called 'Lady in White'. which was bought by Thompson D. Croal in 1921 from Spink & Sons. Several years ago Joseph tried to locate the picture, which is reproduced here, but was told by the Courtauld Institute that it had been destroyed during the Second World War when a bomb fell on the City building where it was displayed. John Rothenstein, one-time Director of the Tate Gallery, who also lived and painted in Thackeray House,[2] said that by 1910 Orpen was 'the most successful portrait-painter of the age'.[3] Alice of course was never a member of high society, but Orpen painted her as if she was, and she is seen in his picture dressed accordingly. Obviously that was how he chose to see her. The fact that he painted her at all underlines the link between Sickert and Alice, since Orpen knew them both.

Some of Joseph's detractors have cast doubt on Joseph's claim that he was the natural son of Walter Sickert[4] and that his mother and grandmother were connected with Walter, who would have supported them rather than allow them to rely on Poor Relief and the workhouse.[5] Joseph remembers his mother telling him how she and Annie were hounded, particularly when Walter was not in London. Even so, the records at the Greater London Records Office show that it was illness that caused Alice to resort to Poor Relief. There are only five entries for admission into workhouses against the name Alice Crook. The first was on 18 April 1885 when she was born at St Marylebone Workhouse; the second when she was 3 years and 9 months old and she spent a day with her mother at St Giles's Workhouse. Of the remaining three two are for one day only. When she was sick Alice knew she would be taken care of in the workhouse, because upon admission all applicants were medically examined and if they were sick were sent to a sick-ward. The remaining entries record her admission into infirmaries because of illness. Three entries of admission – those for 1905, two for the workhouse and one for an infirmary – were in the year Charles was born. Joseph does not know in which month the birth took place, only that Charles was born in 1905, the same year Walter returned to live permanently in London after spending six years in Dieppe. He had visited London the previous year to make his arrangements for moving back, and it was then that he met Alice again and fathered her child.

When Joseph was a boy in London a certain Captain Vernon Ely looked out for him, taking care of his interests and passing on the money which Walter sent for him.

Joseph remembers a game from his childhood which he and his father played during their infrequent times together. When he wished to visit Walter in his room or studio, Joseph would rap on the door and call out: 'Permission to come aboard, Skipper.' Walter would reply: 'Come aboard.' The room was referred to as his 'cabin'.

A pictorial reference to this can be seen in a painting I discovered in the Witt Library at the Courtauld Intitute. I came across it only a week before the final manuscript of this book was passed to the publisher. Painted in 1940, it is one of Sickert's few self-portraits, and shows him reading with his third wife, Thérèse Lessore. Behind them is a large bookcase. Sickert is wearing a nautical hat, and the picture is entitled 'In the Cabin'.

Another nautical reference is found in a letter to Joseph, dated 1959, from Walter's friend Harry Jonas. The letter ends with the words:

> Don't forget to do a good painting. When I return use your Skipper's easel, it is yours by right anyway.

This was the easel Walter had used when he stayed with Harry. It was left to Joseph when Harry died in February 1990. Joseph also owns one of his father's palettes, and his top-hat made by the hatter to the Royal Family.

*

After Charles's birth Walter Sickert married his second wife, Christine Drummond Angus, and began to encourage a romance between Alice and his friend the boxer William Gorman. Despite her deafness Alice was an able woman. She could speak fluent French, and she was an expert embroiderer. It is important to realise that Alice was not born deaf. Otosclerosis often gets progressively worse with the years, so that those who have the disorder can sometimes learn to speak as any child does, though they often become completely deaf in old age. When Alice was a teenager and could still hear to some extent, others thought she was 'stone' deaf, and that is how hospital records usually described her. Like many deaf people, including her father, Prince Eddy, she tended to retreat into her private thoughts, so that she often appeared to others as not fully in charge of her faculties. It was this negative attitude, as we have noted, that led many to believe that Eddy was stupid and 'backward'. It should be remembered that in Victorian and Edwardian times people's attitude towards the deaf was not as enlightened as it is today.

William Gorman, on the other hand, did not have otosclerosis, a fact verified by the Rev. Daniel Harrison, the Administrator at St John's Catholic School, Boston Spa, Yorkshire, which William attended from December 1880 until January 1887. St John's was the first Catholic school for the deaf in this country. The school records are very detailed and give the cause of his deafness as 'Scarlet Fever 3 yrs'. This is an important fact, refuting any suggestion that Joseph inherited his deafness from William Gorman rather than from his mother Alice and his grandfather Prince Albert Victor.

William remained a deaf mute. This was before techniques had been developed which could be used to teach the deaf to speak. He became proficient in the use of sign language, which Alice found very difficult, though she learned to lip-read. After St John's Catholic School William was returned to his parents in London. He had two sisters, one of whom married a Mr Maxwell of Maxwell Laundries in Wells Street near Cleveland Street.

Between 1902 and 1918, the year she was married, Alice and her mother Annie and grandmother Sarah lived at 5 Pancras Street (now Capper Street), off Tottenham Court Road. Alice gave this address as her mother's when she registered her death in 1920, even though her mother, because of epilepsy and increasing dementia, had spent her last seventeen years in various workhouses and infirmaries. When Sarah died in 1916 Alice went to live at 195 Drummond Street, where she continued to live with Gorman after their marriage.

In 1911 Sarah and Alice worked together as market porteresses at Messrs Deaton of Covent Garden. That year Sickert painted a picture of them, 'Two Women'. It shows Alice sitting with her head in profile and Sarah standing behind looking over her shoulder. Both women are shown wearing coster-mongers' hats, a common feature of Covent Garden at that time. The painting hangs in the Harris Museum in Preston. When it was painted, Alice's mother was spending most of her time in infirmaries. Sarah, though she was getting old, took on the role of mother to Alice, which prompted Sickert to do a second, almost identical, version of 'Two Women' called 'Lou! Lou! I Love You'. He used this pen-and-ink drawing as a study for a second painting of them, 'Mother and Daughter' (1911).

He also did a pen-and-ink drawing in 1911 of Alice alone. Its title – 'Alice' – could not be simpler. It portrays her sitting in a smoker's-bow chair which stands upon bare floorboards. The background, like Alice's own background, is in deep shadow, and the picture gives an air of resigned isolation and loneliness. The sketch was reproduced in *The New Age*, 22 June 1911, but today the whereabouts of the original are unknown. When these pictures were made Alice's mother had been in infirmaries for eight years and Alice was becoming more and more lonely. Her grandmother too was succumbing to epilepsy and old age. Two years after these pictures were finished, Sarah entered Tooting Bec Mental Hospital, before being removed to Caterham Mental Hospital, where she died in 1916. With her mother insane and her grandmother dead, Alice became completely and hopelessly alone. This loneliness exacerbated the isolation which her deafness had already forced upon her. Walter, aware of her plight, encouraged the romance between her and William Gorman.

Alice may have been searching for a father-figure as a substitute for the father she had never known, and in William Gorman she recognised a good man who was hardworking and able to take care of her. When they married on 14 July 1918 Alice was thirty-three and William forty-five.

The marriage certificate shows that Alice told the Registrar that her father was 'William Crook' – her grandfather's name. The true identity of her father had led to a great deal of horror and unhappiness in the past, and widespread knowledge of it was therefore to be avoided. Even so, if she had given his real name, Prince Albert Victor, the priest would hardly have believed her. She took the easiest way out.

The Catholic wedding ceremony between William Gorman and Alice was conducted by the parish priest Father Timothy O'Doherty, at St Aloysius' Chapel in Phoenix Street off Euston Road. All their children were baptized Catholics and attended St Aloysius' School.

*

When Gorman married he was no longer active in the boxing ring, though he remained physically powerful. He was once attacked at three in the morning on his way to work at a fish-smoking yard near Gloucester Avenue by two men armed with knives. With professional expertise he knocked one of them down at a blow. This discouraged his accomplice, who ran off. After trying to revive the unconcious man, Gorman called the police. They said later that the man was dead. Gorman appeared at Bow Street Magistrates Court but was released because the man had been clutching a knife when the police arrived and Gorman pleaded self-defence. Joseph told me that his step-father had close links with the IRA, and perhaps this connection with an illegal organisation, hated by most English people, was what led to the attack. Incidentally, some of Walter Sickert's forbears on his mother's side were Irish. An early painting by him, 'Sinn Feiners', now hangs in the Atkinson Art Gallery, Southport. Sinn Fein is the political branch of the IRA.

One reason Walter encouraged the romance was to ensure that any further children Alice might have would be born in wedlock and be accepted as Gorman's. He may have been following orders when he encouraged the romance, for he was probably a Freemason, though Joseph does not know for certain. He knew a great deal about Freemasonry. He may well have been introduced to the brotherhood by the famous actor Sir Henry Irving, in whose troupe, as we noted, he worked before he took up painting. Irving is one of the ten notable 'Men of the Theatre' proudly named in Pick & Knight's *Pocket History of Freemasonry*.

Irving links Sickert and Lord Randolph Churchill, for he was a friend of both. He met Lord Randolph Churchill in Ireland, and boasted that he had introduced him to the plays of Shakespeare.[6] Randolph often visited him backstage at the Lyceum Theatre,[7] which he offered to Lady Churchill for one of her charity concerts.[8] Randolph was on such close terms with Irving that he could introduce his son Winston to Irving's secretary, Bram Stoker, the future author of *Dracula*.[9] Irving was among the close friends who attended Lord Randolph's funeral in Westminster Abbey.[10]

In 1920 Walter's wife Christine died, and four years later, when he was living in Noel Street, he again entered intimately, but briefly, into Alice's life. The following year she gave birth to his second son, Joseph. Seven months later Walter married his third wife, Thérèse Lessore.

Joseph respected and admired his stepfather, whom he called Billy, but always felt he was resented by him. Gorman knew he was not Joseph's father. Even so, he always treated him well, as Joseph readily admits. 'I loved that man,' said Joseph, adding: 'He was dependable. Not like my dad, who was hardly there.'

*

A harrowing event overtook Joseph when he was three: he almost fatally drowned in the Serpentine in Kensington Gardens.

He is vague about the details:

I don't know how I got there. I can't remember anything before it happened, or what happened afterwards. It was very hot and sunny, and I just remember standing by the water. There was a bank, a sort of grassy bank, and lots of children playing on the other side. I kept seeing their heads appear over the top as they were playing, and I wanted to be with them. They were mostly bigger than me, but I wanted to join in the fun because everyone seemed to be enjoying themselves and I could hear them laughing. Then I felt someone push me in the back. Next thing, I was in the water. It was all green. I was looking up through the water and it was all green. I could see the sun through the water. I can see it now. I'll never forget it. I could see the sun through the water as I pushed my arms out, reaching up.

Next thing, I was being pulled up. Someone had pulled me out, but I don't remember anything about it after that. They took me to nearby St George's Hospital, but I don't remember that either.

The man who passed by and fortunately saw Joseph and dragged him out before he drowned was John Robbins. During his childhood Joseph saw him several times but eventually lost touch with him.

At the end of the war, on Palm Sunday 1945, Joseph spent the afternoon at a youth club held in the Whitefield Tabernacle in Tottenham Court Road, a few minutes walk from his home. (The American Church in London now stands in its place.) When he left he strolled up the road, and on reaching the corner he heard a terrific explosion behind him. A German rocket had landed on the youth club and almost totally destroyed the building and killed virtually everyone inside, some of whom were Joseph's pals. He went into shock. His friends had been killed, and he realised that if he had stayed a few minutes longer he would have been killed too. He expressed his pain and horror to a bystander. As he was visibly shaken, the man offered him the English panacea, a cup of tea, saying he lived close by.

As they walked the few yards to Pancras Street where the stranger lived, Joseph told him it was not the first time he had been near death and said he had almost drowned when he was three. The stranger recalled that his brother had saved someone from drowning years before. As they approached the door of No. 5 Joseph remembered that this was the house in which his mother Alice, his grandmother Annie Crook and his great-grandmother Sarah Crook had lived in 1902. The afternoon was becoming imbued with surrealistic overtones. To Joseph's amazement the person who opened the door was none other than John Robbins, the man who had saved him in the Serpentine all those years before.

*

Forty years later, by another of those strange but happy coincidences, Joseph discovered, much to his delight, that Robbins's nephew, Robert, was a caretaker on the estate into which he had recently moved. When I met Robert Robbins he confirmed Joseph's near-drowning story, which he says was frequently mentioned by older members of the Robbins family when he was a child.

On another occasion, when Joseph was a boy staying with relations who lived at 9 Sandwich Street near Cartwright Gardens off Euston Road, he was playing in the street with some local children who had befriended him when a man on the other side shouted to him. Being already deaf in one ear by this time, Joseph did not hear the man call, but one of the other boys heard and ran over to see what he wanted. A horse and cart which had been slowly moving down the street suddenly broke into a gallop, running him down. The boy was seriously hurt but luckily survived. The man who had shouted to Joseph disappeared down the street as quickly as the horse and cart. Onlookers who had seen and heard everything were certain that the name the man had shouted was 'Joseph', and they said as much to Joseph's relations who had come outside to see what the commotion was about. It was concluded that the whole incident had been deliberately choreographed, with Joseph as the intended victim. If so it was clearly well-organised. The man driving the horse and cart could not have known for certain who Joseph was. Otherwise he would not have driven his horse into a gallop towards the wrong boy. The two men were plainly hired killers.

Since it was the Royal Alpha Lodge Freemasons who had undertaken the Ripper murders, so closely linked to the affair of Annie and Eddy and their daughter Alice, it does not seem far-fetched to suppose that high-ranking members of the fraternity, backed perhaps by members of the Royal Family, were responsible for all the ills suffered by Alice and Joseph.

By the time Joseph was pushed into the Serpentine only one member of the original Ripper gang was alive – the elusive John Courtenay. Neverthless Alice did not believe that Courtenay was involved in the attempted drowning, or in Joseph's abduction. Courtenay appeared on the scene when Joseph was a boy and stayed around to keep a watchful, and indeed benevolent, eye on him and his mother. Perhaps he was showing remorse for what had gone before.

The Gorman family home at 195 Drummond Street, where Joseph spent most of his early years, was rented from the owner, Leonard C. Warren. In addition to No. 195, which comprised a house and two shops, he owned No. 197 consisting of a house and one shop, and he lived himself at No. 193, a house with a cottage in the rear. The three houses – Nos 193, 195 and 197 – concealed a large yard which was not visible from Drummond Street but was entered through an alley between the houses. To the left was a long wall, and opposite on the right was a series of old barns. Between the wall and the barns, facing the alley, was an old farmhouse from a previous century. It was divided into two cottages. One was Joseph's home where he lived with his mother and stepfather. It was here that John Courtenay sometimes visited, staying in a spare room.

As an old man in the 1920s and 30s, Courtenay became well-known as a local character. Because of his tramp-like habit of stuffing layers of newspapers between his clothing as insulation against the cold, he was known as 'Paper Jack'. He could not conceal his aristocratic bearing, however, though he concealed his identity and told people his name was Charles Grey. Joseph describes him thus:

> He was tall, about 6 feet 2, and very gaunt-looking. There was something about him that my mother and I found a bit frightening, just something sinister about him. But at the same time – I know this sounds strange – whenever he was there we felt safe. I don't know why, we just did. My mother called him Uncle Jack.

It is difficult to know whether Joseph remembers Courtenay as sinister because he looked sinister or because Joseph and his mother knew about his involvement in the Ripper murders and simply assumed that he must be sinister. It is sufficient to understand that though they felt safe whenever he was around they were uncomfortable in his presence and somewhat relieved when he died.

*

Joseph's mother died in 1950. Not only did her deafness become complete, but her eyesight too began to fail. Joseph told me that her last few years were spent miserably enduring profound deafness and total blindness.

The two attempts on her life by Netley in her early childhood had left her in poor health. She had never known her father. Her firstborn child had been cruelly taken from her. Her mother she watched slip into madness and early death. Her son Joseph was nearly drowned and once shot. She spent part of her adolescence, and the years before her marriage, in poverty, often sleeping rough in Covent Garden.

Alice's spirit finally succumbed when she was 65. Her funeral took place at St Anne's Roman Catholic Church, Seaton Place, near her home in Drummond Street.

At 25 Joseph was now alone, and the isolation and sadness forced upon him by the death of his mother gave him a nervous breakdown, so that he was unable to deal with the funeral arrangements. For some reason, his mother was cremated. This may have been why the priest refused to conduct the service, because in the 1950s there was still a strong Catholic aversion to cremation. Nevertheless, though Alice had been in humble circumstances, the service was conducted by no less a dignitary than Cardinal Godfrey, and was attended by Sister Clare, Mother General of the Sisters of Charity of St Vincent de Paul.

T.O. Lloyd took Alice's ashes to Windsor Castle. There he scattered them near the Albert Memorial Chapel, which houses the tomb of her father, Prince Albert Victor, Duke of Clarence and Avondale.

PASS-GRIP OF A MASTER MA-SON —Take hold of each other's hands as in ordinary hand shaking and press the top of your thumb hard against the space between the second and third knuckles. Should the man whose hand you shake be a Mason he may return or give any previous grip.

PASS OF MASTER MASON—Tubal Cain. It is the name of this grip.

CHAPTER SIX

Minedalex

After Edward VIII's abdication in 1936, when he was created Duke of Windsor, a curious legend arose about him and his bride, Mrs Simpson. It was rumoured that when they left for France they took with them jewellery which belonged to the Crown and was therefore part of the Crown Jewels. The story begins with Queen Alexandra.

When Princess Alexandra arrived in England on 7 March 1863, she brought with her a collection of jewels which had belonged to the Danish Royal Family and were intended to be a token of union between the two Royal Families. They came to be known as 'Alexandra's Emeralds'.

No one today is sure how the story of Alexandra's Emeralds began, or whether indeed they ever existed. Alexandra did possess some emeralds, which she had received as wedding presents. There was a flower-spray brooch, for example, from the Duchess of Cambridge, and there were a few small emeralds in the bracelet given her by the Ladies of Manchester. A suite of Indian jewels from Queen Victoria also contained some small emeralds but was mostly of pink rubies and diamonds. The best were employed within the design of a pair of earrings and a badge given by the Ladies of South Wales. None of them, however, was sufficiently remarkable to create the legend.

When the Prince of Wales returned from his visit to India in 1876, thirteen years after his marriage, he arrived with innumerable presents from the many Rajahs he had met. Among them were some massive emeralds, and a diamond-and-pearl crown with emerald drops given by the Taluqdars of Oudh. Today the whereabouts of almost all these pieces are unknown.[1]

In 1904 a magnificent Indian necklace of diamonds, set with nine rubies, was dismantled for Queen Alexandra. The stones were remounted to become the *collier resille* (hairnet) in which only the diamonds were employed, the rubies and emeralds being returned to the King and Queen. In 1907 a diamond-and-emerald choker was also dismantled, and once again the emeralds – eleven of them – were returned unused to Edward and Alexandra. These stones, twenty-nine in all, may have formed the basis of the legend.[2]

*

Thirty-two years later, in 1936, before Edward VIII's abdication, there were many people at Court who wished to discredit Mrs Simpson. They fed the rumour that she had left England for France with a collection of gems, given to her by Edward, which had once belonged to Queen Alexandra. It was believed that Mrs Simpson had taken Alexandra's Emeralds, a view which appeared to be endorsed when the Prime Minister ordered the jewels to be collected from her.

Stanley Baldwin, the only premier to have held office during the reign of an uncrowned king, asked the lawyer Theodore Goddard to call upon Mrs Simpson in Cannes. This he did 48 hours before the Abdication. Goddard was acting for Mrs Simpson during her divorce. Stanley Baldwin's niece, Monica, described him as 'a man whom every crook employs by reason of his cleverness', adding that he was 'a man of blameless reputation but extraordinary ingenuity'.[3]

Most of Baldwin's biographers have believed that the purpose of Goddard's mission was to ask Mrs Simpson to give up King Edward by withdrawing her divorce petition. No doubt this was intended. But recently a second reason for the visit has gained acceptance: namely, that when Mrs Simpson left England she took Alexandra's Emeralds with her, and that Goddard's purpose was to bring them back to England. This was certainly the view of Viscount Davidson, who had been Baldwin's Private Secretary and was a close friend of Edward VIII's brother Bertie, later George VI. Davidson claimed to know that Goddard had been sent to Cannes by the Royal Family specifically to recover the emeralds.[4]

There is no record that Goddard returned with any jewels, however. The simple truth is that the Danish jewels were never part of Alexandra's bequest to Edward and could therefore never have come into Mrs Simpson's possession.

The belief that Mrs Simpson had the emeralds persisted for another fifty years. There was even a rumour that they were stolen from her when she and the Duke were visiting England in 1946. Being unwelcome at any Royal palace, the Duke and Duchess were staying at Ednam Lodge, Sunningdale, the home of the Earl of Dudley. On the evening of 16 October 1946 only the servants were at home, the Windsors and the Dudleys being in London. While they were having supper, between 6.30 and 7, a thief shinned up a rope into the house and entered the Duchess's bedroom.

The Duchess had brought all her jewellery to England and kept it in a large trunk along with many items of the Duke's fabulous collection of Fabergé boxes. Lord Dudley's butler suggested that the trunk should be placed in the strong-room. The suggestion was opposed by the Duchess, who preferred, as always, to keep it under her maid's bed. In fact the thief found it in front of the fire in the Duchess's bedroom. One of the Fabergé boxes was discovered on a window-sill, while the trunk and about eighteen non-matching earrings were found scattered in a bunker on Sunningdale golf course.

Scotland Yard immediately sent in a Detective Inspector, a Detective Sergeant and a Superintendent, who was a fingerprint expert. Two days later the Assistant Commissioner, R.M. Howe, head of the Criminal Investigation Department, and Deputy Commander W.R. Rawlings took charge.[5] They discovered some odd circumstances. No one in the house had heard anything, and the detective who had been specially posted there to guard the house during the Duke's visit had seen nothing suspicious. Odder still, none of Lord Dudley's guard dogs had barked. Not surprisingly the Duchess believed that the theft was an inside job, and she asked that the servants be interrogated. Lady Dudley refused, however, explaining that, except for one kitchen maid, they had all been with the family for years and were devoted family retainers.[6]

The crime remains unsolved to this day, and after forty-two years not a single item has surfaced anywhere in the world. After the robbery many rumours were rife, the main one being that the Royal Family had master-minded the theft in order to recover Alexandra's Emeralds.

*

Whatever the truth, the Royal Family suspected that a large collection of Alexandra's jewellery went missing at her death in 1925. Their suspicions were investigated, and next year Queen Mary ordered a thorough survey and cataloguing of all the royal jewels.[7]

The fact is, however, that the jewels which the Royal Family knew were missing had not been given to Alexandra's grandson, the future Edward VIII, but to her grand-daughter.

In 1925 two men entered a courtyard behind the houses in Drummond Street. The yard had long ceased to be a farmyard, and the cottage they were walking towards had not been used as a farmhouse for at least seventy-five years. Queen Alexandra died intestate, but before her death she had determined to give a bequest to her grand-daughter who was expecting a child. The two visitors to 195 Drummond Street were delivering it.

Alexandra knew that her eldest son, Prince Eddy, had fathered a child by Annie Elizabeth Crook. The child, as noted, was born in 1885 and christened Alice Margaret. In 1925 Alice was 40. She was married and living in Drummond Street with her husband, William Gorman, and their son William, born the previous year. Gorman was not the father of her unborn child. Early that year she had renewed her friendship with a man twenty years her senior with whom she had first had an intimate affair in 1904, Walter Sickert.

On 22 October 1925, not long after she opened her door to the two men with the package sent by Alexandra, Alice gave birth to Joseph. Next month Alexandra died.

The package contained a magnificent collection of jewels comprising a triple-row diamond-and-emerald necklace with matching earings and bracelet; a single-row dark-red ruby-and-sapphire necklace with a central pear-drop, and matching earrings and bracelet; a single-row diamond necklace; a triple-row necklace of blue-and-red-fire opals; a pair of diamond oval brooches, one framing a picture of the Duke of Clarence, the other a picture of Queen Alexandra and her father, Christian IX of Denmark; and, lastly, a pair of gold cuff-links which had belonged to Prince Eddy.

This king's ransom was contained in a black-lacquered metal box about eighteen inches long, a foot wide and a foot high, with several removable trays. The lid was decorated with two gold-painted capital 'A's entwined, surmounted by a crown. The initials are those of Alice and Alexandra.

*

When Alice died in 1950 the jewels became the property of her only living son, Joseph. Ever since Alexandra's death the Royal Family have been looking for the missing jewels. In 1926, as we have noted, Queen Mary had all the Royal jewels catalogued in order to establish exactly which jewels Alexandra had given away. She may not have known the whole story about Eddy and Annie Crook, but her husband, Eddy's younger brother, George V, certainly did, and he knew that Eddy was Alice Crook's father.

Joseph was told by his mother that, even though the Danish Royal Family was comparatively poor by Royal standards, some of the jewels did in fact come from Denmark. Most of them, however, came from Russia and were given to Alexandra by her sister Dagmar, the Empress Marie of Russia. Dagmar often sent Alexandra presents of rubies, pearls and sapphires, some of which were produced by mines in Siberia. After Bertie's death, rather than turn it over to the Crown, she encouraged her sister to keep her jewellery as personal property. The sisters often holidayed together, staying in the white Italianate villa at Hvidore near Copenhagen, which they bought jointly to avoid imposing on their family when they visited Denmark. The villa became Dagmar's home when she was finally persuaded to leave the Crimea after the Russian Revolution, during which her son, Tsar Nicholas II, was murdered with his wife and children. Under her bed she kept a box full of jewels which she had managed to take out of Russia.

*

When Joseph first told me about the jewels he enigmatically referred to them as the 'Minedalex' jewels, adding that Alexandra had a good reason for not giving them to an 'accepted' member of her family and a specific reason for giving them to Alice.

Some of the Minedalex jewels once belonged to Princess Alexandra's father, King Christian IX of Denmark. They were presented to her, as we have noted, on the occasion of her marriage to Edward, Prince of Wales, to be handed down to each successive queen. When at Edward VII's death in 1910 their younger son became George V, and George's wife, Princess May, became Queen Mary, Queen Alexandra ought to have given the Danish jewels to her. As we have seen, she chose not to.

*

Mary's parents were the Duke and Duchess of Teck. Teck, a castle of Württemberg, Kirchheim in Germany, lent its name to a duchy dating from the twelfth century, but the family became extinct in 1439. From 1495 to 1806 the title was held by the Dukes of Württemberg. In 1863 Alexander (1804-1885), a member of the Württemburg family who had made a morganatic marriage, was created Prince of Teck. His son Francis, who became the Duke of Teck in 1871, married Mary Adelaide, the daughter of Queen Victoria's cousin the Duke of Cambridge. They lived at White Lodge in Richmond Park. It was their daughter May who married, in 1893, Eddy's brother George, the future George V.

Queen Alexandra's hatred of Germans and everything German was renowned. Although Princess May was brought up in England – indeed she had been born in the same room in Kensington Palace as Queen Victoria – Alexandra could still not bring herself to give May the Danish jewels. She had strong personal reasons for giving them instead to her grand-daughter, Alice Crook.

*

The history books tell of the circumstances of Eddy's untimely death. To the Royal Family the weeks surrounding Christmas were known as the 'Sandringham Season'. Edward, who in 1891 was still Prince of Wales, celebrated his birthday on 9 November, while Alexandra celebrated hers on 1 December. Eddy's was the following month, on 8 January. In the middle of these family occasions were the Christmas and New Year celebrations. Since all these events were so close together, convenience normally dictated that the Royal Family should gather at their Norfolk home at Sandringham from early November until mid-January.

In 1891 Eddy was officially betrothed to Princess May of Teck. They were to be married in St George's Chapel, Windsor Castle, on 27 February 1892. As noted, the Princess married Eddy's younger brother George instead. Early in January 1892 Eddy's sisters, Victoria and Maud, who were with the rest of the family at Sandringham, were suffering from influenza. On 7 January Eddy was suddenly taken ill with dizziness and abdominal pains which forced him to return from a shooting party. Next day, his twenty-eighth birthday, Princess May went to his room and read to him while his brother George sat in an adjoining room answering his congratulatory telegrams. Next morning Eddy's condition worsened. He developed a fever, and his father's physician, Dr Francis Laking, diagnosed incipient pneumonia.

By 13 January Eddy had become delirious and in the early hours could be heard shouting various names. Some he emphatically cursed. To others he expressed devotion. Against Lord Salisbury and Lord Randolph Churchill, neither of whom was present, he cried out in fury.[8] His betrothed looked at him from above a screen, but not once did she hear him call her name. His delirious mind meandered in and out of his life's romances, and he called out 'Hélène! Hélène!' (see Appendix 6). By the 14th his lips had become livid and his finger-nails had turned blue. At 9.35 that morning he died.

*

Thirty-two years later, in 1924, Alexandra decided to give the Danish jewels to Eddy's daughter Alice, who was pregnant with Joseph. Alexandra realised that she must soon decide what to do about the jewels, since she was frail with little hope of life.

According to Joseph the codeword 'Minedalex' was a hybrid constructed from parts of three names – Minny, Eddy and Alexandra. Minny was the nickname of Alexandra's sister Dagmar, whose Royal title was Marie Feodorovna, Empress of Russia. Minny had married the Grand Duke of Russia at a magnificient ceremony in the Winter Palace on 9 November 1866.

Most ladies of fashion in Victorian England were prolific letter-writers. Queen Alexandra was no exception. She particularly enjoyed writing to Minny, her favourite sister, and it was in these letters that the Minedalex code was used after Eddy's death. It was simply their means of communicating their feelings when exchanging thoughts about Eddy and the jewels.

*

The reason Alexandra did not give the jewels to Queen Mary had less to do with Mary's Germanic background than with her firm conviction that Mary had no right to be Queen. We shall see why.

After Eddy's death his brother George was next in line to the throne, and the rest of the Royal Family thought he too should now consider marriage. Various candidates were suggested by the Press, among them 'Alicky', Princess of Hesse, who had previously turned down Eddy, and

Princess Helena Victoria, daughter of Prince and Princess Christian of Schleswig-Holstein. Some, including Queen Victoria, were in favour of Princess May, but months were to pass before he would even consider it. He still thought of May as 'Eddy's girl'. Nevertheless by the autumn of 1892 it was being taken for granted by those close to the throne that George and May would marry. The following spring George proposed and was accepted.

In 1911, at George's coronation, Alexandra was still zealously holding onto the Minedalex jewels because she believed that the only person entitled to them was Eddy's daughter, Alice. As Eddy had died without ever coming to the throne, his daughter had little claim to them. Why then should Alexandra believe that Alice was the only one who was entitled to them?

The answer is simple. *Eddy was not really dead, and the whole story of his death was a fabrication.* He lived hidden from the world until his actual death, at the age of 69, in 1933 (see Chapter 9). By then his younger brother had reigned in his place for twenty-two years. Alexandra knew that Eddy was alive and well and felt that George had no right to the throne. Since George ought not to have been king his wife ought not to be Queen and therefore had no right to the Minedalex jewels.

Eddy had no children apart from Alice, and Alexandra believed that Alice was the only one entitled to the jewels. Eddy's marriage to a Roman Catholic had made it unlikely that he would ever occupy the throne. Even more unlikely was that Alice would ever be openly recognised as his legal heir. Alexandra must have realised this; so we can assume that she chose to see things from a human, rather than a constitutional, standpoint.

Believing as she did that George and Mary were not the rightful King and Queen, she saw no reason why the Danish jewels should be passed on to any of their children. This was why she chose not to give them to George's son David, Prince of Wales, later briefly to be Edward VIII.

Eddy was 61 when Alexandra gave the jewels to Alice. At that time he was living in Scotland, remote from the world, long forgotten by everyone except the Royal Family. Alexandra could not give the jewels to Eddy. What could he, a virtual prisoner, do with them? Nor could she allow them to be found among her personal belongings after her death; they were too important to be forgotten or gleefully claimed by the future wife of one of George's descendants.

For thirty years or more Alexandra and everyone around her in the palace had been living a lie. Alexandra could not face the thought that she might die before correcting this terrible injustice. She may have been trying to salve her conscience for allowing Eddy to be supplanted by his younger brother. She was essentially a good woman, with strong feelings of justice. She came to realise that there was only one thing she could do to make amends. As her life edged to its close, she decided that the Minedalex jewels rightfully belonged to her 30-year-old grand-daughter, a wife and mother living in obscurity in Drummond Street with her husband and two children. As Alexandra knew, she had little to pass on to her children, and she was expecting again. She owned only two items which had once belonged to members of the Royal Family: a purse given her by Eddy, and a brooch given her by Alexandra herself.

*

Just before Alice's third birthday in 1888, Prince Eddy had racked his brains to decide what to give her for her birthday. He approached his favourite sister, Maud.* Maud and her two sisters had each been given a tiny purse by their aunt, the Empress of Russia. Maud had little or no use for a purse. It was thought unseemly for young princesses to leave the palace to go shopping. She gave the purse to Eddy for him to give to Alice. It was fashioned from silver inlaid with gold, engraved on both sides and lined with water-mark silk. Joseph gave it to his daughter Carol on her twenty-first birthday. Somewhere in the coffers of Buckingham Palace, or some other Royal residence, there must be two more purses identical with the one given to Alice.

The second item, the brooch, was given to Alice when she was three, after Netley's first attempt on her life.

Late in 1888, just after the Ripper murders, Netley was trying to ingratiate himself with his masonic masters. Joseph was never sure whether or not Netley was a Freemason, but I am able to state categorically that he was, a fact I discovered from a Freemason who wishes to remain unnamed. Though he never rose above the second degree, that of Fellow-Craft, Netley felt that by killing Alice he would be helping his masonic masters who would repay him by elevating him to the third degree of Master Mason. I also discovered that Netley's lodge met at a public house, The Gibraltar, in Prince's Yard, opposite the 'Ragged School' in George's Yard, which is itself off Whitechapel High Street. It was demolished in the 1950s. In 1888 the landlord of The Gibraltar was John Percy Sutton, Netley's brother-in-law. The public house stood more or less at the geographical centre of the five Ripper murder sites, providing a convenient operational base and a place to return to quickly after the murders.

George's Yard was itself the scene of a murder in 1888. Martha Tabram's body was found on the common staircase of George's Yard Buildings on 7 August. She had been stabbed 39 times. There were those who, without any evidence, later chose to link her death to the Ripper murders.

Netley tried to run Alice down in his coach. She was taken to the

* Maud had married her first cousin Prince Charles of Denmark, who was voted King Haaken VII of Norway in 1905. She had a reputation for bravery, and was nicknamed 'Harry' after her father's brave friend Harry Keppel.

nearest hospital, the Charing Cross in Chandos Place, just behind the Strand. A few days later Princess Alexandra visited her bedside to see for herself how well her granddaughter was recovering. (Presumably it was Walter Sickert who had told her what had happened to Alice.) Half a century later Alice recalled the event clearly. She remembered the lady unclipping a diamond brooch and giving it to her, announcing, as she did so, that she was Princess Alexandra and Alice's grandmother. Alice still had the brooch when Joseph was a boy, but it was stolen during a burglary.

Four years later Netley made a second attempt to run Alice down. Joseph was not the only one to repeat this story. It has been corroborated independently by two people, one of whom was with Alice at the time. Both accounts are given in the next chapter.

*

The burglary took place on the day of Walter Sickert's funeral in January 1942. Walter had died at Bathampton, and Alice and Joseph left their London home to attend the funeral. While they were there someone broke in and stole the brooch, together with some apostle spoons. Much of their furniture was also smashed. Alice believed that the thieves could not have been Catholics because they did not find other important items hidden behind a picture of the Sacred Heart (valuables and important papers were often kept behind religious pictures in the belief that they would be safe).

The two Royal items, the brooch and the purse, are, by Royal standards, of little worth. Alexandra may not even have known that Alice had the purse, but she must have realised that she had nothing of great value. She wanted to make certain that Alice had something special, something truly regal.

*

In 1920 Alexandra was almost completely deaf, and her eyesight had also begun to fail. Her mental faculties remained unimpaired, however, and she must have been acutely aware of her physical limitations. In October 1923 she wrote to King George: 'My old head is coming to a break-down soon.'[9] That she was facing up to her impending death can be seen from what she wrote to him in March 1925. 'I feel completely collapsed – I shall soon go.'[10] Only twenty-nine days after Joseph's birth she died at Sandringham. She had made certain that before she died she had given the Minedalex jewels to their rightful heir.

*

Three years after Joseph told me about the Minedalex jewels, a story was published which confirmed much of what he had said. Unfortunately I only discovered the story in 1991 – just a few months before publication of this book.

After the death of the Duchess of Windsor it was announced in several newspapers that her jewellery was to be auctioned in Geneva in April 1987. One article was written by the journalist Suzy Menkes, and after it appeared she received a telephone call from an elderly gentleman called John Neilson. She subsequently related their conversation:

> On the day we published the news that the Duchess of Windsor's fabulous collection of jewelery was up for auction, a lovely old gentleman called John Neilson phoned me.
>
> He was, he said, 97, and had been in service to her Majesty Queen Alexandra for many years. He wanted to explain why the Queen's famous emeralds would not be found in the Windsor collection.
>
> 'It is simple,' he said. 'Her Majesty, just before she died, gave them to Mrs Alice Gorman. They would normally have gone to Queen Mary, but Queen Alexandra did not like Germans after the affair with Denmark.
>
> She had decided to give them to her favourite grandson, David, Duke of Windsor and he would, of course, give them to his wife, who was to be the Duchess of Windsor.
>
> But when, the old gentleman went on, the Duke of Windsor fell out with his father, King George V and they never spoke again, Queen Alexandra changed her will.
>
> But who, I asked, was Mrs Alice Gorman?
>
> 'Ah,' he said, with the secrets of generations in his voice, 'Queen Alexandra believed her to be her grand-daughter. She was, you see, the mother of Joseph Sickert, who handed over all the information for Stephen Knight's book, *Jack the Ripper: The Final Solution.*'

THE BERNER ST. VICTIM.
ST GEORGES IN THE EAST MORTUARY.

CHAPTER SEVEN
Eddy

On 6 January 1864 the ice on Frogmore Lake, Windsor, was thick enough to support a band and a crowd of skaters. It was a scene from a Christmas card, the sending of which had become *de rigueur* among fashionable society in the 1860s. That evening Princess Alexandra gave a children's party.

Although she was pregnant with her first child, she was determined to drive to Virginia Water next day to watch the skaters. Ignoring some twinges of pain, she spent the day on a sledge which had been placed on the ice so that she could watch the skaters and be close to her party. At dusk they returned to Frogmore House, and her lady-in-waiting, Lady Macclesfield, realised almost at once that she had gone into labour. Next day, 8 January, she gave birth to a son two months prematurely. At the insistence of Queen Victoria he was christened Albert Victor Christian Edward, but almost everyone except Queen Victoria called him Eddy. He was the heir apparent.

*

Throughout his life many of Eddy's contempories and most of his family thought he was a dullard who showed little interest in his future role as king. Within a month of his birth Queen Victoria was bemoaning his backwardness. How she was able to discern it, when Eddy was so young, it would be interesting to know. But the matriarch had spoken, and for the remainder of Eddy's life her negative view was echoed in Court circles.

It hardly needs a psychologist to tell us that children often grow up to become the type of person others depict them as. For example, if a child is constantly told he is a poor reader he may well remain one. Another, repeatedly told that he is bad or wicked, may turn out bad and wicked. This process was at work to some extent with Eddy, and though he was not unintelligent he certainly showed little interest in matters which it was important for a future king to know.

On 3 June 1865 Alexandra gave birth to her second son, George, who everyone agreed was altogether more intelligent and lively than his brother. Disregarding their differences, however, the princes became great friends.

When Eddy was 13 they were sent to HMS *Britannia*, a naval training ship at Dartmouth. Their father, the Prince of Wales, wanted his sons to mix with other boys rather than be segregated as he himself had been as a child. They joined the *Britannia* two months later than intended, because that summer Eddy was struck down with typhoid. His father had almost died of the disease six years before, but had been nursed to health by Dr William Withey Gull. In recognition of his skill and devotion to duty in fighting the dread disease – Eddy's grandfather, Prince Albert, had died of it in 1861 – Gull was created a baronet and appointed Physician Extraordinary to the Queen. He therefore became the natural choice to attend Eddy, and under his care Eddy made a complete recovery.

The brothers spent two years aboard the *Britannia* under the tutelage of the Rev. John Neale Dalton, the curate to Canon Prothero, Rector of Whippingham near Osborne. Unfortunately Dalton somehow failed to arouse in Eddy any deep academic interest.

A child's brain is amazingly receptive, but without stimulus it often fails to realise its potential. This stimulus comes above all from parents, but further interest is usually provided through interchanges between the learning child and his peers and teachers. Deaf children start life at a disadvantage because one of their major senses is unable to respond to all the necessary communication signals. This is what happened to Prince Eddy who, as noted, suffered from otosclerosis.

Some of Eddy's and George's biographers have suggested that while Eddy was 'backward' George was bright and accomplished. It is true that George was a better sailor than Eddy, but there was nothing odd in this. Eddy simply did not like sailing and should not have been expected to be as keen on it as his brother. George enjoyed it from the beginning and was known as the 'Sailor Prince'. Eddy's lack of enthusiasm for the life of a midshipman made him seem dull by comparison.

The sad fact remains that both brothers lacked a proper education. If proof were needed that George was hardly more intelligent than Eddy, we should note that the standards of the Navy entrance exam had to be lowered to enable George to pass as a cadet aboard the *Britannia*.

In September 1879 the princes were sent on a three-year world cruise. Before they left, their father's mistress, Lilly Langtry ('Jersey Lilly'), gave Eddy a souvenir which he attached to his watch-chain. 'I had to take off grandmother's locket to make room for it,' he said.[1] They sailed under Captain the Rt. Hon. Lord Charles Scott, aboard HMS *Bacchante*. Because of their different heights they were known by the crew as 'Herring and Sprat'. They sailed the Mediterranean, the Caribbean, the South Atlantic and the Pacific. They also toured Australia. From there they returned to the Mediterranean via the Suez Canal, arriving home on 5 August 1882.

A year later, in October 1883, the Prince of Wales took Eddy to Trinity College, Cambridge, where he was left to struggle with life as an undergraduate. During the previous months at Sandringham a tutorial staff under the direction of J.K. Stephen had crammed him in preparation for university. Stephen was later to write to Dalton:

> I do not think he can possibly derive much benefit from attending lectures at Cambridge ... he hardly knows the meaning of the words to read.[2]

Trinity, which was founded by Henry VIII, has always maintained a close association with Royalty. Indeed it is the only Cambridge college whose Master is appointed by the Crown. Eddy was at Cambridge until June 1885. On 8 June 1888 he returned to receive the honorary degree of Doctor of Laws. Later he dined in the College hall before attending a reception in the drawing-room of the Master's Lodge. Among those present were the Marquess of Salisbury and Lord Randolph Churchill.[3] It was three months before the Ripper murders.

Nine days after he received his degree the *London Gazette* announced that he had been commissioned Lieutenant in the 10th Hussars, a regiment whose Colonel-in-Chief was his father, the Prince of Wales.

Alice was born on 18 April 1885, but Eddy was not in London for the event. In fact he was not even in England but with his parents in Ireland. They left a week before she was born and returned twelve days after.

*

In July 1889, seven months after the last of the Ripper murders, the police raided a homosexual brothel at 19 Cleveland Street, two doors from where Sickert's studio at No. 15 had stood (until 1887), and directly across from the confectionery shop at No. 22 where Annie Crook had been working when she met Eddy. The story is as follows.[4]

On 4 July 1889 PC Hanks was called to the headquarters of the General Post Office in St Martin's-le-Grand in the City to investigate a series of thefts of small sums of cash. During an interview with a messenger-boy, Charles Swinscow, the constable discovered that he had been earning extra money by sleeping with men at 19 Cleveland Street. The proprietor of the establishment, he said, was one Charles Hammond.

The man brought in the next day to lead the investigation was none other than Inspector Frederick George Abberline who, officially at least, was still searching for Jack the Ripper. It did not take Abberline long to secure a warrant for the arrest of Charles Hammond and a post-boy called Henry Newlove.

They were charged:

that they did unlawfully, wickedly and corruptly conspire, combine and confederate and agree to incite and procure George Alma Wright and divers other persons to commit the abominable crime of buggery.

On 7 July, while PC Hanks was taking him to the police station, Newlove remarked on how unfair it was that he was being arrested while men in high positions were allowed to walk free. He repeated this to Abberline, adding that Lord Henry Somerset, the Earl of Euston and a Colonel Jervois had been regular visitors to Cleveland Street. On further questioning Newlove named a 'clergyman' called Veck who was in truth a Post Office worker and one of the worst offenders against young boys. Evidence against Veck was secured by 9 July, and the following day Abberline ordered his men to watch the Cleveland Street premises. They saw furniture being removed, but did nothing to stop it though it must have been obvious to them that Hammond was about to take flight. This he did. It later transpired that he had left for France, furniture and all.

Lord Arthur Somerset who, it may be remembered, was the 38-year old son of the 8th Duke of Beaufort and an Extra Equerry and Superintendent of the Stables of the Prince of Wales, also left for France and so escaped arrest. The Prince, who was Somerset's friend and fellow mason, wrote to the Prime Minister, Lord Salisbury, expressing satisfaction that Somerset had been allowed to escape. Salisbury also saw to it that Hammond was not extradited from France to face charges.

After the escape of Hammond and Somerset Veck was arrested, six weeks after evidence against him had been obtained. He was jailed for four months, and Newlove for nine. Veck received less than half the sentence of one of his victims. Clearly a deal had been struck with the prosecuting authorities. He had been given a short term in return for a promise not to reveal the names of certain eminent men who had visited the brothel.

In the Cleveland Street file of the Director of Public Prosecutions one person mentioned as a frequent visitor is referred to by his initials rather than by name. The initials 'P.A.V.' can refer to only one man, whose name the compilers of the file wished to keep hidden – Prince Albert Victor: Eddy.

According to Walter Sickert, Veck, though actually a Post Office worker, held some sort of lay-preaching position at St Saviour's Chapel in Maple Street, around the corner from his lodgings in Howland Street. He therefore worked in the very place where Annie Crook and Eddy went through a form of marriage. Walter claimed that he was involved with the ceremony in some way. Since Eddy was linked to the Cleveland Street brothel he almost certainly came into contact with Veck there, and it may have been Veck who performed the service at St Saviour's. Even if he did not he may have arranged it.

If Veck was not an ordained priest and yet performed the service, the marriage could not be canonically recognised. Nor could it be registered with the authorities. Eddy's marriage to a Roman Catholic commoner, whether or not it had been canonically recognised, would have been a major embarrassment to the Royal Family and the Establishment.

Eddy liked to smoke Turkish cigarettes, and he was known to be a heavy drinker; but, worse than this, by 1889 it was also becoming accepted among certain sections of society that he was bi-sexual. He seems to have been a familiar figure at several homosexual establishments, where he was known as 'Victoria'. Whether Eddy was bisexual, or homosexual, by inclination, or whether it was something into which he had been led, is difficult to assess. We should remember, however, that because of his deafness he would often misunderstand what was going on around him and could easily be drawn into situations which he might otherwise have rejected. (The same might be said of his association with Annie.) Once in those situations he was open to further influence and possible corruption.

There is reason to believe that Eddy did visit Cleveland Street – not with Lord Somerset, but with his equerry Capt. George Holford. Somerset's sister, Lady Waterford, wrote the following to Reginald Brett, a friend of the Prince of Wales and Eddy:

> Please correct any impression that Arthur and the boy ever went out together. Arthur knows nothing of his movements and was horrified to think he might be supposed to take the Father's money and lead the son into mischief of any kind. I am sure the boy is straight as a line, and as to George Holford, even the blackguard [Hammond] who chantaged A[rthur] never mentioned him or thought of him. I am so glad – dear nice boy.[5]

Lord Euston claimed that he went to the Cleveland Street brothel in the belief that he would see *poses plastiques* – tableaux of naked women in poses imitating classical paintings. These were a Victorian substitute for striptease. Hammond touted for business with cards printed with the words '*poses plastiques*' at the top. Clearly it was in his interest to pimp for women as well as for men and boys. Hammond had long been associated with women – particularly French prostitutes. Indeed his wife, known as Madame Caroline, was herself one. Eddy may therefore have attended for the pleasure of female company, making the same mistake that Lord Euston claimed to have made.

Whatever his motives, it was imperative that his name be kept out of the subsequent scandal and not be associated in any way with Cleveland Street, since it was there that he met and married Annie Crook. A cover-up had to be mounted. But unfortunately for those wishing to hide Eddy's possible homosexual diversions, as well as his secret marriage and fatherhood, one man threatened to reveal all after the trial of Veck and Newlove.

Ernest Parke, editor of the *North London Press*, attacked the police for allowing Hammond to escape with his property to France. He suggested that men of title had also been allowed to escape justice because 'their prosecution would inculpate more highly placed and distinguished personages'.

This was an astute and accurate interpetation, as can be seen from the candid statement made to the police by John Saul, a male prostitute:

> The young Duke of Grafton, I mean the brother to the present Duke, was a constant visitor at Hammonds...I saw him myself last night. I know him well. He went to Hammonds with me on one occasion. He is not an actual sodomite. He likes to play with you and then 'spend' on your belly.[6]

The Duke of Grafton's brother referred to was Lord Somerset's friend Lord Euston. As I revealed in Chapter 4, both were members of the Ripper coterie.

Lord Euston sued Parke for libel. Unbelievably, the main witness against Lord Euston, John Saul, was dismissed by the judge, Sir Henry Hawkins. The reason, given in all seriousness, now seems almost comical. He was unreliable because he was a homosexual!

Parke was found guilty of criminal libel and sentenced to a year's imprisonment. This, by Victorian standards, was an extremely lenient sentence for one found guilty of libelling a member of the nobility, and he may have done a deal with the prosecution by promising not to reveal more names. Joseph – who met him a few years before he died in 1946 – was told that he served his entire sentence in the prison hospital. After prison he moved to the Midlands, where, despite his conviction, he became a Justice of the Peace in his native Warwickshire.

Parke's defence lawyer was the Liberal MP for East Fife, Herbert Henry Asquith, who three years later was appointed Home Secretary and Privy Councillor. He was Prime Minister between 1908 and 1916 and later ennobled as the 1st Earl of Oxford.

*

The Establishment had closed the door to further speculation by the Press. Other journalists would now think twice before pursuing Parke's assertion that 'more highly placed ... personages' had visited the Cleveland Street brothel. His prison sentence would effectively hang like a sword of Damocles over the head of any enterprising enquirer asking questions in Cleveland Street. Otherwise any journalist worth his printer's ink would have gone directly to Cleveland Street and spoken to the locals. Anyone living across the street from the brothel or next door to the shop at No. 22 could have told the story of the prince and the shop-girl, Annie Crook. If it had become common knowledge, the monarchy, the government and the Freemasons would have found themselves staring at disaster.

*

Aleister Crowley, the infamous black-magician and drug-addict who called himself 'The Great Beast', also connected Prince Eddy and Annie Crook with Cleveland Street. *In The World's Tragedy* (Paris, 1910), he claimed to possess some compromising letters from Eddy to a boy called Morgan living in Cleveland Street. The boy's mother was Mrs Hannah Morgan who ran the shop at No. 22 where Annie Crook and Mary Kelly worked. Jean Overton Fuller enlarged upon this after talking to Timothy D'Arch Smith, author of a book on Crowley, *Love in Earnest*. According to her, D'Arch Smith, after consulting his notes, found 'a relation of Annie Elizabeth Morgan of 22 Cleveland Street'. Fuller suggested that 'someone [had] mistaken Annie for a sister of Morgan'.[7]

*

After being snatched from her home in the basement of No. 6 Cleveland Street, Annie Crook was taken directly to Guy's Hospital in a coach driven by Netley, where she was kept for 156 days. Walter told Joseph that Annie underwent an operation at Gull's hands which resulted in partial paralysis. Her dormant epilepsy surfaced also at this time. In the 1880s many believed that epilepsy was evidence of madness, and it was not unusual for epileptics to be certified insane, or at least confined. It would therefore have been easy for Gull to keep Annie at Guy's and have her certified insane. To compound her misery, she lost her memory.

Once Gull believed that she posed no danger to him and his friends she was released. During her imposed stay in Guy's Walter sent Alice to Dieppe, where she was looked after by his relations. Despite Annie's impaired memory the powerful bond between mother and child was not easily broken, and upon her release from Guy's she returned to Cleveland Street to look for Walter and Alice.

*

At the corner of Mortimer Street and Cleveland Street stands the Middlesex Hospital. One of its more eminent surgeons at the turn of the century was Sir John Bland-Sutton. He entered the Middlesex in 1878 and was made Demonstrator and Lecturer in Anatomy, becoming a surgeon in 1886. He is commemorated by the Bland-Sutton Institute of Pathology, which stands a few yards behind the site of Walter Sickert's studio. In 1888 he was only five years Sickert's senior and enjoyed more than a passing acquaintance with him. He also knew Annie Crook, who often served him in the shop where she worked, and whom he regarded as a bright and healthy young woman. Once when she returned to Cleveland Street after her incarceration at Guy's, Bland-Sutton was astonished by the change in her. She was no longer the cheerful, confident woman he remembered. Her eyes had lost their sparkle and she had a haunted look. He examined her and discovered what had happened to make such a profound change. Half a century later, with tears in his eyes, Walter related the story to Joseph, who was then about fifteen.

Bland-Sutton and Gull were ostensibly friends, but some reports suggest that Bland-Sutton despised his elderly mentor, and when he was informed by Sickert of Gull's part in Annie's incarceration he set out to discover how her previous good health had been impaired. Eventually he was able to tell Walter the dreadful news that Gull had not only performed the abominable operation which left Annie with partial paralysis, but had also injected her with drops of blood contaminated with syphilis. Gull, an ardent vivisectionist, had already experimented with animals by injecting them with syphilis and observing the results. It may have been the syphilis, then incurable, that triggered the dormant epilepsy inherited from her mother. It may also have been a major factor leading to the diagnosis in her case notes dated 12 March 1913: 'spells of amentia. Is an epileptic.'[8] Walter believed that the diseased blood given to Annie had been taken from Lord Randolph Churchill, who ordered the procedure.

*

In 1920 Annie died, hopelessly insane, at the early age of fifty-five.

The first time Alice was run down by Netley, Eddy was told that she had died, but because of his angry reaction to the news (see Chapter 8) this was later denied. He was also told that Annie was being well looked after and he did not discover what had really been going on until much later, when it was too late for him to do anything about it. In fact by this time he no longer had any control over his own life, let alone anyone else's. It is not difficult to appreciate the effect upon him of learning first that Alice was dead and later that Annie had been incarcerated. He also realized that others at court, notably his father the Prince of Wales, were planning to prevent his succession and arranging for his younger brother George to take his place.

Admittedly, because of his deafness Eddy was at a severe disadvantage. His knowledge of European history was sadly lacking. He rarely read anything except letters from friends, and he was unable to hold a conversation on social problems or politics. His feeble knowledge of the constitution, coupled with his heavy drinking and dissolute ways, not to mention his rumoured bi-sexuality, proved to the satisfaction of those at Court that he would make an extremely poor monarch. His life style would have been unacceptable in a man of low social standing. In a future King it was unthinkable.

*

Though he does not know the original source of all the information his father gave his mother and himself, Joseph does remember meeting many eminent people within his father's circle. Through them, their children and their friends he has himself been able to meet various members of the aristocracy who have supplied some of the missing pieces in the puzzle of his family background. For instance, he learned that Eddy twice set alight to Sandringham, the royal residence in Norfolk.

The first time was when he was told the lie that Alice had died from injuries sustained under Netley's coach wheels. He was heartbroken and apparently so overcome with grief that for days he was seen holding a large cover over his head.

The terrible events that had overtaken his wife and daughter depressed him deeply. Eventually his grief turned to frustration and anger and he set fire to some furnishings. Alexandra tried to stop him, only to discover moments later that her dress was alight. Fortunately the flames were quickly put out and she was not injured.

The second time was when he first realised that he was to be prevented from ascending the throne. He knew that his mother, to whom he was deeply attached, would not be at risk since she was in the Crimea with her sister, the Empress of Russia.

This second fire became public, though of course Eddy was never openly held responsible. It took place on Sunday 1 November 1891. Smoke was seen by a letter-carrier named Emerson who was walking across Sandringham Park at 7.30 a.m. He immediately informed PC Middleton, the policeman on duty. The fire started in a bedroom on the nursery floor at the top of the house – in itself suspicious since there were no children staying there. It destroyed the top floor and part of the roof and badly damaged the dining-room and some valuable Goya tapestries. It was still burning at noon.

The day before the fire Eddy and George had arrived at Marlborough House from Ireland. The Court Circular in *The Times* on 2 November stated that they were to travel that day to Culford Hall, Bury St Edmunds, to visit the Earl and Countess of Cadogan. The 2nd of November was a Monday, but the Court Circular did not state where Eddy and George were on Sunday, the day of the fire, and readers would assume that they remained in London. If, however, the story Walter told Joseph is true, they must have travelled by train that day to Sandringham. This would have been convenient for their planned visit to Culford Hall, which was much closer to Sandringham than to London. They would remove there five days later, after visiting the Cadogans, for Bertie's birthday party.

In fact, according to the Court Circular of 3 November, Eddy's father travelled to Sandringham on the 2nd to assess the fire damage, returning to London the same day. If Sickert was right, Bertie may also have gone there to remonstrate with Eddy and return him to London, because that evening Bertie, Eddy and George were to be seen watching Joan of Arc at the Gaiety Theatre. They would not have wished to stay at Sandringham, because the roof was open to the weather and needed several days' repair work before Bertie's birthday celebrations could take place.

Eddy and George's vist to Culford Hall was postponed until the 3rd, and they returned to London on the 7th. That day they left for Sandringham to attend Bertie's fiftieth birthday party on the 9th.

The fire, as a result of which the celebrations were nearly cancelled, was the final straw and Bertie became more than ever determined to ensure that his eldest son should never ascend the throne.

*

In her biography of Queen Mary, Anne Edwards acknowledged her gratitude for help given by 'historians, royal observers, librarians, archivists and those members of Queen Mary's Household who shared their memories' with her. She states that some members of the Court thought that there was a plan afoot to have Eddy 'committed' because of his 'irrational behaviour'.[9] This may have been the original plan, but a more permanent solution was soon found. Nine weeks after the second fire the announcement was made that Eddy had died.

At the height of the Cleveland Street affair Eddy had been sent abroad. He sailed first to Greece, then to Egypt and then to India. He returned in May 1890 after the affair had been swept under a rather plush carpet. It has been said that on his return he slipped back into the nether world of the Victorian 'Mary-Anne'. Though the Cleveland Street brothel had been closed down, there were other establishments that pandered to homosexuals. Oscar Wilde was a frequent visitor to W. Jones's establishment at 13 Little College Street near the Houses of Parliament where MPs met rent-boys. The Crown in Charing Cross Road, The Pakenham in Knightsbridge and The Windsor Castle in the Strand were three well-known public houses frequented by homosexuals. It was said that Eddy became a regular guest at The Hundred Guineas Club where the members assumed feminine names and where Eddy was known, as we have remarked, by his grandmother's name, 'Victoria'.

That he may often have been misled by his deafness into situations he might otherwise have avoided has already been argued, but it should be stated categorically that there has never been anything but circumstantial evidence to show that Eddy was homosexual or bi-sexual. The rumours were widespread, however, and these rumours, coupled with the fact that his name is to be found in the file on the Cleveland Street scandal, make it likely that he was involved in bi-sexual activities.

On 4 September 1883 Queen Victoria had conferred upon Eddy the Order of the Garter. He was only 19, and many thought it strange that he was given the honour while still a minor. His brother George was not admitted till long after his majority. Equally strange was that the ceremony, instead of being private at Balmoral, was held publicly in St George's Chapel, Windsor. As a contemporary wrote:

> The exceptional character of the distinction was proof of the high favour in which her Majesty held her grandson.[10]

After his association with Annie, the birth of their daughter Alice and the Cleveland Street scandal, such an honour was never again shown to him by members of his family. Indeed they decided to dishonour him instead.

*

In 1890 Eddy was created Duke of Clarence and Avondale, but this grand title was in fact little more than an insult. A cursory glance at the lives of the previous Dukes of Clarence shows the low esteem the title had fallen to by the time it was conferred on Eddy.

The first two Dukes of Clarence were quite respectable. The first Duke was Lionel of Antwerp, the second surviving son of Edward III. His wife was the heiress of the Clares whose land he inherited and whose name formed the basis of his title. The second was Thomas Plantagenet, the second son of Henry IV and an aide to his elder brother, Henry V. He served his brother faithfully, took part in preparations for the French war and was killed at Anjou while rashly attacking the French and their Scottish allies. At his death he was heir to the throne, but since he was childless the title became extinct.

It was revived when George Plantagenet became Duke of Clarence, and it now began its decline. George was involved in various conspiracies against his brother, Edward IV. Eventually, in 1478, Edward realised that Clarence was aiming at the throne and revealed the charges to Parliament. Not only had George slandered him, but he had received oaths of allegiance and prepared a rebellion. He was sentenced to death and secretly executed in the Tower. Soon afterwards the rumour gained ground that he had drowned in a butt of malmsey wine.

After this debacle there was no further Duke of Clarence until George II's grandson, Prince William Henry, who later ascended the throne as William IV. The Royal Marriage Act of 1772 severely limited William's choice of spouse. He was not permitted in law to marry a Catholic, and until he was 25 needed the sovereign's permission to marry. Over that age twelve months notice had to be given to the Privy Council, or the sanction of Parliament obtained, before a marriage could be contracted. George IV was not willing that any heir presumptive or heir apparent should mingle his blood with any less blue. Consequently William had to search for a wife among princesses of northern Europe, a prospect he found daunting. A more alluring alternative was Dorothy Jordan, an actress renowned for her figure and her legs though not her beauty; added attractions were her voice and her laugh, which combined both gaiety and sensuality. Though they could not marry, Mrs Jordan took upon herself the role of wife and mother, living for a time in a house in Forest Hill. She bore William ten children: five sons and five daughters. It was over twenty years before they parted and William married Adelaide of Saxe-Meiningen.

The two dukes who held the title immediately before Eddy were like him both in character and actions. George Plantagenet was a fool who was easily manipulated, particularly by Richard Neville, Earl of Warwick. Eddy was also considered a fool by many of his friends and family, and he allowed himself to be led by others into dissolute habits and pastimes. As Queen Victoria once said, he 'never seemed to mind what happened to him'.[11] Though Prince William, Duke of Clarence, did not actually go through a wedding ceremony with Mrs Jordan, he was married to her in all but name and was the father of her children. Eddy's association with Annie was similar. Like Mrs Jordan, Annie was a commoner who bore the child of the heir presumptive.

On 24 May 1890 Eddy, who was christened Albert Victor and was thereafter formally addressed by both names. He was saddled with another doublet when he became the Duke of Clarence and Avondale. Henry Labouchere, the outspoken editor of *Truth* and a close friend of Lord Randolph Churchill, tellingly wrote of the new title:

> The only Duke of Clarence who is known in history is the numbskull who was deservedly drowned in a butt of malmsey, and during the present century the title was associated with the aberrations and extravagances for which William IV was unenviably notorious.[12]

*

I have said that Eddy did not die in 1892. This claim was made to me by Joseph Sickert not long after I met him in the mid 1980s. Subsequent research revealed that after his reported death there were in fact rumours that he was still alive. Indeed I have met a number of people in their eighties who maintain that the rumour was going strong at least until the First World War.

In August 1960 Dr T.E. Stowell told Colin Wilson that in the 1930s Sir William Gull's daughter, Caroline Acland, asked him to inspect her father's private papers. From them he learned that Eddy did not die of influenza at Sandringham House, but in a mental home near Sandringham, of 'softening of the brain' due to syphilis.[13]

The rumour that the official story of Eddy's death was false re-surfaced in 1978 when Frank Spiering reported an anecdote allegedly told by Dr Stowell. Spiering claimed that Stowell had met W. Watters who had been head gardener at Sandringham in 1892, the year of Eddy's reported death. When Stowell made a casual reference to Eddy's dying there, Watters replied, 'Did he? Not while I was there.'[14]

Stowell had already created a sensation in 1970, when he wrote a cryptic story in the November 1970 issue of the *Criminologist* in which he claimed to have learned the identity of Jack the Ripper from Gull's private papers. Throughout the article he referred to his suspect as 'S', and he seemed to be pointing the finger at Eddy. He described 'S' as the heir to power and wealth and as having a grandmother who outlived him, adding that he had a 'beautiful mother and a gay cosmopolitan father'. 'S' went on a cruise at the age of 16 with a number of other youths of his own age and contracted syphilis in the West Indies. Stowell claimed that his suspect was commissioned into the army when he was 21 and resigned when he was 24, 'shortly after the raiding of some premises in Cleveland Street'. 'S', says Stowell, was nicknamed 'Collar and Cuffs'.

We can compare these details about 'S' with what is known of Eddy.

It is not uncommon for deaf people to tilt their heads to one side in order to catch what is said to them. It was noticed that Eddy had this habit. The Court tailors were asked to cut his shirts and army tunics with a collar higher than was usual. This was to prevent him holding his head in a less than regal fashion. It also covered a small scar on his neck, the result of a minor operation. Because of his high collars and wide cuffs his father nicknamed him 'Collar and Cuffs'. As a boy Eddy, like 'S', went on a cruise which included the West Indies (though he was 15 at the time and not 16).

No one has yet produced evidence that Eddy had syphilis, but once, when he ran a high temperature in Scarborough, he was treated by a doctor of his own age named Alfred Downing Fripp.[15] Fripp never disclosed the specific nature of Eddy's illness, but after he died his biographer found a prescription made out for Eddy which suggested that he was being treated for gonorrhoea.[16]

If for argument's sake we accept the official view that Eddy died in 1892, then it is true that, like 'S', his grandmother outlived him. Moreover Eddy's mother, Queen Alexandra, was a beautiful woman, while his father, Bertie, did have a notorious reputation for cosmopolitan living. Eddy was commissioned into the army at the age of 21, and though he never actually resigned when he was 24, as 'S' was said to have done, he had little active life in the army after that age.

Even allowing for the inaccuracies and Stowell's later denial, it is at once apparent that Stowell was identifying Eddy as Jack the Ripper. His denial was written on 5 November 1970 and published in *The Times* four days later. Stowell stated that he 'at no time associated His Royal Highness, the late Duke of Clarence, with the Whitechapel murders, or suggested that the murderer was of Royal Blood'.

Stowell's one-time medical superior had been Theodore Dyke Acland who, as we have noted, was married to Gull's daughter Caroline. Through this family connection and, like his father-in-law, being a Freemason, Acland may have learned something, though probably not everything, about the Whitechapel murders. Stowell not only worked with Acland but enjoyed his hospitality in Bryanston Square. Both were Freemasons, and Acland may well have told him something of what he knew about the murders.

In his article Stowell stated (p. 49):

It was said that on more than one occasion Sir William Gull was seen in the neighbourhood of Whitechapel on the night of a murder.

Stephen Knight suggested that Stowell was really accusing Gull, and not Eddy. According to the official Masonic Yearbook for 1970, Dr T.E. Stowell was appointed a Senior Grand Deacon (Craft only) in 1949, and Past Grand Sojourner (Royal Arch) in 1967. In his will he left his PZ jewel to the Cheselden Chapter.[17] Knight suggested that in concealing the truth of Gull's involvement in the East End murders he may have had in mind the words he would have used in the closing of the Royal Arch Chapter.

Companions, nothing now remains but, according to ancient custom, to lock up our secrets in a safe repository, uniting in the act of Fidelity, Fidelity, Fidelity, Fidelity.[18]

It may be that, whatever Stowell knew about the Ripper story, he decided to lock it up as 'secrets in a safe repository', by obscuring it in his strange mixed-up story of 'S'.

One thing that stood out in Stowell's letter of denial was that 'it remains my opinion that he [Jack the Ripper] was the scion of a noble family'. Lord Randolph Churchill was a scion of the Duke of Marlborough. 'S' might equally have signified Lord Randolph, since the initial stands for Spencer in his surname, Spencer-Churchill. The first Duke of Marlborough was John Churchill, but the dukedom passed to Charles Spencer, Earl of Sunderland in 1733. 'Churchill' was tagged on to 'Spencer' by the 5th Duke in 1817. In his autobiography Winston Churchill wrote of his time at Harrow:

The names of the new boys were printed in the School List in alphabetical order; and as my correct name, Spencer-Churchill, began with an 'S' …[19]

It should be remembered that Stowell was vehement in his declaration that he 'at no time … suggested that the murderer was of Royal Blood'. Perhaps his intention was to hide his clues by mixing various characteristics of several persons associated, both directly and indirectly, with the Ripper crimes. Eddy was known as 'Collar and Cuffs' and had a 'gay cosmopolitan father'; Lord Randolph was a 'scion of a noble family, and his name began with 'S'. 'S' was also the initial of several other members of the Ripper coterie: Lord Salisbury, Lord Arthur Somerset and J.K. Stephen – and also of the one figure who linked them all: Walter Sickert.

Though Winston Churchill had nothing to do with the murders Stowell may have had him in mind to point to Randolph's involvement. He wrote that 'S' was '21 when he was gazetted into the army'. Winston was, in the words of his autobiography, which Stowell might have read, in his '21st year'[20] when he was gazetted into the 4th Hussars. 'S' 'resigned his commission at about the age of 24'. Winston resigned his when he was 24, in 1899. It is also significant that Stowell released his article only after Winston's death, yet this was several decades after he claimed to have got his information from Gull's papers.

*

Stowell died a few days after publication of his denial, and his son burned all the papers and notes upon which he claimed to have based his story.[21]

Almost every author who has since written about Jack the Ripper – except Howells & Skinner, but including Jean Overton Fuller, Michael Harrison, Stephen Knight, Wilson & Odell and Peter Underwood – have claimed that Stowell died on the eighty-second anniversary of Mary Kelly's death, 9 November 1970. Inspection of Stowell's death certificate proves this to be incorrect. The public scandal he had caused and the resulting pressure upon him were perhaps too much for his constitution, and at the grand old age of 85, Dr T.E. Stowell died of 'Dissecting Aneurysm' and 'Arteriosclerosis', or, in layman's language, a ruptured aorta caused by hardening of the arteries – old age. He died on 8 November 1970.

The interesting point is that the mistake was first made in *The Times*, which, on 10 November 1970 reported Stowell's death as having occurred the day before. Subsequent authors copied this without checking, and others copied them. *The Times* is generally regarded as an accurate newspaper; so much so that in 1970 it was the only newspaper whose text could be quoted as evidence in a British court of law. This makes it all the more curious that it made a basic error of fact. Was it simply an error? If so, why was a correction not published within a few days? Or was *The Times* deliberately misinformed in order to create another masonic joke, by making it appear that Stowell had died on the anniversary of Mary Kelly's death?

Walter Sickert: 'Mother and Daughter', 1911

CHAPTER EIGHT
The Diaries

Joseph's family, as we have seen, suffered terribly at the hands of powerful people. His grandmother died insane in 1920, after deliberate medical malpractice and thirty-two years of suffering. His mother was twice almost murdered by John Netley's coach. She was imprisoned without cause and had her baby taken from her, never to be seen again. Joseph himself suffered three attempts on his life and was abducted when he was five. His grandfather has been accused more than once of being the Ripper. Little wonder that he wishes to set the record straight in order to vindicate his family's name and make sense of their suffering.

Joseph's assertion that Eddy lived considerably beyond the age of 28, when he is officially supposed to have died, is supported by a photograph published here for the first time. Joseph was told by his father that it was taken by Queen Alexandra when Eddy was 46 in 1910. (Alexandra, while yet a princess, was the first member of the Royal Family to become a keen photographer. In 1908 she published *Christmas Gift Book: Photographs from my Camera*.) The photograph shows a man sitting painting before an easel, a man who for all the world looks like Eddy in middle age. He has the same hooded eyes, the same long lean appearance; and, with the addition of a beard, he looks remarkably like Eddy's younger brother George, who sported a beard from 1886. If we compare the picture with other certain photographs of Eddy the likeness is remarkable. He is seen wearing a shirt with wide cuffs, a reminder of his nickname 'Collar and Cuffs'. Of course when the photograph was taken Eddy no longer had to worry about keeping his head straight with a high collar. Having lost his regal status, he was no longer required to maintain a regal bearing.

According to Walter Sickert, Alexandra, fearful of a revolution in England, sent a black metal box, containing certain items of sentimental value for safekeeping to her sister Dagmar, the Empress of Russia. Among them was this photograph of Eddy. The irony of course is that it was Russia not England that had the revolution and the Russian rather than the British monarchy that was deposed.

When I asked Joseph how he came to have the picture, he said it had been one of several items in the black metal box that had been returned to his father.

'Who returned it?' I asked.

'Harry Gibbs,' he replied. 'He was tutor to the Tsarevitch. After the Revolution he sent the box back here and came himself years later.'

'Did you ever meet him?'

'Yes, when I was a boy he used to talk to me and my father about English and Latin.'

I went to the library to check on Harry Gibbs. Joseph had said that the Tsarevitch to whom Gibbs had been tutor was Queen Alexandra's great-nephew Alexis, the haemophiliac son of Tsar Nicholas II who was murdered with his family by the Bolsheviks at Ekaterinburg in 1918. I checked the indexes of various books on the Romanovs but found no mention of Harry Gibbs. I did, however, find an English tutor to the Tsarevitch whose name was 'Sydney Charles Gibbes'.

When I telephoned Joseph with this information he repeated that he remembered the man only by the name 'Harry'. A mistake perhaps, due to a trick of the memory? Joseph must have sensed, even over the telephone, a note of misgiving in my voice, because he then said:

'We always called him Harry. I'll always remember him. He was tall and always wore a hat. After he left Russia I believe he travelled abroad a lot. But he visited England occasionally and called on my dad when he stayed with us at Drummond Street. My dad once had a studio around the corner at 13 Robert Street, off Hampstead Road, but he still had friends in Robert Street, and he introduced them to Harry, and through them Harry later found a place to live – just a couple of doors away from Dad's studio. Harry became a Russian Orthodox priest with the name Father Alexis. He wore a black robe that went right down to his feet, and he carried a stick. He had a long white beard. He often had Russian friends come to visit him. He opened a Russian church in Oxford. When he came out of Russia he brought a Russian boy with him, an orphan who was adopted and brought up as his own son. I never met the son, but I think he lives in Oxford – if he's still alive. I think he was older than me, and he might be dead by now.'

I did not know what to think. There was only one English tutor to the Tsarevitch who had a name like Harry Gibbs, and that was Sydney Gibbes. I wondered why Joseph could remember so much about the man and yet forget his Christian name.

That evening I pondered over what Joseph had said. I decided to check for the name Gibbes in the London telephone directory. There was one entry with that spelling. On impulse I dialled the number. I explained to the man who answered that I was writing a book and that part of my research had led me to look for someone with the same name as his own – someone who was related to a man who had been tutor to the Tsarevitch. I felt sure it all sounded very improbable.

'That was my grandfather,' said the man immediately, adding: 'You need to talk to my father, George Gibbes. He knows more about him than

I do.' He told me his father lived in Oxford, and gave me his telephone number.

I rang the Oxford number and once again explained my problem to a total stranger. I proceeded to relate the description of Harry Gibbs that Joseph had given me, adding that Gibbs had adopted a Russian boy.

The man in Oxford replied, in an educated voice, but with a slight foreign accent, as follows:

'That was a perfect description of my father, and I am that Russian boy. But I have never heard my father called Harry. I don't know why anyone should call him Harry.'

'When your father was in London where did he live?'

'In Robert Street. No.17.'

I had already learned from biographies of Walter Sickert that in the 1890s he did have a studio in Robert Street, at No. 13 – two doors away from Sidney Gibbes, as Joseph had said.

Apart from the discrepancy over Gibbes's Christian name, everything was exactly as Joseph had said. Joseph still insists that he remembers Gibbes by the name Harry, but he also remembers that he was known as Father Alexis. According to George Gibbes, his step-father became a monk of the Russian Orthodox faith in 1934, when he adopted the name Alexis in honour of his pupil, the Tsarevich. After he was ordained, he assumed the name Father Nicholas in honour of his pupil's father, Tsar Nicholas II.

This account shows that Walter and Joseph knew Sidney Gibbes, but it does not prove that Gibbes posted certain items to Walter Sickert – items which had been sent to Russia by Queen Alexandra. When I spoke by telephone to George Gibbes in Oxford he suggested that I read *Tutor to the Tsarevich* (1975) by J.C. Trewin, based on documents and photographs in his (George Gibbes's) possession.

When I did I found that many things belonging to the Imperial Russian Family had come out of Russia after the Revolution. Some of them are now to be found in the Gibbes collection at Oxford. (According to Trewin, until it disappeared in 1935 there even existed a suitcase containing the mortal remains of the murdered Tsar and his family, found in the mine shaft.) That Gibbes could have sent certain items to Sickert is not impossible, but in the circumstances in Russia at the time I believe it was unlikely. More probably Gibbes left Russia with them and later brought them to England himself.

Further confirmation of Joseph's story was provided by other contents of the 'black tin box' he showed me. One of the most interesting was a black ostrich-feather hat-decoration in the form of the Prince of Wales's feathers. Joseph was told that Alexandra wore it at funerals, and indeed photographs and newsreels do represent her with such a decoration. He also showed me a Russian Orthodox cross which Gibbes gave his mother. The feathers are reproduced here.

When I first began to visit Joseph in 1984 he showed me several curious things. One of the most interesting was a diary. He held it before me but made no move to give it to me when I held out my hand. When I asked to look at it, he said I could but not that day, adding that it was not the only diary he possessed. He described these as 'my father's', and I assumed he meant that the diaries were journals which his father had himself written. I was to learn later that this was true of only one of them.

There are six volumes in all. Two are notebooks. The rest are purpose-made diaries. Two of the diaries consist of ruled pages without pre-printed days or dates. The diarist could therefore insert the dates himself, omitting, if he wished, days and even weeks at a time, and writing down only important or significant events. These two volumes, bound in black leather, identical except that one is slightly larger than the other, have metal locks, to which Joseph has keys. The third, bound in maroon leather, was manufactured for a specific year, 1896. Three days of the week are printed on the odd pages and four, ending with Sunday, on the evens.

This diary was the one Joseph first showed me. It was sealed with wax across the leaves so that it could not be opened and read without the seals breaking. When I asked why he had not unsealed it and read it, he said that his father had told him the contents of all three diaries before leaving them with him and his mother. He had later unlocked the two to which he had a key, keeping intact the diary sealed with wax. Walter had said of the sealed volume: 'Don't open this, or it'll explode in your face.'

Joseph had always resisted the temptation to break the seal because as a child he believed in the literal possibility of an explosion. Since Walter had told him what was in the diaries, he was content to keep this one sealed until such time as he might wish to confirm his father's description of its contents.

*

It was not until much later that Joseph told me that it was Inspector Abberline who wrote three of the diaries. The fourth, he said, was written by his father, which came as no surprise since the diaries had already been described to me as Walter's. The fifth is really nothing more than a notebook. It was written by John Netley and supports Joseph's contention that Netley was the coach driver used in the East End murders. This revelation astounded me. Though Netley's name and involvement had been revealed by Joseph on television as early as 1973, this was the first time he claimed to have documentary evidence. Obviously, if Netley admitted his involvement nothing could be more damning. It was to Inspector Abberline, however, that I first turned my attention.

'How on earth did you get Abberline's diaries?'

'I met him when I was little. He was a friend of my dad's. He visited us at Drummond Street when I was three. He sat me on his knee. My dad said he was a policeman and if I didn't behave he would take me away.'

'What was he like?'

'I can remember him smelling of tobacco. He was chubby and had a white moustache, and underneath it you could see his shiny white teeth. His hair was white too, but he was bald. He wore a bowler hat. We called him Freddy. He was very gentle. He was a lovely man.'

'When did he die?'

'He visited us three times: in 1926, 1927 and 1928. The last time was when I met him. That's when he gave my dad the diaries. He died not long after.'

Abberline began his diaries after the police file was closed in 1892, the year he retired from the force. The volume, sealed with wax, was made by Charles Letts & Company Ltd. The front cover is embossed '1896'. This was the main one, begun after the death of Lord Randolph Churchill in 1895. It names Lord Randolph, J.K. Stephen, Sir William Gull and John Netley as those chiefly responsible for the murders. A photograph of the diary is shown here together with a home-made notebook which has been made up from pages of a closely-ruled writing pad or exercise book, and has a rough cardboard cover. The first page, or title page, of the notebook, has the words, hand-written in fading black ink:

Extracts
Fr.......y
Exposed

Freemasonry Exposed (1827) was a book written by an American Freemason, William Morgan, who, as we have noted, may have been murdered for trying to expose what he had come to believe was a wicked organisation. The notebook contains only extracts from *Freemasonry Exposed*, giving secret passwords, secret hand-shakes, or grips, and a short version of the legend of Hiram Abif. When he learned that the murders had a masonic connection, Abberline obtained a copy of Morgan's book hoping to discover what he could about the craft, recording what he felt might be helpful to his enquiries.

As noted, it is the 1896 Letts diary, the one sealed with wax, that names Lord Randolph and the other members of the Ripper gang. At the top of one page, that for 18 to 20 May, which has been torn from the volume, Abberline has written in brackets the words 'to be kept apart'. He has then signed it and written the date for this entry – 1903. The page contains the name HRH Duke of Clarence, followed by the names of the principal persons involved in the Ripper murders. Against each name is a number. No. 1 is 'Rt. Hon. Lord Randolph Spencer Churchill'. No. 2 is 'Sir William Gull'. No. 3 is omitted. No. 4 is 'J.K. Steven' (sic). Nos 5 and 6 are omitted. No. 7 is 'John Netley'. The entire page is reproduced here.

Walter Sickert as a young actor in
Henry Irving's troupe.

2. Joseph Sickert.

3. Walter Sickert in his last years.

4. The Duke of Clarence and Avondale ('Eddy').

5. Princess (later Queen) Alexandra.

6. Annie Elizabeth Crook.

7. Alice Margaret Crook.

Sir Charles Warren, Chief
Commissioner, Metropolitan Police.

9.   Sir William Withey Gull, Royal
     Physician.

10. *Left:* Sir Robert Anderson, Deputy
     Chief Commissioner, Metropolitan
     Police.

11. John Charles Netley, coach driver.

12. Berner Street, showing the entrance to Dutfield's Yard, scene of Elizabeth Stride's murder.

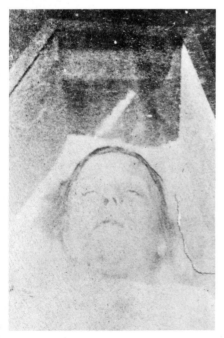

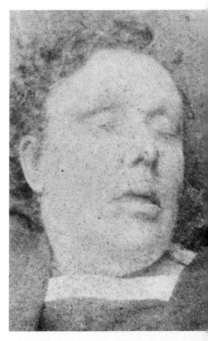

13. Mary Nichols.   14. Annie Chapman.

Plan of Mitre Square
and sketch of
Catherine Eddowes'
body, both prepared
for the inquest.

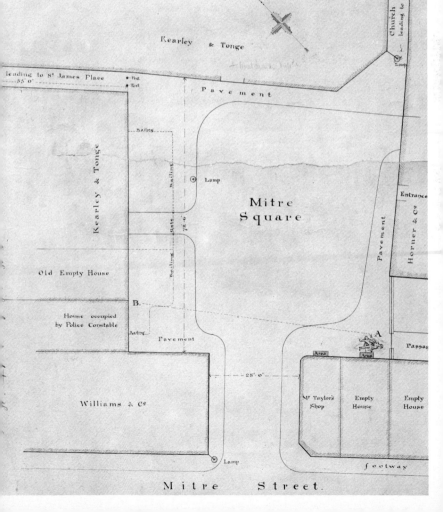

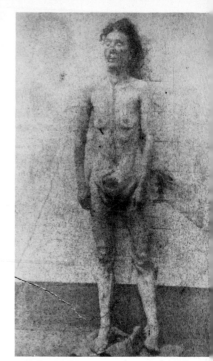

16. *Above:*
    Elizabeth Stride.

17. *Above, right:*
    Catherine
    Eddowes

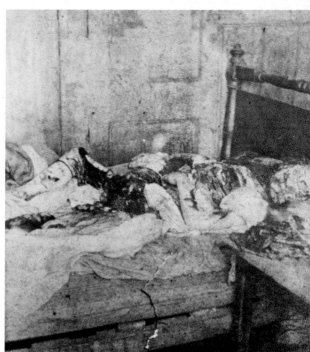

18. *Right:* Mary Kelly.

IS HE THE MURDERER?

Sketch taken from George Hutchinson's description of the last person seen with Mary Kelly.

20. Lord Randolph Churchill.

21. The Duke of Connaught, Edward Prince of Wales and the Duke of Clarence wearing their Masonic regalia.

22. J.K. Stephen.

23. Alice Margaret Crook, by Sir William Orpen.

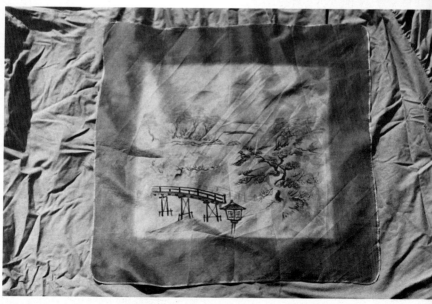

24. Walter Sickert's scarf, which inspired his Camden Town Murder series.

Queen Alexandra's ostrich-feather fan and 'Prince of Wales' hat decoration.

The Duke of Clarence's sketchbook and the purse he gave to Alice Crook.

27. The Duke of Clarence in 1910, aged 46, eighteen years after his official death in 1892.

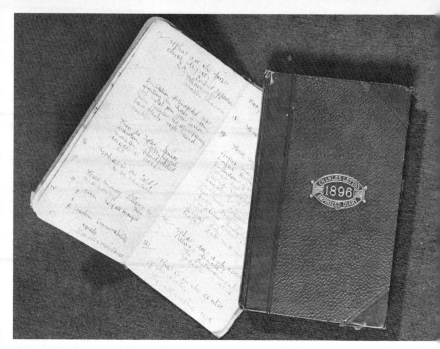

28. Inspector Abberline's 1896 diary and notes on Freemasonry.

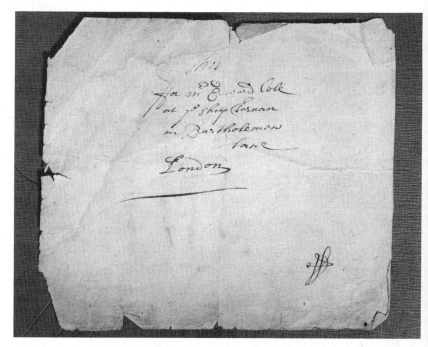

29. A 300-year-old piece of paper found in Mary Kelly's room.

Grand Duke Nicholas, later Tsar Nicholas II, and the Duke of York, later George V.

Crossword with a hidden Masonic message.

Poet who swam the Dardanelles (5).

Artist who founded the Camden Town group (7).

Relationship of Pantagruel to Gargantua (3).

Wading birds with long elastic bills (7).

Orchestra Barbirolli conducted (5).

French name of the chief port of Belgium (6).

Town associated with shoe-manufacturing and B B C radio (8).

Insect in the stage between larva and imago (4).

Surname of the author of: "Trilby" (2, 7).

DOWN

Ursa Major (5, 4).

Small African buck whose (Dutch) name relates to its habit of plunging into the bush (6, 3).

First Christian martyr in England (5).

King of Jordan (7).

American vagrant (4).

What word is missing from the brackets?
ASTER (STAR)
GREBE (BERG)
ABBEY (----) (4).

God worshipped by the Philistines (9).

King, grandson of Alfred the Great (9).

Morse distress signal (3).

9. Creased (8).
10. Small (6).
13. Fatigued (5).
14. Wickerwork boat (7).
15. Inn room (3).
16. Snake, commonly (7).
17. Crucifix (5).
21. Impede (6).
22. Liqueur (8).
23. Inflamed swelling (4).
24. Explain clearly (9).

4. Tall building (5).
5. Flier (7).
6. Forgery (4).
7. Raced (4).
11. Musical instrument (9).
12. Unhurried (9).
14. Vehicle (3).
15. Overdue (7).
18. Swindler (5).
19. Son of Adam (4).
20. Record (4).

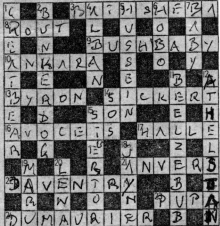

YESTERDAY'S CROSSWORD SOLUTION

ACROSS.—6, Launching-pad; 8, Fuss-pot; 9, Lilac; 10, Junk; 12, Strain; 14, Apply; 15, Cheese; 16, Aida; 19, Extra; 21, Tornado; 22, Mollycoddle;

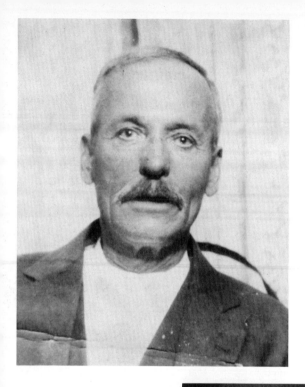

32. George Hutchinson (18
1938), who gave the pol
a detailed description
the last person se
entering Mary Kelly's ro
(p. 179). This photogra₁
the only one in existen
is published here for ₁
first time.

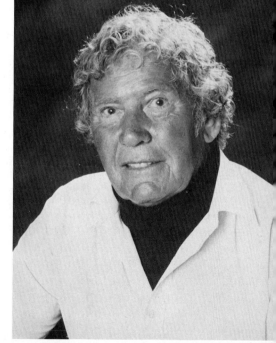

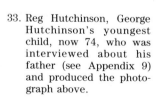

33. Reg Hutchinson, George
Hutchinson's youngest
child, now 74, who was
interviewed about his
father (see Appendix 9)
and produced the photo-
graph above.

The two locked diaries were written between 1892 and 1915, and the second locked diary repeats the names revealed in the 1896 diary.

As we saw in Chapter 2, Inspector Abberline was brought into the Ripper enquiry after the first murder, the murder of Polly Nichols in Bucks Row. He did not lead the investigation. It was led by Detective Chief Inspector Swanson. He was brought in because of his invaluable experience gained over thirteen years in the East End. At the time of the murders he was with the Central Office of Scotland Yard, but having previously been the head of Whitechapel CID he had an intimate knowledge of the East End and its criminals. It was his job to co-ordinate the enquiry at ground level. According to Melville Macnaghten, writing in 1914, Abberline 'knew the East End of London as few men have known it ...'.[1]

In the 1988 television series starring Michael Caine as Abberline the writer/director David Wicks chose to portray Abberline as an East Ender brought up in Whitechapel, and Caine played the part with a cockney accent, though Abberline came from Dorset. This was the least of the programme's inaccuracies, however, for there were slurs on his character. In one of the opening scenes he was shown waking up with a hangover in a police cell, surrounded by half-empty whisky bottles. Throughout the programme he was shown struggling with a 'drink problem'. Then it was hinted that he had an affair with a woman named Emma Prentice – an odious touch since Emma happened to be the name of his second wife. (His first wife, Martha, died of consumption at 25 in 1868, two months after their honeymoon. He married Emma Beament eight years later.)

Frederick George Abberline was born 8 January 1843 at Blandford Forum in Dorset, not far from Bournemouth, where he and Emma eventually retired. He joined the Metropolitan Police on 5 January 1863, three days before his twentieth birthday, rising to Sergeant on 19 August 1865 and to Inspector eight years later. His diaries show his London address in 1892, when he retired from the force, as 41 Mayflower Road, Clapham, SW.

Although he wrote some unpublished memoirs – what he called his 'reminiscences' – they contain nothing about the murders or the Cleveland Street scandal, and the existence of diaries had never been suspected. Indeed such a treasure trove of inside information about the Ripper murders was more than any criminologist could have hoped for. I should add that the handwriting in the diaries is the same as that in the reminiscences known definitely to be written by him.

Abberline reveals that before the murders in 1888 he was taken out of Whitechapel and given a special assignment in the West End. In an undated entry in the first of the two locked diaries he stated:

> Saw Walter with E in Spitalfields, Feb 1887. I asked why they were there, but E told me to mind my own business. I reported this. Told to keep an eye on E and Capt G. H. Later transferred to A Div.

E is of course Eddy. Capt G. H. can only be Captain George Holford, a friend of Eddy's who was to become his Equerry-in-Waiting (and later Edward VII's). Eddy was still in the 10th Hussars but often returned to London at weekends. Walter told Joseph that Eddy and Capt. Holford had been painting the town a lurid shade of red, and that those who considered it their prerogative to look after the Royal Family's public image thought it prudent to have them watched. Eddy was regarded as the future King and they needed to know at Court of any trouble or scandal he might land himself in. Abberline told Walter that his duties had included attendance on the young Prince whenever he was in London. The real nature of his job – that of guardian and watchdog – was kept from Eddy, who was simply informed that he was an unofficial bodyguard.

*

Walter told Joseph that Eddy met Annie Crook for the first time in 1883 or 1884. He was introduced to her not by Walter Sickert, as was stated by Stephen Knight, but by Eddy's Cambridge tutor, J.K. Stephen. Annie Crook and James Stephen were related by marriage. Annie's mother, Sarah Annie Crook, whose maiden name was Dryden, married William Crook, whose mother was a Stephen. In fact she was a sister of James Stephen's grandfather. J. K. Stephen and Annie Crook were therefore second cousins.

Sarah and William Crook had four children, but only two survived: Annie Elizabeth and Alice. Annie later named Joseph's mother after her sister, who was born on 10 May 1868, three years after Annie. Unlike Annie, who suffered a terrible fate at the hands of wicked men which ultimately led to her premature death in 1920, sister Alice lived to 93, dying in 1961. She married Alfred John Richard Jackson, the grand-nephew of John Jackson MD, who was the father of Julia Jackson, the second wife of J.K. Stephen's uncle, Leslie Stephen, and the mother of Virginia Woolf. Annie Crook was therefore related to J. K. Stephen in two ways.

Virginia Woolf, incidentally, wrote a pamphlet *Walter Sickert: a Conversation*, published in 1934. According to Joseph's mother she called Walter a 'cradle snatcher' because he was 45 and she only 20 when their first son, Charles, was born.

Annie's sister, Alice Jackson, had ten children, of whom only two are alive today: Florence Edith and Ellen May. (Ethel Brown, who took Joseph to the orphanage in Mill Hill, was their sister.)

I recently met Ellen, Joseph's first cousin, who told me the following:

> My name is Ellen May Lackner, and my grandparents were Sarah Annie Crook and William Crook.
> I was told – I forget who told me, it must have been my mother or my

eldest sister – that Sarah Annie Crook, my grandmother, whose maiden name was Dryden, was born in Oban in Argyleshire, Scotland. I was told that she left Edinburgh in 1851 to come to England to visit the Great Exhibition. She was 18. She lived for a time with relatives in their bakery business in Nassau Street, near Cleveland Street. [According to the 1851 census there was a bakery at No. 12 Nassau Street, which in 1851 was the business of John Fletcher and his family. One of his bakers who lived on the premises was William Ramsey who, according to the census return, was born in Scotland.]

She was treated like an unpaid servant and so found employment in domestic service which gave her wages as well as food and a roof over her head. My grandfather, William Crook, dined at her employer's house, saw her and fell in love. His guardian, Uncle Ned Stephen, threatened to disown him if he persisted in the romance. This is just what did happen. Before doing so he set him up in a workshop in Rathbone Place, with tools, a bench, plus a boy as an apprentice. He worked as a cabinet-maker making pianos.

Four daughters were born to William and Sarah but only two survived: Annie Elizabeth, my auntie, and her sister Alice, my mother.

My mother was born on 10 May 1868. I never knew her sister Annie's birthday but I believe she was three years older.

Mother died aged 93 in 1961, and she remembered a lot that happened to her sister Annie, and Annie's daughter Alice – my cousin. My father was Alfred Richard Jackson. His brother William was murdered in America, but I know nothing about that except that his body was found in the river. Another of the Jacksons had a newsagent's shop in Phoenix Street.

The Jacksons were all involved with church work, being bell-ringers at St Anne's Church, Soho Square.

My father's grandfather was a well-known London figure, referred to as 'the old patriarch'. He was left behind by mistake after a church outing and not missed until everyone had arrived home. He died from exposure by the River Lea. L-e-a or L-e-e, I've forgotten which. Or at a place called Lee, I'm not sure. My father was six years old when it happened.

My father had been taught tailoring by nuns at St Joseph's Roman Catholic School in Macklin Street, Holborn, but fell on hard times when his small business failed. After some heavy snow falls men were taken on to clear the snow and Father was kept on and put in charge of stores. I believe he became head of the refuse collection service for the whole of Holborn.

Going back to William Crook, my mother said he was educated at Eton with two of his cousins named Stephen. He wanted to be a boat-builder but this went against the grain at Eton and he left when he was only 15. Apparently he had relatives living in Windsor, St Albans and Devizes. Other family names I can remember were Turner and Quartermain.

I also have a vague recollection that my grandmother, Sarah Crook, apart from a brother called Walter, had a sister who married a man named Protheroe who was something to do with the police.

On one occasion my grandfather William Crook visited the Stephen family. He was let in and asked to wait in the hall. On the wall was a painting. My grandfather pointed to it and said. 'That's my cousin.' That's all I know about that. I was never told who the cousin was. Whoever let them in – a servant, I suppose – came back and said that the family weren't at home. They wouldn't see him, you see. Grandfather had taken with him my father, Alfred Jackson, and my mother and my eldest sister, who was a newborn baby, their first child. Grandfather Crook thought the baby would bring about a reconciliation between him and the Stephens. Perhaps it did eventually, because when Grandad died two years later the Stephen family solicitor settled the funeral bill. I can remember the name of a solicitor – De la Rue – but I can't remember whether it was this particular solicitor. There was a definite decline in my grandfather's fortunes after the Stephens rejected him for marrying Sarah. I was told by my mother that one day when he was getting dressed up for something and was wearing a 'dickie' [a false shirt-front worn under a dinner-jacket] made of paper instead of laundered linen, he looked down at it and said, 'What would my people say if they could see me now?' And then he cried.

William made a piece of furniture for a relative called Lady Turner* and he'd promised to deliver it by a certain date, but that day he couldn't find anyone and decided to take it himself using a hand-cart. Well, he slipped and broke his leg and he was taken to the Middlesex Hospital by the end of Cleveland Street.

I remember talking to my mother and eldest sister. We were discussing my cousin, Alice Margaret Crook, and I said, 'Fancy that, you'd think she'd be a bit artistic since her father was Walter Sickert.' You see, as a teenager I understood that Annie Crook had had a deep love affair with an artist named Walter Sickert which resulted in my cousin Alice Margaret. My mother said, 'No that's not correct at all. It was nothing to do with the artist.'

'Why have we always been led to understood that then?' I asked.

She said it was a cover-up.

'A cover-up for what?'

'Her father was a member of the Royal Family.'

'Who?'

'We don't want to speak about it.'

And that was that. She told me that Sickert was well up with the Royal Family and their friends who, to conceal the truth, pretended he was Alice's father.

Another little item I remember – Sickert used Grandfather Crook's hand as a model in one of his paintings.

My eldest sister, Alice Elizabeth, was only four years younger than Alice Margaret Crook and was familiar with most events in her life. She said that Alice Margaret had a sad life and sometimes slept on a cart in Covent Garden, but the police had been told not to move her on but to leave her alone. She said Alice Margaret – considering who she was – really roughed it.

My mother was terrified of having Alice Crook in her house because of her association with Jack the Ripper, but she would never tell us anything more about it. Also, she always refused to have her photograph taken. She didn't want anyone seeing it and realising that she was related to Alice. Do you know, I don't even have one photograph of my own mother. I once drew her but she was offended and I tore it up.

To get my mother out of danger during the Ripper affair my grandfather, William Crook, got two lady friends to give her a home.

When I questioned my father about my grandmother, Sarah Crook, I

* 'Lady Turner' (Mary Anne, Lady Page-Turner), who ordered furniture from William Crook, was the wife of Sir Edward Page-Turner. Sir Edward died without issue and was succeeded by his cousin, Sir Henry Leigh Dryden.

asked if she was nice.

'She was a Tartar,' he said.

My brother Charles said that Sarah was over six feet tall, which was very tall for a woman, especially in those days.

My mother also told me that one day she was with her sister Annie and their mother Sarah, standing in a garden. A lady arrived in a carriage. It was Uncle Ned Stephen's wife, and she offered to take Annie and have her educated properly. Sarah ordered her away but my mother never knew why. William later told Sarah: 'You did a very foolish thing, because by taking Annie away they would have eventually taken her daughter Alice, who never would have suffered as she did.'

William Crook died on 4 December 1891 in St Pancras Infirmary. His death was registered by his widow Sarah, who gave his address as 9 Pancras Street.

At this point in Ellen's narrative I asked her if she had ever met Sarah Crook:

No, I never set eyes on her, as I remember. But I've been sitting here thinking about all this over the weekend and I remember this. We lived in Kenton Street and I remember standing outside the house with my sister Florence. I was about 6 or 7 and she was three years and ten months older than me. And there was this funeral that came to the house. I think they brought the coffin, so presumably the body hadn't lain indoors, and there were no flowers. My sister was very emotional. She was only a young girl and she started crying. I said, 'Why are you crying? You don't know her.' But she said, 'She's our grandmother.' It was Sarah Crook.

I next asked her if she had ever met Annie Elizabeth Crook:

Yes, I visited her once in hospital, with my mother, but I don't remember Annie at all. I can only remember the hospital. My sister said my mother only used to visit Aunt Annie on high-days and holidays. It wasn't out of affection of one sister for another, it was just somewhere to go on bank-holidays.

I also remember my mother saying that Annie was once arrested for attacking a man with a bottle, and she was put in prison. In fact she was in a solicitor's office at the time of the attack, and he came forward and she was set free.

Clearly everything Ellen said corroborated Joseph's understanding of his own background, as well as that of his mother Alice and grandmother Annie Crook. I noticed that Ellen spoke certain words with a Scottish accent. She had been born and brought up in London but picked up the accent from her mother, who was also born in London. It will be remembered that Walter told Joseph that Eddy was attracted to Annie partly because of her Scottish brogue, which gave an edge to her diction so that he could hear what she said despite his deafness. The two daughters of Sarah Crook, Annie and Alice, grew up hearing their mother's brogue. So great was its influence that it had filtered down to Sarah's grandchildren. I was glad I had met Ellen because she had provided independent testimony confirming Joseph's.

*

To return to J.K. Stephen, in recent years much has been made of his supposed hatred of women, particularly whores, and after reading some of his more infamous poetry published by his detractors in recent years, notably Michael Harrison in *Clarence*, his biography of Prince Albert Victor, it is difficult to deny the charge of misogyny. One poem goes:

> If all the harm that women have done
> Were put in a bundle and rolled into one,
> Earth would not hold it,
> The sky could not enfold it...

and

> But if all the harm that's been done by men
> Were doubled and doubled and doubled again,
> And melted and fused into vapour and then
> Were squared and raised to the power of ten,
> There wouldn't be nearly enough, not near,
> To keep a small girl for the tenth of a year.[2]

Another ends:

> I do not want to see that girl again:
> I did not like her: and I should not mind
> If she were done away with, killed or ploughed.
> She did not serve a useful end:
> And certainly was not beautiful.[3]

The following poem, however, may show otherwise. It concerns an occasion in July 1882 when Stephen was in a railway carriage in Belgium. He was rudely awoken by a fellow passenger who accidentally stood on his foot.

> Oh mayst thou suffer tortures without end:
> May fiends with glowing pincers rend thy brain,
> And beetles batten on thy blackened face!

This shows that he was just as capable of unspeakable thoughts against men as against women, and perhaps exemplifies nothing more than a lively black humour, as Martin Howells and Keith Skinner have suggested.[4]

Joseph believes that James Stephen was in love with Eddy. There is no reference in Abberline's diary to a homosexual affair between them, but Joseph thinks that Stephen, knowing that Eddy had been drawn into a homosexual milieu introduced him to Annie Crook to divert him. According to Joseph, Stephen could handle the thought of Eddy with a woman, but became jealous if he was with other men and hoped that a relationship with Annie would serve to exclude them. He also saw that Annie was the image of Eddy's mother, Alexandra, to whom Eddy was deeply attached, and that this alone might attract Eddy to her.

*

Abberline recorded another interesting fact. In his earliest diary, written in 1892, he stated that after Mary Kelly's death in November 1888, her landlord, John McCarthy, received a postcard sent from Scotland. Abberline wrote:

> J McCarthy received anonymous card from Scotland. It said, Now we've done the fourth one, we shall go for the mother and daughter.

McCarthy handed it to the police, but until now no mention has ever been made of this anonymous communication. Abberline discovered that Sir William Gull had a house at Killiecrankie, thirty-two miles from Perth, and that he was there when the postcard was sent. He believed it was Gull who sent it. He told Walter Sickert as much. The wording, it may be thought – with expressions such as 'we've done' and 'we shall go for' – hardly seems of a quality to be expected from one of the country's leading physicians. Perhaps Abberline inaccurately recorded the words from memory. Or, if they are accurately recorded, Gull may have adopted the style on purpose to make it appear the work of someone from the lower classes.

Knight saw the card during his researches, when the Home Secretary, Roy Jenkins, allowed him to see the Scotland Yard and Home Office files. Knight told Joseph and Harry Jonas that he had seen the card and that he believed it referred to Annie and Alice Crook. Yet for some reason he never mentioned it in his book. He may have told Scotland Yard what he thought, hoping they could help him by applying their trained police skills to the questions it posed. If Scotland Yard officials realised the import of the discovery, it may explain why the card disappeared. Wherever it is now it is not in the files, having been removed at some point since Knight saw it. The files, which have been open to the public at the Public Record Office at Kew since 1985, now contain little of value. Many other items went missing after Knight saw them. He was not allowed to remove any himself or even to make photo-copies, but his original hand-written copies of the documents now missing are to be found among his papers in the possession of Paul Begg, who had permission to use them for his recent book *An A – Z of Jack the Ripper*.

Abberline believed that the purpose of the postcard was to announce the intended murder of Annie and Alice Crook. But that is not the only information it reveals. The reference to 'the fourth one', rather than the fifth – since there were five victims – supports the contention that the death of Catherine Eddowes was not counted by the murderers as one of their masonic series. As I have explained, Eddowes was killed by mistake, because she gave the name Mary Kelly to the police when she was taken drunk to Bishopsgate Police Station. In the 1970s Scotland Yard did not know that Joseph had Abberline's diaries. They therefore had no reason to suspect the existence of an independent record of the postcard and believed they could destroy or hide it without fear of discovery.

*

Eddy may or may not have approved of the murder of the five women, but he definitely knew who was responsible for them. Since he wished to preserve the monarchy, and because he was a Freemason, he was pledged to uphold and conceal the action of his 'brothers', especially as he had passed through the Holy Royal Arch. But the threat to his wife and daughter was too much for him, and his loyalty evaporated when he learned of their plans.

When the schism in the Ripper group occurred Eddy was not alone. Loyally at his side was J.K. Stephen. It was due to his love for Eddy and his loyalty to his Royal Alpha brothers that he had become involved in the murderous conspiracy in the first place, but now he too found his loyalty under strain. It was Lord Randolph's feverish mind which formulated the plan to kill Annie and Alice. This was too much for Stephen. His love for Eddy and his regard for Eddy's feelings towards his wife and daughter overcame his loyalty to the brotherhood. Nor did he wish to be involved in the plot to kill two of his own relations, one of whom, Annie, he knew quite well.

Realising that he had to do something before Lord Randolph put the plan into action, Stephen told Inspector Abberline the truth about the Ripper murders and their connection with Freemasonry. Abberline spent time researching Freemasonry and the backgrounds of all the people involved in the murders, both perpetrators and victims, discovering things about both which no one else knew and which later formed the basis of the entries in his three diaries.

Nor did the Prime Minister, Lord Salisbury, have any relish for the murder of Annie and her child. He was also distantly related to Annie

Crook. One of his forbears, the 2nd Earl, had married the youngest daughter of the 1st Earl of Suffolk, the son of the 4th Duke of Norfolk. Norfolk's great-great-granddaughter, Elizabeth Howard, was the wife of the poet Dryden, who was an ancestor of Annie Crook. As can be seen from her sister Alice's birth certificate, their mother had been born Sarah Annie Dryden. Lord Salisbury, who knew all the Ripper gang, and Annie Crook, around whom the Ripper plot revolved, were both descended from the 4th Duke of Norfolk.

So far we have seen that two members involved in the Ripper conspiracy, Lord Salisbury and J.K. Stephen, were related to Annie Crook. They were not the only ones. As we have noted, James Stephen's uncle, Leslie, married Julia Jackson, daughter of John Jackson M.D., whose niece, Isabel, Julia's cousin, married Lord Henry Somerset, an elder brother of Lord Arthur Somerset who absconded to France during the Cleveland Street scandal and was also a member of the Ripper coterie. Lord Arthur was therefore also distantly related to Annie Crook.

But the family web is even more tangled.

Reading the entry in the *Dictionary of National Biography* for Major-General Sir Charles Warren (1766-1838), father of General Sir Charles Warren, the Metropolitan Police Commissioner who organised the cover-up during the enquiry, I noticed to my astonishment that the Commissioner's grandmother was called Elizabeth Crook. I asked Joseph if he knew of any relationship between his family and Warren's.

'Yes,' he replied. 'My father always said that the whole thing was one big family affair.' It was at this point that he first informed me that he was a descendant of Dryden.

Dryden was born in 1631 in the reign of Charles I. His father was Erasmus Dryden, his mother Mary, daughter of the Rev. Henry Pickering. Both the Pickerings and the Drydens took the Parliamentary side in the Civil War. We may therefore assume that the Drydens were Puritans. In fact Dryden's first cousin, Sir Gilbert Pickering, was one of the judges at the trial of Charles I in 1649.

When Dryden began his writing career he was a member of the Church of England, and in various works, notably his *Religio Laici* written in 1682, he defended the Anglican Church and satirised the Catholics. In 1672 Charles II had issued a Declaration of Indulgence, giving his subjects religious liberty, but next year this was set aside by Parliament, who passed the Test Act, ordering every office-holder to take the Sacrament according to the Church of England. It was aimed mainly at Catholics and remained in force until it was repealed in 1828. Charles II died in 1685, having become a Catholic on his death-bed. His brother, the Duke of York, who openly professed the Catholic faith, succeeded him as James II, and that year Dryden converted to the religion of his new king. After his appointment as Poet Laureate, he wrote another verse essay poking fun at the Church of England.

James II replaced Anglican churchmen with Romanists and finally issued, without Parliament's consent, a new Declaration of Indulgence. This was similar to the one issued by Charles II giving complete religious liberty to his subjects. It was followed by another a year later, which had the merit of trying to set aside the Test Act and other measures passed after the Restoration oppressing Roman Catholics and Dissenters. Unfortunately these measures were never put in force. The leaders of both Parliamentary parties combined to call in James's Protestant brother-in-law, William of Orange, who landed at Torbay on 5 November 1688 – exactly two hundred years before the Ripper murders. James fled the country, taking refuge with Louis XIV. William of Orange and his wife, Mary, ruled jointly and were styled 'King and Queen of England, Scotland, France and Ireland'. Ireland, which was mainly Roman Catholic, became James's base for further struggle, but he was routed at the Battle of the Boyne on 1 July 1690.

Dryden was now ousted as Poet Laureate, and the ludicrous Shadwell was installed in his place. Though most of his family remained Protestant, Dryden's sons were faithful to Rome. His second son, John, was placed in the care of the Roman Catholic ex-Master of University College, Oxford, Obadiah Walker. His third son, Erasmus, became a Dominican priest, and his eldest son, Charles, was appointed Chamberlain to Pope Innocent XII.

I have included all this as background to Joseph Sickert's claim that the two lines of descent to Annie Crook and Sir Charles Warren converge at some point within the Dryden family tree, with Warren on the Anglican side and Annie on the Catholic. According to Joseph, his father had said on more than one occasion that the Ripper murders only happened 'because you're all bloody Catholics'.

The name Warren has been associated with Joseph's family also in another way. The cottage in which Joseph grew up, behind No. 195 Drummond Street, along with the two houses on either side, Nos 193 and 197, was owned by Leonard Warren. He was an old man when Joseph was a boy, but Joseph remembers that his son sometimes visited him and his mother. The property had ceased to be a working farm in the nineteenth century, but was still known by its original name, William's Farm, when it was demolished more than thirty years ago. I asked Joseph if he knew of any relationship between Leonard Warren and Sir Charles Warren, but he admitted frankly: 'I think he was a distant cousin of mine, and that's how my mother came to rent the place, but I don't know if he was related to Charles Warren.'

*

Inspector Abberline discovered that, when Lord Randolph Churchill revealed his plan to have Annie and Alice Crook murdered, Eddy was horrified and decided on a counterplan of his own. Unfortunately Eddy's plan, like Randolph's, exhibited a touch of melodrama, as well as a lack of mental stability. Eddy announced that it was his grandmother, Queen Victoria, who should be murdered!

Both his parents, but especially, as we have seen, Alexandra, had instilled in Eddy a hatred of everything German, and he came to regard Victoria as the embodiment of Germany. Alexandra's parents were King and Queen of Denmark, and two of the Danish duchies, Schleswig and Holstein, though not part of Denmark proper, had dominated German politics. War against Denmark in 1850 was declared nominally by the German Bund, but in reality was waged by Prussia, aided by other German States. Alexandra hated the Prussians, who at this time were contending with Austria for German leadership. In 1864, after a short war, Schleswig-Holstein was taken from Denmark by Prussia and Austria. After the inevitable squabbles, resulting in the Seven Weeks War, Austria renounced it, and it was annexed to Prussia. Alexandra was crestfallen and passed many a sleepless night worrying about her parents' problems.

Meanwhile her husband Bertie was indiscreetly heaping abuse upon the arrogant Prussians. Alexandra's hatred became obsessive and profoundly personal, and she thereafter did everything she could to snub members of the Prussian Royal Family, encouraging her relations and those around her to do the same. In 1867 she refused to meet the King of Prussia at Wiesbaden, claiming that she was too ill. Her attendance at a funeral there, however, proves that it was a rebuff. Queen Victoria had been pro-German on the Schleswig-Holstein question, and the snub made her 'extremely angry'. Victoria's father was a Hanoverian, Hanover being a province of Prussia. Moreover her mother was Mary of Saxe-Coberg-Gotha, a former German state, while her husband had been Prince Albert of Saxe-Coberg-Gotha. Her daughter Victoria, the Princess Royal, became the Crown Princess and Empress of Germany and the mother of Kaiser Wilhelm, against whom Britain fought the First World War. Queen Victoria had been born in London, but everything else about her was German. Her love of everything that was German was in inverse proportion to Princess Alexandra's hatred. Since Alexandra exerted a great influence over Eddy, he was bound to emulate her obsessive hatred of Germans in general and Prussians in particular. Abberline came to believe that his hatred of Germany was later extended to hatred of his grandmother, Queen Victoria.

The Prince of Wales considered Eddy a complete numbskull. Like others around Eddy he failed to realise how much his ability to learn or concentrate was due to his deafness. He condemned his elder son absolutely. Joseph, however, feels that there was another reason why he hated Eddy. His real hatred was of John Brown, but he expressed his feelings against Eddy, using him as a whipping boy.

John Brown was Queen Victoria's faithful Highland servant, or gillie.

There is evidence that Victoria used John Brown as a spirit medium to gain contact with her dead husband, Prince Albert.[5] After Albert's death in 1861, she came to rely upon Brown for a variety of purposes. He became a combination of groom, footman, attendant and companion. They were rumoured to be lovers. In high society Victoria was nicknamed 'Mrs Brown', a sobriquet once shouted at her in public. Disraeli, aware of how besotted she had become with Brown, regularly asked after Brown in his letters.[6]

One of the Prince of Wales's lovers, the famous courtesan Catherine Walters, known as 'Skittles', told another of her lovers, Wilfred Scawen Blunt, everything she knew of the affair betweeen Brown and Victoria. Blunt confided the information to his diary which was not opened until 1972. He claimed that Brown had a bedroom next to Victoria's, and that the household staff called Brown 'the Queen's Stallion'. He also learned that after Prince Albert's death Victoria imagined that his spirit had passed into Brown. He was convinced by what he saw of Brown's familiarities with the Queen that she allowed him 'every conjugal privilege'.[7] There was some suggestion that they had secretly married and had a child which was sent to live in France (a story remarkably parallel to that of Eddy and Annie, whose daughter Alice was sent to Dieppe). The *Lausanne Gazette* even dared to print the rumour as fact.[8]

In 1979 several newspapers reported that Dr Michael McDonald had evidence, in the form of a death-bed statement made by a minister of the Church of Scotland, that Queen Victoria had indeed had a child by John Brown. Death-bed statements must be taken seriously. The claim was later amplified by 79-year-old John Stuart, who had been a clerk at Coutts, bankers to the Royal Family for several generations.[9] Stuart said that he had been required to read certain letters from one Louise Brown in Paris. His curiosity aroused, he delved into one of the Royal accounts and discovered that every quarter £250 was paid to Louise Brown and debited to an account marked 'His Royal Highness Prince Albert Edward Prince of Wales'. Stuart first thought that Louise Brown must have been the Prince's illegitimate daughter, until he read other letters from her which referred to the Prince as 'dear generous Bertie' and mentioned the all-too-infrequent visits of 'dear Beatrice', Bertie's favourite sister. Since Louise Brown addressed Bertie and Beatrice in the same manner, using the term 'dear', there is the underlying inference that she regarded them as equals to one another, as well as equal to herself. Had Bertie been her father, as Stuart originally suspected, Louise would surely have adopted a different attitude to Bertie from Beatrice. Louise's surname and the fact that she lived in France support the theory that John Brown was her father, and also the rumour, strongly held in some quarters, that Victoria had a child by him who was sent to France.

There are two reasons why Queen Victoria might have chosen to sleep with her servant. The first is that, despite the belief popularly held today that she was a prude, she enjoyed sex. Her husband, Prince Albert, held the narrow view that sex was solely for procreation, and Victoria had noticed that he was always more relaxed when she was pregnant. Apparently Albert found the sexual act distasteful, and once his 'duty' in that direction had borne fruit he was able to enjoy the nine months respite afforded him. During the intervals between her pregnancies Victoria became bad-tempered, and she was often to be found knocking on her husband's locked bedroom door. After the birth of her daughter Beatrice she was told by her doctor that she was to have no more children and she asked him, 'Oh, doctor, can I have no more fun in bed?'[10]

The second, less obvious reason why she chose a servant as a lover was that she had little choice. It was an age when a woman's virtue or, more accurately, the preservation of its public image, was of paramount importance. The Queen of England could hardly have an affair with one of her courtiers or dignitaries without other courtiers knowing. Her lover would risk being frequently seen by the palace staff entering and leaving her bedchamber, and all kinds of official duties would have to be invented to explain his presence. A trusted servant would have reason to be on hand, and his presence in the palace would not arouse suspicion. The rumour that she had a lover did eventually surface, and it would surely have surfaced sooner if she had chosen a more 'suitable' lover from among her courtiers.

In 1872 a Fenian, Arthur O'Connor, pointed a pistol at the Queen outside Buckingham Palace. John Brown, without demur, leapt from the carriage and seized him by the throat. Not long afterwards the Queen established a gold 'Victoria Faithful Service Medal' to be awarded for 'any special act of devotion to the Sovereign'. It was awarded to John Brown. None has been awarded since.

Brown died in 1883. Next year Victoria threatened to publish a memoir of him, but was strenuously dissuaded by the Dean of Windsor, Randall Davidson, who even offered to resign over the issue.

Robert Wilson, in his exhaustive biography of Victoria, claimed that Brown's private papers which were left when he died, and which might have shed light on his relationship with Victoria, were impounded by Sir Henry Ponsonby acting on the Queen's behalf.[11]

The Queen treasured the presents given her by Brown, and she always ate her breakfast egg from the seaside souvenir egg-cup he gave her. Among the strict instructions she left regarding her burial was that a number of objects should be placed in her coffin to console her in her after-life – a concept worthy of Ancient Egypt. Two of the last items to be put there were a photograph of John Brown and – that most hackneyed 'Victorian' symbol of romance – a lock of his hair.

After her funeral the Prince of Wales took a delight in destroying the many statuettes and mementoes of John Brown scattered round the various royal residences. Many of them he smashed himself. If he detested the memory of John Brown, there had been little he could do to assuage his anger without incurring the royal wrath. J. K. Stephen, as we have noted, told Inspector Abberline that Bertie had turned instead to Eddy, magnifying the irritation he felt towards him and using him as a scapegoat. Being meek as well as deaf, Eddy was an ideal victim.

By the autumn of 1888 Brown had been dead five years and Victoria had become the personification of all that Eddy detested, not only for her affair with Brown, but because she represented all that Eddy's mother had taught him to hate: Germany.

In answer to Lord Randolph Churchill's latest idea to have Annie and Alice Crook murdered, Eddy's tortured mind formulated the madcap scheme of having his grandmother murdered. Apart from his mother, brother and three sisters, Eddy cherished Annie and his daughter Alice above anyone. Lord Randolph cherished the Establishment. A scion of a noble family who had been surrounded with all the trappings of wealth since birth, he was the embodiment of the ruling class and a fervent monarchist who had already had five women murdered in order to protect the monarchy and the established order which underpinned it. When he revealed his plan to kill Annie and Alice he did not count on Stephen's devotion to Eddy. He certainly never expected him to run to Inspector Abberline and tell him who was responsible for the Whitechapel murders. Stephen knew that Abberline got on well with Eddy, and also that he had developed a fatherly regard for Annie Crook, even to the extent of telling her off for allowing Mary Kelly to take Alice into the East End, where she met her cronies. According to Abberline, Stephen told him that it was he who informed Eddy of Lord Randolph's plan to murder Annie and Alice, and Eddy made the counter-suggestion that Victoria should be the one killed. When Lord Randolph heard this he asked, according to Abberline: 'Who? The great whore herself?'

*

Abberline realised that he had to be cautious, because his superior officers, Warren and Anderson, were involved in the murders and, like Churchill, were high-ranking Freemasons. One point should be made clear. Warren and Anderson did not involve themselves directly in the actual killings, though Anderson was more closely involved in the whole operation than Warren. As I showed in Chapter 4, Anderson was employed in helping to locate the victims. That he did not himself wield a knife, and was not present in the East End when the murders were committed, hardly reduces his guilt. Warren may have vacillated. He may have been drawn into an intrigue which prudence and discretion told him to avoid. That he helped in the police cover-up there can be no doubt. As we have noted, he hid facts from the Press and destroyed forensic evidence.

On two separate occasions Abberline told Walter that he feared for his own life. Twice he was called to a house where a crime was supposed to have been committed, and both times he suspected, rightly or wrongly, that if he had gone there his life would have been in danger. This was in 1892, just before the Ripper file was officially closed. He told the head of his department, Robert Anderson, that he had taken the precaution of putting down in writing all that he knew about the murders, keeping the document in a secret place with instructions that it was to be made public in the event of his sudden death. That document was the first of the three diaries. It was begun early in 1892, after Stephen's death in a lunatic asylum in Northampton. (It is astonishing how many people connected with the Ripper story ended up, or are reported to have ended up, insane.) While he was in the asylum, Stephen was told of Eddy's death on 14 January.* From that day on, it was said, he refused all food, dying on 3 February. Abberline retired from the police force four days later.

Eddy's 'death' had been a shock to Abberline, and when he heard that Stephen had also died soon after he came to believe that Stephen had been silenced for breaking his masonic oath in telling the truth behind the murders. He did not then know that Eddy was not dead, but he heard the rumours, widely circulated at the time, that after his death his hands and feet had turned black, which suggested poisoning.[12]

Before Stephen gave him details of the murders Abberline had already become aware of aristocratic involvement. His presence as Eddy's unofficial body-guard and his resulting proximity to Annie Crook and Walter Sickert had made him aware of the special circumstances in which Eddy and Annie found themselves. He knew about Annie's pregnancy almost as soon as she knew herself, and he knew who Alice's father was before she was born. Nor did he fail to observe the arrival, from the East End, of the nanny, Mary Kelly.

Sickert told him of the abduction of Annie from Cleveland Street and the stage-managed brawl which distracted onlookers away from Annie as she was bundled into Netley's coach (see above, p. 9).

*

When Mary Kelly's body was found, Abberline realised, even before her room was entered, that there was a connection between her death, and the deaths of the other four women, and Annie Crook. When the room was finally forced open by the police at 1.30 in the afternoon of 9 November, Abberline was one of the first into the charnel house, and he discovered something which has never been reported before – a piece of paper. It

* On the page from the 1896 diary, which Abberline said should be kept apart, and which he dated 1903, he mistakenly put Eddy's death as the 16th instead of the 14th.

contained a name and an address on both sides. Between Abberline's death and Walter's death only Joseph had ever seen it. Since Walter's death in 1942 only Joseph and his mother have known of it. On one side of the yellowing scrap is written:

> This
> for Mr. Edward Cole
> at Ye Ship Tarvan
> in Bartholomew
> Lane
> London
> J F [possibly I F]

On the reverse it says:

> This
> for Mr Edward Cole in
> Bartholomew Lane
> (an illegible word)
> op Ent London

Scotland Yard must have sent it to a handwriting expert, because Abberline told Walter that the writing dated to about 1690. When I took it to the Manuscript Section of the British Museum I was told by a curator that it was late-seventeenth-century.

I can think of no reason why Mary Kelly, who occasionally turned to prostitution in order to eat, and who turned to drink in order to drown the terrors of poverty, would possess an address on a piece of paper two hundred years old. Equally unlikely is that it was dropped by one of her paying customers who, in the main, would have been ordinary East Enders with little opportunity of possessing an antique document. On the other hand it might have been dropped accidentally by one of the murderers. Abberline claimed that there were three men in the room at Millers Court to kill Mary Kelly. He wrote:

J.K. said the three men in room 13, were L.R.C. – W.W.G and – J.C.N.

L.R.C. was Lord Randolph Churchill, the leader. W.W.G. was William Withey Gull, who performed the actual murder and mutilations. J.C.N. was John Charles Netley, the coach-driver. Three men were present, like the three apprentices who in the masonic legend murdered Hiram Abif. Since aristocrats like Churchill had access to private libraries and family archives, Abberline presumed that the paper was dropped by him.

At first I could find no significance in either the name or the address on that paper. It was months later, when I was reading about London coffee houses, that I stumbled across information which seemed pertinent. There were two separate Ship Taverns in Bartholomew Lane, which today runs up the eastern side of the Bank of England. One was in Threadneedle Street but had an entrance on the west side of Bartholomew Lane and was usually described as 'behind the Royal Exchange'. The second is the one we are interested in. It stood in the middle of the east side of Bartholomew Lane. Its site was later called Ship Court, and later still Capel Court, which still exists. The Ship Tavern began life as an eating house, later becoming a tavern and later still a coffee house.

Coffee houses sprang up all over London in the 1650s. Their customers formed themselves into coteries. Lloyd's, the insurance institution, grew out of just such a coffee house. So great was the political influence of coffee houses that Charles II tried to suppress them. In 1668 Samuel Pepys prepared a dinner party at the Bartholomew Lane Ship Tavern.

Another coffee house in Bartholomew Lane in the years 1702-14 was Coles, or Wat Coles. It is not unlikely therefore that the Edward Cole addressed on the paper found by Abberline was in some way related to the Wat Cole of the tavern of that name, since the establishments were almost next door to one another. Since Edward Cole is not referred to as 'care of the Ship Tavern', or 'staying at the Ship Tavern', we may safely assume that Edward Cole was the proprietor. Significantly for us the Ship Tavern was used for masonic lodge meetings up to 1724.

In John Wilson Croker's 1831 edition of *Boswell's Life of Johnson* (p.308) we are told that the landlord of another meeting place for Freemasons, The Mitre Tavern in Fleet Street, was also named Cole. A possible descendant of any one of these, a certain G. Cole, is listed in 1838 directories as the proprietor of another Cole's Coffee House at 11, Bedford Court, Covent Garden. Yet another was listed from 1702 until 1833 at No. 1, Ball Court, Birchin Lane, Cornhill.[13]

Without having to look very far we have found five Coles who kept taverns, two of which were definitely used for masonic meetings. It seems likely that the Coles were Freemasons who, in the late seventeenth and early eighteenth centuries, specialised in tavern-keeping throughout London – the sons learning their trade from their fathers, as was the custom of the day.

There is a historical connection between Lord Randolph Churchill's family and the name Cole, though the Cole in question is hardly a tavern-keeper. In 1780 William Cole (1753-1806) was appointed tutor to George, Marquess of Blandford, the son of the 4th Duke of Marlborough, to whom he became chaplain. In 1792 he was installed prebendary of Westminster and he was eventually buried in Westminster Abbey. Of course we have no way of knowing whether or not William Cole was related to the Edward Cole on the paper found by Abberline, but if he was, any Blenheim Palace archive material about him or his family was

'The Reward of
Cruelty'. Woodcut by
John Bell after
Hogarth

'Cruelty in Perfection'.
Woodcut by John Bell
after Hogarth

(see above, p. 68)

accessible to Lord Randolph. The foregoing makes it all the more intriguing that this interesting piece of paper was discovered in Kelly's room.

*

Abberline also wrote of finding papers in Millers Court linking Mary Kelly with Cleveland Street. In particular he cites a letter from the Bellord Domestic Agency which was instrumental in getting Mary Kelly a position with 'a west-end family in Cleveland Street'. Edmond Bellord, a solicitor, was a partner in a firm of estate agents in Cleveland Street, Perkins and Bellord. He was asked by Walter Sickert to find a young woman to fill the shop vacancy at 22 Cleveland Street, where Annie Crook worked (above, p. 10).The letter was sent to Kelly where she was staying in the East End – the Providence Row Women's Refuge, of which Edmund Bellord was a founder and committee member.

*

Other revelations in one of Abberline's diaries unravel two previously unexplained mysteries: the locked door of Kelly's room and the fierce fire in her grate. The door to 13 Millers Court could not be entered until it was broken open by the landlord, John McCarthy. Why not? The bolt could easily have been drawn, as Kelly had drawn it after she lost the key – by reaching through the broken window pane. Abberline reveals the answer:

> The door was blocked by a heavy washstand with a marble top.

This, the heaviest piece of furniture in the room, was not mentioned by anyone at the time – neither by the police nor by journalists clamouring for every detail.

By this late stage the Press, as they well knew, were clearly being denied information by the police. After the Mitre Square atrocity the *Yorkshire Post* of 1 October reported that 'the police apparently have strict orders to close all channels of information to members of the press'. On the same day the *New York Times* was more specific, claiming that the police 'devote their entire energies to preventing the press from getting at the facts. They deny to reporters a sight of the scene or bodies, and give them no information whatever.'

Sir Charles Warren, in an apparent attempt to show that police secrecy was necessary to help capture the murderer, admitted the following to the Guardians of Whitechapel.

> It is most important that our proceedings should not be published and the very fact that you are unaware of what the detective department is doing is only the strongest proof that it is doing its work with secrecy and efficiency.

That the police should deny the press a sight of the bodies was not unreasonable. They might have kept certain facts secret, which only they and the murderer would know. This too was not unreasonable. But to 'devote their entire energies to preventing the press from getting at the facts', and to 'give them no information whatever', was not only unreasonable but unusual, and served no useful purpose in the hunt for the murderer. It helps to explain why no newspaper reported the marble-topped washstand which barred the door to Kelly's room. It also explains why other information reported in Abberline's diary is found in no contemporary news account.

Most contemporary reports state that there were two tables in Kelly's room. One even mentions a third table standing between the bedhead and the wall; yet it is not shown in the photograph, where the wall behind can clearly be seen. One of the tables, the one piled with Kelly's flesh, can be seen beside her bed. The photograph is rather indistinct; but what is clear is that the table has no table-cloth upon it, and yet the table top is white, like marble. The structure of the leg and the stretcher, which can just be seen, suggests a table rather than a Victorian washstand. Washstands usually have turned or carved legs, rather than square tapered ones like those in the photograph. Stands with square tapered legs do not have a front stretcher, which would inconvenience anyone leaning over a wash bowl. Nevertheless a table with a marble top, of the kind employed in kitchens, would have been an ideal subtitute for a washstand upon which to place a washbowl and a pitcher of water, and such tables were frequently used for that purpose.

When Dr Phillips entered Kelly's room the door knocked against the table in the photograph. It has often been described as a bedside table, for no reason except that it was beside the bed. Lack of space in the twelve-foot-square room is also suggested as the reason why the door struck the table.

I recently drew a scale diagram of Kelly's room and its contents. Allowing for the apparent foot of space between the bed and the far wall, and assuming the bed to be a standard 5' 6'' wide double, which it appears to be, and allowing 2' 6'' for the width of a standard door, and about 2' from the door to the outside wall which can be seen in the photograph taken outside, I worked out that only about a foot was left between the bed and the door. The table in the photograph, however, seems much longer – two feet at least – and the nearest edge goes out of the picture. It would appear therefore that the table is much larger than a bedside table. I suggest that this is Abberline's marble-topped 'washstand' used to block the door.

Since the door could not be locked in the ordinary way, as there was no key available, the furniture against the door could only have been put there to stop anyone entering while the murder and mutilations were taking place. The murderers then left though the window, leaving the door blocked to any visitors arriving the following day. There is no other explanation.

The first police to arrive, when they could not open the door because of the table, must have assumed that the door was locked. Abberline, however, categorically stated at the inquest that the door was not locked. Breaking it down must therefore have been an unnecessary mistake.

Kelly's body might have remained undiscovered for days had it not been for the persistence of a rent-collector. A fierce fire, hot enough to melt the spout of Kelly's kettle, had burned in the grate, and many authors have concluded that it was lit to illuminate the gory work in hand. Abberline discovered from James Stephen that the three men present in Millers Court – Gull, Netley and Lord Randolph – removed their clothes so as not to get them covered in blood. Contemporary news reports state that Kelly's entrails festooned the picture rail, hanging like sausages in a butcher's shop, with lumps of flesh hanging from nails where once pictures had graced the walls. In his port-mortem report, however, (above p. 46) Bond stated that 'the intestines [were] by the right side & the spleen by the laft side of the body. The flaps removed from the abdomen and thighs were on a table'; also that 'the right wall by the bed & and in line with the neck was marked by blood which had struck it in a number of splashes'. Obviously the murderers could not avoid being splashed with blood and washed down afterwards, the water mingling with the blood on the floor. The November night was cold and windy with intermittent sleet and snow, and the fire was lit. Abberline claimed that, when the Assistant Commissioner, Robert Anderson, entered the room he slipped on the floor, which was slick with the mixture of blood and water.

PC Walter Dew (later to achieve fame as the officer who arrested Dr Crippen) was on duty in Millers Court the day Kelly's body was found. He too claimed to have slipped on what he described as the 'awfulness' on the floor of Kelly' room. He would not have slipped if there had been only blood on the floor. They entered the room about eleven hours after the murder, by which time the blood would have congealed and dried out, especially as the room must have been warm for some time, both during and after the murder, owing to the presence of the 'fierce' fire. The water mingling with the blood on the floor obviously delayed the process, leaving the floor slippery.

Another fact not mentioned at the inquest was reported by Abberline:

> The kidneys and other parts were picked up with a fork, the marks could be seen in the flesh.

When Abberline gave Walter the diaries and the piece of paper found in Kelly's room, he mentioned that one of the murderers, to keep the blood from his hands, had picked up parts of the body which had been removed, using a fork found in the room. The prongs left distinct marks in those portions of flesh found on the table beside the bed.

It is difficult to believe that Abberline found the letter from the Bellord Domestic Agency and the paper addressed to Edward Cole without the knowledge of the other officers who went with him into Millers Court. Obviously some of the police officers or, at the very least, the senior officers who were in the court, knew that entry to Kelly's room was barred by a marble-topped washstand, or table. Since we know that the existence of the washstand did not become public knowledge, we can assume that the papers mentioned by Abberline were also known to the other officers who entered Kelly's room but, like the washstand, were kept secret. I believe that Abberline removed them from the file before it was closed so that he would have something to bargain with. With these important pieces of evidence in his possession, he could say to those in the conspiracy, 'Leave me alone, because if you don't I shall expose you through the evidence I have.' With this parting shot across their bows he retired from the police force, and that year the Ripper file was officially closed for a century.

*

Abberline also discovered that Kelly had two children. This was merely hinted at during Kelly's inquest, and it has been treated as rumour by those who have studied the Ripper case. According to Abberline's diary:

> The youngest child was adopted and the other sent to Canada by the convent.

Abberline did not name the convent, but we may confidently assume that it was the Providence Row Night Refuge, Crispin Street & Raven Row, where Kelly had been recruited for the job in Cleveland Street. Curiously, when I first examined the official Ripper file several years ago I discovered among the documents an envelope containing two identical posters. Printed in red ink using wooden blocks, these late-nineteenth-century posters advertised six 'NIGHT REFUGES' for 'THE DESERVING HOUSELESS POOR'. The first one listed is 'THE PROVIDENCE ROW NIGHT REFUGE, Crispin Street & Raven Row'.

I know of no reason why the posters should be in the file unless they had, in the minds of those investigating the murders, some connection with the murders themselves. Only Abberline's diary makes known what that connection is.

Apart from naming the Ripper coterie, Abberline also gave background details of the victims (Appendix 7) – details which, until now, were not known. A few of his findings actually contradict some of the details given in contemporary newspaper accounts and at the inquests. These are mostly minor details, it is true, such as the birth dates of the victims and information about their parents and brothers and sisters – where they were brought up, whom they married, which church they were married in and so on – but they serve to demonstrate the accuracy of the diaries as well as Abberline's skill in uncovering the truth.

Abberline realised that some of the facts he had discovered were particularly significant, and that they supported what he had already been told by J.K. Stephen: for instance, that Mary Jane Kelly was the intended last victim and that Catherine Eddowes was killed in mistake for her. When he investigated Eddowes's background he discovered that she did not know any of the other victims. He stated categorically:

No connection with any of the others.

That very statement implies that he had discovered that the remaining victims did know one another and were connected in some way, thus confirming one detail of another of Stephen's claims: namely, that four of the victims – Nichols, Chapman, Stride and Kelly – had been working together in a blackmail attempt.

Contemporary newspaper reports and witnesses' statements at Eddowes's inquest stated that two pawn tickets were found in a mustard tin by the body. One was for a flannel shirt in the name of Emily Birrell. In the last few days before her death Eddowes had worked with Birrell in the hop fields of Kent, and since she was returning to London and Birrell was not Birrell gave her the pawn ticket. The second ticket, variously reported as having been in the name 'Anne Kelly' or 'Jane Kelly', was for a pair of men's boots. We have already noted that when Eddowes was taken drunk to Bishopsgate Police Station she gave the name Mary Anne Kelly (some reports say Kate Kelly) because she lived with a man called John Kelly, to whom the pawned boots belonged. Abberline's diary notes about Eddowes, however, claim a slightly different name on the pawn ticket. He wrote:

Pawn ticket in the name M.J. Kelly.

In an interview with *The Star* reported in the *Yorkshire Post* of 4 October 1888 John Kelly stated that Eddowes had pawned the boots in the name 'Jane Kelly'.

Used together, the initials M for Mary Kelly, the name Eddowes assumed, and J for Jane Kelly, the name John Kelly reported, form the initials of the final Ripper victim: Mary Jane Kelly.

When Eddowes was asked her name by the pawnbroker, Mr Smith, Church Street, Spitalfields, she may have first intended merely to say 'M. Kelly', the name she had lately assumed, but as the pawnbroker began writing the initial 'M' she may have decided to add the initial J for John, since the shirt was in fact John Kelly's. Either way the name sealed her fate. Because the Ripper gang were looking for someone called Mary Jane Kelly, killing Eddowes would be an easy mistake to make.

The pawn ticket was evidence and would normally have been clipped to the file on the case. The first person other than a police officer to see the

Home Office files was Stephen Knight in 1974. He made no mention of it, and we can assume that it was removed from the file by Abberline before it was closed in 1892.

Walter Sickert described Robert Anderson, the Assistant Metropolitan Police Commissioner, as 'the look-out man' whose job it was to ascertain the whereabouts of the intended victims. Clearly, then, he must have primed certain police officers in the East End to report back to him any information they had, or might come across, of a woman named Mary Jane Kelly. That no policeman mentioned this to the press after Mary Kelly was discovered in Millers Court, when the significance of the pawn ticket must have become apparent, was just another aspect of the conspiracy of silence the Press complained of.

In Abberline's diary notes about Annie Chapman he shows that she was from a respectable family, and that her father was George Smith who at the time of his marriage to Annie's mother was a private in the Life Guards stationed at Knightsbridge. Abberline added: 'The Smiths' children were all well educated.'

The diary states that before her marriage Annie Chapman called herself Eliza Ann Smith, and that the Smith family lived at eminently more respectable addresses than did Annie during the last twenty-one months of her life, after her husband, John Chapman, died on Christmas day 1886. According to Abberline's notes, the Smiths lived variously at: Montpellier Place, Knightsbridge; Rutland Terrace, Knightsbridge; Albany Street, Regent's Park; and Middle Row North, Knightsbridge. There were also periods spent at Windsor when, presumably, Annie's father was on duty at Windsor Castle. Their address there was 12 Keppel Terrace. Annie married John Chapman, a coachman in Windsor who was two and a half years younger than she and related to her mother, whose maiden name was Ruth Chapman. They also lived for a while at 1 Bruton Mews, Bayswater. There was another London address mentioned. At the end of his section on Chapman Abberline observed:

> Her address in 17, Bruton Mews was only 3/5 min round the corner from 74, Brook Street, Sir William Gull.

74 Brook Street was Sir William Gull's address from the mid 1870s, and although Abberline had noted that the Smith family lived at Bruton Mews in 1873, fifteen years before the Ripper murders, and could therefore have had no particular significance, quite clearly he could not divorce from his mind Gull's connection with the death of Annie Chapman and the other Ripper murders.

*

Abberline gave the dates of birth of all the Ripper victims, and for nearly every one he differs from contemporary accounts. Most writers, for instance, claim that Annie Chapman was 45. Abberline stated in his diary that she was born in June 1841, and when I checked the General Register of Births I found he was correct. Chapman was actually 47. Most writers have stated that Catherine Eddowes was 43. Abberline states 46. Again I checked with the birth records and found he was correct. Abberline also gave the dates of the victims' marriages, plus those of their parents. In every case his diary seems to be correct. It thus proves to be an extremely accurate document.

At the end of his notes about the first Ripper victim, Mary Anne Nichols, Abberline claimed that she:

Was a friend of Emma Smith.

Emma Smith has sometimes been regarded as the first of the Ripper victims, a claim generally dismissed in recent years because her killer's modus operandi was markedly different from that in the other murders; the main difference being that no attempt was made to cut her throat.

After J.K. Stephen's death, following two-and-a-half months in a mental asylum, Abberline could act only on information he already had. He may have thought it prudent to begin at the bottom of the ladder and, on learning of John Netley's involvement, he immediately tried to find him. He discovered that Netley lived at the Lisson Grove end of Bell Street. He lived with friends who were in some way connected with his line of work – coachmen, cab drivers, harness-makers – whose living and business quarters were concentrated in that area. Bell Street was also close to Netley's employers, Thompson and McKay & Co., who had a depot at the Great Central Railway Station, Marylebone.

After finding his home address and making enquiries of his family, Abberline obtained a photograph of Netley from his sister. He next visited Annie Crook to ask if she could recognise the man in the picture. She was in hospital, and the authorities there would not allow him to see her. But they did show Annie the photograph, which was returned to him with the words 'I do not no him' written on the photograph in pencil above Netley's head. The writing shows that Annie was not illiterate as Stephen Knight and others have believed. On the other hand the misspelling of 'no' for 'know' and the scratchy uncertain writing may suggest that her mental state was confused. Abberline gave the photograph to Walter Sickert along with his diaries. It is reproduced here for the first time and is the only photograph known of Netley.

Either Annie could not recognise Netley from the photograph or she had not actually met this man who had driven Eddy to meet her in Cleveland Street. After alighting from the coach Eddy would enter Annie's home and the coach would probably be driven to the nearest trough, where the horses could be watered. Meanwhile Netley could repair to a tea-stall until the prearranged hour when he was to return to collect his royal charge. If Annie opened her door to Netley he would no

18 MONDAY [139—227]

1 Q Jan 1892 ?
         H.R.H. Duke of Clarence

3rd. Feb 1892
    J. the Steven.   (4)

19 TUESDAY [140—226]

Sir William Gull 1892 (2)

Rt Hon Lord Randolph Spencer (1)
                    Churchill.

~~John Kitty 1892~~ Brown

20 WEDNESDAY [141—225]
☽ First Quarter, 6.21 a.m.

believe to have drown (7)

Sir Charles Gull 29 Jan 1890
    H.R.H. Duke Clarence   BB
        16 Jan 1892 ?
    J.K. Steven 3rd Feb. 1892   Beg
    Lord Spencer Randolph Church   SS

96

30 Days.   NOVEMBER, 1896.   NOV. 23 to 29.

26 THURSDAY [331—35]

J. K. Stevens 1892

3rd Feb 1892

14 Jan 1895   Butcher Baker
Candle Stick maker
Lord Randolph Spencer
Churchill   1895

27 FRIDAY [332—34]

H.R.H. Duke of Clarence.
Tinker Tailor Soldier Sailor 1892

Netley
Reverse old.

Sir William W. Gull

Pages from Abberline's diary listing the names of HRH Duke of Clarence, Sir William Gull, Lord Randolph Churchill, John Netley (crossed out) and J.K. Stephen.

doubt have been wearing a hat, the normal street attire of those who worked in the open air, such as coachmen. The studio photograph shows Netley without a hat, making it less easy for Annie to recognise him from it. It must also be remembered that by this time she had undergone surgery by Sir William Gull which had left her partially paralysed and affected her memory.

Netley learned that Abberline was looking for him and decided to disappear. The best way to disappear, he reasoned, was to die, and the best way to die was to fake it. He may have thought that Abberline was working for Lord Randolph or some other person in his masonic entourage who, he thought, had already silenced Prince Eddy and James Stephen. Less than a month after the announcement of Eddy's death, and three days after Stephen's death on 3 February 1892, he made his second attempt to run Alice down. This was two months before her seventh birthday. Walter Sickert later learned that Netley ran away from the scene to escape from passers-by who were angry with him for what had happened. He ran down to the Thames, threw himself in and apparently drowned. Unknown to Sickert at the time, he did not drown but was fished out and taken to Westminster Hospital where he gave his name as Nickley, a name Stephen Knight established as belonging to no one born between 1857 and 1878. On 7 February 1892 the incident was reported in the *Observer*:

> Shortly before one o'clock yesterday, [there was an] attempted suicide from Westminster Pier. A respectably dressed young man took off his boots and coat and hid them under a seat in a waiting room, jumped off the pier and swam a few yards. Rescued by Mr Douglas, Pier Master, but struggled. Taken to Westminster Hospital. Gave name of Nickley, but refused his address.

Anyone seriously intending to commit suicide by drowning would hardly take off his coat and boots. Heavy Victorian boots would help a drowning man to sink, if drowning was what he really intended. By removing his boots and coat Netley hoped to make it easier to swim away. The *Observer* specifically noted that he 'swam a few yards'. Perhaps he meant to hide beneath the pier so that onlookers would believe him drowned. He could retrieve his hidden clothing later and make off, lying low for a few days until Abberline learned he was dead and called off the search. Obviously Netley was in desperate fear of his life to throw himself into the fast-flowing Thames at the beginning of February.

*

That Alice was run down by a coach has been confirmed by Jean Overton Fuller. Florence Pash was there when it happened.

Alice told Joseph that she was with a lady friend of Walter's when it occurred, but she omitted to mention her name. It was Pash, who mistakenly thought that the murder attempt was against herself, not Alice:

> She had not witnessed the murders, which took place in the East End. But an attempt had been made on her own life, in broad daylight, near Charing Cross. Coming from St Martin's Lane ...
>
> On Trafalgar Square, then, in front of St Martin's-in-the Fields. Not in front of the church. Where it broadens out at the junction with the Strand, near Charing Cross. They were making for the station. She had been taking a little girl out for a walk and meant to take her back to her place for tea. They were stepping off the curb when a coach came straight at them. Florence had jumped back on to the pavement and tried to lift the child back on to it but the coach mounted the pavement and the child was hit by the wheel, and had to be taken to hospital. Florence felt dreadful having to go back, alone, and tell Sickert the child he had confided to her care had been injured and was in hospital. He had been very nice about it and told her not to blame herself. He said he was sure it was a case of attempted murder!
>
> Florence had been very specific about the location because, while she had not seen the murders in Whitechapel, this was one thing to which she had been witness, and the details were etched into her mind as though it had happened yesterday.
>
> Probably she accepted what Sickert told her about it because it was part of the whole situation. She had always been told an illegitimate child for the heir to the throne could be a target, and this seemed to prove it. It enforced her conviction she must never speak of it to anyone.[14]

When she did speak of it, to Violet Fuller, Violet Fuller told her daughter Jean: 'She says she could even be bringing me into danger by telling me, which I find hard to believe.'[15]

Florence Pash thought that the murder attempt was against her because she knew about Alice's Royal father.

It should be noted that the streets from the junction with the Strand where the coach incident occurred – Craven Street, Northumberland Street and Northumberland Avenue – lead directly to the Embankment and Westminster Pier where Netley threw himself into the Thames.

Some years later Alice was shown the photograph of Netley, and a few years later still she recognised him when she happened to pass him in the street. Netley did not recognise her because she had blossomed into a young woman of 18. Later that year Netley was murdered.

The *Marylebone Mercury* and *West London Gazette* of 26 September 1903 reported that John Netley, aged 43, had been thrown from his seat while driving his coach along Park Road and had been kicked in the head by one of his own horses. When Dr Norris arrived he was already dead.

The Coroner, George Danford Thomas, held an inquest on 23 September and recorded that Netley suffered a 'fracture of skull and other injuries' after a 'fall from his van under the wheel of it colliding with rest in roadway'. The jury returned a verdict of accidental death.

That Netley was thought by Walter Sickert and Abberline to have drowned, despite the *Observer* report that he was saved, which neither can have read, is confirmed by Abberline's diary. Abberline only discovered that Netley had not drowned when he learned of Netley's actual death in 1903. In the page of his 1896 diary, on which he wrote 'to be kept apart', he wrote: 'John Netley 1903.' The name is crossed through and underneath is written:

drown

believe to have drowned.

Abberline, in the pages of his last diary completed in 1915 when he was 72, maintained that Netley was murdered. In an entry dated 12 November 1903, he wrote:

J.C. Netley murdered under his own coach. Payment for Alice?

Netley had apparently died in the same manner in which he had twice attemped to kill Alice Crook: by being run down by a coach – his own. As a further example of the Freemasons' evil sense of humour, Netley had been found dead at an entrance to Regents Park, the name of which linked him with Prince Eddy: Clarence Gate.

*

Joseph always maintained that there had been two attempts by Netley on his mother's life. This was later confirmed by his cousin Ellen Lackner who had already given me a good deal of information about Sarah and William Crook (above, pp. 148ff). This is what she told me:

It must have been after Grandfather Crook [William] passed away that things went badly wrong for Grandmother Crook [Sarah] and the little Alice Margaret who lived with her. I don't know if he was still alive when the first attempt was made on her life, but I think he must have been, as she was only four. After the first time, she was left blind for four years. The second time she was about eight. The coach ran her down and the crowd chased the driver because they saw that it was deliberate.

Joseph had told me that the first time his mother was run down it was at the height of the Ripper murders when she was three – not four as Ellen stated. In fact she was 3½, so the discrepancy is small. The second time, as Ellen Lackner stated, was 'about four years later': that is, two months before Alice's seventh birthday.

Walter told Joseph that Netley was killed by another member of the

Ripper gang, whom I have not so far named, Frederico Albericci, an Italian-American noted as a pickpocket: a profession that earned him the nickname 'Fingers Freddie'. In the early 1880s Fingers Freddie had worked as a footman for Sir William Gull and was known to Gull's household as Frederick. Was he the man of 'shabby genteel' appearance who looked like 'a foreigner' seen by Elizabeth Long talking to Annie Chapman, an hour before Chapman was found dead (above, p. 26)?

Early in April 1888 Netley and Frederico Albericci had together murdered Emma Smith, the woman stated by Abberline to have been a friend of Mary Anne Nichols, the first Ripper victim. In their search for the intended victims they questioned Emma Smith and learned that she was a friend of Mary Anne Nichols, and that she also knew Annie Chapman. Emma became aware that Netley and Fingers Freddie were up to something sinister, and from that moment she refused to help them further. The two men, realising that she presented a danger, first threatened her and then beat her up. This was done so brutally that she died from her injuries. Something other than a knife, perhaps a bottle or a stick, was pushed into her vagina with such ferocity that it tore the perineum. She staggered home using her shawl to stem the blood and was taken to the London Hospital in Whitechapel Road, where she died the following day from peritonitis. While she was feverish she claimed that she had been attacked by three, perhaps four, men. But Abberline believed that there was no one apart from Netley and Albericci present at the attack, though he acknowledged that they were working for Lord Randolph. He wrote nothing in his diary about this murder except to say that Emma Smith knew Nichols and Chapman. His views on it were given verbally to Walter Sickert who told Joseph and Alice. Emma Smith was attacked on 3 April 1888, almost five months before the Ripper murders proper began. Though it was not one of the official ritualistic murders ordered by the masonic masters, it was nevertheless committed in their interests.

*

As we have noted, one of the notebooks was written by John Netley. In 1973 an article appeared in Joseph's local newspaper announcing Stephen Knight's forthcoming *Jack the Ripper: the Final Solution* based on information he had been given by Joseph. Netley's name was mentioned and was recognised by Percy Philip Sutton, the nephew of John Philip Sutton who was the husband of Netley's sister and the landlord of The Gibraltar. Percy Sutton got in touch with Joseph through the newspaper. He was in possession of Netley's notebook and had read the contents. As it was of no use to him, he gave it to Joseph to substantiate his claims. Some months later Joseph was told that he had been knocked down and killed on the London-to-Brighton Road.

Netley's book is not a diary as such, but a notebook recording his work as a coachman: a job-book listing the names of his private passengers. It also records destinations and the amount charged for each journey. There is no direct reference to the Ripper murders, but among the names listed as regular passengers are several of the Ripper gang: Lord Randolph Churchill, Sir William Gull, J.K. Stephen, Lord Euston and Lord Arthur Somerset. It records that he often picked up Prince Albert Victor, and took him to Cleveland Street. (The full address there is not stated.) It also names Fingers Freddy, who is called 'American Freddy'. His full name, according to the notebook, was Frederico Bruno Albericci.

The Ripper victims were last seen alive in the company of various men. Chapman was seen with 'a foreigner' and Stride with a short man with a dark moustache and sandy eyelashes wearing a billycock hat (bowler-hat). Stride was later seen being thrown to the ground by a short man with broad shoulders. He must have been the murderer, because she was found dead at the exact spot a few minutes later. According to *The Times* of 2 October, Eddowes was seen with a man 'of shabby appearance, about 30 years of age and 5ft 9in in height, of fair complexion, having a small fair moustache, and wearing a red handkerchief and a cap with a peak'. The Home Office file states that he was wearing a 'reddish handkerchief tied in a knot round the neck'. Kelly was observed in the company of a stout man with a blotchy face. Not long before the estimated time of her death she was seen going into her room with a man dressed like an aristocrat. The only explanation of these different descriptions is that more than one man was involved in the murders. Abberline's list, which included Netley, Albericci, Randolph, Gull and others, supports this explanation.

*

At the start of the inquest on Mary Kelly – which took place at Shoreditch Town Hall on 12 November, before the Coroner for North East Middlesex, Dr Roderick MacDonald – there was a sudden hitch. A juryman observed: 'I do not see why we should have the inquest thrown on our shoulders when the murder did not happen in our district, but in Whitechapel.'

The Coroner's Officer, Mr Hammond, replied: 'It did not happen in Whitechapel.'

The Coroner pompously interposed: 'Do you think that we do not know what we are doing here?'

When the dissident juryman persisted, MacDonald told him: 'It happened in my district.'

He omitted to say that the police ought to have taken Kelly's body to the mortuary in the district in which she had died. Their purpose was to make sure that the inquest was not held before the Coroner for the South Eastern Division, Wynne Edwin Baxter. Baxter had presided over the inquests of Nichols, Chapman and Stride and had asked too many searching questions, the sort of questions which those involved in the cover-up wished to avoid in Kelly's case. The police had clearly been ordered to take Kelly's body into MacDonald's district so that he could make sure that any evidence leading to the actual murderer would remain uncovered. This he did, and, after stating that 'there is other evidence which I do not propose to call, for if we at once make public every fact brought forward in connection with this terrible murder the ends of justice might be retarded', he closed the inquest the same day. Normally an inquest of this kind would have taken two, perhaps three, days, as was remarked on by several newspapers. By closing the inquest prematurely MacDonald had prevented George Hutchinson from being called to give evidence. Hutchinson was a vital witness.

Hutchinson's testimony was given in his signed statement to Abberline, who considered it 'important'. The statement, which can be seen in the Metropolitan Police file on the case, runs as follows:

About 2 a.m. 9th I was coming by Thrawl Street, Commercial Street, and just before I got to Flower and Dean Street, I met the murdered woman Kelly and she said to me, Hutchinson will you lend me sixpence. I said I can't I have spent all my money going down to Romford, she said good morning I must go and get some money. She went away toward Thrawl Street. A man coming in the opposite direction to Kelly tapped her on the shoulder and said something to her, they both burst out laughing. I heard her say alright to him and the man said you will be alright for what I have told you. He then placed his right hand around her shoulders. He also had a kind of small parcel in his left hand with a kind of strap round it. I stood against the lamp of the Queen's Head Public House and watched him. They both then came past me and the man hung down his head with his hat over his eyes. I stooped down and looked him in the face. He looked at me stern. They both went into Dorset Street I followed them. They both stood at the corner of the court for about 3 minutes. He said something to her. She said alright my dear come along you will be comfortable. He then placed his arm on her shoulder and [she] gave him a kiss. She said she had lost her handkerchief. He then pulled his handkerchief a red one out and gave it to her. They both went up the Court together. I then went to the court to see if I could see them but could not. I stood there for about three quarters of an hour to see if they came out. They did not so I went away.

Circulated to A.S. [All Stations]

Description, age about 34 or 35, height 5ft 6, complexion pale. Dark eyes and eye lashes. Slight moustache curled up each end and dark hair. Very surly looking. Dress, long dark coat, collar and cuffs trimmed astrakan and a dark jacket under, light waistcoat, dark trousers, dark felt hat turned down in the middle, button boots and gaiters with white buttons, wore a very thick gold chain with linen collar, black tie with horse shoe pin, respectable appearance, walked very sharp, Jewish appearance. Can be identified.

George Hutchinson.

Lord Randolph was 39 rather than 35, but otherwise Hutchinson had given an almost perfect description of him. Even Randolph's dark bulging eyes might suggest that he was foreign-looking, and photographs of him do give the impression of someone surly. Plate 20 shows how close in appearance he was to the description. (See Appendix 9.)

*

The last person seen with both Kelly and Catherine Eddowes was observed to have a red handkerchief. It is established that Walter Sickert connected a red handkerchief with the Ripper murders. Marjorie Lilly, who knew Sickert from 1911 and remained his close friend until his death in 1942, wrote as follows:

> He had two fervent crazes at the moment, crime and the princes of the Church; crime personified by Jack the Ripper, the Church by Anthony Trollope. Thus, we had the robber's lair, illumined solely by the bull's-eye lantern; when he was reading Trollope we had the Dean's bedroom, complete with iron bedstead, quilt and bookcase. The ecclesiastical flavour so congenial to him was somewhat marred by the red Bill Sykes handkerchief dangling from the bedpost; but the presence of this incongruous article in the Dean's bedroom was not a passing whim; it was an important factor in the process of creating his picture, a lifeline to guide his train of thought, as necessary as the napkin which Mozart used to fold into points which met each other when he too was composing. Sickert was working now on one of his Camden Town murders and while he was reliving the scene he would assume the part of a ruffian, knotting the handkerchief loosely round his neck, pulling a cap over his eyes and lighting a lantern. Immobile, sunk deep in his chair, lost in the long shadows of that vast room, he would meditate for hours on his problem. When the handkerchief had served its immediate purpose it was tied to any doorknob or peg that came handy to stimulate his imagination further, to keep the pot boiling.[16]

As already noted, Mozart was a Freemason. The folded handkerchief on his piano seems to have served as a ritual object which helped him to compose. A similar process was also clearly at work with Sickert.

The Camden Town murder was an actual murder which took place in 1907. Sickert painted a number of pictures known as the 'The Camden Town Murder' series, later also called 'What Shall We Do For The Rent'. The series presents bedroom scenes with a naked woman lying on a bed. In some a man is seen seated or standing at the end of the bed.

As noted by Marjory Lilly, Sickert constantly had Jack the Ripper in mind when he painted the Camden Town Murder series, when he gained inspiration from his red scarf. All the crimes – the Ripper murders and the Camden Town murder – were unsolved, but it is an interesting fact that Robert Wood, who was tried and acquitted for the Camden Town murder, modelled for Sickert and is the man to be seen in the paintings sitting at the end of the bed. Wood's friends, probably led by Sickert, hired a solicitor, Arthur Newton, to defend him. This was the same Arthur Newton who had conspired with the Government to keep Eddy's name out of the Cleveland Street scandal. He proceeded to specialise in causes célèbres and achieved notoriety in 1910 as the solicitor of Dr Crippen. In 1913 he defended himself at the Old Bailey against a charge of conspiracy to defraud, lost the case and was imprisoned for three years.

The name of the nude model in the Camden Town Murder series was Marie[17] – the name adopted by Mary Kelly after her visit to France. The alternative title to the series, 'What Shall We Do For The Rent', is a reference to the fact that Mary Kelly owed six weeks rent when her body was discovered by the rent collector.

The red handkerchief used by Sickert clearly reminded him of the red handkerchief worn by the last person seen with Catherine Eddowes and the one handed to Kelly by the wealthy-looking man seen by George Hutchinson.

Sickert's handkerchief had been hand-painted by him when he was a pupil of Whistler. Whistler was fascinated by Japanese art and used oriental devices in his work. This Japanese interest inspired Sickert to paint a small silk scarf. It is 2ft foot square and has a hand-stiched border. In the centre is a typical Japanese scene, with a wooden bridge, trees and mountains fading into the distance. This is framed by a 4-inch red border which has faded. Sickert's signature and the date – 82 – can just be discerned in the bottom right of the picture. When folded and worn round the neck it looks like a red handkerchief. Joseph owns it, and it is reproduced here.

*

Written on page 96 of Abberline's 1896 diary – the page designated for November 26th, 27th, 28th and 29th reproduced here – is a strange allegory on two familiar nursery rhymes, which he used to represent the men involved in the Ripper crimes. The first was:

Butcher, Baker, Candlestick Maker.

The 'Butcher' was Gull, who killed and mutilated four of the victims. The 'Baker' was a combination of Warren, Anderson and J.K. Stephen, with their officials. Together they mixed the ingredients of the cover-up, kneading them into a final product. The 'Candlestick Maker' was Lord

Randolph Churchill, the initials C and M standing for Churchill and Marlborough.

In his potted biography of Lord Randolph Frank Harris included the words of a speech he once heard him make. One sentence is particularly interesting to us:

> But my feeling is that this earl or that marquis is much more in sympathy with the working man than the greedy nonconformist *butcher or baker or candlestick maker* (my italics).[18]

Abberline seems to have read of the speech and adopted it for his own use. Harris's account was not published until 1916 when Abberline was 73, but I believe Abberline's diary entry was written later, when he was even older, which would explain the uncertain, scratchy writing and the misspelling of J.K. Stephen's name.

The second rhyme was somewhat more complex:

Tinker, Tailor, Soldier, Sailor, Richman, Poorman, Beggarman, Thief.

'Tinker Tailor Soldier Sailor' represents Eddy, under whose name the words appear. Beneath Abberline has written 'Reverse old'. He must have meant 'Reverse ord', for 'reverse order', but again made a slight error due to old age. In reverse order the words coincide with stages of the Duke's life. He served as a midshipman on HMS *Bacchante* – hence 'Sailor' – before becoming a soldier in his father's Regiment, the 10th Hussars. Later he was known as 'Collar and Cuffs', a reference to his sartorial idiosyncrasies; hence 'Tailor'. Athlone, one of Eddy's three titles, was Irish, which suggested an Irish tinker. The Clarence dukedom was created for Lionel, the second son of Edward III, when he married Lady Clare, heiress to the Earl of Clare, from which it derives (Clare is a town in Suffolk). Abberline may have thought it was Irish because another of Lionel's titles was Earl of Ulster and Clare is also the name of a large western maritime county of Ireland. Avondale is the name of a castle and a parish in Scotland. The 4,000-acre estate in County Wicklow owned by Charles Stewart Parnell, foremost champion of Irish Home Rule, was frequently mentioned in newspaper reports about him in the 1880s and early 1890s, and Abbberline could not have failed to notice its name – Avondale – leading him to think that a title of the same name was Irish.

Abberline was correct, however, regarding the Irish origin of the Athlone title. It was first held by Godard van Reede, a Dutch General in the service of William III who distinguished himself at the battle of Athlone in 1691. Athlone is a market town on the River Shannon, 78 miles west of Dublin.

'Richman' symbolised the aristocrats privy to the Ripper murders, such as Euston and Somerset, 'Poorman' the depressed and derelict areas of

Whitechapel and Spitalfields, where they were committed; the East End has always been the 'poor man' of London. 'Beggarman' was a substitute for 'bagman', an old-fashioned word for a commercial traveller which became synonymous with coach drivers and drivers' mates (as in baggage-van-driver), and represents John Netley. The thief was the pickpocket Frederico Albericci.

*

Abberline seems to have had a penchant for the poetic and allusive. With the three diaries he gave Walter, which were contained in a travelling stationery case, was a book of Vanbrugh's plays: a first edition of the second volume, published in 1719.

As I looked through the yellowing pages I discovered something not even Joseph had noticed. On page 4, in tiny hand-written capital letters, were the words:

JAMES KENNETH STEPHEN   FEB 1892

I showed this to Joseph, but he could not read it until he found a magnifying glass. He was astonished. I continued to leaf through the pages and discovered more hand-written names between the lines of the printed text.

Stephen's name was written at the end of the Prologue to a play called *The Confederacy*. The word could apply to the organisation behind the Ripper murders.

The last line of the Prologue reads:

And walk about the streets —— Equip'd —— as I am now.

This line was used by Abberline to refer to the Ripper gang's perambulations round the streets of the East End, equipped with a coach, a lamp and, of course, knives.

It provides further testimony that J.K. Stephen was involved in the murders. The title page says 'Spoken by a Shabby Poet', a clear reference to Stephen, and by placing his name at the end of the Prologue Abberline made it appear that Stephen was signing his name to it. 'FEB 1892', incidentally, is the month of Stephen's death.

At the end of Act 1, Scene 1 was the name and date:

LORD RANDOLPH SPENCER CHURCHILL
JAN 1895

The words in the First Act appearing immediately before his name include:

for fear she should learn the Airs of a Woman of Quality.

This may have been seen by Abberline as applying to Annie Crook, whom Lord Randolph wanted killed and denied an elevated position as a 'Woman of Quality' through her association with Prince Eddy.

'JAN 1895' was the month of Randolph's death.

Overleaf, on page 16, are the words:

H.R.H. DUKE OF CLARENCE 1892 ? JAN.

This is written under the following words spoken by a woman called Clarissa:

Is it not a most horrible thing that I should be but a Scrivener's wife? ——— Come, ——— don't flatter me, don't you think Nature design'd me for something *plus élevée*?

A 'scrivener' is a scribe who draws up contracts or copies out documents. The words 'plus élevée' mean 'more elevated', 'more eminent', 'more exalted'.

It is difficult to see exactly what Abberline had in mind when he placed the Duke of Clarence's name where we find it, but of course it was hardly easy to find words which exactly fitted his idea, so that some obscurity was inevitable.

In the case of Eddy's name Abberline was drawing our attention to the words 'Nature design'd me for something *"plus élevée"* '. As we shall see, he placed these names after 1903, long after he discovered that Eddy had not died in 1892. Hence the question mark after the 1892 date. A question mark was also placed after Eddy's name and official date of death in the 1903 entry on the page marked 'to be kept apart'.

After his apparent death and the coronation of his brother George, Eddy, as rightful king, might well have pleaded that he was designed for a more eminent position than the one in which he found himself. In short, Eddy was 'design'd', or, as Abberline meant, 'born', to be king.

The next name I discovered was written in by Abberline on page 22. It was beneath a text more easily understood than the previous one. Below the words 'Your Servant, good Madam', spoken by a character called Dick, he had written:

John CHARLES NETLEY SEP 1903

'1903', the year of Netley's death, provides a terminus a quo, a date after which these hand-written entries were added.

As a coachman Netley was at the beck and call of his passengers. He also served his masonic masters, placing the murdered bodies where they were to be discovered. Since the murders were intended to protect the throne, he was indirectly serving Queen Victoria. When he agreed to do it, it was as if he was bowing before her, offering his services with the words, 'Your Servant, good Madam'.

In Act II, in a scene called, 'Mr. Gripe's House', on page 29, Abberline had written the final name:

SIR WILLIAM. W. GULL   JAN 1890

The name is written beneath the words:

Look you there now. [Aside] If she has not already conceiv'd that, as the supreme Blessing of Life.

As a physician, Gull was duty-bound to uphold the Hippocratic Oath, alleviating suffering where he could and saving life – 'the supreme Blessing'. When he killed and mutilated four of the five Ripper victims, he was doing the very opposite. It was no doubt therefore with a sense of irony that Abberline placed Gull's name where he did. The 'she' probably represented Annie Crook who 'conceived ... the supreme Blessing of Life' when she conceived a royal child, her daughter Alice.

Since Abberline here named only four of the Ripper gang, as well as Eddy, around whom the whole drama revolved, we can take it that they were those he held chiefly responsible.

Abberline's father was a saddler, his mother a shopkeeper. With such humble origins he was probably not very well educated. But he must have been intelligent, rising as he did to the office of Chief Inspector at Scotland Yard. From the choice of book in which he placed his five names, we may presume that he had some awareness of literature (as well as a sense of humour).

Sir John Vanbrugh, the author of the plays contained in the book in which the five names are to be found, lived between 1664 and 1726. He first made his name as a dramatist, his best-known plays being *The Relapse* (1696), *The Provok'd Wife* (1697) and *The Confederacy* (1705), which, contrary to prevailing practice, introduced humble characters onto the stage. In later years he changed tack, rising to fame as an architect, Castle Howard (used for the TV series *Brideshead*) being regarded as his finest work. What interests us, and what must have prompted Abberline to use a book by Vanbrugh, is that his largest and grandest mansion, built for John Churchill, the first Duke of Marlborough, was Blenheim Palace, the birthplace of Lord Randolph Churchill.

*

That Abberline continued to follow the lives and careers of these five men can be seen from the diary of 1896, the one which was sealed with wax. Abberline noted in it the anniversary of the deaths of three of them – that is, of all of them except Eddy, who he knew was not dead, and Netley, who did not die till 1903.

On 3 February, on an otherwise blank page, he wrote:

Anniversary of The Death of

This was the date of J. K. Stephen's death, though he left a blank where the name should have been. He followed the same procedure on 26 January, the day of Lord Randolph's death in 1895, and on Wednesday 29 January, the anniversary of the death of Sir William Gull. In each case, for some reason, the name of the person whose anniversary it was was left blank.

*

I wrote in Chapter 6 that the Prince of Wales decided that Prince Eddy was to lose his birthright. This was not a decision he made alone. Among those he consulted, according to Walter Sickert, were Lord Randolph Churchill and his Private Secretary, Sir Francis Knollys, who had been Gentleman Usher to Queen Victoria. It was Knollys who, along with Lord Esher, another of Bertie's confidants, destroyed all Bertie's private letters after his death in 1910. Knollys was not only a Freemason but one of Lord Randolph's closest friends, and had been best man at his wedding in Paris. Bertie had a great deal to hide, and not merely the details of his adulterous diversions. His wife Alexandra also requested that her private archive be destroyed after her death. Among the few letters of hers which survived were those written to Eddy's brother George, but those to Eddy were destroyed. Only the existence of Eddy's secret wife and child, and the charade of his official death in 1892, explain why she ordered their destruction.

Everyone at court agreed that George would make a much more suitable king than Eddy. Moreover if Eddy succeeded to the throne, it would be threatened by any discovery of Eddy's Roman Catholic wife and child. Eddy was therefore imprisoned.

No.	When and where born	Name, if any	Sex	Name and surname of father	Name, surname and maiden surname of mother
322	Tenth May 1888 53 Cleveland Place	Alice	Girl	William Crook	Sarah Annie Crook formerly Dryden.

CHAPTER NINE

The Monster of Glamis

In April 1890 Lord Randolph Churchill left England for South Africa to make his fortune in diamonds. He stayed there for nine months. When he returned the following January he put into motion his latest plans for Eddy and J.K. Stephen. Both were to die: Stephen because he had spoken to Abberline; Eddy because he was an inconvenience.

Eddy's official death was put at Sandringham on 14 January 1892, but in fact he was not even there that day. J.K. Stephen told Abberline that some time after the fire at Sandringham on 1 November 1891 Eddy was sent to stay at Balmoral. The Prince of Wales and his masonic friends had still not decided what to do with the unwanted heir to the throne, and until a plan was finalised Eddy was sent out of the way while arrangements were made for his fake death. Where might he be kept for the rest of his life, away from curious eyes, and taken care of in a manner befitting a prince? It was reasoned that he must remain in Britain, where he could be watched, and yet be far enough away not to be seen by the general public. A large estate owned by a trusted friend would be ideal.

While such a place was being sought Lord Randolph formulated his own plan: a plan which held fewer long-term complications. A fake death was not direct enough to solve the problem. Something more final was needed. Eddy had actually to die.

*

Balmoral Castle, the royal Scottish residence, sits by the River Dee at the foot of the Grampian Mountains, north of Lochnagor, nine miles west of Ballater. It was bought in 1848 by Eddy's grandfather, Albert, who bequeathed it to Queen Victoria. Too small for a growing family, the old castle was demolished and rebuilt in the Scottish Baronial style between 1853 and 1855. It soon became a favourite residence of the Queen, from whom it passed to Edward VII and eventually to the present Royal Family.

As children, Alexandra and her sister Minnie were taught by their father to draw, but neither had much talent and they later took up photography instead. Nevertheless Alexandra continued to 'dabble', as she termed it, using pastels and oil-paint. As noted, she asked Walter Sickert to become Eddy's tutor, and the young prince soon became a regular visitor to the studio at Cleveland Street, where he was given lessons. We can be sure that all Sickert taught him about painting was used to good effect during his stay at Balmoral.

Standing at a height of 926 ft and commanding a magnificent prospect of the majestic countryside, Balmoral sits within 25,000 acres of park and deer forest. In the hills above the castle and the valley are many fine views of Lochnagor to the south. It was while Eddy was at one of these vantage points, painting the highland landscape, that two men came out to meet him. They had travelled from London and had recently arrived at Ballater station. Eddy knew one of them – John Netley.

Some furniture had been sent to Balmoral from London, and the two men had travelled with it ostensibly to safeguard its arrival. After they had been assured that it had indeed arrived safely at the castle they sought out Prince Eddy in the grounds. In his notebook Netley wrote down the real reason for his visit to Scotland:

> Randy sent me and American Freddy to Scotland with some furniture. We pushed Eddy over a cliff but he is still alive at Balmoral. Never again enoughs enough. Its alright for him.

Lord Randolph was well aware of all the problems that would have to be overcome if Eddy's existence was to be kept secret after the announcement of his death. Members of the immediate household staff could be sworn to secrecy, or even bribed. But what about the dinner guests over Easter, and their guests' coachmen and maids? What about stable-boys, or postmen, or the man coming to mend the roof, or the plumber to fix the burst pipe? Randolph was right of course. Just how right is shown by the rumours about Eddy that persisted for years. Clearly his fears were justified. It is ironical that from what his own servant Netley wrote we are now able to know the truth about Eddy.

Randolph did not wish the Royal Family to know about Eddy's murder. The assassination was meant to look like an accident. Netley and Albericci pushed Eddy over a precipice and left him for dead. Either he was found alive by the Balmoral staff, or he managed to recover enough to make his way back. Abberline never discovered which.

Though Netley and Albericci failed to kill Eddy, they frightened him into submission, because when he was later told what was to happen to him he had not the strength to fight the decision. His friend James Stephen was in an asylum, his wife had been taken from him, his daughter had been run down and he too had been assaulted. His spirit was broken.

*

The problem now was: where could he be confined? Inspector Abberline provided the answer.

Balmoral was ideally situated as a hideaway. It was remote, the nearest village being nine miles away. It was private, with few visitors, and since it was a Royal residence the public were excluded. But there were drawbacks. When the Royal Family stayed there they would not wish to see Eddy because he would be a constant reminder of their ill-treatment of him. It would be easier if they never saw him again. Some other remote castle would have to be found. An approach was made to a castle-owning Scottish peer, another high-ranking Freemason, the 13th Earl of Strathmore.

The Royal Alpha Lodge masons, who included Eddy's father, made an astonishing promise to the Earl: if he and his family kept Eddy in their castle for the rest of his life, a great honour would be bestowed upon them – an honour greater than any the family had enjoyed in its long and illustrious history: marriage to a future King of England. The Earl's ancestral home is Glamis Castle lying twelve miles north of Dundee and five miles south of Forfar, in the Angus district of that part of Scotland now known as Tayside. It was here that Eddy was sent, and he stayed there for the rest of his life, which ended in 1933.

The 13th Earl died in 1904, but not before the promise was made more specific. His eldest son, Sir Claude George, who became the 14th Earl, had married Nina Cecilia Cavendish-Bentinck, grand-daughter of the 3rd Duke of Portland. When their fourth daughter was born in 1900 it was decided that the masonic promise should be fulfilled. By this time Eddy's father had ascended the throne as Edward VII and, since Eddy was officially dead, Eddy's younger brother George was next in line. It was to George's eldest son, Edward (eventually to become Edward VIII) that the 14th Earl's daughter was promised in marriage. His first daughter, Violet, had died at the age of ten in 1893. The second, Mary Frances, born in 1883, was eleven years older than Edward. Even Rose Constance, born in 1890, was considered too old for him. But when Elizabeth Angela Marguerite was born in 1900 she was the ideal choice.

Although Edward was heir to the throne, he made it clear that he had no intention of becoming king. The promise, he said, would have to be fulfilled through his brother Albert, the Duke of York. Albert married Elizabeth in 1923. He was the Provisional Grand Master Mason of Middlesex and was installed as Grand Master of Scotland after affiliating to the Glamis Lodge No. 99, whose Grand Master was his father-in-law, the 14th Earl of Strathmore. In 1936, after his brother's abdication, Albert ascended the throne as George VI. The promise to the Earl was thus fulfilled. No greater honour could be given to his family than to have a daughter crowned Queen of England. Lady Elizabeth Angela

Marguerite Bowes-Lyon, daughter of the 14th Earl of Strathmore, wife and queen of George VI, is of course the present Queen Elizabeth the Queen Mother.

The Queen Mother's uncle, the Hon. Patrick Bowes-Lyon, was the only aristocrat who sailed with Prince Eddy on HMS *Bacchante* in 1879. He was also with him at Trinity College, Cambridge, where they shared rooms overlooking Neville Court. Later they often met at Marlborough House, as 'benchers' of the Middle Temple (one of the four Inns of Court), and on the hunting field, of which Eddy and his father were devotees.

*

No castle in Britain is as steeped in history as Glamis. In 1034 King Malcolm II of Scotland was wounded in battle on Hunter's Hill and died at Glamis. Six years later his grandson and successor, Duncan, was killed near Elgin by Macbeth. Shakespeare wrongly places Duncan's murder in Glamis Castle, in the vaulted hall subsequently named after him.[1] When the Queen Mother was a child she and her sisters ran at top speed through it, on account of the eerie presence felt there. On the floor of King Malcolm's Room, where Malcolm died, was an indelible bloodstain. Elizabeth's mother had the floor boarded over.[2]

Several stories of ghosts and ghouls lend myth and romance to the castle and its family. The best known is that of the 'Monster of Glamis'.[3]

According to tradition, Peter Proctor, agent to the Glamis Estate, was the first agent to see the monster. His son David also saw him, as did Andrew Ralston who succeeded him from 1860 until 1912. Ralston's son Gavin refused even to speak about the monster. The story of the monster seems to have continued almost until the middle of the twentieth century, though Winston Churchill's cousin Shane Leslie fixed its closing year as 1921.[4]

It is clear from Douglas's Scots Peerage and Cockayne's Complete Peerage that a son and heir was born in October 1821 to Thomas, Lord Glamis, heir to the 11th Earl. It is said that he was so hideously deformed that his parents could not bring themselves to announce him as a future Earl. They therefore decided to have him recorded as still-born, hoping that he would not live too long. He did live, however. On 22 September 1822 another son, Thomas George, was born who was normal, and he became the 12th Earl. The 'monster' was a poor deformed creature shaped like an egg, covered in hair and immensely strong. Since the family could not admit to this embarrassing spectacle, particularly after claiming that he had died, they had him confined to a secret part of the castle. Only four men at any given time knew of his existence and whereabouts: the Earl, his eldest son and heir, the family lawyer and the agent to the estate. The name of the so-called monster – great uncle to Queen Elizabeth the Queen Mother – was never recorded.

There are many parts of Glamis Castle where he could have been kept from prying eyes. For instance, in 1684 the 1st Earl had a secret room built with an entrance from the Charter Room. The 16th Earl told the official family biographer, James Wentworth Day, that he felt sure there was 'a corpse or coffin bricked up somewhere in the walls. They are immensely thick. You could search for a week and find nothing.'[5] Again: 'There are probably half a dozen rooms bricked up in this place.'[6]

According to another Royal biographer, David Duff, when Lady Elizabeth was engaged to the Duke of York it was believed that a dark secret lurked within the castle walls and that the Earl's family were glad of all the ghost stories, which made it 'easier' for them 'to hide their real secret'.[7] This was in the early 1920s, so the monster would have been a hundred years old. Yet what evidence there is suggests that his death occurred some time before 1876. A more likely explanation is that the 'monster' story was deliberately continued and extended after his death in order to camouflage the latest secret: that Prince Albert Victor, Eddy, the man who should have been king, was still alive and locked away in the castle, perhaps in the very same secret parts that had once housed the so-called monster.

The Queen Mother's elder sister, the Dowager Lady Granville, told Wentworth Day that they 'were never allowed to talk about it when we were children. Our parents forbade us ever to discuss the matter or ask any questions about it. My father and grandfather refused absolutely to discuss it.'[8]

*

After the attempted murder at Balmoral Eddy was never the same again. Though he was the rightful heir to the throne it hardly seemed to matter to him now he realised that he was surrounded by at least a dozen people eager to ensure that he never obtained his birthright. The push down the cliff, though it failed in its murderous objective, served as a dramatic lesson to show him just how unstable his position was. Not only did it illustrate his recent enforced abasement, it terrified him into submission. Broken and dispirited, battered and shattered, he submitted himself to a future in humble obscurity.

As can be seen from his photograph taken at Glamis, Eddy spent some time painting. Joseph was told that Eddy was 46 when Queen Alexandra visited him at Glamis and took the photograph, which she later sent to her sister, the Empress of Russia. Because of Edward VII's animosity towards Eddy, Alexandra may not have been allowed to visit her son; but in 1910, after Edward's death on 6 May, she was free to go. Eddy was 46 in 1910.

Joseph has another memento of his grandfather, a sketchbook left behind by Eddy at Walter's studio when he was snatched away and separated from Annie and Alice. It is reproduced here. As can be clearly seen, the embossed front cover has been personalised with an oleograph portrait of Eddy as a boy. It probably once belonged to Alexandra who, as noted, enjoyed drawing and painting, and covered a room at Windsor Castle with her work. When ordering his sketchbook from his art dealer, no doubt he did not ask for it to be decorated with a portrait of himself as a boy; but Alexandra may well have ordered it for the front of the sketchbook she used during Eddy's childhood. The book no longer contains any sketches, but did once contain a hand-written formula for an abortifacient. Joseph lent it to Stephen Knight but it was never returned. The inference that Eddy contemplated an abortion for Annie is not easily discarded. Joseph realises this too, and acknowledges that he may owe his life to his grandmother's Roman Catholic conscience. Walter told Alice that the formula was obtained by Eddy from the Royal Physician, Sir William Gull (see below, p. 210).

Joseph was told by Walter, who learned it from Queen Alexandra, that when he was not painting at Glamis Eddy spent much of his time writing poetry. It would be interesting to know what subjects inspired him. Did he, for instance, versify his feelings of loss for the crown he never wore? Did he vilify those who wrenched it from his grasp? And what about his paintings? In the photograph Eddy is shown at his easel, upon which are two pictures, one a landscape, the other what looks like a seascape. Or is it a painting of one of the Scottish lochs? Did he ever try to capture from memory Annie's likeness? Of course we shall never know, since those in whose charge he remained until his death in 1933 would have destroyed, or at least hidden away, all evidence of his life at Glamis. It may be, of course, that his paintings and poems were sent to the Royal Family for them to see before they were destroyed. Or they may be lying forgotten somewhere in Glamis or Buckingham Palace. No doubt we shall never know.

Apart from painting and poetry Joseph has no idea how his grandfather spent his time at Glamis, or even whether he ever left the Scottish estate. As far as he knows, Alexandra was the only person to visit him. In the 'Family Exhibition Room' at Glamis I saw a photograph of Eddy's brother George standing with the Strathmore family outside the front door of Glamis. It was dated 1894, two years after Eddy's official death. As far as I have been able to ascertain, this was George's first-ever visit to Glamis. It occurred not long after the birth of his eldest son, the future Edward VIII. Edward's birth signalled the first step to fulfilment of the promise made to the Earl of Strathmore, and George may have visited Glamis to suggest that any future daughter born to the Earl's eldest son, Lord Glamis, within the next few years might be allowed to marry Edward, eventually becoming his queen. George may also have wished to make the final arrangements for Eddy and bid his last farewell.

Of course other members of the Royal Family have since visited

Glamis. Princess Margaret was born there. It remains the Highland seat of the Queen Mother's family.

After a tour of Glamis I made in 1989 I heard someone ask our charming guide, Ethel Lauder, whether we had seen much of the castle.

'Oh no,' she replied in her lilting brogue. 'You have only seen a very small portion. There are over a hundred and fifty bedrooms in Glamis.'

Eddy could have had a whole suite of rooms to himself, with a couple of trusted servants to bring him his meals and iron his clothes. A guest could visit the castle without ever venturing into the more inaccessible parts of the building, or knowing anything of the castle's dark secret.

One thing is abundantly clear from the letters Eddy is known to have written before he was sent to Glamis. He was not the educational moron his father Bertie believed him to be. Any educational gaps were due entirely to the ignorance and narrow viewpoint of his family and friends. If he appeared to show little interest in something it was simply that he had heard only part of the conversation, or had mis-heard and therefore misunderstood it. Only his mother, Alexandra, who was also deaf, seemed able to understand the quiet world her son inhabited.

*

Some naïve readers may find it hard to believe that in modern times any close relation of the Royal Family could be kept in seclusion for many years, the very fact of their existence a secret, while false statements of their death are publicly circulated. If so, they should consider the case of the five ladies related to the Queen Mother who in 1941 were all confined in the Royal Earlswood Mental Hospital, Redhill, Surrey. They were forgotten by the world until their existence was revealed by the Press in 1985.

The 21st Lord Clinton, John Hepburn-Stuart-Forbes-Trefusis, died in 1957. He left no sons. But he did leave two daughters, the Hon. Harriet and the Hon. Fenella, who had married, respectively, Major Henry Neville Fane and the Hon. John Herbert Bowes-Lyon, the brother of Queen Elizabeth the Queen Mother. Amazingly, five of Lord Clinton's ten grandchildren were afflicted with mental illness: Idonea, Rosemary and Etheldreda Fane, and Nerissa and Katherine Bowes-Lyon. In 1941, at the height of the war, their families decided that it was best to make them patients at the Royal Earlswood and they entered the hospital on the same day.[9] There these ladies, two of them first cousins of Queen Elizabeth II, remained. Rosemary died in 1972, Nerissa in 1984. The others are still alive and still in the Royal Earlswood. But, despite the intense public interest in the Royal Family, their very existence was generally unknown. By 1960 Idonea and Rosemary were no longer listed in the authoritative Debrett's Peerage. And the 1963 edition of Burke's Peerage even states that Katherine had died in 1940 and Nerissa in 1961; the source of this false information remains a mystery. Not until 1985 did the British press at last make public the existence and strange fate of the forgotten Royals.

Their paths crossed with Joseph Sickert's in summer 1938. When he visited the Bowes-Lyon home in Hertfordshire he met Nerissa and Katherine there, and remembers playing with them in the woods. Katherine was about his age, 13 or so, while Nerissa was 18 or 19. He also met the eldest sister, Anne, who was to marry Viscount Anson, and who became the mother of Patrick, the present Earl of Lichfield, the photographer. When Joseph visited the house again in 1942, he asked after the Bowes-Lyon children, and was told that Katherine and Nerissa had died. He had no reason to doubt it, and was as surprised as anyone else when he read the truth in 1985.

*

During my visit to Glamis I looked for the piece of furniture visible behind the man in the photograph which Joseph claims is of Eddy. I had gone to the castle in the hope that such a distinctive piece, with its lifesize carved violin and its friezes and panels carved with Scottish thistles, might have been retained. Thistles, as we might expect, are ubiquitous at Glamis, forming a distinctive feature on the furniture and tapestries. The piece was not in any of the ten rooms open to the public, and none of the long-serving tour guides remembered ever having seen it. One suggested that I speak to a retired retainer who had worked at Glamis for more than twenty years. He lived in Charleston, a hamlet close to the estate, and when I met him at his front door he told me that he had worked at the castle as a gardener and subsequently in the house, 'looking after the cash'. He said nothing the Earl of Strathmore's family might have considered disloyal. Unfortunately he did not remember ever seeing the carved sideboard. It should be noted that he was not at Glamis before Eddy died in 1933, and anyway he spent the first twenty years working in the gardens and grounds. He did remember, however, that during his time there a great deal of furniture had been sold on two occasions.

Although he had worked in the 'house', which I supposed to mean that part of the castle kept by the present Earl's family as their private quarters, he cannot have been in every part of the castle. The sideboard in the photograph may well be in a part to which he had no access. In a castle with 'over a hundred and fifty bedrooms', to say nothing of other rooms, connecting corridors, attics, cellars, dungeons and the many secret rooms built into the massive walls, even the family are probably not fully acquainted with every part of the building.

The sideboard in the picture has two carved panels on either side of the upper glazed cupboards. On each, above depictions of entwined dolphins, are two shields. The two on the right contain the date:

19

05

The two on the left contain initials which cannot be fully made out, because the photograph is not sufficiently focused. They appear to be:

SH
?B

The lower left-hand initial is quite obscure.

Since the furniture at Glamis is period furniture – Jacobean, Georgian, Regency and early Victorian – the Edwardian piece seen in the photograph would have been regarded, after the Second World War, as out of keeping. It was probably sold along with the other unwanted items mentioned by the gardener.

The Queen Mother's sister, Lady Granville, told James Wentworth Day: 'When I lived at Glamis children often woke up at night in those upper rooms screaming for their mamas because a huge, bearded man had leant over them. All the furniture was cleared out a dozen years ago. No one sleeps there today ...'[10]

Inspector Abberline and Eddy celebrated their birthdays on the same day, 8 January, and the realisation of this created a bond of friendship between them during the time Abberline was Eddy's bodyguard. It was as an old friend that Abberline asked the Royal Family to see him. In an entry dated 'Saturday March 20th', the year not given, he wrote:

I marched with the National Guard then Buckingham Palace Garden & was seen by the King & Queen. Very disappointed I could not go and see him.

It is difficult to believe that Abberline marched with a body of soldiers into Buckingham Palace garden, but in fact such an event did take place, and on the very date Abberline recorded. The Court Circular in *The Times* for 20 March 1915 states that George V commanded the City of London National Guard Volunteer Corps, under G.T.B. Cobbet, to march past him and Queen Mary in the Palace garden that afternoon.

Abberline must have marched with them and used the opportunity to ask the King's permission to go and see Eddy. That he felt free to make this request demonstrates, if nothing else, just how deeply Abberline had been drawn into the intrigue, and the confidence, of the Royal Family.

*

In December 1991 Anne Thompson gave the first edition of this book a favourable review in the *Sunday Post*, a newspaper based in Dundee and covering the area around Glamis. On 27 March 1992 she wrote Joseph Sickert the following letter explaining the local rumours confirming the strong possibility that Eddy was at Glamis after his official death:

Dear Mr Sickert

My late father once told me that when he was a boy, at the time of World War 1, he visited relatives near Glamis, and saw a man who looked like the late King Edward VII.

He was told the man was mentally retarded and lived with his parents in a cottage on the estate. Local rumour was that his mother had been a maid at Balmoral, and had attracted the attention of King Edward when he was Prince of Wales, with the result that she became pregnant.

A man was found to marry her and given a post and cottage at Glamis.

Strathmartine Hospital, Dundee, used to be called Baldovan House and is home for mentally retarded people. There was a story that during the 1930s there was there an elderly inmate who resembled Edward VII and who came from Glamis. I heard it from an old man near Brechin who visited a relative in Baldovan House.

I have not so far found anyone to substantiate these stories, as the people I heard them from are dead, and others who know them got them, like me, second hand.

It's possible the man was simply the retarded son of an estate worker with no connection at all to the Royal Family, and that the resemblance was co-incidental. Or he may have been a byblow of someone other than King Edward.

However, profoundly deaf individuals can appear to be mentally retarded rather than physically handicapped to people who do not really know them, so it fits the theory of Prince Eddy as the Glamis recluse.

The rumour in the village would be excellent cover, keeping people away from him and providing an explanation if he were ever recognised. One would expect Prince Eddy's half-brother to look like him.

If the poor man eventually became mentally feeble in old age, he would be well looked after and given privacy as a private patient at Baldovan, when it might have been difficult to keep him on at Glamis.

With Best Wishes

Yours sincerely,
Anne Thompson (signed),
Sunday Post

CHAPTER TEN

Abdication

Within eighteen months of Eddy's official death Princess May, to whom he had been engaged, married his brother George at the Chapel Royal, St James's Palace. May was soon pregnant and gave birth to a son in June 1894. Three days later Queen Victoria wrote to George asking him to name him Albert after his grandfather. George replied that both he and May had decided long before the birth that they would name a son Edward after his brother, 'darling Eddy'. Victoria replied accepting the name, but she reminded George that Edward was not his brother's real name – that he had in fact been christened Albert Victor.

Eventually the child was christened Edward Albert Christian George Andrew Patrick David, the last four being the names of the patron saints of the four nations in the Union. It hardly mattered, however, because his family and friends were always to call him by his last name, David: the name I shall use until that point in the text when he becomes Edward VIII and, after his abdication, Duke of Windsor.

When David was born *The Times* remarked that never before in English history had the sovereign seen three male descendants in the direct line of inheritance. The three were the Prince of Wales, his son George, the Duke of York, and George's newborn son David. Little did anyone realise a year and a half later, when David's brother Albert was born, that he too would one day occupy the throne as George VI. Bertie, as he was called by his family, was born on 14 December 1895. The event caused mixed feelings. The parents of course were delighted, but Queen Victoria was saddened because the birth took place on the anniversary of Prince Albert's death in 1861. It was also the anniversary of the death, in 1878, of her daughter Princess Alice. But she cheered herself with the thought that Albert was 'a gift from God'. The prince was christened at Sandringham Albert Frederick Arthur George.

On 4 August 1900, three months after David's sixth birthday, the Earl of Strathmore's fourth daughter, Elizabeth, was born at St Paul's, Walden Bury. Her birth set the scene for the fulfilment of the Royal masonic promise given to her grandfather. Lady Elizabeth would be allowed to marry David, ready to be his Queen upon his accession.

Five months later Queen Victoria died peacefully at Osborne. She had reigned almost sixty-four years, longer than any British monarch before or since. At long last her son Bertie, the 59-year-old Prince of Wales, could play the role for which he had been born. Unfortunately Bertie was not able to enjoy his reign for long, because he died in 1910. In the meantime, 500 miles away from his father's final resting place at Windsor, Prince Eddy, who should have succeeded him, was whiling away his time writing and painting behind the walls of Glamis Castle.

*

On the eve of his coronation George and May dined with their sons David and Bertie. Soon after dinner a letter arrived from Queen Alexandra:

> May God bless you both and give a little thought to your poor sad and broken-hearted mother dear.[1]

While they were reading that letter, Alexandra was pacing her rooms at Sandringham crying out: 'Eddy should be King, not Georgie.'[2]

Why was she so broken-hearted? It was, after all, over a year since her husband Bertie had died, and her son George was to be crowned next day. Any tears to be shed should have been in joy over her son's forthcoming coronation.

According to David Duff:

> Alexandra had been a problem to Mary ever since she became Queen. She had never fully accepted that George was the rightful King – she looked back at the ghosts of Eddy and her husband.[3]

It was nineteen years since Eddy's apparent death, long enough for the most sensitive of mothers to have accepted her son's death, if it had actually occurred. If Eddy really had been dead would not his mother have shouted 'Eddy should have been King', rather than 'Eddy should be King', which implied that he was still alive to fill the role? Only in the light of Joseph's claims can her feelings be understood. Alexandra knew that Eddy was still alive. That is why Duff was able to write:

> In truth Queen Alexandra never truly accepted her second son as sovereign. She could never bring herself to address her letters to him as 'The King', but always wrote to 'King George', although she knew full well that this was incorrect, sounding, as it did, as if he was merely one of a number.[4]

On 22 June 1911 the Archbishop of Canterbury, Randall Davidson, presented George to the Peers of the Realm with the words:

Sirs, I present unto you King George the undoubted King of this Realm ...[5]

How many of those peers, one wonders, knew that George was not the undoubted King of this Realm? How many of them knew that Eddy was still alive?

*

David was only 17 when he swore homage to his father at his coronation. Three weeks later he was created Prince of Wales at an investiture at Carnarvon Castle. It was now time for him to be told that it had been promised that he would marry Lady Elizabeth, and that his uncle Eddy was still alive and living at Glamis.

Young men, as is well known, can be fiercely idealistic and often have a vigorous sense of justice, decrying their parents' values or, as they often see it, lack of values. When he was told what had happened to Eddy, all David's youthful idealism surfaced. He was furious.

Walter Sickert enjoyed the friendship of many influential people, some of whom were in positions close to the Royal Family, and indeed to the throne. Through his friends, and later their children, Joseph learned that David, from the moment he heard about the masonic promise and the existence of Eddy at Glamis, vowed that he would never rule as king, reasoning that his father had no right to the throne while Eddy was alive and that he too therefore had no legitimate claim to it.

David was told the details of the Ripper story, and one part of it angered him even more: that it was his father who had brought in Lord Randolph Churchill to deal with the blackmail attempt of Kelly and her three friends.

George spent the years 1886 to 1888 serving aboard a succession of ships in the Mediterranean, returning eight days after the death of Mary Kelly. He spent the spring of 1886 with his father at Cannes. Next year he returned to England for Queen Victoria's Jubilee celebrations. On 4 August he sailed aboard the *Aline* in the company of Lady Randolph Churchill and her son Winston, aged 13. He returned on leave in March 1888 to attend the family dinner for his parents' Silver Wedding. It was probably then that he spoke to Lord Randolph. The following month Netley and Albericci killed Emma Smith. Three months later Lord Randolph, Lord Salisbury and Eddy dined together at Cambridge, and three months after that the Ripper murders began.

George appealed to Lord Randolph as a family friend, merely asking his advice on his brother's behalf. This is what J.K. Stephen told Inspector Abberline. At first David found it almost impossible to believe that his father, without realising it, had instigated the Ripper murders and later stepped into Eddy's shoes. Once his bruised idealism had recovered and he had reluctantly accepted the truth, he took his father's guilt upon himself. Apart from stating categorically that he would never wear the crown, or fulfil the promise to make Lady Elizabeth Bowes-Lyon his wife, he made it clear that he had no wish ever to speak to his father again. They were seen together in public of course, and they spoke to one another in the presence of officials and dignitaries, but at home David did what he could to avoid conversation with his father. Instead, he set out to annoy him.

George V was a stickler for wearing the 'right' clothes, and one way the Prince could irritate his father was to express individuality in his mode of dress. It is commonplace these days for the young to dress in a manner likely to shock their parents, and it has almost become part of modern youth culture to be 'different'. But this was not generally the case before the First World War, and among the aristocracy, with their entrenched insistence on formality, for a good many years afterwards. George belonged to a generation which, as often as not, would judge a man's morals by the cut of his suit. If the Prince of Wales arrived for breakfast wearing American-style trousers with 'cuffs' – or 'turnups', as they were later called in England – the King would sarcastically ask his errant son whether or not it was raining, implying that a man only rolled up his trousers when he was likely to walk through puddles. With a severity which should ordinarily have been reserved for grave misconduct the King often reproved his son for such minor indiscretions of dress and deportment.

On one occasion King George rebuked his son for wearing a bowler hat at a provincial public function, instead of the more acceptable top hat. The King could not understand his son's intentions on such occasions – intentions which became even clearer after his decision not to become king, when he felt free to appear less regal and thus closer to 'the people'.

Not only did George constantly criticise his eldest son: he also spied on him. Lord Esher alluded to this when he wrote of David:

> The Prince can be obstinate, he takes violent likes and dislikes. He has got rid of several of his staff because he suspected them of carrying tales to his father.[6]

During the First World War the Prince of Wales displayed all the qualities of a physically courageous man. For instance, he did not hesitate to go to the front, where he witnessed the Battle of Passchendaele. In 1914 he had visited Lord Kitchener at the War Office and asked to be allowed to go to France. When it was pointed out to him that as the future King this could not be permitted, he replied, 'What does it matter if I am killed?' adding, 'I have four brothers.'[7]

Lord Kitchener said that when the Prince did eventually go to France 'it proved impossible to keep him out of the front line whenever he had the opportunity to go anywhere near it'.[8]

An officer of his regiment reported:

A bad shelling will always bring out the Prince of Wales.[9]

As a prince of the realm and a future king, the Prince of Wales did not need to endure the terrors of the trenches. Nor was it expected of him. But he found it distasteful to display his war decorations, which were largely honorary awards, when those who had really earned them received almost no recognition.

David had known Lady Elizabeth Bowes-Lyon since she was eight, and it is a curious fact, according to David Duff, that:

to certain of her parents' friends she was known as Princess Elizabeth from the time that she could toddle. It was a game. They would bend the knee to her and she hold out her hand to be kissed. It just came naturally. While her sisters had Mary and Rose familiarized into May and Rosie, the baby was accorded the full regality of Elizabeth.[10]

Cynthia Asquith reported a friend's telling her that she:

always addressed her as Princess Elizabeth, kissed her hand and invariably made her a low bow, which she acknowledged haughtily yet courteously.[11]

In the summer of 1909 the Minister of Glamis, the Rev. James Sturton, attended a tea party at Glamis Castle. After tea Lady Strathmore began to play the piano. As soon as they heard their cue, young Elizabeth and her brother David appeared and danced a minuet, she dressed in a long robe, he in a jester's cap. Afterwards, when Elizabeth was asked who she was supposed to be, she replied: 'I call myself Princess Elizabeth.'[12]

As late as 1920, not long before her twentieth birthday, Lady Elizabeth was giving a lift to a friend who remembered driving up the Edgware Road in a car resembling the limousine used by Queen Mary. Mimicking the Queen, Elizabeth sat up straight, raised her parasol and began to bow and wave to passers-by, first to one side and then to the other, giving a foretaste of the very gesture with which she became associated when she became Queen and later Queen Mother.[13]

All this has been passed off by her biographers as mere coincidence, but it takes on a different meaning in the light of Joseph's claim that her family expected her to become a princess and ultimately Queen of England.

Walter Sickert learned that David, as we have noted, was so angry after being told that his father had been party to Eddy's internment that he vowed never to ascend the throne. With perfect logic Queen Mary, displaying a profound understanding of constitutional matters, explained to him that only a king can abdicate. A prince might neglect his duties, might shy away from them and even banish himself from court to assume the role of commoner, but such a course had no legal foundation. Only a sovereign could abdicate.

The Prince of Wales did not abdicate, as many have thought, because he loved Mrs Simpson. This is not to say that he did not love her; no doubt he did. Indeed before he met her he had established a pattern of affairs with women older than himself. This was not unusual in a period when society kept a strict eye on its young women to ensure that they retained their value in the marriage stakes. Divorced women, or women who had wed out of duty, or were bored with their husbands, were a suitable alternative.

Once the Prince made it clear that he had no intention of ascending the throne, or at least that he would abdicate soon after, plans had to be changed so that the promise to the Strathmore family could be honoured. Since the heir intended to abdicate, his younger brother Bertie would have to marry Elizabeth instead. Lady Mabel Airlie, wife of the 8th Earl Airlie and Lady of the Bedchamber to Queen Mary, told Lady Elizabeth: 'The King thinks the Prince of Wales will never succeed him, or if he does, not for long.'[14] This was fourteen years before the abdication. The Prince himself even made a point of making this clear to Lady Elizabeth.

David Duff corroborates what Walter Sickert told his son:

> At the time when Lady Elizabeth Bowes-Lyon was considering the problem of whether to marry the Duke of York, she was talking one day to the Prince of Wales. He said to her: 'You had better take him and go on in the end to Buck House.'
>
> The words were of interest on two counts. Firstly, it had been Queen Mary's original idea that the Lady Elizabeth should marry her eldest son and thus begin the sure road towards the Palace. Secondly, some indication was given that *the Prince had early considered the possibility that he might not reach the throne* or that some event might cause him to withdraw from the right of succession. In the event *the seeds of abdication were sown long before the Prince met Mrs Wallis Simpson at Craven Lodge*. (My italics).[15]

Here Duff unwittingly supports Sickert's two assertions: that Lady Elizabeth was expected to marry David, and that David had decided against the crown long before he met Mrs Simpson. Unfortunately for David, his father's death was unexpected and found him unprepared to put into action his plans for withdrawing from the line of succession. His official biographer wrote of the period:

> In the little circle that made up informed London, there were rumours that Edward VIII would renounce the throne, or at least that he had only accepted it with reluctance ... it is harder categorically to gainsay the belief

of Alan Lascelles that the Prince had been caught napping by the King's death and that given a few months more he would have opted out of the line of succession and retired into private life with Mrs Simpson. Once he had told Lascelles that he was keeping the Canadian ranch so as to have somewhere to which he could retire. 'You mean for a holiday, Sir?' asked Lascelles. 'No, I mean for good.' Hardinge was equally certain that another six months would have seen the Prince out of line of succession.[16]

The Duke of York, who was more like his father than were any of his brothers, particularly David, was only too glad to marry Lady Elizabeth, for the simple reason that he fell in love with her. It is not difficult to understand why. All the Queen Mother's biographers have drawn attention to her charm. The picture painted by those fortunate enough to have met her is one of radiant beauty and compelling warmth. This, along with her ability to put everyone at ease, made her an extremely agreeable and attractive young woman.

Lady Elizabeth twice refused the Duke of York. Rumour had it that she was tilting her cap at his handsome Equerry, James Gray Stuart, a Captain in the Royal Scots. (Joseph was himself told this by the 7th Duke of Portland, whose wife, the niece of the 6th Duke of Richmond, had been Maid of Honour to Queen Alexandra.) Queen Mary was determined to see Lady Elizabeth marry one of her sons, and she arranged for James Stuart to be sent to Canada, where he was appointed to the Governor General's staff. To the end of his days the Duke of York never learned that it was his mother who contrived to have Captain James Stuart sent away, after she had been told by one of her ladies-in-waiting that Lady Elizabeth was 'very much in love with the Duke of York's equerry ...'[17] Nor did he learn that the King had said to his Private Secretary, Lord Stamfordham, 'Well, order the silly bugger to go. Tell him he's sacked.'[18]

With the eligible equerry out of the way, Elizabeth, on 15 January 1923, finally consented to marry the Duke of York. This was just ten days after the *Daily News* made the following odd announcement:

SCOTTISH BRIDE FOR PRINCE OF WALES.
HEIR TO THRONE TO WED PEER'S DAUGHTER.
An official announcement imminent ...[19]

That weekend Lady Elizabeth was staying with friends at Firle in Sussex, and this news item prompted them to tease her by bowing and calling her 'Ma'am'. It shows that even at this late date, only three months before she married Bertie, Lady Elizabeth was expected, in some circles at least, to marry David.

*

Princes of the Blood were usually married in private chapels. Edward VII and his two brothers, the Duke of Leopold and the Duke of Connaught, were all married in St George's Chapel, Windsor. As noted, Edward's son George was married in the Chapel Royal, St James's. This tradition was interrupted when George's son Bertie married Lady Elizabeth in Westminster Abbey, even though no king's son had been married there for 541 years. The marriage, on 26 April 1923, put the thirty-year-old promise to the Earl of Strathmore on the sure path to fulfilment. It was also the first time an English Prince had married a commoner for 263 years.

In the week of the royal wedding *The Times* carried the announcement of Captain James Stuart's engagement to Lady Rachel Cavendish, 4th daughter of the Duke of Devonshire. They married later that year.

Joseph Sickert was told by his mother that at about this time she was visited by two VIPs at her home in Drummond Street. One was England's leading lay Catholic, Bernard Marmaduke Fitzalan Howard, Duke of Norfolk, who later became Joseph's friend. The other was David, the Prince of Wales. (The Duke of Norfolk once told Joseph that the Prince had Catholic leanings. Lady Diana Cooper, third daughter of the 8th Duke of Rutland, reported that when she was a guest of the Prince aboard the yacht *Nahlin*, she had seen him wearing not one, but two, crucifixes round his neck. Conversion to Catholicism was one way in which the Prince could have escaped from the line of succession, and Alan Don, the principal adviser to the Archbishop of Canterbury at Lambeth Palace, said in his diary that 'this was told me by a Diocesan Bishop who had just been talking to an ex-Cabinet Minister'.)[20] The Prince was there to pay his respects to the daughter of Prince Albert Victor, Duke of Clarence and Avondale, whom he regarded as the rightful King of England. He referred to Alice as 'cousin'. She told Joseph that when she met the Prince he kissed her on both cheeks and both hands.

He paid her a second visit early in 1926 soon after Joseph was born. It was early evening, but darkness had fallen – an ideal time for someone wishing to remain unnoticed. Children were playing around the car, which was driven, not by one of the palace staff, since the Prince did not wish his family to know of the visit, but by a friend. After the Prince entered the house his friend asked David Walsh, Alice's neighbour from a few doors down, to keep an eye on the limousine and stop any children messing with it. In 1926 cars of any kind were unusual in Drummond Street.

Of all members of the Royal Family it is well known that the one who showed most resentment towards Mrs Simpson was Queen Elizabeth the Queen Mother. Not surprisingly it has always been assumed that the main reason was that she blamed Mrs Simpson for the early death of her husband, George VI. It is true that Mrs Simpson's marriage forced Bertie to become king, and the weighty burden he had to shoulder put a strain on his health, which had never been robust. But her attitude to Mrs Simpson may have been tinged with jealousy. A recap of events leading to the abdication shows why.

First of all, as we have seen, the Earl of Strathmore had been promised that his family would be honoured in return for keeping Prince Eddy at Glamis Castle, and the promise was made specific when Elizabeth was born: she could marry Prince George's son David. Unfortunately David made it clear that he had no intention of marrying Elizabeth, or of being crowned. He suggested that the promise be fulfilled through his brother Bertie, who was next in line. Elizabeth, who no doubt found David attractive, as many women did, twice refused Bertie's proposal of marriage. She finally accepted him after David's intention became clear. Being turned down by the most eligible bachelor in the world, and left to stand by later and watch him fall hopelessly in love with an older married woman for whom, ostensibly, he spurned the throne, must have been hard to bear.

Long before he became king, and before his marriage to Mrs Simpson, David had already become the black sheep of the family. He had had several affairs with older married women. His first serious liaison, which began in 1915 when he was still 20, was with the Earl of Leicester's daughter-in-law, Viscountess Coke. Two years later he proposed to Lady Rosemary Leveson-Gower, the younger daughter of the 4th Duke of Sutherland. (We know this because Lady Rosemary told her close friend Lady Bridget Paget, who was interviewed by Michael Thornton in 1972.)[21] Though she was ten months older, she was single, and in every other respect an eminently suitable bride, and he suggested as much to his father, who was now King. Six months earlier, at the height of the First World War, the King, as a sop to public opinion, had renounced all his German titles and proclaimed the establishment of the House of Windsor. On 17 July 1917 he noted in his diary:

> I also informed the Council that May and I had decided *some time ago* that our children would be allowed to marry into British families. It was quite a historical occasion. (My italics).[22]

Clearly this was George's way of introducing to the country the idea that David could marry someone other than a foreign princess. Yet in spite of this decision George refused to allow David to marry Lady Rosemary Leveson-Gower, a member of one of Britain's most eminent families. We can only surmise that he was still hoping that his son would change his mind and accept Lady Elizabeth Bowes-Lyon, and that permission to marry into British families was specifically intended to encourage public acceptance of Lady Elizabeth as wife to the Prince of Wales.

Lady Rosemary's closest friend, Lady Bridget Paget, had also been

David's mistress. When she met Joseph Sickert she told him all about the affair, which had occurred before her marriage to Captain Lord Victor Paget, brother of the 6th Marquess of Anglesey. Bridget's father was Baron Colebrook who had been Lord-in-Waiting to Edward VII. He later held the same position to George V, until the King's death in 1936. In that year he was Master of the Robes to David, for the short time he ruled as Edward VIII.

Contrary to what several of David's ex-mistresses have declared, Lady Bridget told Joseph that David was an exceptionally good lover, and she impressed upon him that, if there was one thing that he could do really well, it was satisfy a woman. She is reported to have said more than once: 'How vulgar of those American women to call him David. Either one calls him Sir or one calls him Darling.'[23]

It was not only the women in his life who made the Prince of Wales the black sheep. According to Lady Paget his father hated the way he mixed with the common people, objecting in particular that he had been seen gambling in the street with the 'lower classes'. This was not the sort of behaviour expected of a future King of England.

*

Perhaps I may be forgiven for a small digression at this point. While Joseph was at St Paul's he made friends with Timothy Patrick Bowes-Lyon, who was the second son of the Earl of Strathmore and who later, in 1949, himself succeeded to the title. Timothy, who was a few years older than Joseph, was ill and needed a nurse in constant attendance. They met again several years later and swapped memories. The Earl mentioned that when Eddy was attending lectures at Cambridge he would suddenly stretch, yawn loudly, stand up and leave the room. He was bored stiff, for the simple reason that he was too deaf to hear what the lecturer was saying. Usually he went off fishing. I mention this in passing to reinforce Joseph's view that his grandfather's education was greatly handicapped by his deafness, which led many to believe that he was uninterested in anything other than the pleasures of the flesh.

*

Another story related to Joseph by his father may also have provided David with a reason for refusing the crown. Walter Sickert claimed that he was once told by Eddy that his brother George was in reality only his half-brother – that Edward VII was not George's natural father. Walter made the remarkable claim that, according to Eddy, his father and mother had travelled to Denmark where they met the future Tsar of Russia, and the Tsar had a brief fling with Alexandra and became George's natural father.

George was born the year after Eddy, on 3 June 1865. Counting back nine months from George's birth, we arrive at the approximate date of his conception. Since, like all Alexandra's children, he was thought to be about two weeks premature, we can take it that George was conceived between 12 and 26 September. After making this simple calculation I checked all the biographies of Edward VII and Alexandra to see whether there was any possibility that Alexandra met the future Russian Tsar in Denmark between those dates.

I found that on 3 September 1864 Edward and Alexandra boarded the *Osborne* and set sail from Dundee, docking at Elsinore four days later. They were visiting Alexandra's family and her eldest sister, Dagmar, nicknamed Minny, who was eagerly awaiting the arrival of the man she was to marry: Grand Duke Nicholas, son and heir of Tsar Alexander II. Dagmar and Nicholas became engaged on 28 September, but they never married, because next year Nicholas died of tuberculosis. The following year she married his younger brother, who became Tsar Alexander III.

I found no report that Tsaravitch Alexander was in Denmark during the period in which George was conceived. But, as noted, his brother Nicholas was there at that time. Walter could easily have mixed up the story related by Eddy, confusing Nicholas, who was then thought of as the 'future Tsar', with his brother Alexander, who did in fact become Tsar. If Eddy's story is true, he was right in saying that George was fathered by the future Tsar of Russia, since Nicholas was regarded as such when Alexandra met him.

The son of Alexander and Dagmar became Tsar Nicholas II, the last Russian Tsar, who was murdered in 1917. The remarkable likeness between him and George V may well be the result of their fathers having been brothers: Grand Duke Nicholas and Alexander. The photograph of George and Nicholas together, reproduced here, certainly suggests such a possibility. They are so alike that they could be taken for twins.

If David knew of this he would have realised that his father had no natural right to the throne of England, since he was not the natural son of Edward VII, thus adding weight to his own refusal of the crown.

If this story of adultery is true, and the evidence is only circumstantial, it would provide another reason why Alexandra ordered all her private archive to be destroyed after her death (above, p. 186).

*

In November 1986 the astonishing claim was made that King George V had been given an injection on his deathbed to hasten his demise.It was made by Francis Watson, the biographer of George's Physician-in-Ordinary, Lord Dawson of Penn, who was President of the Royal College of Physicians.[24] Lord Dawson's notes clearly show that he agreed to a request from Queen Mary and her son David, the Prince of Wales, not to prolong the king's life. The notes, which were later verified by experts at

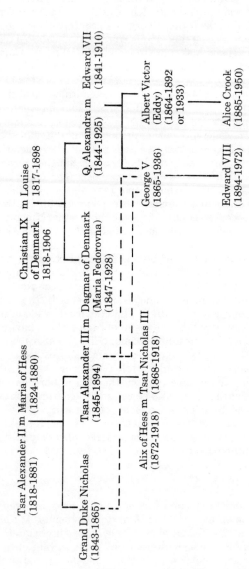

Tsar Alexander II m Maria of Hess
(1818-1881)   (1824-1880)

Grand Duke Nicholas
(1843-1865)

Tsar Alexander III m Dagmar of Denmark
(1845-1894)   (Maria Fedorovna)
                   (1847-1928)

Alix of Hess m Tsar Nicholas III
(1872-1918)   (1868-1918)

Christian IX   m Louise
of Denmark   1817-1898
1818-1906

Q. Alexandra m Edward VII
(1844-1925)   (1841-1910)

Albert Victor
(Eddy)
(1864-1892
or 1933)

George V
(1865-1936)

Alice Crook
(1885-1950)

Edward VIII
(1894-1972)

*According to Walter Sickert Prince Albert Victor said that his brother,
George V, was fathered either by Grand Duke Nicholas, then regarded as the
future Tsar of Russia until his death from tuberculosis the following year, or
by Nicholas's brother who became Tsar Alexander III.*

KEY: —————— Line of official descent.

        - - - - - George V's possible lines of descent according to Walter
                  Sickert.

Windsor Castle, show that his death was hastened by a euthanasia injection of morphia and cocaine into the jugular vein. Queen Mary told Lord Dawson that she did not wish her husband's life prolonged if his illness was going to be fatal. Lord Dawson's notes also admit that it was more appropriate for the King's death to be announced by the BBC in time for the first Press comments in *The Times* than in the evening tabloids or, as he put it, 'the less appropriate evening journals'. While it was courageous of Lord Dawson to have left these notes, it would have been even more courageous and honest not to omit the most important part of the episode.

The real reason why King George's death was hastened was explained to Walter Sickert by two different men: the 16th Duke of Norfolk, England's premier Duke and Earl Marshall, and Lord Trenchard, Principal Air ADC to King George from 1921 to 1925 and Commissioner of the Metropolitan Police from 1931 to 1935, who was later to bear the sword at George VI's coronation.

These two told Walter that as George V became aware that he was dying he was overtaken by feelings of guilt for his part in Eddy's incarceration at Glamis and began to express remorse for accepting his brother's crown. In front of nurses and servants he began to shout hysterically, and to beg for Eddy's forgiveness. This was extremely disturbing for Queen Mary who knew the true import of his outbursts and was worried that those who heard might understand the significance of what he was saying. George had to be silenced.

George V died at five minutes to midnight on 20 January 1936, in time for an announcement to appear in the *The Times*. Eleven days later Lord Dawson's services were rewarded when he was created a Viscount.

*

Upon the death of her husband Queen Mary took hold of David's hand and said. 'The King is dead, long live the King.'[25]

She then went in to her room and wrote in her diary: 'The sunset of his death tinged the whole world's sky.'[26] When David realised that his father was dead and that he was now King Edward VIII, he was observed to display strong signs of mental anguish. Lady Hardinge, whose husband had been equerry and Private Secretary to George V, as he was later to be to Edward VIII and George VI, described his grief as 'frantic and unreasonable'.[27]

> To anyone with an intimate knowledge of his relationship with his father this must have suggested that the grief had causes other than mere bereavement.[28]

Royal biographers believe that Edward was fretting over the new responsibilities that would come with kingship. No doubt. But what has not been generally understood is that the Prince now realised that he had a long struggle ahead to convince those around him that he was determined to abdicate. If he did grieve for his father, which is doubtful, his grief was short-lived, as can be seen from the way he insulted his memory. Holding him responsible for what had happened to Eddy and for taking his place on the throne, and as a final rebuff to his name, the newly created Duke of Windsor married Mrs Simpson on the anniversary of his father's birthday, 3 June 1937.

4 May 1877

**Sandringham,
Kings Lynn.**

Sir William Gull's prescription for Princess Alexandra (see below, Appendix 11).

CHAPTER ELEVEN
A Ripper Interlude

Two years after Joseph Sickert appeared on BBC Television's programme 'Jack the Ripper', and before publication of Stephen Knight's *Jack the Ripper: The Final Solution*, a series of 'ripper' crimes began in the Midlands.

When Peter Sutcliffe was arrested in the red-light district of Sheffield on 3 January 1981 for having false number-plates on his car, the two arresting officers did not realise that they had in their grasp the serial murderer dubbed by the press the 'Yorkshire Ripper', the man responsible for the maiming of seven women and the murder of thirteen. His own nickname for himself was 'The Streetcleaner'.

After he appeared on television Joseph was inundated with telephone calls and letters, many from cranks. Several of the calls and three of the letters had been from Peter Sutcliffe.

*

One evening early in 1975 Joseph was visiting his lifelong friend Harry Jonas. During the evening he received a telephone call from his 18-year-old daughter Carol. She was alone at home and rather distraught, and she asked her father to return immediately because there was a man at the door demanding to see him. She had told him that Joseph was not in, but he would not go away and was still outside the house. Though she was frightened, she did not then realise that she had every reason to be. The stranger at the door was Peter Sutcliffe. She later said to me: 'I'd told him Dad wasn't in, and I shut the door, but he kept banging on it. I wouldn't open it again because I was alone and there was something about him – the way he smiled. He had a moustache, and when he smiled there was this gap between his two front teeth. I don't know what it was about him – just something that scared me. He was creepy.'

Sutcliffe left before Joseph returned, but a few days later he began to pester him over the telephone, saying he wished to discuss the Ripper case with him. Joseph's number and address were in the London telephone directory. Sutcliffe must have followed him from his home, because one day while Joseph was having a cup of tea in a café in Cleveland Street he came up to him and asked if he could share his table. Joseph made no objection and he sat down.

'You're Mr Sickert, aren't you?' he said.

He introduced himself as 'Mr Bruni', adding that he was a private detective working for a client from one of the southern states of America. His client was living in London and had seen Joseph on television and had hired him to speak to Joseph to find out more about Jack the Ripper.

Joseph told me:

I didn't really mind meeting him. I had all sorts of people ringing me from all over the place. He seemed all right at first. He spoke very quietly. I met him twice, the first time in a café when he just came up to me and sat down. This was before the Yorkshire Ripper murders started. The next time I saw him was in 1976, after the murders had begun. Stephen Knight's book had just been published. I had left Harry's house in Myddleton Square, and as I was crossing the street a car hurtled towards me. But I stepped out of the way and it caught my hand. I went to the Royal Free Hospital, which was near where I lived, and was told that I had a hairline fracture in my wrist.

I had seen who was driving the car. It was Peter Sutcliffe, whom I knew then as Bruni. What was odd, though, was that he had a passenger with him, another man. He can't have realised that I'd seen that it was he who tried to run me over, because a few months later he rang to ask me to meet him again.

I refused. I didn't tell him that I knew that he'd tried to run me over. I didn't want to give him any reason to try it again, did I? Anyway, I later agreed to meet him at Harry's. [Shown here is a statement signed by Harry Jonas in 1984, confirming that Sutcliffe visited his house for 'about 1½ hours'.] He was different this time: he was sweating and seemed very agitated. He talked about Jack the Ripper for most of the time; but we also mentioned the Yorkshire Ripper, and he said the culprit ought to be shot. He kept going on about the difference between reality and fantasy, and how they could be confused.

I could tell he was a bit odd. He never told me his real name, but when I had first met him he said he was from Yorkshire. At first I didn't see the connection between him and the murders. It was only after the newspapers talked of the 'Yorkshire Ripper' that I realised it could be him.

I sent the three letters from Sutcliffe to the Yorkshire Police, and I phoned them too. I also spoke to Scotland Yard, but the Yorkshire Police had told them they didn't want any outside interference. I suppose they wanted the credit for themselves, when they eventually caught him. Besides, said Yorkshire, Scotland Yard hadn't caught their own Ripper yet, meaning Jack!

Eventually a London policeman agreed to go with me to Yorkshire to try to identify the man who had come to talk to me about Jack the Ripper. We arranged to go, but Sutcliffe was shortly arrested.

I was asked to appear in court at his trial to testify that he had shown a

Nov 23rd/84
39 Myddelton Square
E.C.1.

Dear Joseph,
and to whom it may
concern : —

Re 1975–1976 & Re Mr Sutcliffe –
Sutcliffe was here at above
address with Mr Joseph & self
to discuss the 'Ripper' Case of
1888. He stayed for about
1½ hours

Yours

H M Jonas

Harry Jonas's confirmation that Peter Sutcliffe, the Yorkshire Ripper, visited his home with Joseph Sickert morbid interest in the Ripper murders, but I didn't want to get involved in any more publicity, and they never pressed me to go.

*

Many years before, Harry Jonas had been told something which was later shown to have some significance for Joseph. Harry Jonas's life had close parallels with that of Joseph's father, whom Jonas had known since he was a young man. Like Walter, Harry, who was the son of a tobacco broker, started out as an actor, but in silent films rather than on the stage. On the advice of Philip Wilson Steer and Egerton Cooper he became an artist. During the 1920s he travelled on the continent, settling for a while in Paris where he became a close friend of Utrillo and met other artistic luminaries including Modigliani and Picasso. (He claimed that Picasso was known to many of his contemporaries as 'that shit'.) Harry regularly exhibited at the Grosvenor and Leicester Galleries. One such exhibition opened on 23 July 1937 at the Leicester Gallery, Leicester Square. The list of 200 exhibitors reads like a Who's Who of modern artists. It included Braque, Dali, Degas, Dufy, Epstein, Gauguin, Henry Moore, Pissarro, Rodin, Wilson Steer and Vlaminck.

With Francis West and Joseph Sickert, Jonas formed a small group of artists called the Guild of St Luke (Luke being the patron saint of artists) to foster the talent of young painters, to whom Harry was always generous with encouragement. When I first met him he was sitting in an armchair from which the horsehair upholstery had long since fallen away leaving little except the wooden frame. He was 92, and still taking snuff and drinking copious glasses of whisky. A marvellous old character, he retained the resonant voice of an actor performing Victorian melodramas. But he was clearly an educated man. A convert to Roman Catholicism at the age of 16, he displayed a deep understanding of theology and spoke with authority on many subjects. His work as an artist was recognised by the Establishment when one of his portraits, of John Armstrong ARA, was hung in the National Portrait Gallery. Other subjects included Lady Iris Mountbatten, Lady Montague and the Earl of Cromartie.

He had also painted Lord Beaverbrook, whom Walter Sickert also knew. Sickert's own portrait of Beaverbrook, which hung for many years in the Manchester offices of the *Daily Express*, was colossal, and was refused entry into the Royal Academy's annual exhibition on the grounds that smaller works would be overwhelmed. Beaverbrook was also a friend of Churchill, who appointed him Minister of Aircraft Production during the war. As owner of the *Daily Express*, he knew everyone of any consequence in Fleet Street.

When he sat for Harry Jonas their conversation turned to Freemasonry, and Beaverbrook mentioned that newspaper crosswords had been used by Freemasons to pass secret messages. (In 1944 several codewords of the D-Day landings had appeared in the *Daily Telegraph* crossword.) According to Beaverbrook Freemasons passed information to their brothers through the crossword in a well-known tabloid. It was chosen, he said, because of its left-wing views and because it represented the working classes and would therefore not be suspected of carrying messages for the Freemasons, who were generally considered bastions of the Establishment. Jonas accepted what Beaverbrook told him and thereafter regularly completed the crossword in the hope that he would find something of interest. He often found connections between the answers to various clues, but none so interesting as one he found in 1973.

As we have noted, this was the year Joseph Sickert appeared in the six-week BBC series 'Jack the Ripper'. It was during the course of this series, but before Joseph's appearance in the final episode, that Harry Jonas found in the crossword a direct refence to Joseph. Joseph was known among his friends and family as 'Hobo'. In 1973 the following question was being asked by a person or persons unknown: 'Who knows the true story of Jack the Ripper?' The answer was given in the crossword, which is reproduced here. The answers to clues 14 and 15 across and 6 down are respectively 'Sickert', 'son' and 'Hobo'. The crossword therefore seemed to show that information about Jack the Ripper could be provided by Walter Sickert's son, Joseph Sickert, known as 'Hobo'. Joseph has no idea who wanted this information or why. Nor did he discover who provided the answer. It was as if someone was keen to advertise his connection with the murders before it was made known in the BBC programme. Some kind of separate communicating channel must have been used to give the numbers of the pertinent clues. The question remains why this Boy's Own, cloak-and-dagger method was necessary. Foreign spies in wartime would have found such methods crucial, since they would have had difficulty meeting without risk from the security services. The Freemasons, however, meet regularly in their own lodges. They can also talk openly to one another by telephone. I can offer no definite solution to this question, but I suggest that messages passed by means of crosswords were meant to be seen by Freemasons who were too numerous to be reached by telephone or other practicable means.

*

A sad but intriguing postscript to the friendship between Harry and Joseph occurred when Harry telephoned him on 27 February 1990. Joseph was in Ireland, and Harry spoke to Joseph's wife, Edna. He said he was sorry not to be able to speak to Joseph and added: 'Say goodbye to Joseph for me. That's really why I rang – to say goodbye.' With that he rang off. The following day, five months before his 97th birthday, he died.

*

In 1987 Joseph received a visit from two Australian prison warders who were in Britain to study the British penal system. One was the amateur Ripperologist Leonard Baker (above, p. 86). He has also made a study of Freemasonry. He gave Joseph a map of London's East End as it was in 1888. Pencilled lines had been drawn upon it in the shape of a diamond, the points of which touched the spots where four of the Ripper victims' bodies had been found. None of the corners pointed to where Kelly's body was found in Millers Court, because Baker accepts that her body should have been placed in Mitre square where Eddowes was placed after being killed in error. He explained that if the diamond was cut out and folded in half it became a triangle, like a Freemason's ceremonial apron when folded and put away. This, he claimed, was another feature of the Ripper murders that showed that they were masonic.

Using callipers for accuracy I have measured the distances between the points on the map. There was just two millimetres' difference between the two longest parallel lines, and just eight between the other two. These almost negligible differences, when translated into the actual distances between the places where the bodies were found, would represent only a few yards. This was an incredible feat, and the murderers themselves must have consulted a map before deciding where to dump the bodies. Eddowes and Nichols were found almost a mile apart. That four bodies many hundreds of yards apart were found in this near-perfect configuration is certainly beyond the realms of coincidence.

In the first chapter of *Jack the Ripper: the Final Solution* Stephen Knight explained how Paul Bonner, a television producer, and Elwyn Jones, a script-writer, tried to get in contact with Joseph Sickert when they were making the series. Hoping to glean information from the closed files of Scotland Yard, they had lunch with a senior Yard man. He was said to have informed them that Joseph Sickert knew of the marriage between the Duke of Clarence and an Alice Mary Crook, and that the marriage took place at a St Saviour's Church. Though he mixed up the names of Annie and Alice Crook he apparently knew more than any police officer had previously admitted, or, for that matter, has admitted since. Scotland Yard have always maintained that they have no information about Jack the Ripper other than what is in the official file. Clearly this is not so. The implication that some people at Scotland Yard have known all along that Joseph, his mother, his grandmother and his grandfather, the Duke of Clarence, were in some way connected with those infamous murders, cannot easily be dispelled.

The 'senior Yard man', as he was described by Knight, who revealed the Sickert connection to the BBC wished to remain anonymous. Knight wrote of him (p. 17):

> Though his name cannot be disclosed, he is regarded as an impeccable source.

It has been suggested that the information came indirectly from Sickert himself. On 23 June 1976 Nigel Morland, editor of the *Criminologist*, claimed that after publication of Stowell's article (see above, pp. 137ff.) Joseph Sickert approached him 'asking if I could use the material he had ...'. Joseph says that it was the other way round, and that it was Morland who got in touch with him. Joseph's version is as follows.

When land and property in the area of Maple Street, Howland Street and Cleveland Street were being purchased in the 1960s, just after the building of the GPO (now Telecom) Tower, various people from round about were interviewed for television. Among them was Harry Jonas. During this period the actor Oliver Reed, who played Bill Sykes in the musical *Oliver*, was told that Harry Jonas had been served an eviction order on his studio at 35 Maple Street. Hearing that the studio had once belonged to Thackeray, had featured in his novel *The Newcomes* and had been frequented by famous artists such as William Orpen, Walter Sickert and Augustus John, he announced on 21 April 1969 that he was setting up a trust fund to restore and repair the premises. As a result of the public interest aroused, he was interviewed privately by Eamon Andrews. Andrews claimed an interest in Jack the Ripper, and Harry mentioned that the crimes were due to events which began in Cleveland Street. This, he said, had been told him by Walter Sickert.

The developer Sir Max Rayne, later Lord Rayne, eager to demolish Harry's studio to make way for offices, and hearing that Harry was a deeply committed Roman Catholic, persuaded him to move to a house in Myddelton Square which had once been a Carmelite Convent. It remained his home until his death in February 1990.

Meanwhile Andrews got in touch with Nigel Morland, whom he knew to be a Ripperologist, and relayed what Harry had told him about the Cleveland Street connection. Morland got in touch with Harry, who invited him to his new home in Islington with Joseph.

Morland is no longer alive, but it may have been he who told Scotland Yard of the connection of Sickert with the Ripper story. Even if it was, Joseph still believes that his family was already known to them for its Ripper connection. He remembers that as early as the 1940s an Aliens Officer attached to Albany Street Police Station told Joseph's mother that he had heard that there was some connection.

As noted in Chapter 8, Annie Crook was arrested by the police on 29 April 1894 for hitting a man over the head with a bottle and was released because she had been with her solicitor at the time of the alleged incident. Alice too, we heard, was arrested, in 1905 and taken to Holloway, when her son Charles was removed from her. Also Alice's husband, William Gorman, appeared at Bow Street Magistrates Court on a murder charge, but was released on a plea of self-defence. As noted in Chapter 5, two BBC researchers discovered that Alice's first-born, Charles, was taken to live with the Royal Family.

In 1988, the centenary year of the Ripper murders, a Scotland Yard spokesman proclaimed in a television programme:

> It is often said that there's a set of records kept at the Home Office that tell us who it is. That's nonsense. At least, if they do exist I've never seen them. I can certainly say that we do not keep a set of records here at New Scotland Yard.

Whether or not it has been seen, a file of sorts must exist. Since the police amassed a whole catalogue of information on several of Joseph's relations, and since researchers were able to discover highly sensitive material connecting Alice Crook with the Royal Family, who can deny that some members of the police Establishment have, for several decades, known of the Sickert/Ripper connection?

The 19 August 1988 edition of the *Guardian* reported that Scotland Yard had announced that several photographs and letters, which for decades had been lost from the Jack the Ripper file, had 'come into [their] possession'. It was claimed that they had been posted to Scotland Yard in a large brown envelope via a Croydon pillar-box. According to the *Guardian*, the Yard claimed that they had been sent to them anonymously by the family of a deceased ex-police officer who, before he left the force, had been using them as visual aids when giving lectures to other officers. Further, it was stated that Scotland Yard had said that the photographs were the original police photographs of the Ripper's victims and that one of the documents was the original letter – the first letter received by the Yard in 1888 signed 'Jack the Ripper'. While the pedigree of all these documents and photographs is not in question, the identity of the person who sent them is.

Early in 1988 Joseph informed both the Metropolitan and the City of London Police that he owned Abberline's diaries. It was suggested to him that he should give two of them to Scotland Yard's Black Museum, since Abberline had been a Metropolitan man, and that the third should go to the City's Police Museum because one of the Ripper murders, that of Catherine Eddowes, had taken place on City territory. The City of London Police Museum in a letter representing the City Commissioner, dated 18 March 1988, invited Joseph to attend the Police History Society's annual conference to be held in the McMorran Hall at Wood Street Police Station on 24 September 1988. They wrote:

> And if you decide to present the diary/diaries you have to the City of London Police, what a perfect opportunity to do so. I'm sure our Commissioner, Mr Owen Kelly, would be pleased to accept them from you officially.

On 10 April 1988 the Police History Society also wrote to Joseph with the same invitation to attend their annual conference. Joseph decided not to.

*

Joseph told me that the Special Branch had forcibly entered his home and taken away material in his possession. He believed they had been looking for Abberline's diaries which, unknown to them, were not at his home. They took what they could. In fact Joseph presented them with a few items to prevent his home being ransacked. Among them were the original 'Jack the Ripper' letter and the police photographs of the victims. They had been given to Joseph's father by Abberline with the diaries. As noted, Scotland Yard had informed the *Guardian* that the letter had been sent to them anonymously along with the photographs. In 1990, however, they told me on the telephone that the letter still in its original envelope had been sent to them separately, and that they had 'no idea where it came from or who had sent it to them'. Had they known where the letter came from, they would hardly have admitted it, since this would have invited questions from the Press clamouring to know why Joseph had it in the first place – a risk the police could not take since Joseph's connection with the Ripper case and its association with the Royal Family would have proved positive.

It is possible of course that it was not Special Branch but another organisation falsely claiming to be Special Branch who raided Joseph's home. Whoever it was, they were certainly acting in secret on behalf of the Establishment. There are several possibilities, including the Secret Service. Nor can we rule out the chance that it was someone working covertly for the Royal Family.

The photographs in question – of Mary Ann Nichols, Annie Chapman, Elizabeth Stride and Mary Jane Kelly – are now back in Scotland Yard's Ripper file, apart from the one of Kelly, which they deem to be so ghastly that it is retained in the Black Museum. Exactly why is a mystery, since it is one of two out of several photographs which the police made in 1888; one has been published several times and is seen here. The other is no more gruesome. It was taken from the opposite angle from the published picture – that is, from the other side of Kelly's bed – and shows in close-up her right leg and the abdominal cavity which was left gaping when the internal organs were removed.

It is of course impossible to say who ordered the raid on Joseph's home, and without evidence I cannot suggest who was responsible.

As several books and countless newspaper articles in the past five years have shown, Freemasonry is an organisation with many members in police forces across the country, and with none more than in the City of London and Metropolitan forces.

If the diaries had been collected from Joseph's home at the same time as the letter and photographs, doubtless they would have been kept secret once their true import had been perceived.

*

Another curious train of events is worth noting. On 19 November 1973, soon after Joseph's appearance on television, Joseph met Stephen Knight at Harry Jonas's studio and agreed that he would give him the information he needed for his book, and that all subsequent profits would be shared equally, Sickert's share going to societies for deaf and blind children. A contract to that effect was hastily typed out on a battered old typewriter, signed by both parties and witnessed by Jonas and another friend, Keith Parker. They later celebrated with a meal at the Angel Inn Restaurant, St John Street, London EC1, where the contract was witnessed by the proprietor.

Several weeks later Knight asked for Joseph's copy of the agreement in order, he said, to have it drawn up properly by a solicitor. Knight never returned the agreement and Joseph did not receive a penny of the royalties, even though it was he who provided the most pertinent information upon which it was based.

In 1984, after Knight published *The Brotherhood*, an exposé of Freemasonry, Joseph was told by more than one Freemason that there were members of their organisation who were 'out to get' Knight. Indeed many Freemasons today believe that their brotherhood was responsible for Knight's death at thirty-three in 1985. He died of a brain tumour, but recent masonic legend holds that it was somehow chemically induced. Some Freemasons I have spoken to have even claimed a sinister connection between Knight's exposure of the 33° masons and his age at death.

At about 6 o'clock in the evening one day in July 1985 Joseph was sitting in his living room when his infant grandson came to him with an envelope which had been pushed through the letter-box. Inside he found the original typewritten agreement between himself and Knight. Though he did not realise it at the time, it was the very day that Stephen Knight died.

*

Early in 1986 Joseph asked me to let him read a copy of the first draft of this book, since he wished to get the opinion of some friends who for some years had been looking after his family interests. A couple of weeks later he told me that they thought it might be seditious. Unknown to me, they had sent it to the Crown Prosecution Service and asked them their view. On 10 May a number of CPS officials visited Joseph at home. They told him that the book had politial implications and could embarrass the Royal Family, and they questioned his need to publish. He let them believe that he was the author and agreed to change any parts thought to be seditious or treasonable. They took away some documents and gave him a receipt.

Two days after this visit three men came to see him. They produced Warrant Cards and said they were from Special Branch. They knew he had written a book, they said, adding that they were there to check whether it was treasonable. They took away some photographs and letters including some from Walter Sickert to Frederick Abberline, and some from Nigel Morland to Walter.

Nigel Morland had known Sickert during Sickert's final years and had also met Abberline during his retirement in Bournemouth. He claimed that he found Abberline working in his front garden. At first Abberline refused to answer any questions about the Ripper. Finally he relented. Morland reported their conversation in the *Evening News* of 26 June 1976:

> I visited Abberline many years ago when he was living in retirement in Dorset.
>
> In spite of my efforts he was very cagey and said he had no intention of discussing the case in detail. He was sick of the whole business. But when I mentioned two friends of mine – Edgar Wallace and Henry Battley, who became Chief Inspector in charge of the fingerprint bureau – he relented a little.
>
> The case, he said, was tightly shut. 'I've given my word to keep my mouth permanently closed about it.'
>
> But he let slip some revealing comments.
>
> 'There was a lot of material never entered in any records,' he said. 'Hearsay stuff, word-of-mouth information and orders in 1888-9 to forget all about the affair.'
>
> 'Then neither you nor anyone else knows who the Ripper was?' I asked, as I was ushered firmly out of the house.
>
> 'I know,' he said, 'and my superiors know certain facts.' He was not going to give the details to me or anyone else. But he added, and I remember distinctly his exact words:
>
> 'It wasn't a butcher, Yid or foreign skipper, as he was supposed to be ... you'd have to look for him not at the bottom of London society at the time but a long way up. That's all I will ever say. Goodbye.' And the door was firmly closed.

In his introduction to Frank Spiering's *Prince Jack* (1978) Morland said that when he asked Abberline about the identity of the Ripper, Abberline answered with the words: 'I cannot reveal anything except this – of course we knew who he was, one of the highest in the land.'

It will be remembered that it was Nigel Morland, who knew nothing of Abberline's diaries, who published in his magazine the *Criminologist* Dr Stowell's article implicating the Duke of Clarence. The visits to Joseph's home by the Special Branch and the Crown Prosecution Service were reported on the front page of the *Camden and St Pancras Chronicle* for 25 May 1989. The reporter, Gary Henson, made enquiries at Scotland Yard and the CPS to no avail. Both claimed to know nothing of any investigation concerning Sickert. The CPS was quoted as saying: 'If Mr Sickert is in possession of a receipt on CPS notepaper I'd be interested in looking into it.'

I include here a photograph of the said receipt. It is hand-written on CPS Headquarters stationery and says:

> Received ref Mr Sickert
> in respect of Col Matthew Baker.
> 1 set of sealed documents.
> 14.40pm.
> 10th May '89.   signed illegibly

In a telephone call to the CPS headquarters, whose number was on the receipt, I was told that no Colonel Matthew Baker worked there.

It may be that those who visited Joseph's home had no connection with either the Crown Prosecution Service or the Special Branch and merely used them as cover to hide their true identity. Even so, Joseph and I decided not to show the receipt to the CPS. We decided, on reflection, not to pull the ears of a dog which might turn to bite.

Crown Prosecution Service   Headquarters

4/12 Queen Annes Gate
London SW1H 9AZ

Telephone 01-273
Switchboard 01-273-3000

Director of Public Prosecutions
Allan Green QC

Deputy Director and Chief Executive
D. S. Gandy OBE

With Compliments

Fax 01-222-0392   Telex 945310 CPS HQ   Britdoc DX2328 Victoria

CHAPTER TWELVE

Mary Kelly: The Final Twist

In Chapter 8 I dealt with Abberline's diaries and revealed, among other things, some of the information, previously unknown, that he provided about four of the Ripper victims: Mary Ann Nichols, Annie Chapman, Elizabeth Stride and Catherine Eddowes. I omitted most of the information he gave about Mary Kelly.

Abberline claimed that Kelly was born in August 1865. In 1888 newspapers variously reported that she was 24 or 25 at her death. The brass plate on her coffin stated that she was 25. According to Abberline, her age was 23 years and 3 months.

This, however, was the least important piece of information in Abberline's diary. The following notice of a letter sent to him early in 1889 has never been revealed before and provides a final twist to this most controversial of all murder stories. In January 1892 he wrote:

> Through a letter sent to me in Jan 1889, from Miss Nora O'Brien of Roofer Castle, Limerick, Ireland, who stated that Marie Jeanette Kelly was her niece, daughter of her brother who was in the army, officer of the Inniskilling Dragoons. Her real name was Mary Jane O'Brien. Kelly was the name of a distant relative. She had been receiving letters from her in the name of Mary Jane Kelly, but after her letters stopped coming she had found out about the Whitechapel murders.

O'Brien is the family name of the Barons Inchiquin, legitimist kings of Ireland. The family seat was Dromoland Castle, County Clare. Despite its aristocratic association O'Brien was by 1890 the sixth commonest surname in Ireland. Kelly was the second commonest and therefore a good name for an Irish woman to use who wished to hide her true identity.

Kelly's landlord, John McCarthy, was quoted in the *Western Mail* of 10 November 1888 as saying that Kelly sometimes received letters from Ireland which he believed were from her mother. Joseph Barnett was obviously kept in the dark by Kelly, since she withheld certain details from him about her background. We know this because he said she never corresponded with her family. Clearly she did; otherwise they would not have known where to send her the letters seen by McCarthy. All the mai addressed to Millers Court would have been delivered to the landlord, as was customary in these yards where each room in a house became a separate family dwelling. The responsibilty for distributing letters to their intended recipients would in this case have been McCarthy's, who would have noticed any Irish postmarks and would therefore have been able to state categorically that Kelly had received letters from Ireland.

As we saw above, Abberline said that Nora O'Brien made it clear in her letter to him that her niece had been writing to her under the name Kelly, so presumably Nora's replies were addressed to Mary under this name rather than under her actual name, O'Brien. If not, how would McCarthy have known whom the letters were for? Mary had definitely been lying to Joseph Barnett. Had she not told him that she had married a collier in Wales called Davis who died in a mining explosion? Yet at St Catherine's House the marriage registers have no record of any Mary Jane Kelly married in Wales between 1874 and 1884. Perhaps her lies to Barnett were intended to inspire pity for the plight she was claiming to have found herself in as a destitute young widow. By this subterfuge she hoped he would excuse her for resorting to prostitution, the very thing he most strongly objected to.

Barnett apparently knew nothing of the name O'Brien. Nor did he know that Kelly's aunt lived in a castle, or he would certainly have mentioned what, in the East End at least, would have been a particularly interesting item. Roofer Castle, however, was not an actual castle with dungeon, moat or castellated towers. Neither Limerick City Reference Library nor the Archivist at Limerick County Library could find any reference to a castle of that name. In reply to my enquiries Dr S.C. O'Mahony of the Limerick Regional Archives wrote as follows:

> We have not been able to locate anyone who ever heard of Roofer Castle, or to find it in any guide. 'Castle' frequently occurs in placenames. When it occurs in the name of a family home, it does not mean that someone is claiming that their home is a castle; rather it denotes that a house has been built on to an earlier castle or near it. I don't think it is used to make their home sound more grand. The word 'House' is much more effective in this respect: e.g. Seafield House would leave one in no doubt that the occupants thought they lived in the principal house in Seafield.

Another explanation is that Roofer Castle was the name of a public house.

Notwithstanding the foregoing, Barnett was aware that Kelly came from a good family. In the interview given to the Press Association published in the *Western Mail* for 10 November 1888 he stated that they were 'fairly well off'. In the same report a Mrs Carthy, with whom Kelly once lived at Breezer's Hill off Pennington Street, said that Kelly's family were 'well-to-do-people', adding that Kelly was 'an excellent scholar and an artist of no mean degree'. The day after the murder *The Times* reported that Maria Harvey, who had stayed overnight with Kelly for a few nights before her death, had said that Kelly's status was 'much superior to that of most persons in her position in life'. That Kelly was from a respectable background is to be presumed from the letter sent to Abberline. As we have seen, by the standards of her East End contemporaries she was something of a lady, if not an aristocrat.

Abberline found a definite link between Mary Kelly, as Mary O'Brien called herself, and Cleveland Street, where Walter Sickert had brought her to work as a nanny to Annie Crook's daughter, Alice. As we noted in Chapter 2 and Chapter 8, Abberline revealed that Sickert had approached the solicitor Edmond Bellord, a partner in a firm of Cleveland Street Estate Agents and a founder committee member of the Women's Refuge in Crispin Street, asking him to find a girl to work with Annie in the shop. Bellord was more than a solicitor, as we can see from the following information found in Abberline's first diary:

> Bellord Domestic Agency helped her to acquire service to a West-End family as a nanny in Cleveland Street. Had made friends with a house-parlourmaid, Winifred May Collis, 20, of 27 Cleveland Street, Great Portland Street, who went to stay with Mary Jane Kelly in Dorset Street in Nov 1888, due to an unwanted pregnancy. Never heard of again?

There was a particularly startling revelation made to our intrepid detective. After noting that Kelly's letters to her ceased in early November 1888, Nora O'Brien claimed, in Abberline's words, 'but in January 1889 she received a christmas card from Kelly ...'

The reader will be forgiven for thinking how inefficient the postal system was between England and Ireland in 1888. It was not. In many ways it was enviably better than it is today. The number of letters was much smaller, and local letter deliveries were often made three times a day, and sometimes four.

Why then did it take Kelly's card more than a month to arrive in Limerick, assuming that she posted it in London before her death in November? The simple answer was supplied by Nora O'Brien. She told Abberline that it had been sent, not from London, but 'from Canada'.

Only two explanations are possible. Either Kelly gave the card to a third person who travelled to Canada and posted it there on her behalf, or the body found in room 13 at Millers Court was not that of Kelly, who had travelled to Canada and posted the card herself from there.

Two statements of Abberline's help us to reach the correct conclusion. First, he said of Mary Kelly:

> I believe she was a P.A.

Joseph was told by his father that in police parlance of the day a PA was a 'police agent': that is, someone not in the police force but working for them in some way, either for money or favours – what an old lag in a 1950s British B movie might call a 'copper's nark'.

Secondly, Abberline claimed that he

was advised not to pursue any more of this investigation.

Kelly would have little, if anything, to gain by pretending to her aunt that she was living in Canada at a time when she was in fact living somewhere else. Abberline gave no indication that Kelly was deceiving her. We therefore have no reason to believe that in this instance there was any deception on her part.

If Mary Kelly was still alive and in Canada around Christmas time, after her supposed murder, several questions present themselves:

(1) Whose body was found in Millers Court?

(2) Who provided the means for Kelly to sail to Canada?

(3) Why did Abberline think that Kelly was an agent of the police?

(4) Why was Abberline told not to pursue his investigation further, and by whom?

*

Abberline's diary of 1896 is the sole extant source naming Kelly's previously unknown friend Winifred May Collis. He added that, after Kelly's apparent murder, Collis was

Never heard of again?

This statement, with its incongruous question mark, was surely his way of informing us that it was Collis, not Kelly, who was murdered in Millers Court. He knew of Collis from his time in Cleveland Street with Prince Eddy, where he had also met Kelly. After the discovery of the body in Millers Court, on being told that room 13 was rented by Kelly, Abberline must have feared that evidence would be found there which was potentially dangerous to the Royal Family. No doubt he entered the room with the intention of retrieving anything that could be connected with Eddy and Cleveland Street. Among the things he found were some papers which had belonged to Winifred Collis. They were merely lists of household items: four pages of crockery and cutlery, much of it silver, and a fifth page of household linen, with the word 'Parlourmaid' at the top. Abberline's diaries do not reveal why he believed that these pages belonged to Collis, but that is what he told Walter Sickert when he gave them to him with the diaries. Knowing that Collis was a parlourmaid in Cleveland Street, he simply assumed the obvious – that the lists were connected with her household duties. Incidentally No. 27 Cleveland Street, where Abberline said Collis worked, was the only house in a block

of business premises listed as a private residence in the Post Office
Directory of 1888.

Of Kelly, the diarist wrote:

> I now know she was never an unfortunate. No record of Workhouse or of
> infirmary or of any other help or assistance.

The first sentence flies against everything that was said about her.
Statements given to Abberline by Kelly's friends or neighbours show that
they believed her to be a prostitute. Twenty-year-old Lizzie Albrook, a
friend of Kelly's, said that when Kelly last spoke to her it was to warn her:

> About the last thing she said was, 'Whatever you do, don't you do wrong and
> turn out as I have.' She had often spoken to me in this way and warned me
> against going on the streets as she had done. She told me, too, that she was
> heartily sick of the life she was leading and wished she had money enough
> to go back to Ireland where her people lived. I do not believe she would have
> gone out as she did if she had not been obliged to do so to keep herself from
> starvation.

Kelly's lover, Joe Barnett, even stated:

> she told me that she had obtained her livelihood as a prostitute for some
> considerable time before I took her from the streets ...

He added that it was 'her resorting to prostitution' that caused him to
leave her. The night before her death he wasn't able to give her any
money, which suggests that she asked him for some, so presumably she
had none of her own. Florence Pash, a friend of both Sickert and Kelly,
also said that Kelly became a prostitute. All of which makes Abberline's
statement that Kelly was not an 'unfortunate' even odder. He must have
considered her a shrewd and able young woman. For instance, he
discovered that not only was she well-educated – an opinion which, as we
have seen, he shared with Maria Harvey and Mrs Carthy – but she had
an illegal arrangement with an unnamed man who worked at the London
Hospital in Whitechapel Road. This man had the job of 'laying out'
persons who died in the hospital. Many bereaved relatives could not
afford shrouds and therefore buried their dead in their Sunday-best.
Between the time the relatives viewed the body in the coffin and its
arrival at the cemetery the man who 'layed them out' removed the
clothing, later selling it to Mary Kelly, who re-sold it to second-hand
clothing shops or to individuals. This, said Abberline, was how she made
her living after she left Cleveland Street.

Prostitution was therefore a last resort, inconsistent with Kelly's true
inclination and adopted only when the second-hand rag trade was at a
low ebb. Nevertheless she was a prostitute, and Abberline, one of the
Yard's best detectives, knew this. On the day the body was discovered

Barnett, as we have noted, told him he had left Kelly because she had returned to prostitution. Perhaps Abberline had grown to like Mary and, because of her respectable background in Cleveland Street and her family connections in Ireland, decided to leave her in death with a better name than she had earned in life. Joseph recalls that Abberline spoke slowly and seemed to be a kind man, as we hear from other reports. He may have found it easy to repay Nora O'Brien for the information she gave him by concealing ill of her errant niece.

Though Nichols, Chapman and Stride were told by Kelly that Prince Eddy married Annie Crook, they had proof to back this assertion. Abberline stated that Kelly did have proof:

> Kelly left Cleveland Street with Annie's marriage certificate. Left it with nuns at Women's Refuge, for safe-keeping. Also other papers which E left in J.N's carriage.

What were these papers left by Eddy in John Netley's coach? Abberline did not say. If Walter knew that Kelly had the marriage certificate, the Ripper gang probably also knew: or at least they suspected something of the kind. The threat this posed to the monarchy was serious. The certificate gave Kelly power; it could buy her life and her passage to Canada.

*

As noted in Chapter 8, Abberline stated that Kelly had two children: one adopted and the other sent to live in Canada by the Sisters of Mercy of the Women's Refuge in Crispin Street. In a Press Association syndicated interview, in *The Times* of 10 November 1888, an unknown woman claimed that Kelly had a little boy and that the day before she was found dead she had seen her at 10.30 p.m. with a respectably dressed man who had given her money and accompanied her to her room. It was stated that while he was there Kelly's son had been taken to a neighbour's house. When the boy was returned to Kelly the next morning the man she was with gave him some money and sent him on an errand. The woman may have been confusing Kelly with someone else, since she mentioned that Kelly lived on the second floor when in fact she lived on the ground floor. Of course though she may have been been acquainted with Kelly – drinking with her, sharing gossip and so on – she may never have actually visited her room and may have made an incorrect assumption based on something Kelly said.

There were other unsubstantiated reports that Kelly had a son, but neither her landlord, John McCarthy, nor her ex-lover, Joseph Barnett, mentioned it. Abberline, however, was specific on the point:

Kelly's son Michael sent to Canada by nuns at Womens Refuge.

If this is true, the child was clearly sent there before Kelly lived in Millers Court – before she knew either Barnett or McCarthy.

Canada may seem an odd place to send a child, but it was customary at the time. Professor Fishman notes that it was common practice for Boards of Guardians to send pauper children to Canada. Here is one such example of these heartless bureaucratic decisions. It is copied here in full:

Whitechapel Union

I, the undersigned, being one of the Magistrates of the Police Courts of the Metropolis sitting at the Thames Police Court do hereby Certify that I have this day personally examined [as listed above except Mary Clifford] at present maintained at the Forest Gate District School chargeable to the Whitechapel Union etc ... and that they have severally consented to emigrate to Canada.

As witness my hand on the 6th day of April 1888.

Sgd. Franklin Lushington

Whereupon it was resolved:

That the six orphan and deserted children ... having consented to emigrate to Canada, the necessary steps be taken to effect the emigration and that a sum not exeeding eleven pounds be expended for each child and charged upon the Common Fund of the Union.[1]

Professor Fishman told me that Dr Barnado's Homes also sent destitute children to Canada. By 1890 they had purchased large tracts of land there. Indeed by 1927 *Harmsworth's Universal Encyclopedia* could state:

over 26,000 boys and girls have been sent overseas, by Dr Barnardo's, chiefly to Canada.[2]

Whether or not the Sisters of Mercy placed Kelly's son in the clutches of the local Board of Guardians who later sent him to Canada, or whether they arranged his emigration through Dr Barnado's, I cannot say, but the child was a substantial reason for Kelly's wishing to go herself to Canada.

Abberline did not record what happened to the unnamed child, except to say that it was adopted; perhaps the adoption was also arranged by the Sisters of Mercy. Nor did he record who looked after the second child, Michael, before Kelly arrived in Canada. She may have had relations in Canada, perhaps a brother or sister. Abberline did not elucidate, and we can only speculate. Walter told Joseph that Michael eventually worked for a publishing company in Vancouver, and that after she arrived in Canada Kelly changed her name to Claston. Since he knew this, we may confidently assume that he kept in touch with Kelly after 1888.

When Abberline described Kelly as a 'PA' he was, according to what

Walter told Joseph, hinting that she did a deal with the Ripper gang leaders. Walter claimed that Annie's marriage certificate was given in exchange for her life and a new start in Canada, and that it was through him that this arrangement was made.

But it was unlikely that Lord Randolph would permit her to escape. The killers had done too much and gone too far to stop, now that they were so close to killing their most important victim. But, unknown to Lord Randolph, Winifred May Collis went to Millers Court and became a subtitute for Kelly. Apart from Kelly herself, only Walter Sickert, and later Abberline, knew that Kelly did not die in Millers Court.

*

If Kelly was alive after the body was found that was thought to be hers, we might reasonably expect to discover other supporting evidence from the time. Only Abberline's diary makes sense of the statement given to the police by Caroline Maxwell. In this statement, which I quoted in full (above, p. 44), Mrs Maxwell claimed to have seen and spoken to Kelly hours after the doctors said she had been murdered. She repeated this, giving further information when questioned at Kelly's inquest. Here is the court clerk's hastily written report of what she said:

> I live at 14, Dorset Street, my husbands name is Henry Maxwell he is a Lodging House Deputy I knew deceased for about 4 months as Mary Jane I also knew Joe Barnett, I believe she was an unfortunate girl. I never spoke to her except twice – I took a deal of notice of deceased this morning seeing her standing at the corner of the Court on Friday from 8 to half past. I know the time by taking the plates my husband had to take care of from the house opposite. I am positive I saw deceased I spoke to her I said why Mary What brings you up so early she said Oh! I do feel bad! Oh Carry I feel so bad! she knew my name – I asked her to have a drink, she said Oh no I have just had a drink of ale and have brought it all up, it was in the road I saw it – as she said this she motioned with her head and I concluded she meant she had been to the Brittania at the corner. I left her saying I pitied her feelings – I then went to Bishopsgate as I returned I saw her outside the Brittania talking to a man – the time was about 20 minutes to half an hour later about a quarter to nine – I could not describe the man I did not pass them I went into my house I saw them in the distance, I am certain it was deceased, the man was not a tall man – he had on dark clothes and a sort of plaid coat – I could not say what hat he had on – Mary Jane had a dark skirt – velvet body – and maroon shawl & no hat – I have seen deceased in drink but not really drunk.[3]

In the light of the doctor's testimony regarding the time of Kelly's death it was thought that Mrs Maxwell had mistaken the day she claimed to have seen Kelly. This is most unlikely, because she originally made the claim in her statement to Abberline on the day the body in Kelly's room was found. Unless she was a complete cretin she would hardly confuse the morning's events with those of the day before. Her statement, which was clear, lucid and uncluttered by speculation and yet full of details, indicates that she was no cretin. Alternatively, if she had been drunk we should not expect her to have recalled details so vividly.

Mrs Maxwell's testimony was corroborated by that of others, for she was not the only one to see Kelly early that morning. On 10 November *The Times* reported that an unnamed woman saw Kelly between 8.30 and 8.45 a.m. – the very time that Maxwell claimed to see Kelly again. A week later the same newspaper said that Maurice Lewis, a tailor from Dorset Street, saw Kelly leave her room at 8 a.m. and return soon afterwards. He claimed to have seen her in the Horn of Plenty, a public house on the same side as Millers Court on the corner at the Crispin Street end of Dorset Street. She was with a woman called Julia (Julia Venturney? See below, p. 234) and a man called Dan who sold oranges in Billingsgate and Spitalfields markets and with whom, according to Lewis, Kelly had lived until recently.

Two hours later Lewis was illegally playing pitch-and-toss in Millers Court, and when their lookout boy shouted 'Copper!' they ran down to The Britannia at the corner of Dorset Street and Commercial Street. Lewis was positive that he saw Kelly sitting with some women, one of whom was called Julia. It was just past 10 a.m., only fifteen minutes after Maxwell said she saw Kelly standing outside the same public house.

Kelly's decision to let people believe that the body in her room was hers was probably reached in a moment of opportunism. Two witnesses at Kelly's inquest, Elizabeth Prater from the room above Kelly's and Sarah Lewis who was staying opposite, claimed that at about 4 a.m. they heard someone cry out feebly 'Oh murder!' It is most unlikely that a woman suddenly confronted by a man with a death-dealing blade would half-whisper 'Oh murder!' She would scream 'Help!' at the top of her voice or, alternatively, be rendered utterly speechless through fear.

If Kelly discovered her dead friend horribly murdered, her blood, gore and flesh besmirching the floor and walls, a stifled cry of 'Oh, murder!', with a hand at the mouth to stifle the overwhelming urge to vomit, is exactly what we might expect. When Kelly went to the broken window pane to reach through and release the bolt on the door, she would be able to see, by the light of the fire, what had occurred. The horror in the room would have precluded her entry and forestalled any intention she may have had of retrieving the papers which Abberline later discovered. Even if she managed to suppress her fear she could not have opened the door, because it was barred by the marble-topped table, and old sash-cord windows are more difficult to open from the outside than from the inside. She probably wandered around in shock for the next four hours. During this time she must have realised that she had been the intended victim.

In the previous weeks, according to Barnett's testimony at the inquest, Kelly had said several times that she was afraid of someone. When the

Coroner asked Barnett, 'Did she express fear of any particular individual?', he answered, 'No, sir.' If she was frightened of someone, but not of one 'particular individual', was she frightened of more than one person, perhaps a group of people? The Ripper gang? Barnett also told the Coroner, 'I bought newspapers, and I read to her everything about the murders, which she asked me about.' This seems to suggest that Kelly had more than a passing interest in the Ripper murders. Indeed since she had attempted blackmail with the first three victims it is clear that she knew of the thread linking them. The death of Catherine Eddowes, whom she probably did not know and who was no part of the blackmailing coterie, might well have served to confuse Kelly at first. Later, after she read that Eddowes had given the name Kelly to the police, she might have realised that the murderers had confused Eddowes with herself, thus lulling her into a false sense of security which kept her openly on the streets.

*

When it dawned on Kelly that she, not Collis, was the intended last victim, she probably steeled herself to return for the incriminating letters connecting her with Cleveland Street and Prince Eddy. Unable to overcome the nausea resulting from the horrific spectacle beyond the covering of her window, she walked back into Dorset Street, where she was sick in the roadway, the results of which she pointed out to Maxwell.

Kelly had no reason to think that anyone would call on her early in the morning. If they did they would get no reply from their knock at her door and would go away. As far as she knew, the body in her room need not be discovered for some time, giving her the opportunity to gather her thoughts and have a drink at The Britannia to steady her nerves, where she was seen by Lewis in the company of others.

Whatever she decided, and whatever the final arrangements, and whoever made them, one thing appears certain: Mary Jane O'Brien, alias Kelly, was not the person murdered in Millers Court.

*

The body was identified as Kelly's by her one-time lover, Joe Barnett. The torso was in such a terrible state that the police would have covered it, leaving only the head showing for identification purposes. Not only was the forehead skinned, but (above, p. 45):

> The ears and nose had been clean cut off – while the face was slashed about, so that the features of the poor creature *were beyond all recognition*. (My italics)

The *Illustrated Police News* of 17 November reported that a certain Dr

J.R. Gabe of Mecklenburgh Square saw Kelly's body. He said that, as well as the forehead, the cheeks were skinned. The *Western Mail*, a week before, had also reported that 'the flesh of the cheeks and forehead [was] peeled off'.

The body and face were so disfigured that the only features Barnett claimed to recognise, according to the written copy of his oral statement given to the inquest, were 'the ears and the eyes'.

Barnett was afflicted with a stutter, which during his testimony was probably exacerbated by the solemnity of the occasion and the emotional trauma of his bereavement. This may have led whoever took notes of the proceedings to mishear what he said, because on 17 November the *Illustrated Police News* reported that he said 'the *hair* and eyes' (my italics).

The *Western Mail* of 10 November reported that Kelly answered to the nickname 'Fair Emma'. The *Illustrated Police News* of that day stated that Kelly was nicknamed 'Ginger'. Florence Pash, who was Kelly's friend, said she had 'good hair, dark, bushy'. The several paintings by Walter Sickert of a certain Mrs Barrett, one with the alternative title 'Blackmail', which he claimed were really of Kelly, also show her with dark bushy hair. 'Fair Emma' might easily have referred to Kelly's comeliness rather than her colouring and have indicated that she was fair of face. On the other hand, I know of no one nicknamed 'Ginger' who did not have red hair. The Irish, like the Scots to whom they are related, are noted for having a higher proportion of red-haired people than other nationalities. From the nickname 'Ginger', the paintings of Sickert and the description by Pash, it is safe to assume that Irish-born Mary Kelly had dark red hair.

Much of the blood in room 13 at Millers Court came from the woman's throat and lay in a large patch by the side of the head. Much of it would have been soaked up into the hair lying in it on the pillow. Also, the skinning of the forehead and cheeks would have caused blood to seep into the hair line. We do not know the colour of Collis's hair, but if it wasn't red like Kelly's, it might, at a glance, have appeared red, covered as it must have been in blood. This is immaterial, of course, if Barnet identified the body by the ears and the eyes, as reported at the inquest, and not by the 'hair and the eyes' as reported in the *Illustrated Police News* (a penny-dreadful for the masses which had no connection with the police).

The police already believed that it was Kelly who had been murdered, and Barnett was asked to formalise this belief. He went to the room already expecting to see Kelly's body. After all, whose body would he have expected on her bed? If Collis had eyes of the same colour as Kelly's, Barnett could easily have been mistaken in his identification. He is not likely to have looked very long at the butcher's mess before him on the bed. He is more likely to have been horrified by what he saw upon entering the room, to have averted his eyes, to have taken a quick sideways glance at the skinned head, and, sickened with revulsion, to have averted his eyes swiftly before rushing away.

It may be worth noting that in the police photograph purporting to be of Kelly the blood appears black because the orthochromatic photographic plates used in 1888 were not red-sensitive (panchromatic film emulsion was invented in 1906). The hair, which can just be seen, appears much lighter than the blood. If this was a photograph of Kelly, whose hair was dark red, the hair would reproduce as dark as the blood. Clearly this is not a photograph of Kelly.

When Maxwell spoke to her several hours after her apparent death, Kelly told her: 'I have the horrors of drink upon me as I have been drinking for some days past.' This suggests that she had been in a state of intoxication for several days. Yet she had not been drunk when Barnett visited her at 8 p.m. the previous evening, and, although she was drunk, by the time Mary Anne Cox saw her at 11.45 p.m. she appeared to have sobered up when George Hutchinson saw her at 2 a.m. An evening spent in the public house, with periodic breaks taken when she was seen with different men going into her room, hardly constitutes several days of intoxication. One resident of Millers Court, a German woman called Julia Venturney, knew both Barnett and Kelly well and testified that, far from being a drunkard, Kelly was only occasionally the worse for wear. Joseph Barnett said that he 'always found her of sober habits'. As already noted, when she spoke to Maxwell at 8.30 a.m. Kelly had just been sick and pointed to some vomit in the roadway. If she was sober by 2 a.m. why was she being sick when presumably she had slept off the drink of the previous night? It would appear that Kelly was deliberately misleading Mrs Maxwell when she gave drink as the reason for being sick. Was she perhaps sickened by the thought, or even by the sight, of Collis lying butchered in her room?

*

It is common knowledge that pregnancy may be a cause of early morning sickness. Abberline stated in his diary that Collis went to stay with Kelly 'in Dorset Street due to an unwanted pregnancy', but he didn't make it clear who was pregnant, Kelly or Collis. The inference is that Collis went there either for an abortion herself or to perform one on Mary Kelly. It seems likely that it was Collis who was pregnant; otherwise Abberline would have probably written that she went to Dorset Street to 'perform an abortion'. While rumour at the time held that Kelly was not quite three months pregnant, no evidence was ever presented which indicated that the body in Millers Court was that of a pregnant woman. The post-mortem report showed that no part of the body, not even the uterus, was missing. Obviously if Kelly was pregnant, as rumour suggested, it could not have been her body that was found in her room. Alternatively, an abortion could have been performed on either woman before the murder happened.

*

A young woman called Kennedy claimed in the newspapers to have gone into Millers Court to visit her parents at 3.30 a.m. She saw a woman who may have been Kelly standing with either one man or two, and another older woman standing in the background. No other women came forward to say they had been in the Court at the time, making it almost certain that it was Kelly whom Kennedy saw. Obviously, in order to assert her belief that the woman she saw was Kelly, she must have known what she looked like. She regularly visited her parents in Millers Court, and had probably seen Kelly several times. Moreover, since Kennedy wasn't sure whether or not the women had been speaking to one or two men, she may also have been mistaken when she said that the second woman she saw was older than Kelly, particularly since this woman was standing in the background. It should be remembered that Millers Court was a dark yard with only a gas-lamp at the end and was entered through an unlit passage. It is not inconceivable – in fact, since no other women admitted being there at that time, it is more than likely – that the two women Kennedy saw were Mary Kelly and her friend Winifred Collis.

*

As noted, Walter was the one who arranged Kelly's escape to Canada. He told Joseph that when Kelly left England he gave her one of his paintings entitled 'The Boy I Love Is Up In The Gallery'. It was a Music Hall scene, he said, with a female artiste performing on the stage, while in the foreground were three men in the audience wearing bowler hats. The three men, he said, represented the three apprentice masons in the Hiramic legend: Jubela, Jubelo and Jubelum. The girl represented Annie Crook, and the boy up in the gallery – an elevated position – Eddy. Sickert often painted different versions of the same theme, and one known version of this is called 'Little Dot Hetherington At The Bedford Music Hall' (*c*.1888-9).

Abberline did not say who it was who advised him not to pursue any more of this investigation – the word 'advised' perhaps employed to convey a veiled threat. It could only have been someone representing the murderers, or the murderers themselves. It must have been his police superiors, Chief Commissioner Warren and his Assistant, Dr Anderson. Abberline would only have taken such advice from his superior officers. The other members of the Ripper gang – particularly Lord Randolph Churchill, Lord Arthur Somerset and the Earl of Euston – would not have wished to show their faces.

Walter was helped to arrange Kelly's escape to Canada by James Stephen. His feelings for Eddy prompted him to do anything to recover the marriage certificate which would have jeopardised Eddy and his family.

We will never know all the answers, of course, but how glad we can be that Stephen ultimately had the strength of character to go to Abberline with the truth. We should also be grateful to Abberline himself, for he alone had the courage to document the reasons why the Ripper murders were committed, and by whom.

To Abberline's courage we should add that of Joseph Sickert, without whom we would have never have been able to solve what has been, until now, one of the most enduring mysteries in the annals of British crime.

*

P R O L O G U E;

Spoken by a Shabby Poet.

These Benefits are such, no Man can doubt
But he'll go on, and set your Fancy out,
Till for Reward of all his noble Deeds,
At Last like other sprightly Folks he speeds:
Has this great Recompence fix'd on his Brow
As fam'd Parnassus; has your leave to bow
And walk about the Streets—Equip'd—as I am now.
JAMES KENNETH STEPHEN   FEB 1892.

Her Father (who is a Citizen from the Foot to the Forehead of him) lets her seldom converse with her Mother-in-law and me, for fear she should learn the Airs of a Woman of Quality. But I'll take the first Occasion: See there's my Lady, go in and deliver your Letter to her. Lord Randolph Spencer Churchill [*Exeunt.*
Jan 1895.

16   *The* CONFEDERACY.

Scrivener's Wife ?——Come, —— don't flatter me, don't you think Nature design'd me for something *plus elevée* ? H.R.H. Duke of Clarence 1892 ? Jms.
Flip. Nay, that's certain; but on t'other side, methinks, you ought to be in some measure content, since you live like a Woman of Quality, tho you are none.

22   *The* CONFEDERACY.

Flip. Ne'er fear, I'll take care of 'em.
Aml. How he traps 'em; let *Dick* alone.   [*Aside*
Dick. Your Servant, good Madam.   [*To his Mother.*
John CHARLES NETLEY SEP 1903   [*Exit Dick.*
Aml. Your Honour's most devoted.—— A pretty.

The CONFEDERACY.   23

Flip. Then you envy her, I find ?
Cor. And well I may. Does she not do what she has a mind to, in spite of her Husband's Teeth ?
Flip. Look you there now. [*Aside.*] If she has not already conceiv'd that, as the supreme Blessing of Life. SIR WILLIAM W. GULL JAN 1890

Page 4 from Inspector Abberline's copy of Vanbrugh's plays (1719) with names of the Ripper gang inserted in handwriting (see above, p. 183).

Appendixes

Appendix 1: Walter Sickert's studio at 15 Cleveland Street

According to Stephen Knight, Prince Albert Victor was visiting Sickert at 15 Cleveland Street right into the year 1888.[1] But Donald Rumbelow showed that Sickert could not have had a studio there in 1888 since No. 15 had been torn down to make way for the Middlesex Hospital's Trained Nurses' Institute. Knight, as I noted in the Preface, quarrelled with Joseph before he finished his book and was left with an incomplete story; his imagination was a poor substitute for Joseph's narrative. This is not to say that Walter never had a studio there. Joseph has made it clear to me that Prince Albert Victor met Annie Crook about two years before the time suggested by Knight and well before No. 15 was demolished. The Post Office Directory recorded no occupants of 15 Cleveland Street during the years 1885, 1886 and 1887. (It was demolished in 1887 and the new Nurses' Institute completed and occupied in 1888.) But this does not prove that it was unoccupied. As long as a building is standing someone will find a use for it. Take as an example No. 19, two doors along. The Directory does not mention No. 19 either after the year 1884. But it clearly existed. Until 1889, five years after its disappearance from the Directory, it was definitely in use, because in that year it was the address of the male homosexual brothel which featured in the 'Cleveland Street Scandal' of 1889 (see Chapter 7). While it is true, therefore, that Walter Sickert could not have used 15 Cleveland Street in 1888, when the Nurses' Institute was completed, there is no reason to doubt Joseph's account that he used it from 1882 to 1886.

Sickert's habit was to lodge at one address while renting separate rooms for use as his studio. In the file on Sickert at the London Division of the Historic Buildings and Monuments Commission I discovered that he usually had more than one studio at a time. Though he was living in Claremont Square from 1881, and at 13 Edward Square, Kensington from 1884 until he married in 1885, I found no evidence that he had studios at those addresses. Indeed Marjorie Lilly, who was Sickert's student and a friend until his death, claimed in her biography that 'he never worked from home'.[2] Clearly he must have had a studio somewhere, and the empty house at 15 Cleveland Street would have been perfect, situated as it was in a colourful area. As a squatter, Sickert avoided rent and rates: a prime consideration for an artist at the outset of his career. (After his marriage he lived at 54 Broadhurst Gardens, Hampstead.) He was often drawn back to Fitzrovia, and early this century he occupied the 'Frith' at 15 Fitzroy Street (named after W.P. Frith, the painter of 'Derby Day', one of his favourite pictures). He was later to occupy No. 8 opposite, which had been Whistler's old studio. Later still, when Joseph was a boy, he sometimes stayed at Thackeray House (named after the novelist, who once lived there). This was 35 Maple Street, just off Cleveland Street, close to where Telecom Tower now stands, the home of Walter's friend and fellow-artist Harry Jones. Walter's easel was still there after his death in 1942. Jonas, who died in 1990, gave it to Joseph.

One day, at a private view of the Royal Society of British Artists in December 1885, Walter Sickert met 23-year-old Florence Pash, who remained a life-long friend. She is an important witness to the events of Cleveland Street, since, according to Jean Overton Fuller, she often met Sickert at his studio there, 'only a couple of doors down' from a brothel 'at which boys were available to men'.[3] As noted, the Cleveland Street brothel stood at No. 19, while according to Joseph his father's studio was at No. 15 – 'a couple of doors down', as Florence Pash claimed. Fuller was told this by her mother, Violet Overton Fuller, in 1948. Violet was a friend of Florence Pash, who told her also that Sickert 'knew who Jack the Ripper was'.

During the 1970s the Greater London Council decided to erect a blue plaque in memory of Walter Sickert, but they found it more difficult than they had at first imagined, because he had rented so many addresses over the years. In the GLC Press Office letter No. 610 of 29 November 1974 it was acknowledged that 'Sickert lived or worked at more than thirty London addresses'. There is no evidence against Joseph's claim that early in the 1880s one of those addresses was No. 15 Cleveland Street.

Appendix 2: Annie Crook's Scottish origins

The assertion that Annie Crook was of Scottish descent, first made by Joseph and repeated by Knight, was denied by Rumbelow, who stated categorically that Annie 'was born in north London on 10 October 1862' and that her mother Sarah 'was born on 31 August 1838, according to Poor Law entries, at 22 Great Marylebone Street'.[4]

Sarah's death certificate states that she was 75 when she died in 1916. If this is true she must have been born in 1841, not in 1838 as stated by Rumbelow. An entry in the Marylebone Workhouse records, however, for 19 August 1880, gives her age as 42, thus supporting 1838. In the St Pancras Board of Guardians Rough Examinations Register 1879-83 an entry of 13 May 1882 states that she was 42. This would mean that she was born in 1840. But the record of her entry into Cleveland Street Infirmary on 23 October 1905 gives 1839, while the entry for 22 February 1913 gives 1841. Which, if any, of these four dates is correct?

The authors who have criticised Joseph's claims, made through Knight, took their information from the Poor Law entries kept at the Greater London Records Office. Even if Annie was born in London, as Rumbelow claims, it has no bearing on whether or not she was of Scottish descent. Rumbelow and others ought to have checked their information with the more accurate records at the General Register Office, St Catherine's House. If they had, they would have discovered, as I did, that there is no record of Annie Crook's birth in October 1862 and none of Sarah's birth in August 1838. Checking all possible years, I found no record that either was born in England. (Unfortunately, without knowing the name of the parish she was born in it was impossible to check Sarah's birth records in Scotland, because there the name of the parish is needed to locate records before 1855.)

Annie Crook's death certificate, dated 23 February 1920, says that she was 56 when she died. The information was supplied by her daughter Alice. Accordingly,

Annie must have been born in 1863/4, not 1862, as Rumbelow asserts. There were a number of Annie Elizabeth Crooks born in London, but an examination of their birth certificates proved that none was the Annie Crook we are concerned with.

It is easy to see why Poor Relief records are inaccurate. For one thing, people applying for relief frequently told lies. Those who had nowhere to live, or were ill, thought nothing of lying to gain entry into an infirmary or workhouse. In the nineteenth century, in order to appear 'respectable', unmarried women accompanied by their children would invent a marriage date. Others would lie about their age in order to appear older in the hope of gaining more sympathy, just as people nowadays often lie to avoid embarrassing or seemingly pointless questions when applying for Income Support, the inadequate modern equivalent of Poor Relief.

Rumbelow also claimed that Sarah was married to William Crook in 1863, but admitted that there is conflicting evidence, showing that even he did not entirely trust the Poor Relief records. The General Register of Marriages confirms that Sarah and William Crook were definitely not married in London in 1863. In fact I checked all eighty volumes of marriage records under the name Crook from 1849 to 1868 and found no record of their marriage in England. Either they never married or they married elsewhere – perhaps in Scotland.

Human error also plays its part in official records. Using Alice Crook's birth certificate dated 1885, Rumbelow (p. 203) calculated that she was 31 when she married in 1918; but 1918 minus 1885 produces 33, not 31.

Questions are sometimes misunderstood and the answers misheard. This was probably a common occurrence in the entrance-halls of workhouses and infirmaries, crowded as they often were with homeless families – the bored children running around, the babies crying through hunger. Sarah and Annie Crook, who suffered from various illnesses including epilepsy (and, as Rumbelow was quick to point out, often drunk), might well have answered unreliably. Information from Alice Crook would be especially liable to error because, as the Poor Relief records state, she was 'stone deaf'. I found that almost every time Sarah, Annie or Alice entered a workhouse they did so because of illness. They were often put in the sick ward and given an 'invalid's diet'. In the days before the National Health Service, persons who could not afford doctors' fees could go to the workhouse claiming that they were destitute, knowing full well that they would be given a medical examination upon admission and, if found to be ill, be sent to the sick ward, where they would have free medical care.

Appendix 3: St Saviour's

Donald McCormick related a yarn told by a certain Dr Thomas Dutton, a graphologist who studied many of the letters sent to Scotland yard signed 'Jack the Ripper'. He quotes Dutton as saying that 'Annie Chapman, Mary Nichols and Mary Kelly all attended a clinic at St Saviour's Infirmary in Westmoreland Road, Walworth'.[5] Dutton said that Jack the Ripper worked there as a part-time assistant. It was recently claimed by Melvyn Harris that Joseph 'borrowed' the name St Saviour's from McCormick's account and wove it into his own.[6] But why should he do this when all he had to do, if he was inventing his story, was to look for a church close to where Annie Crook worked in Cleveland Street? Why would he need to lift the name St Saviour's from a story when there were two churches by that name close to Cleveland Street? The one in Osnaburgh Street was less than seven hundred yards from where he spent his childhood in Drummond Street. And why should he have chosen a Protestant church in which to place a Catholic ceremony? If this part of his story was invented, would he not rather have chosen a Catholic church – St Mary Magdalene's, for instance, two hundred yards from St Saviour's in Osnaburgh Street and a stone's throw from his home. Joseph knew the denominations of the churches in his area, including St Saviour's, and if his story was an invention he would surely have been careful to pick a Catholic Church in which to place a Catholic wedding. The fact that he did not makes his story more, rather than less, credible.

Appendix 4: The effect of Prince Albert Victor's secret marriage

Donald Rumbelow has said that Eddy's marriage to Annie would have been put aside by the authorities as illegal under the Act of Settlement (1701) and the Royal Marriage Act (1772), and that since no marriage had taken place in law a scandal could not have resulted.[7] I suggest the contrary. It seems perfectly obvious that, if word had leaked that the heir to the throne had secretly married a commoner, and that the marriage was illegal, quite the opposite result would have occurred and it would have been a *cause célèbre*.

Howells & Skinner have stated that, since there is no record of the marriage at the General Register Office, the marriage could not have taken place.[8] Nonsense, I say! Those in power can make sure the records say whatever they wish them to say – especially to save the throne.

Appendix 5: Whether or not Annie Crook was a Roman Catholic

Howells & Skinner,[9] Rumbelow,[10] and others have sought to show that Annie Crook was not a Roman Catholic, in an attempt to discredit Joseph Sickert's account. But they were using the Workhouse Creed records, part of the Poor Relief records which I have already shown (Appendix 1) to be inaccurate. The first time Annie entered a workhouse was on 18 April 1885, the day she gave birth to Alice. (Significantly, it was from this moment that Annie's life took its downward course.) Against Annie's name in the Creed Records are the initials 'C.E.' (Church of England).

Women about to give birth generally enter hospital only after their contractions have begun, and we have no reason to think that Annie Crook's case was different. From her home in Cleveland Street to the Marylebone Workhouse, where Alice was born, was quite a distance for a woman to walk in the initial stages of labour. Even if she had taken a cab she would probably have been accompanied by a relation, or a friend or neighbour. Whoever accompanied Annie and spoke to the receptionist may not have known which denomination she belonged to and have given the commonest and most likely-seeming answer. If it was her friend Walter Sickert, he may have deliberately given false information.

Whatever the case, Walter told Joseph that after the birth she was given good cause to avoid the authorities and felt her life to be in jeopardy. Under this pressure it would not be surprising if Sarah, Annie and Alice concealed or denied their Roman Catholic faith. Annie certainly brought up her daughter as a Roman Catholic. It could be argued that she converted to Roman Catholicism before she met Eddy, but there is no evidence. More probably she was born a Catholic.

It was not until late in my researches, after I had almost finished the first draft of this book, that I discovered that Annie Crook had a sister called Alice, after whom Annie's daughter was named (see Chapter 8). Alice's daughter Ellen Lackner told me that her mother was a Protestant and her auntie, Annie Crook, a Catholic. She never knew, she said, why the two sisters were of different faiths. If, for the sake of argument, we assume that Sarah and her husband were also of different faiths – Sarah Roman Catholic, her husband Church of England – they may have agreed for the sake of fairness to have Annie baptized a Catholic and her sister Alice baptized an Anglican.

At all events Annie's mother, Sarah Crook, went into the Poland Street workhouse on 3 February 1907, and the records categorically state that her religion was Roman Catholic. In December that year they show the initials 'R.C.' against her name, but this is crossed through and 'C. of E.' inserted in its place. Did Sarah momentarily forget herself and give her correct religious denomination, only to change it when she realised what she had said? Walter and Alice both told Joseph that it was being a Roman Catholic that had led to Annie's troubles. It is not surprising therefore that Sarah and Annie, and later Alice, should have denied their denominational allegiance when confronted with figures in authority such as those at the workhouse.

Appendix 6: Eddy and Princess Hélène d'Orléans

In 1890, two years after the Ripper murders, Eddy, having been rejected by Princess Alix of Hess and refusing to consider Princess Margaret of Prussia, proposed to Princess Hélène d'Orléans, daughter of the Pretender to the French throne, the Comte de Paris. The princess was a Roman Catholic and the proposal created consternation in royal circles. In May that year Queen Victoria, hearing about the affair through her well-organised network of family spies, wrote to Eddy castigating him for even thinking of such a thing, and told him that the marriage was 'utterly impossible' and that he 'should avoid meeting her as much as possible'.[11] Nevertheless at the end of August 1890 they became engaged at Mar Lodge while staying with the Duke of Fife. Alexandra hated the idea of any German marriage and against all advice encouraged the match with Hélène, suggesting to the young couple that they should go to nearby Balmoral to seek Queen Victoria's support. This they did on 29 August. Alexandra knew that Victoria was a sentimentalist, and her plan worked. Eddy wrote of the visit to his brother George:

> I naturally expected Grandmama would be furious at the idea, and say it was quite impossible etc. But instead of that she was very nice about it and promised to help us as much as possible.[12]

What brought about this change of mind in Victoria? Surely not mere sentiment. Alexandra too was well aware that marriage to a Catholic Princess was not possible if Eddy was to retain his right to the throne. Why should a princess from Denmark – a staunchly Protestant country where her father, King Christian IX, was head of the Evangelical Lutheran Church – support her son in a marriage to a Roman Catholic, a marriage which she knew would end his right to the throne? She may have had Catholic leanings herself. (By her bed at Marlborough House she kept a small replica of Thorwaldsen's statue of Christ, and above the bed hung a four-foot crucifix.)[13]

Nevertheless Walter Sickert told Alice, who later told Joseph, that the story of Eddy's wish to marry Hélène d'Orléans was a fabrication dreamt up by the Royal Family. They were worried that the Vatican was aware that Eddy had married the Catholic Annie Elizabeth Crook and might decide to make political capital out of it. The intended marriage to the French princess was invented to test the Vatican's reaction. The Princess, however, seems genuinely to have fallen in love with Eddy, and offered to defy her father by renouncing Catholicism and joining the Church of England. Her mother, a woman of independent mind who enjoyed smoking pipes while shooting, favoured the marriage. There was no reason why the Vatican should forbid the marriage, unless of course there was an actual canonical impediment. The Pope refused permission, however, and advised Hélène – who travelled to Rome to plead with him personally – to remain faithful to Rome. This, said Walter, was the Vatican's way of indicating to the British Royal Family that the Holy See knew that Eddy was already married. It is pertinent to add that, according to Pope-Hennessy, there is documentary evidence to show that during this apparent love match, Eddy was in love with Lady Sybil St Clair Erskine.[14]

When Queen Victoria and Lord Salisbury expressed their feelings against the proposed marriage to the French princess, it was as if they were really expressing what they had felt two years before at the time of Eddy's marriage to Annie. Queen Victoria said that the marriage to Hélène would have 'the very worst effect possible',[15] while Lord Salisbury warned the Prince of Wales that the 'anger of the middle and lower classes might endanger the throne if it became known that he had advanced or even contemplated it'.[16] Salisbury must have felt that since the throne was in danger over the mere contemplation of Eddy's marriage to a Catholic Princess, it was definitely doomed if his marriage to a Catholic commoner, Annie Crook, became known.

Appendix 7: Abberline's account of the five Ripper victims

The following are the background details of the Ripper's five victims, as discovered by Inspector Abberline, and copied verbatim from his diaries.

Mary Anne NICHOLS
was born August 26th 1845.

Father – Edward Walker. Tradesman, locksmith – later blacksmith. It was her mother who was married at the age of 12, not Mary. Mary Walker married William Nichols on Jan 4th 1864.* William Nichols was a printer by trade, from Oxford. After the wedding, they lived at a lodging house in Bouverie Street† for a while and then both moved in with Mary's father at 131, Trafalgar Street, Walworth, (in St. Saviour's District) south of the Thames. At the last address she

---

* [Abberline here refutes contemporary reports which stated that Mary Nichols was only 12 when she married. Checking the marriage records at St Catherine's House, I discovered that Abberline was correct in his assertion that it was her mother who married at that age, and not Mary herself. Abberline was the only person either then or since to make this discovery.]

† [Bouverie Street was off Fleet Street – a convenient place for a printer to choose to live having recently arrived in London.]

gave birth to two children, the first was a son, Edward John Nichols – born in Camberwell in 1866. The second and third children were named Percy George; born July 18th 1868, and Alice Esther born in 1870. In 1874, they moved to 68, Peabody Building, Stamford Street, off Blackfriars Road. While at the last address gave birth to Eliza Sarah in 1877, and Henry Alfred in 1879. In 1880 she left her husband, and took to drink. From there on, lived in the Lambeth Workhouse from Sept. 6th 1880 until 31st May 1881. She stayed briefly with her father. From thereon a life in various workhouses. Ending Oct 25th. 1887, she was at St Giles Workhouse, Endell Street. Mary Anne Nichols was also known as Mary Gray. Then she went to the East -End, and there met her death on the night of August 31st 1888, just a few days after her 46th year.

She was still married to William Nichols. Mother of 5 – was a friend of Emma Smith, who had explained Annie Chapman.

Annie CHAPMAN
June 1841 – Sept 8th 1888.

Annie Chapman – mother Ruth Chapman married George Smith in 1842, Feb at Paddington. Her father was a private in the life guards at Knightsbridge. The Smiths' children were all well educated. Annie's sister Emily baptised at Holy Trinity Church, Brompton Road. Address then was No. 3 Montpelier Place, Knightsbridge, and then to No 4, Rutland Terrace, Knightsbridge. – 1856 they moved to 12, Keppel Terrace, Windsor. Then the third daughter Georgina was born. George Smith stated the birth giving the birth address as 32, Upper Albany Street, Regents Park. Two years later, in 1858, another daughter Miriam was born, this time at Windsor. Then in 1861 a birth of the only son, Fountain Smith, Middle Row North, Knightsbridge, then back to Windsor, leaving Annie behind in London, taking up respectable employment. After the death of her father the family return to London to 29, Montpelier Place, Knightsbridge. Mother died in 1893. She had called herself Eliza Anne Smith. Annie on May 1st 1869 married John Chapman at All Saints Church. John a coachman, 2 years younger than Annie, was related to Annie's mother. They lived at No 1, Brook Mews, Bayswater. Another address was 1873 at 17 South Bruton Mews, Berkeley Square. In 1886 her husband died Dec 25th. In 1887 went into East-End and so died Sep 8th 1888.

Her address in 17, Bruton Mews, was only 3/5 min around the corner from 74, Brook Street, Sir William W. Gull.

Elizabeth STRIDE
1846 – Sept 30th 1888

Elizabeth arrived in London 1866 from Sweden as a domestic servant to a gentleman near Hyde Park. Married John Thomas Stride 7th March 1869. She lived in at 67 Gower Street, St Pancras, and her husband lived at 21 Munster Street, Regents Park. Husband a coffee-room owner in 1870/1, Upper North Street, Poplar. They lived both together at 178 Poplar High Street. 3 years later Elizabeth Stride left her husband, 1875. On 21st March 1877 she was an inmate at the Poplar Workhouse. Nothing was heard of her until 28th Dec 1881. She suffered from bronchitis, and was admitted to Whitechapel Hosp. and discharged on the 4th Jan 1882. She stayed in a Workhouse from then till she moved to 32 Flower & Dean Street. Then on to 35 Dorset Street with a man Michael Kidney. She was aged 42.

Catherine EDDOWES
4th April 1842 – Sept 29th 1888

Catherine Eddowes was born to George and Catherine Eddowes on the 4th April 1842 at Gaisley Green, Wolverhampton. Her father was a tin-plate worker. The family moved to London living at 4, Baden Place, Bermondsey, where her brother was born. Over the next 10 or 11 years the family lived in Long Lane, Bermondsey, and the children went to the St John's Charity School at Potters Field, Tooley Street. In 1851, they lived at 35 West Street, Bermondsey. On Nov 7th, 1855, Mrs Eddowes died of phthisis (T.B. of the lungs). She was 42 when she died. Catherine was only 13 years of age. Her brothers and sisters were sent to the workhouse for the best part of 12 years. At the age of 19 Catherine met an army man, Thomas Conway. She bore him 3 children although she never married him, and they parted in 1880. Conway took the two boys and she took the girl, Annie. In 1880 she took up with another man, an Irish porter named John Kelly. They lived in Flower & Dean Street, Whitechapel. Last record of Catherine was when she was admitted to Whitechapel Infirmary, 14th June 1887, suffering with foot burns. She was known as Kate Conway, and put her religion as R.C. She died age 46, on 29th Sept 1888.

No connection with any of the others.

Pawn ticket in the name of M.J. Kelly.

Mary Jane KELLY
Ref. to Marie Jeanette Kelly. August 1865 – Nov 1888.

Through a letter sent to me in Jan 1889, from Miss Nora O'Brien of Roofer Castle, Limerick, Ireland, when she stated that Marie Jeanette Kelly was her niece, daughter of her brother who was in the army. Officer of the Inniskilling Dragoon Guards. Her real name was Mary Jane O'Brien. Kelly was a name of a distant relative. She had been receiving letters from her in the name of Mary Jane Kelly. But after her letters stopped coming she had found out about the Whitechapel murders. I now know she was never an unfortunate. No record of Workhouse or Infirmary or any other help or assistance. Bellord Domestic Agency helped her to acquire service to a West-end family as a nanny in Cleveland Street. Had made friends with a house parlour-maid – Winifred May Collis, 20, of 27 Cleveland Street off Great Portland Street, who went to stay with Mary Jane Kelly in Dorset Street in Nov 1888, due to an unwanted pregnancy. Never heard of again.

I discovered –

(1) She was not an unfortunate, and she never lacked money.

(2) She mysteriously appeared from nowhere, then dissappeared. I believe she was a P.A.

The aunt received a christmas card from Kelly, sent from Canada after Kelly's murder.

I was advised not to pursue any more to this investigation.

Appendix 8: Letter from Abberline to G.J. Goschen

Among the documents given to Walter Sickert, now in Joseph's possession, is a hurriedly scribbled note written by Abberline to the Chancellor of the Exchequer, G.J. Goschen, on a leaf of official Metropolitan Police stationery (above, p. vi).

In the margin is the number '52983', the same as on Abberline's report on

Kelly's inquest which is in the Ripper file at the Public Record Office, and identifies the note as one of the original documents on the case. The printed heading, 'Metropolitan Police', has been crossed out, indicating perhaps that Abberline considered the note unofficial since the Chancellor of the Exchequer had no jurisdiction in Home Office or police matters.

Goschen, a friend of Lord Randolph's, was Chancellor from 1887 to 1892 after Lord Randolph resigned the post. Before tendering his resignation Lord Randolph was confident it would seriously embarrass the premier, who unexpectedly accepted it. Afterwards he said, 'All great men make mistakes. Napoleon forgot Blücher, I forgot Goschen.'

Abberline's note reads:

Whitechapel   Whitehall

15th day of Dec 1889-92

52983   Sir
                 With respect reference to your last instruction my
                 interview with J.K. Stephen, Lord Randolf [sic] Spencer
                 Churchill, Sir W. Gull were confirmed. I am sending this
                 report for you [sic] personal Attention. No further
                 investigation will be made. I leave this in your hand. I
                 have done our duty. Rest of my report will be sent on. I
                 shall now heed to my burns.
                          Yours respectfully
To G.J. Goschen   D.I. F.G. Abberline (signed)

This document shows beyond doubt that J.K. Stephen named Churchill and Gull as responsible for the Ripper murders.

Why, we may ask, did Goschen instruct Abberline to interview Stephen? Had he heard something on the family grapevine which aroused his curiosity, from his nephew perhaps, who was married to Sir William Gull's granddaughter, Amy Beatrice Cameron Gull, or his former secretary, Moreton Frewen, who was Lord Randolph's brother-in-law? Or perhaps J.K. Stephen had been led by these connections to Goschen, rather than the other way round. Goschen may have found the story implausible, and later, thinking of the possible repercussions, told Abberline to bring to bear all his police experience in an interview with Stephen. No doubt we shall never know the exact background details, but the document is vital evidence for the involvement of Lord Randolph and Sir William Gull.

Appendix 9: George and Reginald Hutchinson

Stephen Knight (op. cit. pp. 253ff.) thought that Hutchinson's description was too elaborate, indeed almost theatrical, and believed that the suspect was Walter Sickert wearing a disguise. Others again have speculated that the description was too detailed to be accurate. Hutchinson's seventy-four-year-old son, Reginald Hutchinson, whom Joseph Sickert and I interviewed recently (May 1992), thinks otherwise. 'Reg' worked with his father for many years and was very close to him. 'Dad took careful note of details,' he said, 'and could remember things accurately. Part of his job was to work out estimates, and, no matter how big the job, he always remembered exactly which materials were needed, and in what quantities, without ever writing it down.'

George William Topping Hutchinson was born in 1866 and celebrated his twenty-second birthday on 1 October 1888, the day after Stride and Eddowes were killed. He followed in his father's and grandfather's footsteps and became a plumber. He was so honest and hardworking that when he became self-employed he was rarely, if ever, without work. His customers recommended him to others.

In 1895, seven years after the murders, he married Florence Jervis. They met when she tripped over his cane after coming down the steps from the stage of the music hall, where he sat in the front row, having watched her performance as a 'Dutch vocalist' (yodeller) and 'skipping-rope-artiste'. After their wedding at Trinity Church, Stepney, they became keen ice-skaters. George was also an accomplished violinist.

'I remember,' said Reg, 'he mentioned several times that he knew one of the women and was interviewed by the police, but I'd never seen his actual statement until today, when you came round. But if that's what he said, that's what he saw. Dad was a very down-to-earth man, and didn't elaborate anything. It just wasn't in his nature. He knew more than he told though, but he kept it close to his chest. Whenever the subject of Jack the Ripper came up, as it often did in the East End in the twenties and thirties, because many people who were there when it happened were still alive, he used to say: "It was more to do with the Royal Family than ordinary people." And when asked who he thought it was he always said: "It was someone like Lord Randolph Churchill." Until you told me that about Abberline's diaries and that he named Churchill, I thought my father was merely saying that in his opinion the murderer was someone high up, like Churchill. Now I can see that he knew all along that the man he saw *actually was Churchill*, but he didn't want to come straight out with it. He said that at the time he was paid a hundred shillings, but he never said why. Perhaps he was paid to keep quiet about what really happened, and say nothing about what he really knew.'

George Hutchinson was working as usual when he suffered a heart attack and died aged 71 in 1938. The previously unpublished photograph of him (Plate 32) does indeed show the honest face of a forthright and 'down-to-earth' man.

Appendix 10: Post-mortem on Mary Kelly

The original post-mortem report on Kelly, written by Dr Thomas Bond, was recovered by Scotland Yard in 1987 and has recently become available:

Position of body
The body was lying naked in the middle of the bed, the shoulders flat, but the axis of the body inclined to the left side of the bed. The left arm was close to the body with the forearm flexed at a right angle & lying across the abdomen. The right arm was slightly abducted from the body & rested on the mattress, the elbow bent & the forearm supine with the fingers clenched. The legs were wide apart, and the left thigh at right angles to the trunk & the right forming an obtuse angle with the pubes.

The whole of the surface of the abdomen & thighs were removed & the abdominal Cavity emptied of its viscera. The breasts were cut off, the arms mutilated by several jagged wounds & the face hacked beyond recognition of the features. The tissues of the neck were severed all round down to the bone.

The viscera were found in various parts viz: the uterus & Kidneys with one breast under the bed, the other breast by the Rt foot, the Liver between the feet, the intestines by the right side & the spleen by the left side of the body. The flaps removed from the abdomen and thighs were on a table.

The bed clothing at the right corner was saturated with blood, & on the floor beneath was a pool of blood covering about 2 feet square. The wall by the right side of the bed & in a line with the neck was marked by blood which had struck it in a number of separate splashes.

Postmortem examination

The face was gashed in all directions the nose, cheeks, eyebrows and ears being partly removed. The lips were blanched & cut by several incisions running obliquely down to the chin. There were also numerous cuts extending irregularly across all the features.

The neck was cut through the skin & other tissues right down to the vertebrae, the 5th & 6th being deeply notched. The skin cuts in the front of the neck showed distinct eccymosis.

The air passage was cut at the lower part of the larynx through the cricoid cartilage.

Both breasts were removed by more or less circular incisions, the muscles down to the ribs being attached to the breasts. The intercostals between the 4th, 5th & 6th ribs were cut through & the contents of the thorax visible through the openings.

The skin and tissues of the abdomen from the costal arch to the pubes were removed in three large flaps. The right thigh was denuded in front to the bone, the flap of skin, including the external organs of generation & part of the right buttock. The left thigh was stripped of skin, fascia & muscles as far as the knee.

The left calf showed a long gash through skin & tissues to the deep muscles & reaching from the knee to 5 ins above the ankle.

Both arms & forearms had extensive & jagged wounds.

The right thumb showed a small superficial incision about 1 in long, with extravasation of blood in the skin & there were several abrasions on the back of the hand moreover showing the same condition.

On opening the thorax it was found that the right lung was minimally adherent by old firm adhesions. The lower part of the lung was broken & torn away.

The left lung was intact: was adherent at the apex & there were a few adhesions over the side. In the substance of the lung were several nodules of consolidation.

The pericardium was open below & the heart was absent.

In the abdominal cavity was some partly digested food and fish & potatoes & similar food was found in the remains of the stomach attached to the intestines.

The fact that her heart was missing was kept from the press. Everything else was accounted for, except her dignity.

Appendix 11: Five letters from Sir William Gull

Early in 1877 it was reported that Princess Alexandra was ill and being treated by Sir William Gull.

Five letters from Gull were purchased at auction in 1990 by Tim Haydock, who generously gave me access to them. Three, dated June 1875, were written to Alexandra on Marlborough House stationery and concern her daughter Victoria, Eddy's sister, who was six and was suffering from a feverish cough. The other two – one from Gull's Brook Street house, the other on Sandringham stationery – are addressed to 'Mrs Jones'. Mrs 'Johnnie' Elizabeth Jones and her sister Mrs Thomas had been called upon from St Bartholomew's Hospital to attend Alexandra and subsequently her husband Bertie during his acute typhoid illness in 1871.[18] Mrs Jones was retained by the Royal Household to care for the children until her death in 1881. The letter from Brook Street is dated 8 March 1877:

Dear Mrs Jones,
So soon as Dr Gream got my note he telegraphed to me that he would come up. He came last evening. If The Princess of Wales would see Dr Gream or allow him to learn particulars from you I think sufficient information for his guidance in advising for the health of the Princess would be quite sufficient. It would not be necessary to trouble her Royal Highness further. I am to see HRH at quarter to 2 today and will ask Dr Gream to accompany me then Her Royal Highness will inform me of her wishes. I got your note of last evening and am quite aware of the circumstances.
Yours faithfully
[signed] William W. Gull
Thursday morning
8th March 1877

The second document sent to Nurse Jones is reproduced here (above, p. 210). It is not a letter but a medical prescription, dated 4 May 1877. The prescription is marked with the embossed stamp of 'H.W. Allen & Willis, Chemists & Co., 55, High Street, Kings Lynn'. The formula, along with chloroform and purified water, contains ergot, a fungus parasite of rye containing various alkaloids. Ergot is sometimes used to treat migraine, but in the nineteenth century it was used in childbirth. It was injected after a birth to make the uterus contract and expel the placenta and to stop any bleeding. Its other main use, both then and now, is to cause miscarriage. I have consulted two doctors and a pharmaceutical chemist, who tell me that Gull's prescription is an abortifacient. Either Alexandra became pregnant and had a spontaneous miscarriage and Gull used ergot to stop any bleeding, or Gull deliberately caused her to have a miscarriage. No pregnancy, however, was ever announced. One explanation could be the remorse she felt over the death, in 1891, of her son John who lived only twenty-four hours. Although she was only 26, 'from now on there were to be no more children'.[19]

Later in May, not long after the date of the prescription, Alexandra was sent on holiday to Greece to recover from her 'illness'.

If the story of Alexandra's adultery with a Russian Grand Duke is true – and the evidence is only circumstantial – and if, as Gull's prescription suggests, she had an abortion in 1877, she had good reason for ordering all her private archive to be destroyed after her death (above, p. 186).

Notes

Chapter One: Clarence's Contretemps

1 For details of Sickert's biography see Wendy Baron, *Sickert* (1973).

2 Osbert Sitwell, *In a Free House, or The Artist as Craftsman, being the Writings of Walter Richard Sickert* (1947), p.1.

3 Michael Thornton, *Royal Feud* (1986), p.157.

4 Compton Mackenzie, *The Windsor Tapestry* (1938), p.254.

5 Michael Thornton, op. cit., p.159.

6 John Law, *In Darkest London* (1889), pp.189-90.

7 Stephen Knight, *Jack the Ripper: The Final Solution* (1976), p.88.

8 Ibid., p.89.

9 *East London Observer*, 11 February 1888.

10 For the background see W.J. Fishman, *East End Jewish Radicals* (1987).

11 Fuller, op. cit., p.48.

12 Greater London Archives, Coroner's Papers, MJ/SPC/NE/Box 3, No.19.

Chapter Two: The Murders

1 Michael Harrison, *Clarence: The Life of HRH the Duke of Clarence and Avondale* (1972), p.184.

2 Sir Melville Macnaghten's notes (1889), Metropolitan Police Report: Mepo 3/141, Fol. 177-183. Public Records Office.

3 Jack London, *The People of the Abyss* (1902), p.134

4 Donald Rumbelow, *The Complete Jack the Ripper* (revised edition 1987), p.26.

5 Arthur Morrison, *Tales of Mean Streets* (1894), p.7.

6 James Greenwood, *In Strange Company* (1883), p.2.

7 Martin Fido, *The Crimes, Detection and Death of Jack the Ripper* (1987), pp. 44-5.

Chapter Three: Masonic Mutilation

1 Eugene Lennhoff, *The Freemasons* (1978), p.284.

2 *History of the Royal Alpha Lodge* (1891), private publication held in the Library, Freemason's Hall, London.

3 Jean Overton Fuller, *Sickert & the Ripper Crimes* (1990), p.15.

4 For details see Frances Edwardes, *Guy Fawkes: The Real Story of the Gunpowder Plot* (1969).

5 Bernard E. Jones, *The Freemason's Guide & Compendium* (1956), p.169.

6 James Dewar, *The Unlocked Secret: Freemasonry Examined* (1966), p.164.

7 Stephen Knight, *Jack the Ripper: The Final Solution* (1976), p.156.

8 William Morgan, *Freemasonry Exposed* (1827), p.120.

9 Coroner's Inquests (L) 1888. No.135, Corporation of London Records.

10 Ibid.

11 Ibid.

12 William Morgan, op. cit., p.82.

13 *Daily Telegraph*, 6 October 1888.

14 Report by Chief Insp. Swanson dated 19 October 1888, to the Home Office. HO/144/221/A49301c 8a.

15 Ibid.

16 Sir Robert Anderson, *The Lighter Side of My Official Life* (1910), p.138.

17 Sir Melville Macnaghten's notes (1889), Metropolitan Police Report: Mepo 3/141/ Fol. 177-83. Public Record Office.

18 John Francis Brewer, *The Curse Upon Mitre Square* (1888), p.70.

19 Bernard E. Jones, op. cit.

20 Stephen Knight, op. cit., p.74.

21 Bernard E. Jones, op. cit., p.450.

22 Ibid., p.312.

23 Ibid., p.313.

Chapter Four: Magister Magistrorum

1 A.P. Moore Anderson, *Sir Robert Anderson* (1919), p.29.

2 Ibid. p.141

3 Sir Robert Anderson, *The Lighter Side of My Official Life* (1910), p.134

4 Marjorie Lilley, *Sickert: The Painter and His Circle* (1971), p.69.

5 Michael Harrison, *Clarence: The Life of HRH the Duke of Clarence and Avondale* (1864-1892) (1972), p. 131.

6 Philip Magnus, *King Edward the Seventh* (1964), p.145.

7 Randolph Churchill, *Winston S. Churchill: Youth 1874-1900* (1966), p.30.

8 Anita Leslie, *The Life of Lady Randolph Churchill* (1969), p.55.

9 R.F. Foster, *Lord Randolph Churchill: A Political Life* (1981), p.253.

10 Ibid., p.10

11 William Manchester, *The Last Lion: Winston Spencer Churchill* (1983), p.120.

12 Philip Magnus, op. cit., p.195.

13 Ibid., p.200.

14 Giles St Aubyn, *Edward VII* (1979), p.248.

15 Michael Harrison, op. cit., p.131.

16 All these letters can be read in *Jennie: Lady Randolph Churchill* (1974), co-written by Julian Mitchell and Lord Randolph's grandson, Peregrine Churchill.

17 Ibid., p.22.

18 Anita Leslie, op. cit., p.86.

19 William Manchester, op. cit., p.104.

20 Giles St Aubyn, op. cit., p.180.

21 Marian Fowler, *Blenheim* (1990), p.000

22 R.F. Foster, op. cit., p.15.

23 Ibid., p.376.

24 *Pall Mall Gazette*, 28 June 1884.

25 Ted Morgan, *Churchill: 1874-1915* (1983), p.18.

26 Ibid. p.54.

27 Marian Fowler, op. cit., p.112.

28 Ted Morgan, op. cit., pp.167f.

29 R.F. Foster, op. cit., p.29.

30 Winston Churchill, *Lord Randolph Churchill* (second edition 1907), p.530.

31 Marian Fowler, op. cit., p.142.

32 Mitchell & Churchill, op. cit., p.61.

33 Winston Churchill, op. cit., pp.24, 25.

34 For Lord Randolph's syphilis see R.F. Foster, op. cit., esp. pp. 58f, 96f, 218f.

35 Winston Churchill, *My Early Life* (1937), p.38.

36 Thomas Dyke Acland, *In Memoriam: Sir William Gull* (1891), p.xxxiv.

37 Ted Morgan, op. cit. p.23.

38 Frank Harris, *My Life and Loves* (1925; repr. 1964), pp.488ff. For Louis Jennings see Foster, op. cit., p.385f.). Professor Foster (p.389) refers to the passage quoted as 'an almost completely unlikely assertion of the manner in which [Randolph] contracted syphilis', but of course Harris nowhere says that Randolph in fact caught syphilis that way (or any other), only that on this supposed occasion he was afraid he had caught it and was relieved to be given a clean bill of health by his doctors.

39 Richard Hough, *Winston and Clementine* (1990), p.543.

40 R.F. Foster, op. cit., p.96.

41 Anita Leslie, op. cit., p.108.

42 Ralph G. Martin, *Lady Randolph Churchill, Vol. 2: 1895-1921* (1971), p.43.

43 *The Westminster and Keystone Lodge* (a private edition in the Library, Freemasons Hall, London), pp. 202, 206.

44 Giles St Aubyn, op. cit., p.30.

45 Anita Leslie, op. cit., p.110.

46 Mitchell & Churchill, op. cit., p.148.

47 Fred L. Pick and G. Norman Knight, *The Pocket History of Freemasonry* (revised edition 1983), p.327.

48 Anita Leslie, op. cit., p. 108.

49 Ibid., p.161.

50 Ralph G. Martin, op. cit., p.272.

51 Mitchell & Churchill, op. cit., p.169.

52 Mary Soames, *Clementine Churchill* (1979), see pages 16, 17-21, 23, 228, 248, 502.

Chapter Five: The Changeling

1 Anne Edwards, *Matriarch: Queen Mary and the Royal House of Windsor* (1984), pp.177, 198.

2 *The Times*, 21 April 1969.

3 John Rothenstein, *Modern English Painters, Vol.1: Sickert to Lowry* (1984), p.187.

4 Martin Howells & Keith Skinner, *The Ripper Legacy* (1987), p.47.

5 Donald Rumbelow, *The Complete Jack the Ripper* (revised edition, 1987), p.205.

6 Ralph G. Martin, *Lady Randolph Churchill: A Biography 1854-1895* (1969), p.281.

7 R.F. Foster, *Lord Randolph Churchill: A Political Life* (1981), p.225.

8 Ralph G. Martin, op. cit., p.247.

9 William Manchester, *The Last Lion: Winston Spencer Churchill* (1983), p187.

10 Ralph G. Martin, *Lady Randolph Churchill, vol. 2: 1895-1921*, p.281.

Chapter Six: Minedalex

1 Suzy Menkes, *The Royal Jewels* (1985), pp. 89, 91.

2 Ibid. pp. 36, 37, 41, 92.

3 Frances Donaldson, *Edward VIII* (1974), p.286.

4 Ibid. p.287.

5 Suzy Menkes, op. cit., p.83.

6 Michael Thornton, *Royal Feud* (1986), pp.234, 236.

7 Suzy Menkes, op. cit., p.102.

8 J. Pope-Hennessy, *Queen Mary 1867-1953* (1959), p.223.

9 Harold Nicolson, *King George the Fifth* (1952), p.410.

10 J. Pope-Hennessy, op. cit., p.537.

Chapter Seven: Eddy

1 Thomas Brough, *The Prince and The Lilly (1975)*, p.192.

2 Philip Magnus, *King Edward the Seventh* (1964), p.178.

3 Michael Harrison, *Clarence: HRH The Duke of Clarence and Avondale* (1972), p.131.

4 Full details of the affair are to be found in H. Montgomery Hyde, *The Cleveland Street Scandal* (1976) and L. Chester, D. Leitch and C. Simpson, *The Cleveland Street Affair* (1977).

5 H. Montgomery Hyde, op. cit., p.59.

6 Stephen Knight, *Jack the Ripper: The Final Solution* (1976), p.120.

7 Jean Overton Fuller, *Sickert & The Ripper Crimes* (1990), p.40.

8 Case notes for Annie Elizabeth Crook at Fulham Road Workhouse (St Stephen's Hospital), dated 12 March 1913, Greater London Records Office. Amentia is a discredited term no longer permitted in English law since 1960. It was what Victorians often called 'idiocy'.

9 Anne Edwards, *Matriarch: Queen Mary and the House of Windsor* (1984), p.43.

10 Robert Wilson, *Life and Times of Queen Victoria* (1888), vol. 2, p.667.

11 J. Pope-Hennessy, *Queen Mary 1867-1953* (1959), p.57.

12 Giles St Aubyn, *Edward VII: Prince and King* (1979), p.105.

13 Donald Rumbelow, *The Complete Jack the Ripper* (revised edition 1987), p.189.

14 Frank Spiering, *Prince Jack* (1978), p.175n.

15 Fripp was later surgeon to Guy's Hospital and to the King. He was knighted in 1903.

16 See H. Montgomery Hyde, op. cit., p.57.

17 PZ means Past Zerubbabel, Zerubbabel being the principal mason among a group who have passed the Royal Arch.

18 Stephen Knight, op. cit., p.205.

19 Winston S. Churchill, *My Early Life* (1930), p.34.

20 Ibid., p.34.

21 Stephen Knight, op. cit., p.204.

Chapter Eight: The Diaries

1 Melville Macnaghten, *Days of My Years* (1915), p.273.

2 *Granta*, February 1891.

3 *Cambridge Review*, February 1891.

4 Martin Howells & Keith Skinner, *The Ripper Legacy* (1987), p.117.

5 Theo Aronsen, *The King in Love* (1988), p.68.

6 Ibid., p.68.

7 Ibid., pp.69f.

8 *Lausanne Gazette*, 10 June 1881.

9 *Sunday People*, 24 June 1979.

10 David Duff, *Albert and Victoria* (1973), p.225.

11 Robert Wilson, *The Life and Times of Queen Victoria* (1888), vol. 2, p.665.

12 J. Pope-Hennessy, *Queen Mary 1867-1953* (1959), p.223.

13 For a comprehensive history of the Ship Tavern and coffee houses, see Bryant Lillywhite, *London Coffee Houses* (1963).

14 Jean Overton Fuller, *Sickert & The Ripper Crimes* (190), p.13.

15 Ibid., p.13.

16 Marjorie Lilly, *Sickert: The Painter and His Circle* (1971), p.15.

17 Ibid. p.47.

18 Frank Harris, *My Life and Loves* (1925; repr. 1964), p.447.

19 Stephen Knight, *Jack the Ripper: The Final Solution* (1976), p.204.

20 Ralph G. Martin, *Lady Randolph Churchill* (1969), p.315

Chapter Nine: The Monster of Glamis

1 For the history of Glamis, I consulted the official guide book by Robert Innes-Smith, obtained from the castle.

2 James Wentworth Day, *The Queen Mother's Family Story* (1979), p.17.

3 Ibid. For the most comprehensive history of the 'Monster of Glamis', see ch. 10, pp.130ff.

4 Ibid. p.140.

5 Ibid. pp.135f.

6 Ibid. p.144.

7 David Duff, *Elizabeth of Glamis* (revised edition 1980), p.30.

8 James Wentworth Day, op. cit., p.135.

9 For a comprehensive summary and family trees, see *London Daily News*, 10 April 1967, p.13.

10 James Wentworth Day, op. cit., p.132.

Chapter Ten: Abdication

1 Georgina Battiscombe, *Queen Alexandra* (1969), p.279.

2 David Duff, *Alexandra: Princess and Queen* (1980), p.254.

3 Id., *Queen Mary* (1985), p.184.

4 Id., *Alexandra: Princess and Queen* (1980), p.255.

5 Harold Nicolson, *King George the Fifth* (1952), p.145.

6 Frances Donaldson, *Edward VIII* (1974), p.101.

7 Ibid. p.50.

8 Philip Magnus, *Kitchener* (1958), p.375.

9 Frances Donaldson, op. cit., p.53.

10 David Duff, *Elizabeth of Glamis* (1965), p.13.

11 Helen Cathcart, *The Queen Mother Herself* (1979), p.31.

12 Ibid. p.32.

13 Ibid. p.66.

14 Richard Hough, *The Windsor Story* (1988), p.223.

15 David Duff, *Elizabeth of Glamis* (1965), p.149.

16 Philip Ziegler, *King Edward VIII: The Official Biography* (1990), p.243.

17 Richard Hough, *Born Royal* (1988), p.220.

18 Ibid. p.220.

19 *Daily News*, 5 January 1923.

20 Philip Ziegler, op. cit., p.243.

21 Michael Thornton, *Royal Feud* (1986), pp.45f n.80 on p.385.

22 Ibid. p.44.

23 Kenneth Rose, *Kings, Queens and Courtiers* (1985), p.232.

24 Francis Watson, 'The Death of George V', *History Today* (Dec. 1986).

25 Frances Donaldson, op. cit., p.174.

26 David Duff, *Queen Mary* (1985), p.201.

27 Frances Donaldson, op. cit., p.178.

28 Patrick Howarth, *George VI* (1987), p.57.

Chapter Twelve: Mary Kelly: The Final Twist

1 William J. Fishman, *East End 1888* (1988), p.95.

2 *Harmsworth's Universal Encyclopedia* (1927) p.927.

3 Greater London Archives, Coroners Papers, MJ/SPS/NE Box 3 No. 19.

Appendixes

1 Stephen Knight, op. cit., pp. 26f.

2 Marjorie Lilly, op. cit., p.12.

3 Jean Overton Fuller, op. cit., pp.8, 17.

4 Donald Rumbelow, op. cit., pp.201f.

5 Donald McCormick, op. cit., p.110.

6 Melvyn Harris, op. cit., p.164.

7 Donald Rumbelow, op. cit., pp.208f.

8 Howells & Skinner, op. cit., p.40.

9 Ibid., p.45.

10 Donald Rumbelow, op. cit., p.208.

11 John Pope-Hennessy, *Queen Mary* (1959), pp.196-7.

12 Ibid., p.198.

13 Princess Michael of Kent, *Crowned in a Far Country* (1986), p.162.

14 John Pope-Hennessy, op. cit., pp.199-200.

15 Ibid., p.196.

16 Philip Magnus, *King Edward the Seventh* (1964), p.220.

17 Wendy Baron, *Sickert* (1973), pp. 149, 152, 154, 158f.

18 *The Times*, 19 December 1971.

19 Georgina Battiscombe, op. cit., p. 113.

Bibliography

Titles by authors whose names are printed in bold type are titles quoted from or referred to in this book. Those marked with an asterisk are recommended background reading.

THE EAST END

* BOOTH, Charles. *Conditions and Occupations of the People of Tower Hamlets 1886-1887*. London, 1887
FISHMAN, William J.
    East End Jewish Radicals 1875-1914. London, 1975
    The Streets of East London. London, 1979
    East End 1888. London, 1988
GREENWOOD, James. *In Strange Company*. London, 1883
JONES, Gareth Steadman. *Outcast London*. Oxford, 1971
LONDON, Jack. *The People of the Abyss*. London, 1903
MEARNS, Andrew. *The Bitter Outcry of Outcast London*. Leicester, 1970
MORRISON, Arthur. *Tales of Mean Streets*. London, 1884
SAMUEL, Raphael. *East End Underworld: Chapters in the Life of Arthur Harding*. London, 1981
* WHITE, Jerry. *The Rothschild Buildings*. London, 1980

JACK THE RIPPER

ANDERSON, Sir Robert. *The Lighter Side of My Official Life*. London, 1910
* BEGG, Paul. *Jack the Ripper: The Uncensored Facts*. London, 1988
BREWER, John Francis. *The Curse Upon Mitre Square AD 1530-1888*. London, 1888
DEW, Walter. *I Caught Crippen*. London, 1938
FARSON, Daniel. *Jack the Ripper*. London, 1972
FIDO, Martin. *The Crimes, Detection & Death of Jack the Ripper*. London, 1987.
HARRIS, Melvin. *Jack The Ripper: The Bloody Truth*. London, 1987
HOWELLS, Martin, & SKINNER, Keith, *The Ripper Legacy*. London, 1987
* JONES, Elwyn and Lloyd, John. *The Ripper File*. London, 1975
* KELLY, Alexander. *Jack the Ripper: A Bibliography and Review of the Literature*. London, 1973
KNIGHT, Stephen. *Jack the Ripper: The Final Solution*. London, 1979
McCORMICK, Donald. *The Identity of Jack the Ripper*. London, 1959
LACASSAGNE, Jean Alexandre Eugène. *Vacher L'Eventreur et les crimes sadiques*. Paris, 1899

* MATTERS, Leonard. *The Mystery of Jack the Ripper*. London, 1929
MONTGOMERY HYDE, H. *The Cleveland Street Scandal*. London, 1976
RUMBELOW, Donald. *The Complete Jack the Ripper*[2]. London, 1987
SHARKEY, Terence. *Jack the Ripper: 100 Years of Investigation*. London, 1987
SPIERING, Frank. *Prince Jack*. New York, 1978
* STEWART, William. *Jack the Ripper: A New Theory*. London, 1939
UNDERWOOD, Peter. *Jack the Ripper: One Hundred Years of Mystery*. London, 1987
* WILSON, Colin & ODELL, Robin. *Jack the Ripper: Summing up and Verdict*. London, 1987

ROYALTY

ARONSON, Theo. *The King in Love: Edward VII's Mistresses*. London, 1988
BATTISCOMBE, Georgina. *Queen Alexandra*. London, 1969
BLOCH, Michael. *The Secret File of the Duke of Windsor*. London, 1985
BLYTH, Henry. *Skittles: The Last Victorian Courtesan*. London, 1970
BROUGH, James. *The Princess and The Lilly*. London, 1975
BRYAN III, J. & MURPHY, Charles J.V. *The Windsor Story*. London, 1979
CATHCART, Helen. *The Queen Mother Herself*. London, 1979
CHESTER, Lewis, LEATH, David, & SIMPSON, Colin. *The Cleveland Street Affair*. London, 1977
CORBY, Tom. *Queen Elizabeth the Queen Mother*. London, 1990
DALTON, John D.D. *The Cruise of Her Majesty's Ship 'Bacchante,' 1879-1882*. London, 1882
DAY, James Wentworth. *The Queen Mother's Family Story*. Robert Hale: London, 1979
DIMOND, Frances, & TAYLOR, Robert. *Crown & Camera: The Royal Family and Photography 1842-1910*. London, 1987
DONALDSON, Frances. *Edward VIII*. London, 1974
DUFF, David. *Alexandra: Princess and Queen*. London, 1980
* *Elizabeth of Glamis*. London, 1980
* *Queen Mary*. London, 1985
EDWARDS, Anne. *Matriarch: Queen Mary and the House of Windsor*. London, 1984
FISHER, Graham & Heather. *Bertie and Alix: Anatomy of a Royal Marriage*. London, 1974
HARDY, Alan. *Queen Victoria Was Amused*. London, 1976
HARRISON, Michael. *Clarence: The life of HRH the Duke of Clarence and Avondale (1864-1892)*. London, 1972
HIBBERT, Christopher. *Edward VII*. London, 1976
HOUGH, Richard. *Born Royal: The Lives and Loves of the Young Windsors*. London, 1988
LANE, Peter. *The Queen Mother*. London, 1979
* LONGFORD, Elizabeth. *The Royal House of Windsor*. London, 1974
MAGNUS, Philip. *King Edward the Seventh*. London, 1964
MAXWELL, Sir Herbert. *Sixty Years A Queen: The Story of Her Majesty's Reign*. London, 1897
MENKES, Suzy, *The Royal Jewels*. London, 1985
MICHAEL, HRH Princess, of Kent. *Crowned in a Far Country*. London, 1986

MIDDLEMAS, Keith. *The Life and Times of Edward VII*. London, 1972

MORTIMER, Penelope. *Queen Elizabeth: A Life of The Queen Mother*. London, 1986

NICOLSON, Harold. *King George the Fifth*. London, 1970

POPE-HENNESSY, James. *Queen Mary 1867-1953*. London, 1959

ROBY, Kinley. *The King, the Press and the People: A Study of Edward VII*. London, 1975

ROSE, Kenneth. *Kings, Queens and Courtiers*. London, 1985

ST AUBYN, Giles. *Edward VII: Prince and King*. London, 1979

SINCLAIR, David. *The Two Georges*. London, 1988

SOMERSET, Anne. *The Life and Times of William IV*. London, 1980

THORNTON, Michael. *Royal Feud*. London, 1986

TOWNSEND, Peter. *The Last Emperor*. London, 1975

VINCENT, James E. *His Royal Highness The Duke of Clarence and Avondale: A Memoir*. London, 1893

WEINTRAUB, Stanley. *Victoria: Biography of a Queen*. London, 1987

WILSON, Robert. *The Life and Times of Queen Victoria*. London, 1888

WALTER SICKERT

BARON, Wendy. *Sickert*. London, 1973

BELL, Quentin. *Victorian Artists*. London, 1967

BLANCHE, Jacques-Emile. *Portrait of a Lifetime: The Late Victorian Era. The London Pageant, 1870-1914*. London, 1937

* BROWSE, Lillian. *Sickert*. London, 1960

EMMONS, Robert. *The Life and Opinions of Walter Richard Sickert*. London, 1941

LILLY, Marjorie. *Sickert: The Painter and His Circle*. London, 1971

ROTHENSTEIN, John. *Modern English Painters. vol. 1: Sickert to Lowry*. London, 1984

SITWELL, Osbert. *A Free House! or The Artist as Craftsman, being the Writings of Walter Richard Sickert*. London, 1947

* SUTTON, Denys. *Walter Sickert*. London, 1976

LORD RANDOLPH CHURCHILL

* CANNADINE, David. *The Decline and Fall of the British Aristocracy*. New Haven & London, 1990

* CHURCHILL, Randolph. *Winston S. Churchill, 1874-1965. Vol. 1: Youth*. London, 1966

CHURCHILL, Winston Spencer. *Lord Randolph Churchill*. London, 1907

ESCOTT, T.H.S. *Randolph Spencer Churchill*. London, 1895

FOSTER, R.F. *Lord Randolph Churchill: A Political Life*. Oxford, 1981

FOWLER, Marian. *Blenheim*. London, 1989

HOUGH, Richard. *Winston & Clementine: The Triumph of the Churchills*. London, 1990

LESLIE, Anita. *The Life of Lady Randolph Churchill*. London, 1969

MANCHESTER, William. *The Last Lion: Visions of Glory, 1874-1932*. London, 1983

MARTIN, Ralph G. *Lady Randolph Churchill: A Biography. vol. 1 1854-1895*. London, 1969

MITCHELL, Julian & CHURCHILL, Peregrine. *Jennie: Lady Randolph Churchill.* London, 1974
MORGAN, Ted. *Churchill, 1874-1915.* London, 1983
* RHODES JAMES, Robert. *Lord Randolph Churchill.* London, 1965
SOAMES, Mary. *Clementine Churchill: By her Daughter Mary Soames.* London, 1979
  A Churchill Family Album: A Personal Anthology. London, 1982

FREEMASONS

* CAHILL, E. *Freemasonry and the Anti-Christian Movement. Dublin, 1952*
COVEY-CRUMP, Rev. *The Hiramic Tradition.* London, 1937
* DEWER, James. *The Unlocked Secret: Freemasonry Examined.* London, 1966
DYER, Colin F.W. *Symbolism in Craft Freemasonry.* London, 1983
FINLAYSON, J. Finley. *Symbols and Legends of Freemasonry.* London, 1889
* HANNAH, Walton. *Darkeness Visible.* Chumleigh, Devon, 1952
  Christian by Degrees. Chumleigh, Devon, 1954
* JONES, Bernard E. *The Freemason's Book of the Royal Arch.* London, 1957
  The Freemason's Guide And Compendium. London, 1975
* KNIGHT, Stephen. *The Brotherhood.* London, 1984
LANE, John. *Lane's Masonic Records.* Grand Lodge of England, London, 1895
LENNHOFF, Eugene. *The Freemasons.* Lewis (Masonic Publishers), London, 1978
LEO XIII, POPE. *Humanum Genus, 1884.* London, 1952
MORGAN, William. *Freemasonry Exposed.* Glasgow, 1836
PICK, Fred L. & KNIGHT, G. Norman. *The Freemason's Pocket Reference Book.* London, 1983
  * *The Pocket History of Freemasonry.* London, 1983
* PONCINS, Vicomte Leon de. *Freemasonry & the Vatican: A Struggle for Recognition.* Translated by Timothy Tindal-Robertson. London, 1928
* SIMPSON, John Percy. *Some Old London Taverns & Masonry.* London, 1939
SHORT, Martin. *Inside the Brotherhood.* London, 1989

MISCELLANEOUS

ACLAND, Theodore Dyke. *William Withey Gull: A Biographical Sketch.* London, 1896
ARNOLD, Bruce. *Orpen: Mirror to an Age.* London, 1981
* BELL, Quentin. *Virginia Woolf: A Biography, 1882-1912.* London, 1972
CHARNLEY, John. *Lord Lloyd & the Decline of the Empire.* London, 1987
CHESNEY, Kellow. *The Victorian Underworld.* London, 1970.
CUNNINGHAM, Peter. *Hand-Book of London, Past & Present.* London, 1850, London, repr. 1978
FRIEDLAND, Martin L. *The Trials of Israel Lipski.* London, 1984
* GULL, William Withey. *A Collection of Published Writings of William Withey Gull:* Edited and Arranged by Theodore Dyke Acland. London, 1894
HARDWICKE, Michael and Mollie. *The Charles Dickens Encyclopedia.* London, 1973
HELLICAR, Eileen. *Prime Ministers of Great Britain.* Vermont, Canada, 1978
LILLYWHITE, Bryant. *London Coffee Houses.* London, 1963

MACNACHTEN, Melville. *Days of My Years*. London, 1915

MOORE-ANDERSON, A.P. *Sir Robert Anderson*. London, 1919

NAPLEY, Sir David. *The Camden Town Murders*. London, 1987

OGG, David. *England in the Reigns of James II & William III*. Oxford & London, 1963

ROSE, Kenneth. *The Later Cecils*. London, 1975

TAYLOR, Robert. *Lord Salisbury*. London, 1975

TREWIN, J.C. *Tutor to the Tzarevich*. London, 1975

VANBRUGH, John. *The Confederacy. Plays, vol. 2*. Printed by F. D. for J. Tonson and M. Wellington: London, 1719

WILLIAMS, Watkin Wynn. *The Life of Sir Charles Warren: By His Grandson*. Oxford, 1941

YALLOP, David A. *Deliver us from Evil*. London, 1981

DOCUMENTS

Corporation of London Records Office, Guildhall
Police Box 3, 13-18, and Coroners Inquests (London), 1888, No. 135, regarding Catherine Eddowes and Elizabeth Stride

Greater London Record Office, Clerkenwell
Board of Guardians Records for St Marylebone and St Pancras
Rough Examination Records and Religious Creed Records
Charing Cross Hospital Admittance Records for 1888 & 1892-93
Guy's Hospital Registers of Admittance & Discharge – H9/GY/B2/4 and H9/GY/B3/11/1
Patients Records for Charing Cross Hospital, National Temperance Hospital and University College Hospital

General Register Office, St Catherine's House
Registers of Births, Deaths and Marriages

Historic Buildings and Monuments Commission, London Division, Warwick Street
File on the many places Walter Sickert lived in London. Includes GLC Press Office letter No. 610

Public Record Office, Kew File DPP 1/95, on the Cleveland Street scandal, 1889
Scotland Yard Files – MEPO 3/140; Mepo 3/141 and Mepo 3/142, relating to the Whitechapel murders
Home Office Files – HO A49301, 144/220; A49301 A, B, C, D, C, D, E, F, G, H, J and K, relating to the Whitechapel murders
Metropolitan Police Register of Leavers 1889-1892 – MEPO/4/339
Metropolitan Police Register of Joiners 1871-1891 – MEPO/4/335
Reports on Vagrants in Trafalgar Square – MEPO/2/ 181 & 182
Army Lists and Navy Lists

London Borough of Camden Libraries
Local History Library, Holborn.
Ratebooks for Camden, Hampstead, Holborn and St Pancras

Local History Library, Swiss Cottage
Census Returns for Hampstead and St Pancras
Collection of photographs of St Pancras
The Heal Collection on St Pancras of maps, books, documents etc

London Borough of Southwark Libraries
Minet Historical Library
Local Census Returns for 1851, 1861, 1871 and 1881. Local Ratebooks

Scotland Yard's Black Museum
Post mortem records on Mary Jane Kelly, and the original letter signed 'Jack the Ripper'. Also the unpublished photograph of Kelly

City of Westminster Libraries
Victoria Library Archives and St Marylebone Library for the local Ratebooks and local Census Returns for 1851, 1861, 1871 and 1891
Marylebone Medical Library, for medical facts

Index